CW00922605

Medieval Latin and Middle English Literature

Essays in Honour of Jill Mann

Medieval Latin and Middle English Literature

Essays in Honour of Jill Mann

Edited by
Christopher Cannon and Maura Nolan

D. S. BREWER

First published 2011
D. S. Brewer, Cambridge

ISBN 978–1–84384–263–7

D. S. Brewer is an imprint of Boydell & Brewer Ltd
PO Box 9, Woodbridge, Suffolk IP12 3DF, UK
and of Boydell & Brewer Inc.
668 Mount Hope Ave, Rochester, NY 14620, USA
website: www.boydellandbrewer.com

A CIP catalogue record for this book is available
from the British Library

Printed in Great Britain by
CPI Antony Rowe, Chippenham and Eastbourne

Contents

Preface

This volume honors the accomplishments, in work and in life, of our mentor, teacher, colleague and friend, Jill Mann. It both celebrates and marks out the extent to which she has achieved pre-eminence in two distinct fields, medieval Latin and Middle English, although even such celebration does not do sufficient justice to her mastery of a wide variety of sub-disciplines within both fields. For Jill is also an editor of the first rank, as well as the kind of textual scholar such editing requires; a close reader of almost unparalleled skill, not least because she is a linguist with an extraordinary command of the ancillary languages to those in which she mainly works (French and Italian, as well as Dutch and German) as well as their medieval forms and grammar and literature; in addition, she is a superb intellectual historian, as at home and incisive in her reading of works of philosophy and literary theory as in her analyses of literary texts. There may be scholars working who have done as much as Jill to heal the breach that has opened wide between attentive criticism of medieval vernacular literature and deep knowledge of its Latin background since Erich Auerbach's *Mimesis* (1946) and his *Literary Language and its Public* (1958), but we do not know of any.

What was immediately apparent upon the publication of *Chaucer and Medieval Estates Satire* (1973) was not only that Jill's knowledge of Latin and its literature is exhaustive, but also that the quality of understanding that she brings to any text and its range of meanings would, by itself, have placed her among the first rank of critics. Her commitment was and is above all (in a phrase she often uses) to the 'words on the page', by which she means not only what is printed on paper, but the various manuscript pages behind any edition. She sees these words so clearly because she does not look at any word in isolation, but, rather, considers words in the light of the various meanings they have accumulated over time, as well as in relation to the various other possible texts and contexts in which they might or have occurred. This incisive method and its interpretative riches have been shared with medievalists in an astonishing series of articles about Chaucer and Langland, the Goliardic poets, the *Ysengrimus*, and the *Speculum Stultorum* (among many other writers and works) that began to emerge from Jill's study in the late 1970s, and continues to this day. Read together, these works demonstrate that she is fundamentally committed to listening to what medieval texts have to say, a commitment perhaps best described using one of her own critical terms of art: 'modest'. This word is Jill's shorthand for scholarship that adheres to the highest standards of proof without making grandiose or extravagant claims. These are, of course, the defining characteristics of her own style, coupled with a prose as controlled as it is artful, and a mode of argument refined with ruthless precision. As she herself has been known to remark, 'just because one has researched a topic doesn't mean that it belongs in the essay or book'. It is also a manifestation of this modesty that these varied and influential essays have as yet never been brought together between covers – that each one was created as but a *minor opus* – although, taken together, they have quietly changed the face of Middle English and medieval Latin literary scholarship.

The books that Jill has also produced alongside these articles – books that seem now to amass at an even faster rate, since retirement from teaching has only allowed Jill more time for her own academic work – have also re-made the various fields in which they participate. What was, until recent years, her *magnum opus*, her edition and translation of the *Ysengrimus* (1987), not only made this work available to all non-Latinists (while also providing a critical edition of the original) but also sneaked in, under the guise of an 'introduction', a monograph-length history of the genres of beast epic and beast fable. Her feminist study of Geoffrey Chaucer (1991; revised edition 2002) – one of the first such works – proved conclusively, through a series of dynamic and fiercely original readings, why as staunch a feminist as Jill could love Chaucer, not only for the beauty and wisdom of his poetry, but also because he really was 'ever woman's friend'. Even as Jill was writing and editing these books and essays, she was working on another monumental project, an entirely new critical edition of the *Canterbury Tales* (2005). This edition is a product of thirty years of labour over textual variants as well as careful attention to an ever-growing body of criticism that is also carefully, clearly and, most extraordinarily, fully absorbed in the edition's notes. Most recently, she has published yet another life's work, *From Aesop to Reynard* (2009), the truly definitive history of the various significant works of beast literature written in medieval Britain. Here Jill provides yet another sequence of rich and original readings and demonstrates conclusively, out of her deep knowledge of the effects and influences of this work (from the elementary schoolroom to the period's best poets), the key importance of writing about animals to all medieval thought and life.

Those who know Jill well will also know that none of these achievements was at all predestined. Jill grew up in the North of England, in an industrial town (Sunderland), and although she was born into a relatively prosperous family, she attended a grammar school (The Bede School for Girls) far from the centres of British higher education. Her clearest advantage, as a girl, was having a father who had himself gone up to Oxford, and who supported Jill when this seemed the obvious course for her. In retrospect, Jill's successes from the moment of her arrival at St Anne's College in 1961 (the beginning of a life-long, and deep, affection for Oxford) must seem like a natural progression, from distinction in her first exams, to First Class Honours in Finals

(1964), her Research Fellowship in Clare Hall, Cambridge (1968), her election to a Fellowship in Girton College (1972) followed by an Assistant Lectureship in the Cambridge Faculty of English (1974), then a University Lectureship (1978), her election to the Chair of Medieval and Renaissance English (1988), then her election as Notre Dame Professor of English (1998). But, as Jill has never forgotten, St Anne's was one of only three Oxford colleges in which she might have matriculated, just as Girton was one of only three colleges in Cambridge in which she might have held a fellowship. She was, then, almost of necessity, the first woman to hold her Cambridge chair (at that point, Jill might have jumped ship from Girton, as other professors had done, but it was part of her feminism to feel – and often to say – that she would never be a fellow of a college that would not have admitted her as an undergraduate). But, as in the careers of so many women of her generation, there were, throughout this steady progress, any number of opportunities for derailment, not least in the moment when Jill followed her first husband to Cambridge, where she was not even a student (she eventually converted a registration for the unpromising degree of B.Litt. in Oxford to registration for a Cambridge Ph.D.), as well as the moment, after receiving her Ph.D., when there was no obvious job (and then, for a few years, only a college lectureship of the kind in which many women in those days were sidelined). Of course a paper given upon her arrival in Cambridge at an informal group of medievalists hosted by the Dronkes (Peter and Ursula), at Derek Brewer's invitation, swept all before her. And the emergence of *Estates Satire* secured her Cambridge and subsequent career. But among the principles underlying much of Jill's more feminist work is the awareness, in all this earned success, that it could so easily have been otherwise.

Jill's second professorship at Notre Dame, in the hands of a less dedicated or less professional scholar, might have amounted to hard earned and just deserts, a chance to throw off the shackles of the most bracing, daily administrative and teaching demands, in order to pull back a little and relax. The move was, however, reinvigorating and reanimating for Jill, not least because, with a chance finally to design all her own courses and to focus only on her favorite texts and subjects, and at last free to throw herself into the most ambitious sorts of pedagogy, she rediscovered her native delight in the classroom. The kind of sociability that Jill embodies, which has always been crucial to her method (she has never been afraid to ask an expert for advice, nor to share her work with any colleague or student; nor has she ever received a reader's report she did not engage with fully), finally had a proper stage at Notre Dame, with its many seminars of the most varied kind, its rich and equally various faculty in the medieval period, and its unusually large concentration of serious and motivated students interested in medieval topics. It is no surprise then, that, in a few short years, Jill had produced an extraordinarily large cohort of successful Ph.D. students, each of them now launched on promising careers.

Those who know Jill, even a little, know that her greatest love – aside from the life of the mind, although in her mind it is much the same thing – is

Michael Lapidge, her partner in life and scholarship. That they have explicitly collaborated only a few times in print is not so much ironic as it is fitting, since almost all of their scholarly work has occurred in adjacent studies, in constant collaboration and consultation, often from dawn until dusk in the astonishing academy of two they convened in Sturton Street in Cambridge over thirty years ago. Those who know Jill just a little better will know that she is as talented and ambitious a cook as she is a scholar (and not in a substantially different style, since you may leave her table, even still, not only happy and sated but also with a bibliography of cookery books to learn from). She is also a keen traveler (and there is bibliography for that too: tell her you are on your way to Istanbul and you will come away from her house not only with a guide-book but with a Turkish grammar and dictionary), and while she is keen to go to places in Europe whose history and literature she knows well, traveling is also for Jill about a more extravagant articulation of her native *joie de vivre*, an extended celebration of the casual pleasures of living she also visibly relishes each day, the native beauty of particular places and prospects, relaxed time with loved ones, a good (and, almost always to her mind, informing) joke, and fine meals and wine.

It would be otiose to spend too much time describing the many public honors that Jill has garnered, her early election as a Fellow of the British Academy (1990), her Presidency of the New Chaucer Society (1992–4), her Chairmanship of the Board of the Faculty of English in Cambridge (1993–5, where she negotiated with aplomb and consequential success the first predations of the government scrutiny that has now become the rule and scourge of British higher education), as well as her many invited lectures. What is perhaps most worth recognizing in print, however, is Jill's unflagging attention – and the quality of that attention – to her students, colleagues, and friends. None of us who have ever asked Jill to read our work has come away short of amazed at the depth of her engagement with the argument and its details, or at the extent to which her learning has been extended on our behalf: she is as likely to read anew the obscure text on which you are working in order to help you understand it better, as she is to find errors, not only in what you thought was your very careful transcription of a Latin or Middle English passage, but also in the critical edition from which you faithfully copied the given lines. Such reading, although it benefits at every level from Jill's learning and intelligence, is itself only a symptom of the fundamental loyalty that characterizes her feelings toward those she cares about: to have her count you as a friend, or to have been her student, is always and forever to be a part of her world – to be able to draw again and again on the enormous generosity that both characterizes and, in so many ways empowers, her enormous capacities of kindness and mind.

Bibliography of Jill Mann's Works

Books

Chaucer and Medieval Estates Satire: The Literature of Social Classes and the General Prologue to the Canterbury Tales (Cambridge: Cambridge University Press, 1973)

Part of the conclusion (pp. 189–202, 290–294) reprinted in the Norton Critical Edition of *The Canterbury Tales: Nine Tales and the General Prologue*, ed. V. A. Kolve and Glending Olson (New York: Norton, 1989)

Extracts from pp. 1–2, 3–4, 4–7, 9–10, and 201–202 reprinted in *Icon Critical Guide to Geoffrey Chaucer's the General Prologue to the Canterbury Tales*, ed. Jodie-Anne George (Cambridge: Icon Books, 2000), pp. 67–72

Parts of the beginning and conclusion (pp. 1–16, 187–202 and 289–294) reprinted in *Geoffrey Chaucer's The Canterbury Tales: A Casebook*, ed. Lee Patterson (Oxford: Oxford University Press, 2007)

The Cambridge Chaucer Companion, ed. with Piero Boitani (Cambridge: Cambridge University Press, 1986); Revised edition (with five new essays): *The Cambridge Companion to Chaucer*, ed. Piero Boitani and Jill Mann, 2nd ed. (Cambridge: Cambridge University Press, 2003)

Ysengrimus: Text with Introduction, Translation and Commentary (Leiden: Brill, 1987)

Geoffrey Chaucer (Harvester-Wheatsheaf Feminist Readings series) (Hemel Hempstead: Harvester-Wheatsheaf, 1991); Revised as *Feminizing Chaucer* (Cambridge: D. S. Brewer, 2002), pp. 13–25 and 129–133 of which are reprinted in the Norton Critical Edition of *Troilus and Criseyde*, ed. Stephen Barney (New York and London: Norton, 2006)

The Canterbury Tales, Penguin Classics (London: Penguin Books, 2005)

The Text in the Community: Essays on Medieval Works, Manuscripts, Authors and Readers, ed. with Maura Nolan (Notre Dame, IN: University of Notre Dame Press, 2006)

From Aesop to Reynard: Beast Literature in Medieval Britain (Oxford: Oxford University Press, 2009)

Articles and contributions to books

'Chaucer and the Medieval Latin Poets: Part B', pp. 172–183 in *Writers and their Background: Geoffrey Chaucer*, ed. Derek Brewer (London: Bell, 1974)

'The *Speculum Stultorum* and the *Nun's Priest's Tale*', *Chaucer Review* 9 (1975), 262–282

' "Luditur Illusor": the Cartoon World of the *Ysengrimus*', *Neophilologus* 61 (1977), 495–509

'Eating and Drinking in *Piers Plowman*', *Essays and Studies* 32 (1979), 26–43

'Satiric Subject and Satiric Object in Goliardic Literature', *Mittellateinisches Jahrbuch* 15 (1980), 63–86

'Troilus' Swoon', *Chaucer Review* 14 (1980), 319–335, reprinted in *Critical Essays on Chaucer's "Troilus and Criseyde" and his Major Early Poems*, ed. C. David Benson (Milton Keynes: Open University Press, 1991)

'Giraldus Cambrensis and the Goliards', *Journal of Celtic Studies* 3 (1981), 31–39

' "Taking the Adventure": Malory and the *Suite du Merlin*', pp. 71–91, 196–207 in *Aspects of Malory*, ed. Toshiyuki Takamiya and Derek Brewer (Cambridge: D. S. Brewer, 1981)

'Chaucerian Themes and Style in the *Franklin's Tale*', pp. 133–153 in *The New Pelican Guide to English Literature*, ed. Boris Ford, vol. I.1 (Harmondsworth: Penguin, 1982)

'Malory: Knightly Combat in *Le Morte Darthur*', ibid., pp. 331–339

'Parents and Children in the *Canterbury Tales*', pp. 165–183 in *Literature in Fourteenth-Century England: The J. A. W. Bennett Memorial Lectures, Perugia, 1981–1982*, ed. Piero Boitani and Anna Torti (Tübingen: Narr, and Cambridge: D. S. Brewer, 1983)

'Satisfaction and Payment in Middle English Literature', *Studies in the Age of Chaucer* 5 (1983), 17–48

'On Translating the *Ysengrimus*', *Revue canadienne d'études néerlandaises/ Canadian Journal of Netherlandic Studies* 4 (1983), 25–31

'Proverbial Wisdom in the *Ysengrimus*', *New Literary History* 16 (1984–1985), 93–109

'La favolistica latina', pp. 193–219 in *Aspetti della letteratura latina nel secolo XIII: Atti del primo convegno internazionale di studi dell'Associazione per il Medioevo e l'Umanesimo latini (AMUL). Perugia 3–5 ottobre 1983*, ed. Claudio Leonardi and Giovanni Orlandi (Perugia: Regione dell'Umbria and Florence: La Nuova Italia, 1986)

'Chance and Destiny in *Troilus and Criseyde* and the *Knight's Tale*', pp. 75–92 in *The Cambridge Chaucer Companion* (see Books), reprinted in *The Cambridge Companion to Chaucer*, pp. 93–111

'Price and Value in *Sir Gawain and the Green Knight*', *Essays in Criticism* 36 (1986), 294–318, reprinted in *Medieval English Poetry*, ed. Stephanie Trigg

(London and New York: Longman, 1993), and also in *Chaucer to Spenser: A Critical Reader*, ed. Derek Pearsall (Oxford: Blackwell, 1999)

'The "Roman de Renart" and the "Ysengrimus" ', pp. 135–162 in vol. I of *A la recherche du Roman de Renart*, ed. Kenneth Varty (New Alyth, Perthshire: Lochee Publications, 1988)

'L'invenzione satirica nell'*Ysengrimus*', *Medioevo e Rinascimento* 2 (1988), 17–32

'Shakespeare and Chaucer: "What is Criseyde Worth?" ', pp. 219–242 in *The European Tragedy of Troilus*, ed. Piero Boitani (Oxford: Clarendon Press, 1989) [also published in *The Cambridge Quarterly* 18 (1989)]

'The Planetary Gods in Chaucer and Henryson', pp. 91–106 in *Chaucer Traditions: Studies in Honour of Derek Brewer*, ed. Ruth Morse and Barry Windeatt (Cambridge: Cambridge University Press, 1990)

'The Authority of the Audience in Chaucer', pp. 1–12 in *Poetics: Theory and Practice in Medieval English Literature: The J. A. W. Bennett Memorial Lectures, Seventh Series, Perugia, 1990*, ed. Piero Boitani and Anna Torti (Cambridge: D. S. Brewer, 1991)

'Chaucer and the "Woman Question" ', pp. 173–188 in *This Noble Craft ...: Proceedings of the Xth Research Symposium of the Dutch and Belgian University Teachers of Old and Middle English and Historical Linguistics, Utrecht, 19–20 January, 1989*, ed. Erik Kooper (Amsterdam: Rodopi, 1991)

'Anger and "Glosynge" in the *Canterbury Tales*' [Sir Israel Gollancz Memorial Lecture 1990], *Proceedings of the British Academy* 76 (1990), 203–223

Apologies to Women [Inaugural Lecture Delivered 20th November 1990] (Cambridge, 1991)

The Narrative of Distance, The Distance of Narrative in Malory's Morte Darthur. The William Matthews Lectures 1991, Birkbeck College (London, 1991)

Langland and Allegory. The Morton W. Bloomfield Lectures II (Kalamazoo, 1992); reprinted in *The Morton W. Bloomfield Lectures, 1989–2005*, ed. Daniel Donoghue, James Simpson, and Nicholas Watson (Kalamazoo, MI: Medieval Institute Publications, 2010), pp. 20–41

'La poesia satirica e goliardica', pp. 73–109 in *Lo Spazio letterario del Medioevo. 1. Il Medioevo latino*, vol. I part II, ed. Guglielmo Cavallo, Claudio Leonardi, and Enrico Menestò (Rome: Salerno, 1993)

'La favolistica', ibid., pp. 171–195

'Sir Gawain and the Romance Hero', pp. 105–117 in *Heroes and Heroines in Medieval English Literature: A Festschrift Presented to André Crépin on the Occasion of his Sixty-Fifth Birthday*, ed. Leo Carruthers (Cambridge: D. S. Brewer, 1994)

'Allegorical Buildings in Mediaeval Literature', *Medium Aevum* 63 (1994), 191–210, reprinted in *Blackwell Guides to Criticism: Middle English Literature*, ed. Roger Dalrymple (Oxford: Blackwell, 2004), pp. 131–138

'The Power of the Alphabet: A Reassessment of the Relation between the A and the B Versions of *Piers Plowman*', *Yearbook of Langland Studies* 8 (1994), 21–50

'Malory and the Grail Legend', pp. 203–220 in *A Companion to Malory*, ed. Elizabeth Archibald and A. S. G. Edwards (Cambridge: D. S. Brewer, 1996)

'Chaucer and Atheism' [Presidential Address to the New Chaucer Society Ninth International Congress, July 23–27 1994], *Studies in the Age of Chaucer* 17 (1995), 5–19

'The Satiric Fiction of the *Ysengrimus*', pp. 1–15 in *Reynard the Fox: Social Engagement and Cultural Metamorphoses in the Beast Epic from the Middle Ages to the Present*, ed. Kenneth Varty (New York and Oxford: Berghahn Books, 2000) [Dutch version printed in *Tiecelijn: Tijdschrift voor Reynaerdofielen* 15 (2002), 141–52]

'Jean de Meun and the Castration of Saturn', pp. 309–326 in *Poetry and Philosophy in the Middle Ages: A Festschrift for Peter Dronke*, ed. John Marenbon (Leiden: Brill, 2001)

'Speaking Images in Chaucer's "Miller's Tale" ', pp. 237–253 in *Speaking Images: Essays in Honor of V. A. Kolve*, ed. R. F. Yeager and Charlotte C. Morse (Asheville, NC: Pegasus Press, 2001)

'Wife-Swapping in Medieval Literature', *Viator* 32 (2001), 93–112 [reprinted in *Feminizing Chaucer*, pp. 152–173]

'Chaucer's Meter and the Myth of the Ellesmere Editor of *The Canterbury Tales*', *Studies in the Age of Chaucer* 23 (2001), 71–107

'Reconstructing the Anglo-Latin Aesop: the Literary Tradition of the "Hexametrical Romulus" ' (jointly with Michael Lapidge), in *Latin Culture in the Eleventh Century: Proceedings of the Third International Conference on Medieval Latin Studies (Cambridge, September 9–12, 1998)*, vol. II, ed. Michael W. Herren, C. J. McDonough and Ross G. Arthur, 2 vols. (Turnhout: Brepols, [2002]), II, pp. 1–33

'Newly Identified Quotations in Chaucer's *Tale of Melibee* and the *Parson's Tale*', pp. 61–70 in *The Medieval Book and a Modern Collector: Essays in Honour of Toshiyuki Takamiya*, ed. Takami Matsuda, Richard A. Linenthal, and John Scahill (Cambridge: D. S. Brewer, 2004)

'Chaucer's Sources and Analogues Revisited' [review of Robert M. Correale and Mary Hamel, eds., *Sources and Analogues of the Canterbury Tales*, vol. 1 (Cambridge: D. S. Brewer, 2002)], *Journal of English and Germanic Philology* 104 (2005), 103–128

'The Nature of Need Revisited', *Yearbook of Langland Studies* 18 (2004), 3–29

' "He Knew Nat Catoun": Medieval School-Texts and Middle English Literature', pp. 41–74 in *The Text in the Community* (see Books above)

'Does an Author Understand his Own Text? Nigel of Longchamp and the *Speculum Stultorum*', *Journal of Medieval Latin* 17 (2007), 1–37

'Messianic Chivalry in *Amis and Amiloun*', *New Medieval Literatures* 10 (2008), 137–159

'Courtly Aesthetics and Courtly Ethics in *Sir Gawain and the Green Knight*', *Studies in the Age of Chaucer* 31 (2009), 231–265

' "Learning, Taste and Judgment" in the Editorial Process: Vance Ramsey and Manly-Rickert', forthcoming in *Studies in the Age of Chaucer* (in a colloquium on 'Manly-Rickert 70 Years On')

'The Poetics of Editing: In Memory of George Kane', to be published in the Occasional Papers of the Centre for Late Antique and Medieval Studies

Contributions to Encyclopedias, Dictionaries and Other General Projects

'Nivardus von Gent' [article on *Ysengrimus*], cols. 1170–1178 in *Verfasserlexikon der deutschen Literatur des Mittelalters*, vol. 6 (1987)

'Beast Epic and Fable', pp. 556–561 in *Medieval Latin Studies: An Introduction and Bibliographical Guide*, ed. F. A. C. Mantello and A. G. Rigg (Washington, D.C.: Catholic University Press of America, 1996)

'Beast Fable and Epic', in *The Oxford Dictionary of the Middle Ages*, ed. Robert Bjork (forthcoming)

'*The Canterbury Tales*', in La Letteratura Europea, vol. 4, ed. Piero Boitani and Massimo Fusillo (Turin, UTET)

Reviews

Huling E. Ussery, *Chaucer's Physician* (New Orleans: Tulane University Press, 1971). In *Medium Ævum* 43 (1974), 195–197

Pamela Gradon, *Form and Style in Early English Literature* (London: Methuen, 1971). In *TLS* November 8 1974, p. 1265

Bert Dillon, *A Chaucer Dictionary: Proper Names and Allusions Excluding Place Names* (Boston, Mass.: G. K. Hall, 1974). In *Medium Ævum* 47 (1978), 159–161

Donald R. Howard, *The Idea of the Canterbury Tales* (Berkeley and Los Angeles: University of California Press, 1976). In *Medium Ævum* 47 (1978), 356–360

Ann Thompson, *Shakespeare's Chaucer* (Liverpool: Liverpool University Press, 1978). In *Book Auction Records* 76 (1978–79), p. x

'Now Read On', *Encounter* July 1980, pp. 60–64 [several books]

Terry Jones, *Chaucer's Knight: The Portrait of a Mercenary* (London: Weidenfeld, 1980). In *The Listener*, 31 January 1980

Patrick Boyde, *Dante Philomythes and Philosopher: Man in the Cosmos* (Cambridge: Cambridge University Press, 1981). In *The Cambridge Review*, 20 November 1981, pp. 82–83

Kenelm Foster and Patrick Boyde, eds., *Cambridge Readings in Dante's Comedy* (Cambridge: Cambridge University Press, 1981). In *The Cambridge Review*, 7 May 1982, p. 222

Carl Lindahl, *Earnest Games: Folkloric Patterns in the Canterbury Tales* (Bloomington, IN: Indiana University Press, 1987). In *Anglia. Zeitschrift für englische Philologie* 107 (1989), 197–199

Gillian Jondorf and David N. Dumville, eds., *France and the British Isles in the Middle Ages and Renaissance: Essays in Memory of Ruth Morgan* (Woodbridge: Boydell, 1991). In *The Cambridge Review*, March 1992, p. 39

Caroline Walker Bynum, *Fragmentation and Redemption: Essays on Gender and the Human Body in Medieval Religion* (New York: Zone Books, 1991). In *Medium Ævum* 62 (1993), 111–112

Elaine Tuttle Hansen, *Chaucer and the Fictions of Gender* (Berkeley and Los Angeles, CA: University of California Press, 1992). In *Medium Ævum* 62 (1993), 328–330

Ronald E. Pepin, *Scorn for the World: Bernard of Cluny's "De contemptu mundi." The Latin Text with English Translation and an Introduction* (East Lansing, MI: Colleagues Press, 1991). In *Journal of Medieval Latin* 4 (1994), 163–169

Derek Pearsall, *The Life of Geoffrey Chaucer: A Critical Biography* (Oxford: Blackwell, 1992). In *Medium Ævum* 63 (1994), 130–132

Ruth Evans and Lesley Johnson, *Feminist Readings in Middle English Literature: The Wife of Bath and All Her Sect* (London and New York: Routledge, 1994); Carolyne Larrington, ed., *Women and Writing in Medieval Europe: A Sourcebook* (London and New York: Routledge, 1995). In *Archiv für das Studium der neueren Sprachen und Literaturen* 149 (1997), 142–145

Leonard Michael Koff and Brenda Deen Schildgen, *The 'Decameron' and the 'Canterbury Tales': New Essays on an Old Question* (Madison, WI: Fairleigh Dickinson University Press, 2000). In *Medium Ævum* 71 (2002), 144–145

1

The Man of Law's Tale and Crusade

Siobhain Bly Calkin

The Man of Law's Tale does not usually leap to mind as a Chaucerian evocation of late medieval crusade, perhaps because it seems determined to skirt ideas of armed conflict over religion, referring only briefly to Romans 'brenn[ing and] slee[ing]' Saracens (II.964) and emphasizing instead Custance's individual religious devotion.[1] Scholars of this tale who do mention historical crusades tend to do so briefly, in a passing reference in their analyses of other matters. For example, in her study of race and religion in the Man of Law's Tale, Carolyn Dinshaw suggests that the text's anxiety about the efficacy of conversion is informed by awareness of the military failures of the crusades, while Brenda Deen Schildgen ties the centrality of Rome in this tale to British support for the Roman papacy and concomitant opposition to French crusading plans during the Papal Schism.[2] Even Geraldine Heng, who describes the tale's relationship to crusade much more fully, argues that this tale represents a distinctive, feminine rewriting of crusading ideals. She writes, 'There should be little doubt that what Custance accomplishes in her story is the enactment of a successful crusade, cultural-style, feminine-style.'[3] As valuable as these studies are, they raise the question of how directly and fully

1 Geoffrey Chaucer, the Man of Law's Tale in *The Riverside Chaucer*, ed. Larry D. Benson (Boston: Houghton-Mifflin, 1987), pp. 87–104. All quotations of the Man of Law's Tale are from this text and are henceforth identified by line numbers in parentheses. I am grateful to the Social Sciences and Humanities Research Council of Canada for a grant that funded research for this article.

2 See Carolyn Dinshaw, 'Pale Faces: Race, Religion, and Affect in Chaucer's Texts and their Readers', *Studies in the Age of Chaucer* 23 (2001), 19–41, p. 24; Brenda Deen Schildgen, *Pagans, Tartars, Moslems, and Jews in Chaucer's Canterbury Tales* (Gainesville: University of Florida Press, 2001), p. 66. Likewise, in his discussion of the colonialist implications of the tale, Christopher Bracken notes in passing that the tale 'perpetuates the crusading idea long after the Crusades themselves had ended in failure': Bracken, 'Constance and the Silkweavers: Working Women and the Colonial Fantasy in Chaucer's "The Man of Law's Tale" ', *Critical Matrix* 8.1 (1994), 13–39, p. 20.

3 Geraldine Heng, *Empire of Magic: Medieval Romance and the Politics of Cultural Fantasy* (New York: Columbia University Press, 2003), p. 189.

Chaucer's Man of Law's Tale engages the fourteenth-century discourse of crusade. Is crusade merely a passing reference in this tale, or something Chaucer depicts only to rewrite? Might one instead perceive a very full, and decidedly less revisionary, engagement of the historical rhetoric and experience of crusading in Chaucer's day? In this essay, I argue the latter. As I will show, many of the ideas that structure the Man of Law's Tale and constitute its substance are ideas that appear prominently in fourteenth-century Latin and French treatises advocating crusade and recovery of the Holy Land. As a result, the Man of Law's Tale can be read as a fascinating Middle English literary assessment of the rhetoric and practices of 'God's War' in the later Middle Ages.[4]

Historians such as Norman Housley, Maurice Keen, Antony Leopold, and Christopher Tyerman have demonstrated the ongoing commitment to crusade to the Holy Land in fourteenth-century Europe, long after the fall of Acre in 1291 and the effective end of the crusader kingdoms.[5] By studying chivalric treatises, papal correspondence, heraldic court records, proposals to recover the Holy Land, and chronicles, these historians have debunked the notion that crusading in Chaucer's day was perceived as a disgraced and antiquated endeavour. At the same time, however, it was not perceived as a practice without limitations or failures. Indeed, many medieval texts explicitly outline the challenges posed by crusade in practice, the past failures of crusading, and the complexity of re-launching eastern crusades after the fall of Acre. This article examines the ways in which Chaucer's Man of Law's Tale engages these and other specific issues discussed in fourteenth-century crusading proposals, those treatises written to outline the need for western Christians to recover the Holy Land and to provide guidance as to how this task might be accomplished. I do not wish to make the impossible claim that Chaucer must have read a particular crusading proposal, or that he directly responds to a certain crusading proponent. Instead, what I will show is that the Man of Law's Tale explores many aspects of crusade as it was portrayed in treatises circulating during the fourteenth century. Specifically, the Man of Law's

4 The phrase is taken from Christopher Tyerman's magisterial *God's War: A New History of the Crusades* (Cambridge, Mass.: Harvard University Press, 2006).

5 Norman Housley, 'Holy Land or Holy Lands? Palestine and the Catholic West in the Late Middle Ages and Renaissance', *Studies in Church History* 36 (2006), 228–49; *The Later Crusades, 1274–1580: From Lyons to Alcazar* (New York: Oxford University Press, 1992); 'Perceptions of Crusading in the Mid-Fourteenth Century: The Evidence of Three Texts', *Viator* 36 (2005), 415–33; 'Costing the Crusade: Budgeting for Crusading Activity in the Fourteenth Century', in *The Experience of Crusading 1*, ed. Marcus Bull and Norman Housley (Cambridge: Cambridge University Press, 2003), pp. 45–59; Maurice Keen, 'Chaucer's Knight, the English Aristocracy and the Crusade', in *English Court Culture in the Later Middle Ages*, ed. V. J. Scattergood and J. W. Sherborne (London: Duckworth, 1983), pp. 45–62; Antony Leopold, 'Crusading Proposals in the Fourteenth and Fifteenth Centuries', *Studies in Church History* 36 (2000), 216–27; *How to Recover the Holy Land: The Crusade Proposals of the Late Thirteenth and Early Fourteenth Centuries* (Aldershot: Ashgate, 2000); Tyerman, *God's War.*

Tale considers the roles of marriage, proselytizing, trade, and money as tools that further crusading goals. It also, I argue, depicts the failures of human plans for conversion and conquest, and the problem of internecine division within Christianity itself, two issues that preoccupied crusade proponents. As the text exposes the human limitations and delusions that beleaguered the crusading movement, however, it also illustrates, and venerates, precisely the type of courage demanded of crusaders. As a whole, then, the tale provides a wide-ranging, unflinching assessment of crusade machinations and motivations that simultaneously condemns crusade and celebrates the form of Christian heroism that its practice ideally demanded.

Custance's Surryen marriage and crusade contexts: proselytizing, trade, money

The extent of the Man of Law's Tale's engagement with crusade first becomes apparent in the depiction of Custance's Surryen marriage. This marriage broaches the text's concern with promulgating Christianity in a context that evokes crusading locales and interactions with Muslims. Chaucer suggests, drawing on source texts by Trevet and Gower, that Christianization might be effected through a Saracen Sultan's marriage to a Christian woman. The idea that Christian women might participate in peaceful efforts to expand the influence of Christianity was not as uncommon as one might think, and was a possibility raised in literature about crusade and crusading locales. The premise was central to late medieval tales of St Katherine of Alexandria, many of which depict her preaching to, and converting, Muslim scholars and soldiers.[6] In romances, women might preach Christianity to their husbands and convert them within the context of inter-faith marriage, as in the Middle English *King of Tars* and its chronicle sources.[7] The same idea also turns up in one crusading treatise, alongside the more traditional plans for violent conquest. In Pierre Dubois' *De recuperatione terre sancte* (dedicated to Edward I of England),[8] Dubois suggests that

> While others are pursuing a policy of inflicting injury on the Saracens, making war upon them, seizing their lands, and plundering their other property, perhaps girls trained in the proposed schools may be given as wives to the Saracen chiefs, although preserving their faith lest they participate in their husbands' idolatry. By their efforts, with the help of God and the preaching disciples so they may

6 See, for example, the version of *Seynt Katerine*, in the 1330s Auchinleck manuscript, Edinburgh, National Library of Scotland, MS 19. 2. 1, fols. 21r–24v.

7 See *The King of Tars: Edited from the Auchinleck MS Advocates 19.2.1*, ed. Judith Perryman (Heidelberg: Carl Winter, 1980), pp. 42–50 and also Lillian Herlands Hornstein, 'The Historical Background of *The King of Tars*', *Speculum* 16 (1941), 404–14; 'New Analogues to the "King of Tars" ', *Modern Language Review* 36 (1941), 433–42.

8 As Leopold notes, however, 'there is no indication that he ever received a copy'; *How to Recover*, p. 31.

> have assistance from Catholics – for they cannot rely on the Saracens – their husbands might be persuaded and led to the Catholic faith.[9]

Here, marriage becomes a peaceful complement to traditional crusade warfare in endeavours to extend Christian control over Saracen territories. Although Chaucer derives his account of Custance's first marriage from the work of Trevet and Gower, he is depicting the kind of inter-faith marriage for which Dubois' tract called, in which the Christian bride converts her husband. Given this motif, it is unsurprising that Custance's first marriage has been read as a meditation on European efforts to convert the East.[10] Ultimately, however, the Surryen marriage in Chaucer's text is not really about conversion in any spiritual sense, wherein a process of theological instruction leads to a change of religious belief. Instead, Chaucer's depiction of this marriage eliminates suggestions of proselytizing efforts on Custance's part and emphasizes the role of trade and 'certein gold' in spreading the Christian faith. In so doing, the tale pointedly evokes the rhetoric and practices of fourteenth-century crusade.

The role of missionary activities in crusade attracted some attention from late medieval crusade theorists, but crusade to the Holy Land traditionally was depicted as a mission to reclaim land unjustly taken from Christians rather than a conversion mission.[11] In the thirteenth century, the idea of preaching conversion to Muslims and other non-Christians attracted increasing attention, as military efforts to conquer non-Christian territories repeatedly proved unsuccessful,[12] but by the fourteenth century, belief that preaching might

9 Pierre Dubois, *The Recovery of the Holy Land*, trans. Walther I. Brandt (New York: Columbia University Press, 1956), p. 124. The Latin reads: 'Forte majoribus Saracenis quibus alii injuriantur guerras movent, auferunt terras suas, alia bona rapiunt, poterunt dari uxores perite provisionis istius, salva fide earum, ut non communicent cum eorum ydolatria; per quas cum auxilio Dei et discipulorum predicantium, et ut subsidium habeant a catholicis, quia de Saracenis non possunt confidere, poterunt ad fidem catholicam induci et perduci.' Brandt's translation captures the spirit of Dubois' suggestion that Saracen rulers be subjected to forceful conquest as well as to wifely encouragement to convert. However, a more precise translation of the first part of the Latin might read: 'Perhaps [as some] wage war against the Saracen chiefs (by whom others are attacked), take away their lands, [and] seize other goods, wives trained in the schools could be given [to the Saracen chiefs], without violation of their [Christian] faith, and with this precaution: that they not participate in their husbands' idolatry.' See Dubois, *De recuperatione terre sancte*, ed. Ch-V. Langlois (Paris: A. Picard, 1891), p. 57.

10 Dinshaw, 'Pale Faces', pp. 24–27; Heng, *Empire*, pp. 181–237; Schildgen, *Pagans*, pp. 48–68.

11 For example, when preaching the First Crusade, Pope Urban is reputed to have said 'Enter upon the road to the Holy Sepulchre; wrest that land from the wicked race, and subject it to yourselves. That land which as the Scripture says "floweth with milk and honey", was given by God into the possession of the children of Israel.' Robert of Rheims, *Historia Hierosolymitana*, trans. Dana C. Munro in *The First Crusade: The Chronicle of Fulcher of Chartres and Other Source Materials*, 2nd ed., ed. Edward Peters (Philadelphia: University of Pennsylvania Press, 1998), p. 28. The Latin reads 'Viam sancti Sepulcri incipite, terram illam nefariæ genti auferte, eamque vobis subjicite, terra illa filiis Israel a Deo in possessionem data fuit, sicut Scriptura dicit, *quæ lacte et melle fluit*.' Robert of Rheims, *Historia Iherosolimitana* in *Recueil des historiens des croisades: historiens occidentaux*, vol. 3 (1866; repr. Farnborough: Gregg Press, 1967), p. 728. See also Leopold, *How to Recover*, p. 101.

12 Housley, *Later Crusades*, p. 381.

succeed where conquest had failed was on the wane. Crusade during this period again became predominantly a matter of violent territorial conquest. Even crusade proponents such as Ramón Lull, who sometimes advocated Christianization through peaceful theological conversion, increasingly called for the use of force alongside preaching.[13] Chaucer's text similarly downplays ideas of preaching Christianity to Muslims. In the Man of Law's Tale, unlike other versions of the Constance story, proselytizing plays no part in efforts to Christianize Surrye. In Trevet and Gower, Constance actively embraces the opportunity to proselytize presented by the Saracen merchants who visit Rome. In Trevet's text, she 'went down to see their riches and asked them about their land and their religion. And when she understood that they were heathens, she preached the Christian faith to them. And when they had assented to the Christian faith, she had them baptized and instructed perfectly in the faith of Jesus Christ.'[14] Similarly, in Gower's *Confessio Amantis*, Constance

> ... was so ful of feith
> That the greteste of Barbarie,
> Of hem whiche usen marchandie,
> Sche hath converted as thei come
> To hire upon a time in Rome,
> ...
> Sche hath hem with hire wordes wise
> Of Cristes feith so full enformed
> That thei therto ben all conformed,
> So that baptesme thei receiven.[15]

In contrast, Chaucer's Custance never even meets the merchants who relay to the Surryen Sowdan the descriptions of her that ignite his desire to marry her.

[13] See, for example, the *Tractatus de modo convertendi infideles*, in which Lull advocates the use of both conversion and force. Ramon Lull, 'Tractatus de modo convertendi infideles', ed. Jacqueline Rambaud-Buhot, in *Beati Magistri R. Lulli opera Latina*, vol. 3 (Palma de Mallorca, 1954), pp. 99–112. For a translation into French, see Ramon Sugranyes de Franch, trans., in *Raymond Lulle, docteur des missions: Avec un choix de textes traduits et annotés* (Switzerland: Nouvelle Revue de science missionnaire, 1954), pp. 129–43. Antony Leopold also notes that, in later works, Lull suggests that the 'threat of a crusade could be used to induce conversion' and that 'Saracen emirs in Africa could be confirmed in their possessions if they converted to Christianity, but would face perpetual warfare if not.' Leopold, *How to Recover*, p. 103.

[14] Nicholas Trevet, 'Of the Noble Lady Constance', trans. Robert M. Correale in *Sources and Analogues of the Canterbury Tales, Volume II*, ed. Robert M. Correale and Mary Hamel (Cambridge: D. S. Brewer, 2005), pp. 296–329, p. 296. The Old French reads: '... marchaunz paens hors de la grant Sarizine, aportauntz [trop] diverses et riches marchaundises, a queux descendi Constaunce pur aviser lour richesses, si lour demanda de lour terre et de lour creaunce. Et quant ele [entendi] q'il estoient paens, lour precha la foi Cristiene. Et puis q'il avoient assentu a la foi Cristiene les fist baptizer et enseigner parfitement en la foi Jhesu Crist', p. 297.

[15] John Gower, 'Tale of Constance', from *Confessio Amantis*, ed. G. C. Macaulay, in *Sources and Analogues*, pp. 330–50, lines 598–609, p. 330.

The Man of Law's Tale presents its heroine as an unwilling, passive vehicle of Christianization who never, in the Surryen portion of the tale at least, preaches Christianity. As a result, Chaucer's text focuses its readers' attention on other forces driving Custance's Surryen marriage, namely the mercantile trade that brings her to the Sowdan's attention, and the subsequent transactions of her father, the Pope, 'the chirche', and 'the chivalrie', those European estates who historically promoted, and participated in, crusades to the east.

The Man of Law's Tale opens with the depiction of eastern merchants and east–west trading interactions:

> In Surrye whilom dwelte a compaignye
> Of chapmen riche, and therto sadde and trewe,
> That wyde-where senten her spicerye,
> Clothes of gold, and satyns riche of hewe.
> Hir chaffare was so thrifty and so newe
> That every wight hath deyntee to chaffare
> With hem, and eek to sellen hem hire ware. (II.134–40)

This opening situates the narrative of Custance's eventual marriage to the Saracen Sowdan in a mercantile context in which, as various scholars have noted, Custance ultimately becomes a commodity traded between men to accomplish Christian goals:[16]

> ... by the popes mediacioun,
> And al the chirche, and al the chivalrie,
> ... in destruccioun of mawmettrie,
> And in encrees of Cristes lawe deere,
> They been acorded, so as ye shal heere:
>
> How that the Sowdan and his baronage
> And alle his liges sholde ycristned be,
> And he shal han Custance in mariage,
> And certein gold, I noot what quantitee;
> ...
> This same accord was sworn on eyther syde. (II.234–44)

Custance herself has no say in the 'accord'; indeed, her comments communicate her distressed response to the plan, opening as they do with the word 'Allas': 'Allas, unto the Barbre nacioun/ I moste anoon, syn that it is youre wille;/ ... / Wommen are born to thraldom and penance,/ And to been under mannes governance' (II.281–87). What intrigues me about this marriage accord, however, is not Custance's pitiable situation, as poignant as it is, but rather the ways in which Chaucer's depiction of the attempted

[16] The fullest discussion of this is Carolyn Dinshaw, 'The Law of Man and its "Abhomynacions" ', in *Chaucer's Sexual Poetics* (Madison: University of Wisconsin Press, 1989), pp. 88–112.

Christianization of Surrye emphasizes the mercantile and earthly aspects of this endeavour, and in so doing evokes the rhetoric and practices of 'God's War'.

In treatises advocating recovery of the Holy Land, trade between Muslims and Christians turns up regularly as a topic. Leopold notes that the Mamluk sultanate's 'reliance on imports for certain vital goods' was perceived as a military weakness that crusaders should exploit, and 'Consequently, the majority of proposals … favoured an embargo on trade with the Mamluks, and several authors discussed the vulnerability of the enemy to economic warfare.'[17] Lull, for example, suggests that Christians not buy goods from 'infidels' unless they do so through an agreement that ensures the Christian merchants have access to an important market, because Christians will thereby obtain profit while the Saracens will sustain loss.[18] He also advocates the destruction of Saracen merchants who carry their wares across the sea, noting that through their destruction the number of Christian merchants will be multiplied and their safe passage across the sea will be enabled.[19] Dubois, too, repeatedly raises the intersection of crusading and mercantile endeavours, usually to signal the trade benefits that would accrue from a successful eastern crusade. He writes, 'valuable commodities, abundant in those regions but rare and highly prized among us, would be transported to us Occidentals in adequate amounts at reasonable prices, once the world were made Catholic', adding later that 'When these [crusading] projects have, by the grace of God, been accomplished, … [t]he Arabs will then be unable to prosper materially unless they share with the Catholics the commerce in their products. This will also be true in the case of oriental peoples.'[20]

Historical actions during the fourteenth century also reveal the role of trading concerns, particularly those of the Italian merchant-states, in western crusade efforts. The slave trade that supplied the Mamluk regiments of the Sultanate's army was a 'lucrative business … dominated by Genoese traders', and agreements involved were believed to prevent Genoese attacks on ships trading with the Muslim sultanate.[21] Such trade engagements not only outraged crusade proponents, but also occasioned papal letters insisting that

17 Leopold, *How to Recover*, p. 119.

18 Lull, 'Tractatus', p. 99. The Latin reads: 'neque emant mercimonia ipsorum infidelium nisi sit sub pacto quod habeant magnum forum, quia ex hoc Christiani lucrum reportabunt et ipsi Sarraceni magnum dampnum'.

19 Ibid., pp. 99–100. 'Et etiam, circa mercatores Sarracenorum qui per mare mercimonia adducunt, destruentur, et, in destruxtione [sic] ipsorum, multiplicabuntur mercatores Christianorum et ire per mare secure poterunt.'

20 Dubois, *Recovery*, pp. 120, 156–7. The Latin reads 'nobis occidentalibus communicari res preciosas, in partibus illis habundantes, nobis deficientes et apud nos carissimas, satis pro modico nobis communicari, mondo catholicum ordinato', and 'Quibus premissis sic per Dei graciam ordinatis, … ita quod bene vivere etiam corporaliter non poterunt Arabes, nisi communicent catholicis commercia rerum suarum; et idem in orientalibus populis.' *De recuperatione*, pp. 53, 89.

21 Leopold, *How to Recover*, pp. 122, 124.

Genoa and Venice, another Muslim trading partner, 'observe the prohibitions against trade' with Muslims.[22] These same mercantile powers, however, often managed the naval logistics of getting crusaders to the East and providing supply lines for crusading activities there.[23] Trading concerns could also prompt these merchant powers to act against Muslims. In 1332 Venice helped form a naval league to attack the Turks, while in 1390 Genoese desires to suppress piracy off the coasts of North Africa led them to help organize Louis of Bourbon's unsuccessful crusade and to contribute shipping and crossbowmen to the enterprise.[24] Mercantile concerns were thus widely understood both to thwart and facilitate efforts to conquer Muslim territories.

When Chaucer depicts Custance as a passive item of news relayed by Saracen merchants rather than as a devout religious proselytizer, he suggests, as did crusading treatises, that mercantile interests take precedence over the preaching of Christianity in East–West engagements. The marriage arrangements further this suggestion by laying bare the role of financial transactions in the Sowdan's conversion. According to the narrator, the Emperor, Pope, 'chirche' and 'chivalrie' all agree that the Sowdan will 'ycristned be,/ And … shal han Custance in mariage,/ And certein gold, I noot what quantitee' (240–42). The reference to 'certein gold' clearly suggests a dowry, but mentioning the gold at the start of a line foregrounds its significance for the Christianization endeavor that is unfolding. Chaucer enhances this effect by appending to this description the narratorial comment 'I noot what quantitee': the reference to 'quantitee' evokes pragmatic, mercantile concerns with a transaction, while the narratorial 'I noot what' makes the reference to such concerns unspecific and, indeed, extraneous. In their very narrative excess, however, these words draw the narrator's interest in gold to the reader's attention. Human interest in quantities of gold is foregrounded in a context that ties this reminder to the clerical and knightly arrangements to marry Custance to the Sowdan. The 'destruccioun of mawmettrie' and 'encrees of Cristes lawe' (II.236–37) in many ways are presented as side effects of a financial transaction. Christianization becomes a financial project as well as a political and religious one, a state of affairs depicted in many crusading treatises.

As Leopold states, 'The huge expense of crusading in the [fourteenth century] made it impossible for an individual, even a ruling monarch, to finance the crusade without assistance',[25] so the acquisition and distribution of 'certein gold' was a central component of most plans to recapture the Holy Land. Dubois, for example, advocates that all the European properties and revenues of the military orders be confiscated and used to fund one combined

22 Ibid., p. 124.

23 Ibid., pp. 124–5.

24 Ibid., pp. 141, 192; Housley, 'Costing the Crusade', p. 52.

25 Leopold, *How to Recover*, p. 72. See also Housley, 'Costing the Crusade'.

military order actively engaged in the recovery of the Holy Land. He also wryly suggests that all monies gathered in local churches since the Fall of Acre to aid recovery of the Holy Land actually be tallied and used for a crusade.[26] Philippe de Mézières, who wrote a letter to Richard II of England advocating peace with France and renewal of eastern crusade, suggests the formation of a new chivalric order to spearhead crusade, and claims that by this measure Richard 'will expend a million florins less than [he] would if the said Order did not exist'.[27] Other examples abound, indicating that 'certein gold' underpinned crusade plans for Christianization by conquest as overtly as it does the plans for Christianization by marriage in Chaucer's text.

In sum, Chaucer's depiction of Custance's Surryen marriage arrangements evokes a great deal of the rhetoric surrounding the planning and practice of 'God's War' in his day. Even though the inter-cultural marriage itself is not a military crusade, its possibility formed part of some crusade plans, while the absence of proselytizing efforts on Custance's part suggests the lack of interest in missionary efforts demonstrated by most fourteenth-century crusade treatises. Furthermore, the central role of merchants and money in effecting Custance's *passagium* to Surrye accurately conveys the importance of trade and finance in historical plans to Christianize Muslim realms. Crusade thus constitutes much more than a passing reference in the Man of Law's Tale. Indeed, the number of intersections between the depiction of Custance's Surryen marriage and crusading rhetoric and practices encourages a reading of this episode as a fourteenth-century reflection on the crusades' efficacy in promulgating Christian influence. In this light, I suggest that the unfolding of events in Surrye can be read as a condemnation of the historical failure of European crusading endeavours.

Crusading/conversion failures and successes

In Chaucer's Surrye, Christianization efforts fail spectacularly because of an unanticipated Saracen uprising that occurs when the Sowdan's mother organizes a feast in which, with the exception of Custance, 'The Sowdan and the Cristen everichone/ Been al tohewe and stiked at the bord' (II.429–30). Chaucer powerfully highlights the Christian failure to plan for Saracen opposition to the imposition of Christianity. This possibility is not even raised in Rome, but is the first thing Chaucer mentions in his depiction of a Surryen

26 Dubois, *Recovery*, pp. 82, 158; *De recuperatione*, pp. 14, 91.

27 Philippe de Mézières, *Letter to King Richard II: A Plea Made in 1395 for Peace between England and France*, ed. and trans. G. W. Coopland (Liverpool: Liverpool University Press, 1975), p. 33. The French reads 'faisant le saint passage comme dit est dessus, quant a finances, qui ne seront pas petites, vous despenderes mains un million de florins que vous ne feries se de la dicte chevalerie n'estoit riens', p. 106.

response to the agreement. The Sowdan's mother 'Espied hath hir sones pleyn entente', and how he

> ... in point is for to lete
> The hooly lawes of our Alkaron,
> Yeven by Goddes message Makomete.
> But oon avow to grete God I heete,
> The lyf shal rather out of my body sterte
> Or Makometes lawe out of myn herte! (II.324, 331–36).

Although the narrator adds another motivation for the Sowdanesse's action about a hundred lines later, stating that she 'Hath ... doon this cursed dede,/ For she hirself wolde al the contree lede' (II.433–34), this narratorial interpolation does not, to my mind, have the same weight as the Sowdanesse's own words in communicating a sense of her motives. Moreover, her speech is given first in the text, long before the narrator's comment, and is the only motivation provided for the massacre before it happens. This insistence on the Sowdanesse's devotion to Islam contrasts markedly with Gower's *Confessio Amantis*, where the Souldan's mother muses that if 'Mi sone him wedde in this manere,/ Than have I lost my joies hiere/ For myn astat schal so be lassed' (647–49). Chaucer instead foregrounds the Sowdanesse's attachment to the 'Alkaron' and to 'Makomete', thereby presenting a historically accurate evocation of Islamic difference which is rare among romances, as Schildgen notes.[28]

Because Chaucer carefully situates Custance's Surryen marriage plans in contexts that evoke historical ideas about crusade, the marriage project's failure speaks to crusade proponents' failures to acknowledge or comprehend cultural differences. Dubois, who also envisioned marriage to Christian women as a way of advancing crusading goals, exemplifies this incomprehension in his depiction of Muslim marriages. Dubois suggests that Muslim women really desire Christian marriages. According to him, Muslim women will

> ... strive the more zealously for this [the adoption of the Christian faith by Saracen chiefs] because each of the [Saracen chiefs] has many wives. All the wealthy and powerful among them lead a voluptuous life to the disadvantage of their wives, anyone of whom would rather have a man to herself (nor is it to be wondered at) than that seven or more wives should share one husband. It is on that account, as I have generally heard from merchants who frequent their lands, that the women of that sect would easily be strongly influenced toward our manner of life, so that each man would have only one wife.[29]

28 Schildgen, *Pagans*, p. 60.

29 Dubois, *Recovery*, p. 124. The Latin reads 'quod plurimum appeterent eorum uxores, eo quod quilibet ipsorum multas habet; vitam enim ducunt omnes divites et potentes intra ipsos luxuriosam,

Dubois' words point to how differently from Chaucer one fourteenth-century writer envisaged a female Muslim reaction to Christianization, and indicate the ways in which Chaucer's comments on religious attachment highlight an aporia present in fourteenth-century crusading rhetoric and plans for peaceful conversion. Of course, proponents of violent Christianization by conquest did anticipate Muslim refusal of Christianity and attachment to Islamic practices. These proponents' failure in perception tended to take the form of assertions of Muslim military weakness and cowardice. In contrast, Chaucer's narrative suggests that the failure of Christians to convert Muslims was caused by the Sowdanesse's deep attachment to her beliefs and to Muslim law.

While Chaucer powerfully identifies non-Christian religious attachments as a reason for the failure of the Christianization plans of the Pope and the Emperor, he also, as many scholars have noted, identifies another reason for this failure. Custance's Surryen marriage is, above all else, a human-designed and human-implemented model of Christianization. Human merchants bear the tidings that foster the Sowdan's human desire for the womanly epitome of goodness and beauty, while human power-brokers negotiate the agreement to bring Christianity to Surrye, and human attachments provoke the Sowdanesse's bloody response to a conversion she has not chosen. Chaucer shows that larger forces doom such human plans to failure. His narrator prefaces Custance's arrival in Surrye with this comment:

> O firste moevyng! Crueel firmament,
> With thy diurnal sweigh that crowdest ay
> And hurlest al from est til occident
> That naturelly wolde holde another way,
> Thy crowdyng set the hevene in swich array
> At the bigynnyng of this fiers viage,
> That crueel Mars hath slayn this mariage. (II.295–301)

He then concludes his invocation of larger forces by stating

> Imprudent Emperour of Rome, allas!
> Was ther no philosophre in al thy toun?
> Is no tyme bet than oother in swich cas?
> Of viage is ther noon eleccioun,
> Namely to folk of heigh condicioun?
> Noght whan a roote is of a burthe yknowe?
> Allas, we been to lewed or to slowe! (II.309–15)

The last line explicitly acknowledges human failure and limitation, and

in prejudicium uxorum, quarum quelibet vellet habere solum magis (nec est mirum) quam quod septem vel plures uxores non haberent nisi unum. Idcirco generaliter prout a mercatoribus qui frequentant eorum terras audivi quod mulieres illius secte de facili multum moverentur ad nostram, ut quilibet vir haberet uxorem unam tantum.' *De recuperatione*, p. 57.

thereby sets the scene for the Sowdanesse's scheme and the collapse of a human-planned Christianization. As Jill Mann has argued, the evocation of astrology and of larger forces at play in Chaucerian texts like this one and the *Knight's Tale* tends to be tied to Boethian ideas of divine 'purveiaunce' and to the difficulty humans experience in accepting failures and reversals of fortune as parts of normal earthly life.[30] Considered in this light, the stanzas quoted above constitute a particularly apt Chaucerian preface to events in Surrye. Once the Sowdanesse has cast Custance out to sea in a rudderless boat, the Man of Law explicitly begins to contrast the events that follow with the human-driven events that culminated in the Surryen conversion fiasco. The narrator prays in line 448 that 'He that is lord of Fortune be thy steere', and henceforth divine 'purveiaunce' replaces human desires in directing Custance's conversion efforts. As Schildgen puts it, 'In this tale, human desires and plans fail, for desires do not shape results; rather divine providence … rules.'[31]

Structurally, Chaucer makes this point clear through his careful pairing of the human-planned (and failed) conversion efforts in Surrye with the divinely guided conversion efforts in Northumbria. As Kathy Lavezzo notes, 'In marked contrast to the Holy Roman "imperialism" that lies behind Custance's journey to Syria, "Goddes sonde" or providence directs the rudderless ship that transports Custance to England (523).'[32] In Northumbria, Custance 'hath so longe sojourned there,/ In orisons, with many a bitter teere,/ Til Jhesu hath converted thurgh his grace/ Dame Hermengyld, constablesse of that place' (II.536–39). In contrast to the Sowdan's conversion, which is motivated by human desire and demands, Hermengyld's transformation is effected through Custance's prayers and Jesus's own grace. The text further emphasizes the idea that divine intervention, not human action, determines events in Northumbria in the episode of Custance's rejected suitor. When this knight attempts to frame Custance for Hermengyld's murder, his nefarious plans, prompted by human desire and resentment, come to nought as a miraculous hand and voice condemn him when he perjures himself on the Bible. King Alla

30 Jill Mann, *Feminizing Chaucer* (1991; repr. Cambridge: D. S. Brewer, 2002), pp. xvii–xviii, 102–12. It should be noted that Jill's chapter on 'Suffering Woman, Suffering God' informs much of my thinking on the Man of Law's Tale. I would also like at this point to acknowledge my general gratitude to Jill as scholar, supervisor, and friend. Her insights preserved me from many pitfalls intellectually and professionally when I was her first Notre Dame doctoral student, and have continued to do so in my subsequent career. I only hope that this article does justice to her formative and ongoing influence on me. Her thoughts inform my thinking in ways that enrich my work as much as they may sometimes surprise her. Here, for you Jill, is an article in which my crusading research is worked into a consideration of Chaucer's texts rather than of those anonymous or Hocclevian texts you read so carefully when supervising me, even as you lamented that 'They just aren't Chaucer!'

31 Schildgen, *Pagans*, p. 60.

32 Kathy Lavezzo, 'Beyond Rome: Mapping Gender and Justice in the Man of Law's Tale', *Studies in the Age of Chaucer* 24 (2001), 149–80, p. 161.

'and many another in that place' (II.685) are converted by this sight – making divine intervention, not human trade and negotiation, the cause of the Northumbrian conversion to Christian belief. Chaucer further states that 'Jhesus, of his mercy,/ Made Alla wedden ful solempnely/ This hooly mayden' (II.690–92). As Paul Beichner notes, Chaucer's description contrasts with those of Trevet and Gower, who describe Alla's love for Constance and do not attribute the marriage solely to divine intervention.[33] Chaucer's words thus repeatedly highlight the difference between the failure of the Surryen marriage and conversion, and the success of the Northumbrian sojourn and the transformation of Alla and his people into Christians.

This well-developed contrast between Surrye and Northumbria heightens Chaucer's condemnation of the human machinations that produced the Surryen fiasco, and signals yet again the ways in which his narrative intersects with crusading treatises. As Leopold notes, late medieval crusade literature 'was grounded on the belief that victories were granted by God, while the sins of both crusaders, and Christendom in general, were responsible for military defeat'.[34] For example, Eustache Deschamps' 'Exhortation à la croisade', dated to approximately 1395, appeals to kings, counts, dukes, knights and barons to conquer the Holy Land,

> Que nous avons par nostre iniquité,
> Par convoitier, comme fiers et felons,
> Aux ennemis de Dieu, dont c'est pitié,
> Laissé long temps. (11–14)
>
> [which we have, through our iniquity, through covetousness, like proud villains, abandoned to the enemies of God for a long time, which is a wretched state].[35]

In another poem, 'Faicte pour ceuls de France quant ilz furent en Hongrie', Deschamps writes in the envoy

> Prince, abisme est li jugemens
> De Dieu et ses pugnissemens;
> Il l'a bien moustré a ce tour:
> En Turquie est ses vengemens,

33 Beichner notes that Alla's motives in Trevet and Gower are mixed. Paul Beichner, 'Chaucer's Man of Law and Disparitas Cultus', *Speculum* 23 (1948), 70–75, p. 75, n. 16. Trevet states, 'because of the great love he had for the maiden and because of the miracles shown by God, King Alla had himself baptized' ('Puis le roi, pur le grant amour q'il avoit a la pucele, et pur les miracles par Dieux moustrez, le roi Alla lui fist baptizer'), *Sources and Analogues*, pp. 311–12. In Gower, Alla 'his hole herte ... leide/ Upon Constance, and seide he scholde/ For love of hire, if that sche wolde,/ Baptesme take', lines 896–99 in *Sources and Analogues*, p. 336.

34 Leopold, *How to Recover*, p. 95.

35 Eustache Deschamps, 'Exhortation à la croisade', in Aziz Suryal Atiya, *The Crusade of Nicopolis* (London: Methuen, 1934), p. 127, lines 11–14. Translation mine.

De loing, par divers mandemens,
Pour nos pechiez pleins de venin:
Je ne voy que tristesce et plour
Et obseques soir et matin. (31–38).

[Lord, the judgement of God and his punishments are an abyss. He has well shown this on this occasion: In Turkey is his punishment, from afar, by exceptional commandment, for our poisonous sins: I do not see anything but sadness and weeping and funeral rites morning and night].[36]

Like the Man of Law's Tale, these crusading texts depict events as subject to God's judgement, assistance, or impediment, and interpret Christian failures as the results of human flaws. The writers of crusade treatises, however, were restricted to describing recent events whose lack of success provided evidence only of divine disfavour. In contrast, the Man of Law's Tale is a romance set long ago; its genre and setting allow Chaucer to depict a divinely inspired and durably successful Christianization of a non-Christian realm.

Northumbria and schism

Many scholars have read the success of Christianization in Northumbria as evidence of Chaucer's commitment to depicting England as a Christian nation forged by divine intervention. Kathleen Davis writes, 'The English conversion … proceeds not from rational calculation or sexual desire, but through divine revelation. The miraculous punishment of the knight who had falsely accused Custance signals God's attention to the English, and effects their permanent entrance into the Christian community.'[37] Similarly, Lavezzo argues that 'through Custance's providential journey, Chaucer's lawyer endeavors to affirm … how the English are set apart from the world as God's chosen people'.[38] Such arguments certainly hold true. I would like to suggest, however, that Chaucer's turn to Northumbria can also be interpreted as a continuation of his engagement with the concerns of crusading rhetoric. Medieval crusading treatises were particularly concerned with religious schisms within Christianity and their implications for efforts to recover the Holy Land. The presence of British Christians in Northumbria distinguishes it from Surrye, and suggests that the land itself harbours a longstanding Christian identity, even if that identity needs some Roman rewriting by Custance. At the same time, this British presence draws attention to the existence of multiple Christianities and to schisms within Christianity. This

[36] Ibid., p. 131, lines 31–8. Translation mine.

[37] Kathleen Davis, 'Time Behind the Veil: The Media, the Middle Ages and Orientalism Now', in *The Postcolonial Middle Ages*, ed. Jeffrey Jerome Cohen (New York: Palgrave Macmillan, 2000), 105–22, p. 117.

[38] Lavezzo, 'Beyond Rome', p. 155.

problematic multiplicity preoccupied many crusading treatises of the fourteenth century, and prompted repeated calls for the unification and homogenization of Christianities. However, though many crusade proponents argued for the forcible resolution of Christian schism through violence and/or submission to Rome, Chaucer's text suggests that variant Christian pasts might intersect in more fruitful ways and perhaps even work together to facilitate the conversion of non-Christians.

Crusading treatises of the late Middle Ages addressed two religious schisms within Christendom: the papal schism of 1378–1417 and, more frequently, the Great Schism between the Roman Catholic and Greek Orthodox churches. Both were perceived as impediments to the conquest of the Holy Land. The papal schism turns up only occasionally, given the smaller number of treatises written during its duration, but it clearly perturbed crusade proponents. Philippe de Mézières devotes one section of his Letter to Richard II to 'the mortal schism in the Church, and the remedy therefore by way of peace between the Kings [of England and France]'.[39] He laments that 'Catholic Christians, making a double-headed monster of their mother, say to one another, not in love but in wrath, I am for Paul, I am for Apollo, that is, I am for Boniface, I am for Benedict.'[40] Philippe then advocates the establishment of 'a saintly Pope in Rome, sole Vicar of Christ our Creator', calling on Richard and Charles of France to use the current peace in the Hundred Years War to 'restore the Church' in this way, and thereby pave the way for a crusade to reclaim the Holy Land.[41] Perhaps unsurprisingly, given his desire to foster peace between France and England, Philippe remains somewhat vague about the precise actions needed to resolve the papal schism. This vagueness regarding the papal schism contrasts starkly with resolutions to the Great Schism propounded by treatise authors, which were specific and often violent. It was this schism that excited most comment in crusade treatises, and by the fourteenth century, most crusade proponents advocated conquest of the Greek Christians and their submission to Rome. Lull, for example, suggests that the Pope send wise and holy men to discuss the Articles of Faith with the Greek schismatics and to threaten them with dispossession and the sword if they do not wish to unite with the Catholic Church.[42] Dubois similarly advocates sending learned 'persons highly skilled in every branch of

39 Philippe de Mézières, *Letter*, p. 21. The French reads 'du mortel sisme de l'esglise et du remede d'iceluy par le moien de la paix des ii roys', p. 93.

40 Ibid., p. 22. The French reads 'les crestiens catholiques, faisans un monstre de leur mere a ii. tetses, respondans l'une l'autre, non pas par charite mais par indignacion, et disans, Je suy de Paul, je suy de Apollo, c'est a dire, Je suy de Boniface, je suy de Benedic', p. 94.

41 Ibid., p. 22. The French reads 'un saint pape de Romme, seul vicaire souverain de Jhesucrist, nostre tres doulz Createur', and 'reparer l'eglise', p. 95.

42 Lull, 'Tractatus', p. 100. The Latin reads 'Dominus Papa mittat ipsos ad disputandum de fide, denunciando eis quod, si se nolverint unire cum Ecclesia, oportebit eos terram amittere et gladium corporale subire.'

knowledge' who 'would outdo the experts of that country in disputing, advising, discussing … so that there would be no one who could withstand the wisdom of the Roman Church'.[43] He also baldly states that any eastern crusade should follow up its conquest of the Holy Land with an attack on the Greek empire, so that Charles of Valois might replace 'the unjust usurper Paleologus' and, 'after gaining the victory and the possession of the [Greek] Empire [might] bring opportune aid to the defense of the Holy Land whenever the need arose'.[44] The historical problem of religious difference within Christianity thus tends to be addressed by calls for a unity rooted not in negotiation and coexistence, but in the submission of all Christian groups to Rome, often enforced by violence.

Just as the Man of Law's Tale raises the problem of deep-rooted attachments to 'Makometes lawe' in Surrye, so too it raises the problem of deep-rooted, non-Roman Christian beliefs in Northumbria. The religious schism between Roman and Celtic Christianity is a well-known part of English history, due largely to the attention paid to it by Bede, who described various meetings between Roman and British Christian leaders as they attempted to negotiate a union of the two Churches. This non-Roman Christian presence is one of the first details conveyed about the land where Custance washes up:

> To Walys fledde the Cristyanytee
> Of old Britons dwellynge in this ile;
> Ther was hir refut for the meene while
>
> But yet nere Cristene Britons so exiled,
> That ther nere somme that in hir privetee
> Honoured Crist and hethen folk bigiled. (II.544–49)

Chaucer makes British Christianity a fact of life which Custance, the Roman Christian, must engage.[45] Unlike Bede's *Ecclesiastical History*, however, the Man of Law's Tale does not depict British Christianity as sinful and flawed. Bede lists among the Britons' 'unspeakable crimes' the fact 'that they never preached the faith to the Saxons and Angles who inhabited Britain with them', and includes in his text a meeting between British and Roman Christians in which the Roman St Augustine warns that if the Britons 'refuse[] to accept peace from their [Christian] brethren, they w[ill] have to accept war from their

[43] Dubois, *Recovery*, p. 120. The Latin reads 'si papa … mitteret aliquem legatum, simul mitteret cum ipso peritissimos in qualibet sciencia duos vel plures, qui peritiores de illa terra, disputando, consulendo, conferendo, et modis omnibus superarent; ut non esset qui posset sapiencie romane ecclesie resistere'. *De recuperatione*, pp. 52–3.

[44] Ibid., p. 156; The Latin reads 'Peryalogum injustum detentorem' and 'habita victoria et possessione Imperii, ad defensionem Terre Sancte tamquam ei ceteris proximior, quociens opus fuerit, subsidium faciet opportunum'. *De recuperatione*, p. 89.

[45] In this, Chaucer's text resembles that of Trevet, but differs notably from that of Gower who does not explicitly raise the issue of British Christianity.

enemies; and if they w[ill] not preach the way of life to the English nation, they w[ill] one day suffer the vengeance of death at their hands'.[46] Bede concludes with the statement 'This, through the workings of divine judgement, came to pass in every particular as he had foretold.'[47] The Man of Law's Tale, by contrast, remains silent on the failure of the Britons to convert the pagans of Northumbria, stating only that the Britons 'Honored Crist and hethen folk bigiled'. Perhaps one is meant to perceive a failure in the contrast between this course of action and the successful conversions enacted by Custance and Jesus, but that negative comparison is never explicitly drawn in the tale. Instead, the narrative presents a conversion process in which British and Roman Christians work together, with God, to Christianize the realm.

This Christian teamwork becomes apparent when a 'blinde Briton' calls upon the newly converted Dame Hermengyld to restore his sight, a request she fulfills only after Custance 'made hire boold, and bad hire wirche/ The wyl of Crist, as doghter of his chirche' (II.566–67). Admittedly, metaphors of spiritual blindness abound, so perhaps this blind Briton is a subtle comment on the flawed spirituality of the British, but even this interpretation of the figure does not change the fact that he plays an essential role in the enactment of Christ's power in Northumbria. His situation prompts Custance's proselytizing speech and Hermengyld's working of a miracle. Moreover, the sight of this miracle 'abasshe[s]' the constable and provokes him to inquire of Custance 'What amounteth al this fare?', a question the Roman Christian answers by declaring 'oure lay [so ferforth]/ That she the constable, er that it was eve[,]/ Converteth, and on Crist made hym bileve' (II.572–74). The British Christian becomes the vehicle through which God's power is manifested, and this power is then explained by the Roman Christian. The two types of Christians work together, with divine assistance, to spread the faith. In case one might think, however, that the British Christian is always consigned to a subservient role in the conversion process, it is worth noting that while Custance may do most of the talking in the Northumbrian conversions, her own life is saved by a miracle facilitated by a British Christian treasure.

When Custance is falsely accused of the brutal murder of her new convert Hermengyld, she prays to God and Mary for succour. Assistance does come from God, but it is God working in tandem with 'A Britoun book, written with

[46] Bede, *Bede's Ecclesiastical History of the English People*, ed. and trans. Bertram Colgrave and R. A. B. Mynors (Oxford: Clarendon Press, 1969), pp. 69, 141. The Latin passages read 'Qui inter alia inenarrabilium scelerum facta … et hoc addebant, ut numquam genti Saxonum sive Anglorum, secum Brittaniam incolenti, verbum fidei praedicando committerent', p. 68, and 'Quibus vir Domini Augustinus fertur minitans praedixisse quia si pacem cum fratribus accipere nollent, bellum ab hostibus forent accepturi, et si nationi Anglorum noluissent viam vitae praedicare, per horum manus ultionem essent mortis passuri', p. 140.

[47] The Latin reads, 'Quod ita per omnia, ut praedixerat, divino agente iudicio patratum est.' Ibid., p. 140.

Evaungiles' (II.666) that saves her. When Custance's rejected suitor falsely swears on this Bible that she is guilty of Hermengyld's murder, 'An hand hym smoot upon the nekke-boon,/ That doun he fil atones as a stoon,/ And bothe his eyen broste out of his face' (II.669–71). A disembodied voice then states that the knight has 'desclaundered, giltelees,/ The doghter of hooly chirche in heigh presence' (II.674–75). The British Bible and God respond to the Roman Christian's prayers and prove her innocence. The text then adds, 'And for this miracle, in conclusioun,/ And by Custances mediacioun,/ The kyng – and many another in that place –/ Converted was, thanked be Cristes grace!' (II.683–86). God and the Bible perform the miracle that saves Custance and then triggers conversions aided by her 'mediacioun'. Once again, British and Roman Christianities work together to convert pagans, thereby providing a model of harmonious, efficacious alliance among Christians of different sects. The Man of Law's Tale thus depicts inter-Christian interactions that differ radically from ideas found historically in the works of Bede and crusade proponents, who advocated the absolute submission of one type of Christianity to another, even if it produced inter-Christian strife. Chaucer presents a vision of cultural interaction that, in its engagement of the issue of religious schism, provides a distinct critique of the historical practices found in the crusading rhetoric of his own day and in the record of his nation's own Christianization.[48]

Admiring the heroics of crusade

Although Chaucer's Man of Law's Tale offers many critiques of crusade, it also communicates an admiration for one aspect of the mindset necessary to crusade in the later Middle Ages: namely, the willingness to venture oneself in a hazardous expedition, usually by sea, with no clear material incentive, and absolutely no guarantee of success or even of survival. By Chaucer's day, crusading had for a hundred years failed to re-conquer the Holy Land, and had become a progressive narrative of financial and military loss, with only a few temporary victories, such as the very brief (and lucrative) sack of Alexandria in 1365. Crusading was generally a very costly business requiring huge expenditures by expedition leaders and participants, and involving many deaths.[49] As

48 Chaucer's consideration of schism in Northumbria also includes intra-European political schisms. These are evoked when the text records that King Alla was 'worthy of his hond/ Agayn the Scottes' (II.579–80), and that he 'is gon/ To Scotlond-ward, his foomen for to seke' (II.717–18). Such references set Custance's story against a backdrop of European war and conflict. Crusading treatises, too, frequently addressed intra-European conflicts, usually bewailing them as impediments to renewed crusade. See, for example, Dubois, *De recuperatione*, p. 3 and de Mézières, *Letter*, pp. 79–83, 86–87. The backdrop to Chaucer's European story of Custance thus evokes the backdrop of European calls to crusade during the fourteenth century, even if Chaucer does not offer any meditation on how such conflicts might be resolved.

49 See Housley, 'Costing the Crusade'; Christopher Tyerman, *England and the Crusades 1095–1588*

Maurice Keen points out, neither of the 1390s crusades 'brought anyone much profit', and very few crusaders survived the attack on Nicopolis to return home.[50] Despite the costs, hardships and danger, however, one finds many knights in the fourteenth century responding to calls for crusade 'and risk[ing] body and fortune by so doing'.[51] Keen reports, for example, that the Soldich de la Trau is reputed to have said that he considered 'to have been present at Bourbon's siege of Tunis, inconclusive as it was, more honourable than to have been at three mortal battles in the field in ordinary war'.[52] Geoffroi de Charny, too, articulated an intense admiration of crusading in his *Livre de chevalrie.* He states,

> the man who makes war against the enemies of religion in order to support and maintain Christianity and the worship of Our Lord is engaged in a war which is righteous, holy, certain, and sure, for his earthly body will be honored in a saintly fashion and his soul will, in a short space of time, be borne in holiness and without pain into paradise. This kind of war is good, for one can lose in it neither one's reputation in this world, nor one's soul.[53]

Geoffroi also advocates honouring those who have ventured themselves 'on distant journeys to foreign parts, for indeed no one can travel so far without being many times in physical danger. We should for this reason honor such men-at-arms who at great expense, hardship, and grave peril undertake to travel to … distant countries.'[54] Perhaps of even more interest in the context of the Custance story are Geoffroi's beliefs that knights, to be truly admirable, had to push their bodies to extremes, and that 'crusading was an activity involving so much suffering and privation that it could be considered as a form of martyrdom'.[55] These references show that even as crusade was esteemed in Chaucer's day, it was recognized as an activity involving privation, suffering and defeat. These aspects of crusade, rather than being passed over in knightly records, were held up as part of what made crusading a heroic

(Chicago: University of Chicago Press, 1988), pp. 75–85, 187–228; Keen, 'Chaucer's Knight', p. 58.

50 Keen, 'Chaucer's Knight', pp. 56, 58.

51 Ibid., p. 60.

52 Ibid.

53 Housley quotes this passage in 'Perceptions', p. 419. The French reads 'qui fait guerre contre les ennemis de la foy et pour la crestienté soustenir et maintenir et la foy de Nostre Seigneur, ycelle guerre est droite, sainte, seure et ferme, que les corps en sont sainctement honorez et les ames en sont briefment et sainctement et senz paine portees en paradis. Ceste guerre est bonne, que l'on n'y peut perdre ne les corps ne les armes.' Geoffroi de Charny, *The Book of Chivalry of Geoffroi de Charny: Text, Context and Translation*, ed. and trans. Richard Kaeuper and Elspeth Kennedy (Philadelphia: University of Pennsylvania Press, 1996), p. 164.

54 Geoffroi de Charny, *Book of Chivalry*, p. 91. The French reads 'en lointains et estranges voiages … car vraiement nulz ne peut aler en telx lointains voiages que le corps ne soit en peril maintes foiz. Et pour ce devons nous telz gens d'armes honorer qui a grant mise et a grant travail et en grant peril se mettent en aler et en veoir les lointains païs', p. 90.

55 Geoffroi's comments in the unpublished *Livre Charny*, as summarized by Housley in 'Perceptions', p. 418.

knightly endeavor, and it is precisely such heroism, in venturing and suffering, that Chaucer's Man of Law's Tale celebrates.

Jill Mann best describes the nature of the Christian heroism celebrated in the Man of Law's Tale. According to Mann, Chaucer 'identif[ies] the strength in the apparently passive role of acceptance, and … insist[s] on this as the truly heroic role for men and women alike'.[56] The Man of Law's Tale, she argues, depicts 'the *strength* necessary to surrender', and the motif of the rudderless boat 'expresses the courage needed to hazard the self to the flux of events'.[57] This willingness to hazard oneself takes the form of a patient acceptance of 'Goddes sonde'. Custance herself states, 'Lord, ay welcome be thy sonde!' (II.826) when she is put out to sea in Northumbria, but her acceptance of fate extends beyond the passive, as her speech indicates. She follows her statement/prayer of acceptance with a full stanza outlining the theology of this acceptance:

> He that me kepte fro the false blame
> While I was on the lond amonges yow,
> He kan me kepe from harm and eek fro shame
> In salte see, although I se noght how.
> As strong as evere he was, he is yet now.
> In hym triste I, and in his mooder deere,
> That is to me my seyl and eek my steere. (II.827–33)

Such willingness to accept, and even welcome, adverse events is not confined to Custance. The converted Alla also displays this courage when, upon reading the false news that his child is a monster, he states, 'Welcome the sonde of Crist for everemoore/ To me that am now lerned in his loore!' (II.760–61). He then adds, 'Lord, welcome be thy lust and thy plesaunce;/ My lust I putte al in thyn ordinaunce' (II.762–63), thereby emphasizing his active acceptance of divine 'purveiaunce'. In these examples, Chaucer highlights the heroism of actively accepting and suffering whatever trials God may send, and attributes it to both men and women.

Crusading texts, too, emphasized the need to accept God's will, whatever form it might take, as part of venturing on crusade. In Baldric of Dol's version of Pope Urban's preaching of the first crusade, Urban articulates the ideals that informed calls to crusade in later centuries:

> Under Jesus Christ, our Leader, may you struggle for your Jerusalem, in Christian battle-line, … even more successfully than did the sons of Jacob … and may you deem it a beautiful thing to die for Christ in that city in which He died for us. But if it befall you to die this side of it, be sure that to have died on the way is of equal value, if Christ shall find you in His army. God pays with the same shilling, whether at the first or eleventh hour.[58]

56 Mann, *Feminizing Chaucer*, p. 142.

57 Ibid., p. 110.

58 Baldric of Dol, *Historia Jerosolimitana*, trans. Krey, in *The First Crusade*, p. 32. The Latin reads 'et

Geoffroi de Charny, writing in the fourteenth century, advises knights to rely 'on God alone, for one often sees that the best men are defeated by lesser men … you on your own can achieve nothing except what God grants you', and adds 'if you are in a state of grace and you die honorably, does not God show you great mercy when He grants you such a glorious end to your life in this world?'[59] Perhaps the most apt summary of the type of chivalric heroism displayed and required on crusade is the following description of 'good knights', also by Geoffroi:

> good knights may have to undergo hard trials and adventures, for it can truly be said to them that when they want to sleep, they must keep vigil, when they want to eat, they must fast, and when they are thirsty, there is often nothing to drink, and when they would rest, they have to exert themselves all through the night, and when they would be secure from danger, they will be beset by great terrors, and when they would defeat their enemies, sometimes they may be defeated or killed or captured and wounded and struggling to recover; this is not to speak of the perilous adventures they may encounter on their journeys in search of deeds of arms such as the danger of crossing sea or river … All these dangers must they endure and come through safely when they can and God grants them grace.[60]

Texts that advocated crusade thus articulate a vision of heroism similar to that demonstrated by Custance and Alla in the Man of Law's Tale.[61] Even as Chaucer's text clearly communicates a sense of the failures and delusions involved in late medieval crusade, his vision of religious heroism endorses many of the ideals preached to crusading knights. At the same time, Chaucer is not an apologist for, or advocate of, crusade. Rather, his reflections on crusade illustrate the abundantly evident flaws in the practice while also

sub Jesu Christo, duce nostro, acies Christiana … melius quam ipsi veteres Jacobitæ, pro vestra Jerusalem decertetis … Pulchrum sit vobis mori in illa civitate pro Christo, in qua Christus pro vobis mortuus est. Ceterum, si vos citra mori contigerit, id ipsum autumate mori in via, si tamen in sua Christus vos invenerit militia. Deus ejusdem denarii est retributor, prima et hora undecima.' See *Recueil des historiens des croisades: historiens occidentaux*, vol. 4, p. 15.

59 Geoffroi de Charny, *Book of Chivalry*, pp. 131–3. The French reads 'fors que Dieu tant seulement, que vous veez assez souvent que par les moins vaillans sont vaincu li meilleur … vous n'avez riens fors ce que Dieu vous donne … se vous estes en bon estat et vous y mourez honnorablement, ne vous fait Dieu grant grace quant il vous donne si honorable fin en ce siecle?' pp. 130–2.

60 Ibid., p. 177. The French reads 'a ces bons chevaliers peut avenir assez des dures vies et aventures, que l'en leur peut bien dire que quant il cuident dormir, il les convient veillier, et quant il voudront mengier, il les faut jeuner, et quant il ont soif, il n'ont rienz a boire moult de foiz, et quant il se cuident reposer, lors les convient travaillier et a tresnuitier, et quant il cuident estre asseur, lors leur viennent il de grans paours, et quant il cuident desconfire leurs ennemis, aucune fois se treuvent desconfiz ou mors ou pris et bleciez et [en] la paine de garir, sanz les perilz et aventures qui leur peuent avenir es chemins et voiages d'aler querir tel fait d'armes, comme en peril de mer, de rivieres … Et tous telz perilz leur convient avoir et passer quant il peuent, et Dieux leur en donne grace', p. 176.

61 Geraldine Heng, too, albeit in a different context, perceives some similarity between the experiences of Custance and crusaders, noting that Custance's 'sexual martyrdom' bears some resemblance to the 'martyrdom won by crusaders'. Heng, *Empire*, p. 189.

acknowledging that to participate in such flawed endeavours required a type of courage that could be seen as admirable.

Conclusion

Although scholars wishing to analyze Chaucer's depiction of crusade often turn to the representation of the Knight in the General Prologue, the Man of Law's Tale is an equally rich source of commentary on the rhetoric, ideals, and practices of crusade in Chaucer's day. The minimal, failed role of proselytizing in crusade is illustrated in Surrye, while a model of successful conversion, with divine assistance, is depicted in Northumbria. The roles of trade, finance, and human desires in crusading projects are directly evoked in the first part of the tale, and the failures of religious endeavours rooted in such human, earthly concerns are forcefully illustrated. The challenges posed by historical Christian schisms, so much a concern of crusade proponents, are directly confronted in Chaucer's text, which also imagines how such schisms might be resolved, or at least managed, so as to promote the Christianization of non-believers. And the model of heroism required by crusading ideals is repeatedly depicted. Chaucer thus engages many of the issues involved in the historical rhetoric and practice of 'God's War' as it was portrayed in treatises circulating in the fourteenth century. As he does so, he offers an assessment of crusade that condemns its historical failures as a way of dealing with religious difference, commends the mindset it ideally demanded of participants, and illustrates how Christianization might be divinely 'done over' so as to be a success.

If, as the Man of Law suggests in his introduction, he cannot tell a tale because Chaucer has already told them all, then it makes perfect sense that Chaucer should tell a tale addressing the issues of crusade. After all, as Simon Lloyd and Christopher Tyerman have shown, crusade was very much a part of religious life in late medieval England, either through participation in it, attendance at church where it was preached, the willing or unwilling provision of monies to fund it, or general cultural awareness of it as a form of Christian aspiration and endeavour.[62] In short, it was a topic of importance in Chaucer's world, and its appearance in the Man of Law's Tale testifies to the contemporary cultural engagements of the *Canterbury Tales.* By deploying crusading rhetoric and practices in his tale of Custance, Chaucer adds another dimension to his wide-ranging exploration of Christianity's ideals, contradictions and corruptions in the *Canterbury Tales.* Other tales illustrate Christian ideals of sainthood (The Second Nun's Tale), reflect on Christian pronouncements about sin and women (The Parson's Tale, The Wife of Bath's Prologue and

[62] Simon Lloyd, *English Society and the Crusade, 1216–1307* (Oxford: Clarendon Press, 1988); Tyerman, *England and the Crusades.*

Tale), depict Christian interactions with non-Christians (The Prioress's Tale), or condemn the corruption of Christian office-holders (The Pardoner's Tale, The Summoner's Tale, The Friar's Tale). It makes sense that one tale at least also considers the failures and heroics of Christian crusades and thereby adds to the fullness of the *Tales*' survey of Christianity and its fourteenth-century ideals and discontents.

The assessment of crusade that I discern in the Man of Law's Tale also befits the nature of the tale's larger engagement with Christianity. As Jill Mann states, 'The Man of Law's Tale does not produce Christianity like a rabbit out of a hat to "answer" the problems of human existence; instead it grounds Christianity in human experience.'[63] The representation of crusade in this tale offers additional support for this claim. As the text considers the challenges posed by interactions between different human cultures, it explores one of Christianity's strongest responses to the problem of religious difference: crusade. Here, however, crusade does not solve the problem of religious difference. Instead, it serves as a Christian activity through which the nature of human success and failure in resolving difference can be explored, and through which the human need for divine assistance, or grace, can be acknowledged. Chaucer's depiction of the role of trade and money in Christianization projects points to the earthly concerns that often preoccupied crusaders, and events in Surrye suggest the problems that can arise when such irreligious preoccupations inform Christian efforts to end religious difference. Events in Northumbria, however, suggest that success in resolving religious difference can result from human willingness to entrust body and fate to the hazards of unplanned sea voyages to distant places. Such courage, relying on nothing but God's grace for survival, models Christian and crusade ideals, and enables Custance, with British assistance, to convert non-Christians. Chaucer thus illustrates how the Christian activity of crusade is imbricated in human behaviours both blameworthy and praiseworthy.

Chaucer's thought-provoking consideration of 'God's War' in The Man of Law's Tale also contributes to the oft-debated unity of Fragment II of the *Tales*, as it suggests connections between tale and introduction, tale and prologue, and tale and teller. The Man of Law, in his introduction, concludes his extensive praise of Chaucer by saying 'I speke in prose, and lat him rymes make' (II.96). The engagement of crusading issues in the tale provides direct evidence of Chaucer's ability to take ideas from prose materials like crusading treatises and render them into poetry. The tale thus exemplifies the artistic achievement explicitly touted by the Man of Law in his Introduction. The specific assessment of crusade provided in the tale also unifies the fragment. As argued above, the Man of Law's Tale juxtaposes an ideal, divinely assisted

[63] Mann, *Feminizing Chaucer*, p. 109.

Christianization effort with a flawed, unsuccessful one. The tale stresses the contrast between man-made and God-made events on the earthly plane, and between a Christian ideal and its corruption. In so doing, it speaks tellingly to both the Prologue of this tale and the occupation of its teller.

The use of Pope Innocent III's text, *De miseria condicionis humane*, in the Man of Law's Prologue has occasioned the frequent observation that the original papal text is seriously misrepresented. Peter Beidler perhaps best describes the disjuncture between the papal and Chaucerian texts. He writes: 'The point of the Innocent passage is that poor people, like everyone else on earth, are miserable [because the human condition is miserable]. The point of the Chaucer passage is that poverty is a miserable condition for which there is a cure: wealth.'[64] The Man of Law's Prologue thus depicts the way in which a religious text, upholding a Christian ideal, can be turned into an articulation of earthly desire for wealth. The prologue and its intertext demonstrate the warping of a Christian ideal by human concerns. This depiction is precisely the vision of crusade provided by Chaucer in the episode of Custance's Surryen marriage. The notion of a Christian ideal corrupted by interests in trade and money thus animates both the Man of Law's Prologue and the first part of his tale, and provides some support for efforts to perceive unity between tale and prologue. The tale, however, follows its depiction of a corrupted model of Christianization with the depiction of an ideal model, directed by 'goddes sonde' and 'purveiaunce'. Human endeavours directed by humans contrast with human endeavours directed by God. This structural contrast befits the tale's attribution to a medieval Man of Law, someone who, as part of his work, necessarily ponders theories about how natural laws, given by God, intersect with positive laws, made by humans. The tale's teller works in a profession where he must regularly consider the contrasts and connections between divine and human models of human interaction. It is therefore entirely appropriate that his tale, too, explores these matters as it reflects on the gap between the historical practices of late medieval crusade and the ideals it promoted.

64 Peter Beidler, 'Chaucer's Request for Money in the Man of Law's Tale', *Chaucer Yearbook* 2 (1995), 1–15, p. 6. Beidler's larger claim is that this prologue does not belong with the tale, thus his article as a whole is at odds with my point here.

2

The Language Group of the Canterbury Tales

Christopher Cannon

To imagine a language means to imagine a form of life.
– Ludwig Wittgenstein[1]

When Kittredge first wrote about the issue of marriage in the *Canterbury Tales* he referred to a 'Marriage Chapter' in the larger 'Human Drama', by means of these simple phrases associating the *Tales* in formal terms with both the novel and Dante's *Divine Comedy*.[2] When he later expanded on these views in his famous lectures on Chaucer, the 'Marriage Group', as he now always called it, was presented as if it were fully substantiated by the fragments of the *Tales* when placed in what we now usually call Ellesmere order: in this account, the appearance of the Wife of Bath's Prologue and Tale at the beginning of fragment III 'starts the debate' and the tales that follow in fragments IV and V are 'occasioned' by her remarks.[3] Such questionable textual presumptions, coupled with Kittredge's old-fashioned confidence that marriage is not usefully discussed by 'theorists',[4] might seem to bring Kittredge's entire discussion into disrepute, and yet his concerns also precisely anticipated the strong sense in any number of important recent studies that issues of gender and sexuality are central to the *Tales* as a whole.[5] The idea of a 'Marriage

1 *Philosophical Investigations*, trans. G. E. M. Anscombe, 2nd ed. (New York: Macmillan, 1958; first published 1953), § 19.

2 George Lyman Kittredge, 'Chaucer's Discussion of Marriage', *Modern Philology* 9 (1912), 435–67 (p. 22).

3 George Lyman Kittredge, *Chaucer and His Poetry* (Cambridge: Harvard University Press, 1924), p. 185. Kittredge also refers to the 'Marriage Chapter' as a 'Group' in the 1912 article (p. 1 n. 1, pp. 5 and 33).

4 Kittredge, *Chaucer and His Poetry*, p. 210.

5 It is a mark of the acuity of Kittredge's anticipation that no note could do justice to the importance issues of gender and sexuality have assumed in Chaucer criticism in the last twenty-five years, but it is probably right to mention the clutch of pioneering works which initially insisted upon this critical agenda: Carolyn Dinshaw, *Chaucer's Sexual Poetics* (Madison, WI: University of Wisconsin Press, 1989); Elaine Tuttle Hansen, *Chaucer and the Fictions of Gender* (Berkeley, CA: University of

Group' has also proved helpful to the least old-fashioned of such approaches, as, for example, where queer readings have demonstrated that Kittredge's 'argument … gains even greater purchase' when the Friar's and the Summoner's tales are shown to be about marriage ('same sex contracts') too.[6]

Kittredge's formulation was important, however, not only for its content but for the presumption that that there are certain important but largely unannounced concerns that cut across the 'infinite variety' of 'form' and 'subject' that comprises the *Canterbury Tales*, organizing as well as uniting its varied and disparate parts.[7] Here, the old-fashioned language and attitudes may obscure the larger formal insight whereby the 'group' becomes a kind of shorthand for the idea or thematic structure ('marriage') which is not just one issue among many but what the *Canterbury Tales* at some fundamental level is 'about'.[8] We might say, then, that while a certain sophistication in critical description has allowed us to realize that the 'Marriage Group' was in many ways too coarse an analytic instrument – that the tales in it are not really concerned with 'marriage' so much as the complex interactions of sex, gender and power – such sophistication may have come at the cost of being able to notice that there are other groupifying ideas in the *Tales*, other thematic structures that are not just equivalent to other meanings but fundamental to the meaning of the whole collection.[9] It was, in part, as a recognition of just this potential in Kittredge's shorthand that Jill Mann explained to me, when I was in my first year of graduate school, that alongside the 'Marriage Group' in the *Canterbury Tales* one must recognize a 'Language Group', a particular set of narratives that unfold a comprehensive understanding of language and its efficacy.

Mann's own description of the 'Language Group' would not, I am sure, take the shape I will give it here, and her own exploration of language in the *Tales* has been deep, wide-ranging, and generally resistant to the use of a shorthand.[10] But this seems the right place to mention this particular pedagogical help not only because it has never been committed to print but because it can

California Press, 1992), and Jill Mann, *Geoffrey Chaucer* (London: Harvester Wheatsheaf, 1991; reprinted as *Feminizing Chaucer* [Cambridge: D. S. Brewer, 2002]).

6 John M. Bowers, 'Queering the Summoner', in *Speaking Images: Essays in Honor of V. A. Kolve* (Asheville, NC: Pegasus Press, 2001), pp. 301–24 (314–15).

7 Kittredge, *Chaucer and His Poetry*, p. 153.

8 Kittredge, *Chaucer and His Poetry*, p. 185.

9 I derive the very useful term 'groupify' from L. O. Aranye Fradenburg, *Sacrifice Your Love: Psychoanalysis, Historicism, Chaucer* (Minneapolis, MN: University of Minnesota Press, 2002), where she uses it in a more precisely psychoanalytic sense (see especially p. 259 n. 79). Fradenburg in turn credits the terminology to Laurence A. Rickels, *The Case of California* (Minneapolis, MN: University of Minnesota Press, 2001).

10 A good summary of Mann's views can be found in the section on 'Words, Deeds, "Entente" and "Termes" ' in Geoffrey Chaucer, *The Canterbury Tales*, ed. Jill Mann (London: Penguin Books, 2005), pp. xxxvii–xlii. All quotations from the *Canterbury Tales* will be taken from this edition and cited by line number in the text.

also stand for the whole of Mann's teaching practice – similarly unrecorded but of deep significance to those it has touched. To the extent that any insistence on the importance of language might now seem old-fashioned, Mann's suggestion is also valuable as a way of drawing out of the *Tales* what developments in Chaucer criticism in the last decades have conspired to help us overlook. If consideration of the 'Language Group' returns us to the moment, now thirty years past, when Chaucer's various styles could be seen as equivalent to particular 'meanings' – a moment also prior to the recognition that such attention to language erred in its capacity to 'de-historicize' Chaucer – the conservatism may be no bad thing.[11] For if part of the repudiation of such New Critical understandings was the concomitant belief that Chaucer was a poet particularly susceptible to dehistoricizing readings because he tended to 'retrea[t]' from the political himself, it must be salutary to discover – or remind ourselves – that language and its theories also constitute a political category.[12] This observation is not equivalent to saying, I would hasten to add, that Chaucer criticism has failed to describe Chaucer's politics or to see his writing as 'political'.[13] Nor is it to disagree in any way with the incisive proof we have had that Chaucer encouraged a certain de-politicization because his own 'horizons of ... social imagination' were presciently coincident with what would become 'bourgeois individualism'.[14] It is to insist anew, however, that the very accuracy of the insight that the study of language was the particular

11 'The "meaning" of a conventional style is partly determined by the meanings of previous poems in that style, but also partly – and this too accounts for its conventionalization – by an inherent fitness-to-mean within the style itself', Charles Muscatine, *Chaucer and the French Tradition: A Study in Style and Meaning* (Berkeley, CA: University of California Press, 1957), p. 2. On the association of this view with New Criticism see Lee Patterson's 'Historical Criticism and the Development of Chaucer Studies', pp. 3–39 in his *Negotiating the Past: The Historical Understanding of Medieval Literature* (Madison, WI: University of Wisconsin Press, 1987): 'The effect of this representation of the Chaucerian context is to dehistoricize history' (pp. 25–6).

12 Lee Patterson, *Chaucer and the Subject of History* (Madison, WI: University of Wisconsin Press, 1991), p. 246.

13 Again, the range of criticism here is too wide to survey in full, but both now-classic and recent studies of Chaucer that present him as a consequential political thinker would necessarily include Paul Strohm, *Social Chaucer* (Cambridge, MA: Harvard University Press, 1989), Larry Scanlon, *Narrative, Authority, and Power: The Medieval Exemplum and the Chaucerian Tradition* (Cambridge: Cambridge University Press, 1994), Steven Justice, *Writing and Rebellion: England in 1381* (Berkeley, CA: University of California Press, 1994), esp. pp. 193–254; David Wallace, *Chaucerian Polity: Absolutist Lineages and Associational Forms in England and Italy* (Stanford, CA: Stanford University Press, 1997). In *Chaucer, Langland and the Creative Imagination* (London: Routledge & Kegan Paul, 1980) Aers' conviction that Chaucer invested himself in the 'individual' included the view that 'Chaucer developed a social psychology which comprised a profound contribution to the understanding of interactions between individual and society' (p. 118) and that he was able to 'penetrate' the 'contradictions' in 'traditional practices and ideologies' by way of a 'thoroughly critical and creative poetic exploration' (p. 160). Patterson, too, introduces *Chaucer and the Subject of History* as an account not only of Chaucer's 'privileging of a socially undetermined subjectivity' but of the ways this deflection failed (how Chaucer was 'too fully a historical creature and too fully aware of it') (p. 46).

14 David Aers, *Chaucer* (Atlantic Highlands, NJ: Humanities Press International, 1986), pp. 35–6.

method whereby criticism left out the 'political' ultimately made it impossible to see that *Chaucer* actually understood language as a potent political instrument.

In what follows I will argue that three tales constitute the 'Language Group' – the Friar's Tale, the Nun's Priest's Tale, and the Manciple's Tale – but so far from 'assert[ing] the freedom of the individual from a determining historical context', these tales understand language as precisely that medium through which the individual may act with larger consequence.[15] Although one might approach the principles Chaucer develops in these three texts from any number of the theoretical angles they anticipate (the Marxist view, say, that language is a 'dynamic and articulated social presence in the world'),[16] I will look here instead at philosophies of language, as I have looked to a philosopher in my epigraph. It is within this discipline, I will argue – and perhaps most precisely in what is sometimes called the philosophy of ordinary language – that it is now easiest to reconstruct Chaucer's bracing and thorough-going commitment to language as an active part of social life.

The work of words

It may be obvious enough that the Friar's Tale, the Nun's Priest's Tale and the Manciple's Tale take up language as an important topic, but it would also seem, on its face, that, in every case such interest denigrates rather than celebrates linguistic possibility. The plot of the Friar's Tale exposes the degree to which people fail to understand the implications of what they say, as, for example, when the summoner, sees no problem in swearing himself the 'brother' (III.1405) of a 'feend' (III.1448). In the Nun's Priest's Tale, Chauntecleer does not understand his own words (' "*Mulier est hominis confusio*/ – Madame, the sentence of this Latin is:/ 'Woman is mannes joye and al his blis' " ', VII.3164–6) and most spectacularly, the fox is so duped by Chauntecleer's taunting that he does not realize that in order to respond to Chauntecleer he must release him from his mouth:

> The fox answerde, "In feith, it shal be done!"
> – And as he spak that word, al sodeinly
> This cok brak from his mouth deliverly,
> And hye upon a tree he fley anon. VII.3414–17

In the Manciple's Tale, when the crow tells the truth about his master's wife's infidelity, the result is a concatenation of disasters that he did not foresee:

[15] Lee Patterson, *Negotiating the Past*, p. 25.

[16] Raymond Williams, *Marxism and Literature* (Oxford: Oxford University Press, 1977), p. 38. In his chapter on 'language' in this volume Williams summarizes a whole history, from Plato onward, of thinking of language as 'constitutive' (pp. 21–44).

This Phebus gan aweyward for to wryen,
And thoghte his sorweful herte brast atwo;
His bowe he bente, and sette therinne a flo,
And in his ire his wif thanne hath he slain –
This is th'effect; ther nis namoore to sayn.
For sorwe of which, he brak his mistralcye,
Bothe harpe and lute and giterne and sawtrye
And eek he brak hise arwes and his bowe.
...
And to the crowe he stirte, and that anon,
And pulled hise white fetheres everychon,
And made him blak, and rafte him al his song,
And eek his speche, and out at dore him slong
Unto the devel, which I him bitake. IX.262–9; 303–8

More disheartening still to any hope that language does consequential work in this tale is the way that Phebus insists that the crow betrayed him simply by speaking the truth (' "Traitor", quod he, "with tonge of scorpioun" ', IX.271) as if words that succeeded most perfectly in their work – reflecting reality, communicating what had actually happened – were somehow, simultaneously, the instruments that could inflict the most harm.

But it is surely equally important – if, in this light, somewhat confounding – that all three of these tales also contain speech acts that are profoundly effective. I have cited one of these already, since, described in its simplest form, we could also say that Chauntecleer's invitation to the fox to boast of his mastery is a speech act that succeeds in persuading the fox to act a certain way. The fox's very act of assenting releases Chauntecleer (' "In feith, it shal be done!" ') and thereby shows, with what might be described as a philosophical wit, that the production of even hypothetical thought in words takes a consequentially physical form.[17] With slightly less complexity – but a similar result – we see in the Friar's Tale that words may be so effective that they reflect our intent perfectly:

"Unto the devel blak and rough of hewe
Yeve I thy body, and my panne also!"
  And whan the devel herde hire cursen so
Upon hir knees, he seide in this manere:

[17] This 'action' is there in Chaucer's likely source for this part of the tale, Branch II of the *Roman de Renart*. As in the whole of the Language Group, however, the workings of language are not important because Chaucer invents them but because he embeds them in a context that focuses on so many of them. For the relevant passages in this source, see *The Earliest Branches of the Roman de Renart*, ed. R. Anthony Lodge and Kenneth Varty (Louvain: Peeters, 2001), ll. 420–39. This action also occurs in another possible source or analogue, Marie de France's *Fables*: see *Les Fables*, ed. Charles Brucker, 2nd ed. (Louvain: Peeters, 1998), no. 60 (ll. 21–5). Jill Mann has carefully described the 'exploitation of a split between words and deeds' in beast fable generally in the introduction to her edition of the *Ysengrimus* (Leiden: E. J. Brill, 1987), pp. 58–77.

"Now Mabely, min owene moder dere,
Is this youre wil in ernest that ye seye?"
   "The devel", quod she, "so fecche him er he deye,
And panne and al, but he wol him repente!"
   "Nay olde stot, that is nat min entente,"
Quod this somnour, "for to repente me
For anything that I have had of thee.
I wolde I hadde they smok and every clooth!"
   "Now, bother" quod the devel, "be noght wrooth:
Thy body and this panne been mine by right.
Thow shalt with me to helle yet tonight ...   III.1622–36

The exchange here could not be more artificial. In the case of the widow's curse there is a subsequent examination of intent (' "Now Mabely ... Is this youre wil in ernest that ye seye?" ') along with a precise repetition of the original speech act, now as an explicit statement of 'will' (' "The devel", quod she, "so fecche him er he deye, And panne and al" '). The possibility that the summoner may repent and save himself is similarly foreclosed by an explicit statement of intent (' "Nay olde stot, that is nat min entente" '). And yet all such explicitness about the relationship of thought to speech makes this story, more generally concerned with the wages of rapaciously thoughtless action, also very much 'about' the possibilities of what J. L. Austin would later dub 'performative speech'. In fact, these statements arbitrate with surprising precision the distinction that Austin would later make between 'locutionary' speech acts (which, like the curses earlier in this tale, simply 'say something')[18] and 'illocutionary acts' (like the events I have just described, the 'performance of an act *in* saying something').[19] As a consequence of this investigation the conclusion of the tale is also parallel to the conclusion of *How To Do Things With Words* in that both the narrative and Austin's lectures demonstrate that a constative ('any true or false statement') *is* performative when it is uttered in a situation that demands 'uptake' – a result.[20] That is, the Friar's Tale insists in the end, not that the summoner's sinfulness sends him to hell, but that words do: it is the *utterance* of the widow's curse and the summoner's refusal to repent that produce his punishment.

Thus, it is part of the demonstration of the power of words in these tales that Chaucer often suggests that it may be dangerous to say anything at all. That danger is also introduced in the most gentle form in the Manciple's

[18] J. L. Austin, *How to Do Things With Words*, 2nd ed., ed. J. O. Urmson and Marina Sbisà (Cambridge, MA: Harvard University Press, 1975; first published 1962), p. 94.

[19] Austin, *How to Do Things With Words*, p. 99.

[20] 'Once we realize that what we have to study is *not* the sentence but the issuing of an utterance in a speech situation, there can hardly be any longer a possibility of not seeing that stating is performing an act', Austin, *How to Do Things With Words*, p. 139. For the term 'uptake' see p. 139 as well. For Austin's definition of a 'constative statement' see p. 3.

Prologue when the Manciple successfully retracts his words to the Cook (' "That that I spak, I seide it in my bourde" ', IX.81) after the Host reminds him of the trouble he may have created for himself by mocking someone whose goodwill may matter (' "Another day he wole, paraventure ... speke wole of smale thinges/ As for to pinchen at they rekeninges,/ That were nat honeste" ', IX.71–5). The same point is made much more strongly, however, in the Manciple's Tale itself, where it is clear that words can actually kill. It is crucial to this demonstration that Phebus murders his wife because the crow has told him of his wife's infidelity (' "For on thy bed thy wif I sey him swive" ', IX.686) and not because he has seen that infidelity or any other evidence of it. When Phebus then silences the crow, he is also making the emphatic point that the representation of an act of betrayal in words is as painful and upsetting (and as fatally motivating) as the betrayal itself.

> And to the crowe, "O false theef!" seide he,
> "I wol thee quite anon thy false tale.
> Thow songe whilom lik a nightingale;
> Now shaltow, false theef, thy song forgon,
> And eek thy white fetheres eveychon,
> Ne nevere in al thy lif ne shaltow speke.
> Thus shal men on a traitour been awreke!" IX.292–8

The Manciple's Tale also registers all the verbal power implied in these transactions when it warns its readers not to spread tidings whether they are 'false *or trewe*' (IX.360), suggesting in this way that words in any form (with any relationship to reality) may cause injury. The long coda in which various proverbial warnings against loose speech are provided is itself notable for the equation it constantly makes between speaking and injury:

> ... keep wel thy tonge, and kepe thy freend. IX.319

> ... ful ofte for to muche speche
> Hath many a man ben spilt ... IX.325–6

> ... of muchel speking ivele avised,
> Ther lasse speking hadde inow suffised,
> Comth muchel harm ... IX.335–7

This admonition is pursued most dramatically in an image that equates speaking with 'cutting':

> Right as a swerd forkutteth and forkerveth
> An arm atwo, my deere sone, right so
> A tonge kutteth frendship al atwo. IX.340–2

All of these equations and cautions are simply a different way of making the point that the whole of the Language Group makes: for whether Chaucer is claiming that words are potentially or necessarily salvific or sometimes or necessarily destructive – whether he is saying that they can save a life or take one – what he is claiming is that words do consequential work. They are not simply equivalent to actions: they *are* actions.

Viewed in this way, the Language Group is also an important classification because it brings into focus Chaucer's emphasis on verbal action throughout the *Tales*. Other important instances include: Griselda's 'oath' in the Clerk's Tale, which weds her not only to Walter but to his implacable 'will' (' "But as ye wol youreself, right so wol I" ', IV.361); both the high valuation placed on Dorigen's pledge in the Franklin's Tale (' "Trouthe is the hyeste thing that man may kepe" ', V.1479) and the extent to which that oath compels action (as Dorigen puts it, she goes ' "Unto the gardin, as min housbond bad,/ My trouthe for to holde, allas, allas!" ', V.1512–13); and the 'trouthe' sworn by the knight in the Wife of Bath's Tale (III.1009), which compels his marriage to the 'olde wif', as well as the correct 'word' (III.1046) he offers in answer to the queen's demand that he tell her what women most desire. That the concerns of the Language Group should also play such an important role in the tales of the Marriage Group need not diminish the usefulness of either classification, for it shows, rather, that issues of language and 'marriage' were of equal importance to Chaucer. (The blurring extends in both directions, for the Language Group's Chauntecleer and Pertelote, a burlesque version of a married couple if ever there was one, insist, as the very material of this burlesque, that gender is a social construction [' "Have ye no mannes herte, and han a berd?" ', VII.2920]). The extent to which the Language Group explores a set of issues important to all of the *Tales* is illustrated best, however, by the predicating fact of the whole collection, for even before Harry Bailey proposes a tale-telling contest as the principle activity of the Canterbury pilgrimage, the narrator has assumed words are equivalent to character (as he promises to be faithful, above all, to 'hir wordes and hir cheere') just as he proposes to proceed under the assumption of the principle (repeated in the Manciple's Tale) that words are akin to deeds ('Eek, Plato seyth ... The wordes mote be cosin to the dede', I.741–2; see also IX.207–8). That the *Tales* also generally illustrate the principle that the potency of words is measured most dramatically by the harm they can do is most emphatically demonstrated by the concluding fact – if the Retractions are indeed a part of the *Tales* – that what one has 'seid', that the merest 'translacions and enditings', may constitute damning and consequential 'giltes' (X.1082–85).

Philosophies of language

'Rhetoric' (and the various ideas and practices that traveled in the Middle Ages under that term) is the most obvious philosophy of language at work in the *Tales*, although it is more conceptually complex and more subtle than it might first appear. Indeed, Chaucer's most overt references to rhetoric take the form of a kind of negative self-consciousness, often describing what a given speaker's language will eschew:

> I sleep nevere on the mount of Parnaso,
> Ne lerned Marcus Tullius Scithero.
> Colours ne knowe I none, withouten drede,
> But swich colours as growen in the mede,
> Or ellis swiche as men dye or peinte.
> Colours of rethorik ben to me queinte;
> My spirit feeleth nat of swich matere. V.721–7[21]

John Manly suggested long ago that such protestations are disingenuous and Chaucer was in fact extensively influenced by what rhetorical theory had to say about the arrangement of texts, the amplification and abbreviation of subjects, and, most importantly, by precisely those figures or ornaments, those very 'colours', that the Franklin so emphatically abjures.[22] Moreover, when Manly measured the proportion of 'larger rhetorical devices' in each one of the *Canterbury Tales*, he found that two of what I am calling the Language Group, the Manciple's Tale and the Nun's Priest's Tale, were among the most highly 'rhetorical' (they are, in this tabulation, comprised of 61 per cent and 50 per cent 'of rhetoric' respectively).[23] But it could be said that what Manly is uncovering with his coarse measurements, particularly in these tales, is not a straightforward use of rhetoric, but a self-consuming critique of rhetorical technique and its emptiness. If the Nun's Priest's Tale is, as Rita Copeland has observed, a 'rhetoric laboratory', and the one work in which Chaucer makes explicit reference to a rhetorical manual, then both the wit and the pleasure of this evocation lie entirely in the poet's deflation of the elevating techniques taught by Geoffrey of Vinsauf.[24] Thus, the exemplary apostrophe to England on the death of Richard the Lionheart from the *Poetria Nova* is deployed to mourn the perils facing a chicken:[25]

> O Gaufred, deere maister soverain,
> That, whan thy worthy king Richard was slain
> With shot, compleinedest his deth so soore,
> Why nadde I now thy sentence and thy loore,
> The Friday for to chide, as diden ye? VII.3347–51

21 For another important passage of this kind see the words of the Host to the Clerk in the Prologue to the Clerk's Tale (IV.16–20).

22 J. M. Manly, 'Chaucer and the Rhetoricians', *Proceedings of the British Academy* 12 (1912), 92–113 (esp. pp. 99–106).

23 Manly, 'Chaucer and the Rhetoricians', p. 107. The Nun's Priest's Tale and Manciple's Tale are only exceeded in Manly's tabulations by the Monk's Tale, 100% of which (according to Manly) was composed 'of rhetoric'. In this calculation the Wife of Bath's Tale also contains 50% 'of rhetoric'.

24 Copeland, 'Chaucer and Rhetoric', p. 139.

25 Chaucer evokes Cicero too on a number of occasions, but always as a writer of sententiae rather than as a rhetorician (see concordance).

The value of rhetoric is similarly undermined by the wholly irrational conclusion to Chauntecleer's attempt to persuade Pertelote that his dream foretells real danger. Lust persuades him, in a mere four lines, to disregard everything he has taken several hundred lines and great forensic care to establish:

> "For whan I feele a-night your softe side
> – Al be it that I may nat on yow ride,
> For that oure perche is maad so narwe, allas! –
> I am so ful of joye and of solas,
> That I deffye bothe swevene and dreem" VII.3167–71

The deflation works by the same principle (if in a more serious register) in the Manciple's Tale where Phebus's elaborately rhetorical address to his murderous hands is part of his attempt to persuade himself that his wife is 'giltelees' of the crime for which he has just killed her:

> "O rakel hand, to doon so foule amis!
> O trouble wit! O ire recchelees,
> That unavised smitest giltelees!
> O wantrust, ful of fals suspecioun!
> Where was thy wit and thy discrecioun?
> O, every man be war of rakelnesse." IX.278–83

In both of these tales the point of rhetoric seems not to be that words do certain work, but rather that, almost in proportion to one's investment in them, words are useless. In this sense, for Chaucer, 'rhetoric' represented a form of language sufficiently ornamental as to be detachable from the activities of thought itself.

The term 'rhetoric' referred to much more than 'ornament' or even 'style' in medieval thought, however, and Chaucer is often most deeply and self-consciously 'rhetorical' in places where his language is neither ornamented nor high-flown. As Robert Payne demonstrated with great care in the *Key to Remembrance*, the devices and techniques we now sometimes count as the sum total of rhetoric (again, 'the colors, the three-level codifications of stylistic decorum, and the catalogues and categories of figures') are actually 'integral parts' of a much larger 'system', a system primarily concerned, not with elaboration, but with the principles by which language as such functions.[26] In this larger view, as Copeland has also observed, medieval rhetoric's concern is how 'discourse acts in the face of contingency', or simply but broadly speaking, with the relationship between language and the larger

[26] Robert O. Payne, *The Key of Remembrance: A Study of Chaucer's Poetics* (New Haven, CT: Yale University Press, 1963), p. 49.

world.[27] Rhetoric is, thus, a set of strategies and terms for interrogating and then stating the function of poetry:

> Poetry is a process of manipulating language so that the wisdom evolved in the past will become available, applicable, and operative in the present. Its most distinctive characteristic as poetry is its ability to stir emotion – to move knowledge into operation.[28]

For Payne, the deepest consideration of these questions in Chaucer can be found in the Prologue to the *Legend of Good Women*, a text as close as Chaucer ever got to an *ars poetriae.*[29] But, in so far as they are also abundantly concerned with how words move knowledge into operation, the Nun's Priest's Tale, the Friar's Tale, and the Manciple's Tale are also deeply rhetorical in this different sense.

Another way to put this last point is that the more 'rhetorical' moments in the *Tales* are not to be found in any concatenation of figures or verbal ornament, but in the passages that look very closely at how language as an entity, process, or phenomenon actually works. The Language Group is often highly 'rhetorical', then, not because its language is often ornamented (although it often is) but because it often also eschews ornament in order to isolate and examine speech acts. When Manly suggested that the 'Friar's Tale' was the least rhetorical of the *Tales*, since 'rhetorical devices do not occupy more than 1 per cent of the text', he was very precisely wrong in that instance, since it is precisely the tale's plain-spoken dialogue and spare plot that lay bare the conditions surrounding each important utterance.[30] The discussion I have already mentioned, between the summoner and the fiend over a carter's wish that the ' "devel, have al, bothe hors and cart and hey" ' (III.1547), in other words is highly 'rhetorical' but in the sense that Payne isolates (and Manly obscures). Similarly, the following scene of instruction by the devil is rhetorical in this larger sense in so far as it provides a careful description of the procedure by which words both do and do not convey knowledge:

> "Nay," quod the devel, "God woot, never a del!
> It is nat his entente, trust thow me wel.
> Axe him thyself, if thow nat trowest me,
> Or ellis stint a while and thow shalt se'.
> This cartere thakketh his hors upon the croupe,
> And they bigonne to drawen and to stoupe.
> "Heit now", quod he, "ther Jesu Crist yow blesse,
> And al his handwerk, bothe moore and lesse!

27 Copeland, 'Chaucer and Rhetoric', p. 124.
28 Payne, *Key of Remembrance*, p. 89.
29 Payne, *Key of Remembrance*, p. 63.
30 Manly, 'Chaucer and the Rhetoricians', p. 107.

> That was wel twight, min owene liard boy!
> I pray God save thee, and Seinte Loy.
> Now is my cart out of the slow, pardee!"
> "Lo, brother," quod the feend, "what tolde I thee?
> Heer may ye se, min owene deer brother,
> The carl spak o thing, but thoghte another.
> Lat us go forth abouten oure viage:
> Heere winne I nothing upon cariage". III.1555–70

To such rhetorical analysis may also be added a linguistic failure I have already mentioned: the summoner's inability to register the ramifications of the knowledge that he is the 'sworn bretheren' (III.1405) of a 'feend' whose 'dwelling is in hell' (III.1448), a particular instance of the way that, throughout the tale, even when speech seems both transparent and efficacious (when intent and meaning are perfectly aligned), a speaker fails to understand the consequences of what he or she has said. Thus, the widow knows she is cursing the summoner just as he knows he is not repenting, but neither is aware that the context in which they speak – before a fiend – will make the curse effective and damn the summoner to hell. All the tales of the Language Group are highly rhetorical in this different sense in so far as they also include figures (such as Chauntecleer or Phebus) who are unable to acquire the knowledge their own language purveys.

The tales of the Language Group may be described as 'rhetorical', then, whenever they show that words can fail, and in so far as this definition of rhetoric is also groupifying, it not only points to the importance of this idea in the Language Group, but in the *Canterbury Tales* as a whole. Chief among the examples of such informative failure in the larger collection must be the moment in the Pardoner's Tale when, after having described his preaching as a 'gaude' (VI.389) and 'false japes' (VI.394), and having also scandalously revealed that his purpose is 'nothing for correccioun of sinne' (VI.406) but, rather, to persuade people 'to yeve hir pens' to him (VI.402), the Pardoner concludes his performance by asking the pilgrims not only to 'com forth anon, and kneleth adoun' (VI.925) but to offer their 'nobles or pens' (VI.930) so that he might 'assoille' them (VI.933). The 'double truth' in which such a performance is caught has been well analyzed psychoanalytically as an embodiment of a general medieval understanding of language as 'partial and fragmentary'.[31] But it is also the case that this double truth is created and an unconscious revealed precisely because the Pardoner proceeds as if his words will not do the work of conveying the knowledge they purvey. Such dysfunction is also general in the *Tales* in so far as the Host's performance in the prologues and

[31] See Dinshaw, *Chaucer's Sexual Poetics*, pp. 156–84. For the phrases I quote see pp. 172 ('partial and fragmentary') and 176 ('double truth').

end-links trails such failure throughout the collection, pairing some of the most serious performances with what are, at times, broadly comical instances of linguistic failure. I refer in particular to the Host's sense (in co-operation with the Merchant) that the conclusion of the Clerk's Tale is an appropriate moment to speak of his ' "wives cursednesse" ' (IV.1239), or his reductive and strange view that the Physician's Tale demonstrates that ' "yiftes of Fortune and of Nature/ Been cause of deeth to many a creature" ' (VI.295–6), or his conclusion that the Shipman's Tale points to a moral about harboring monks (' "Draweth no monkes moore unto youre in" ', VII.442). But most significant of all is the Host's insistence, after the narrator tells his tale of Melibee, that his aggressive wife (' "Whan she comth hoom she raumpeth in my face" ', VII.1904) would learn 'pacience' (VII.1895–6) were she to hear this story, mistaking the manner of Prudence's argumentation for its content, since she repeatedly insists that husbands should heed the 'counseiling of women' (VII.1096). Since Melibee ultimately does just what Prudence counsels him to do, what the Host's most scandalously fails to notice is that this tale demonstrates a woman's complete success in compelling a husband to 'encline to the wil of his wif' (VII.1871).[32]

That the Host 'always misses the point of what he has heard' is not a new observation, of course, and most of the misunderstandings I have noted in individual tales have also been separately noted, but the Language Group both focuses these concerns and analyses such activity with unusual depth and clarity because it presents its own instances of linguistic failure *in the context of* more successful acts of communication.[33] It is particularly in the light of the subsequent success of his words, for example, that we can see that Chauntecleer's decision to 'defie' his extensive argument on the efficacy of dreams is also a registration of verbal potency (and it is itself part of the point of these earlier actions that Chauntecleer acquired the knowledge his words purveyed since that is how and why he can 'defy' them). In the same way, the Friar's Tale does not simply show that speech acts fail or succeed but rather analyzes such a variety of acts and their conditions that, even when it is describing a misunderstanding, its subject remains the processes by which understanding occurs. Further, even when Phebus acts irrationally in response to the crow's words in the Manciple's Tale, his irrationality is visible – the way the import of words can be both known and not known at the same time – only

32 Because the tale is itself so serious and the one consequential production attributed to the *Tales*' narrator, there is a similar generalizing quality to the culminating misunderstanding within it, when Melibee's first response to his wife's lengthy counsel, her 'goodliche wordes' (VII.1743), which counsel him to live in 'pees' with his 'adversaries' (VII.1782), is to do exactly the opposite and to vow to 'disherite hem ... and to putte hem in exil for evere' (VII.1835). On this 'devastating' moment see Lee Patterson, ' "What Man Artow?": Authorial Self-Definition in *The Tale of Sir Thopas* and *The Tale of Melibee*', *Studies in the Age of Chaucer* 11 (1989), 117–76 (p. 157).

33 Derek Pearsall, *The Canterbury Tales* (London: George Allen & Unwin, 1985), p. 39.

because their 'truth' is also abundantly clear. The 'rhetorical' analysis performed by each of these tales is unusually precise then because they explore so many of the trajectories language may take. These analyses are also extraordinarily comprehensive because they occur *by way of* narrative, exploring these trajectories in particular settings, always with an eye to the way speech acts operate in relationships between speakers and auditors, with abundant attention to these operations in the context of a variety of acts and conditions.

As I began by suggesting, what may be described in medieval terms as a 'rhetorical' analysis in the Language Group might also be described as a 'philosophical' analysis in the modern sense, and I think it is worth reframing the concerns of the tales in this way, not so much to suggest that such explorations were ahead of their time, as to register most fully their depth and breadth. We might say, for example, that just as the demonstrations of the power of words in the Nun's Priest's Tale and the Manciple's Tale show how words put knowledge into action, so too do they offer an emphatically affirmative answer to the question Austin poses early in *How To Do Things With Words*: 'Can saying make it so?'[34] Because language is the concentrated subject of the tales of the Language Group, *and* because its analysis always occurs in the kind of situations that Austin finds crucial to the definition of speech acts, such analysis also fleshes out one of Wittgenstein's more global claims that 'to imagine a language means to imagine a form of life'. In fact, with a surprising precision, the analyses that comprise the Language Group can also be said to anticipate a number of the more pointed questions and observations of the *Philosophical Investigations*:

> (1) 'The expression of our thoughts can always lie, for we may say one thing and mean another'.[35]
> (2) 'If language is to be a means of communication there must be agreement not only in definitions but also (queer as this may sound) in judgments'.[36]
> (3) 'Could we also imagine a language in which a person could write down or give vocal expression to his inner experiences – his feelings, moods, and the rest – for his private use?'[37]

The first of these claims says much more than that people lie, for it suggests that language may exceed the capacity of those who employ it to use it accurately or well. Like Chaucer when he has Phebus act as if the crow's observation is the truth even as he describes it as a lie or when he has Chauntecleer prosecute and then ignore his own best arguments, Wittgenstein is noticing that language can

34 Austin, *How to Do Things With Words*, p. 7.
25 Ludwig Wittgenstein, *The Blue and Brown Books: Preliminary Studies for the 'Philosophical Investigations'*, 2nd ed. (New York, NY: Harper and Row, 1960; first edition 1958), p. 42.
36 Wittgenstein, *Philosophical Investigations*, § 242.
37 Wittgenstein, *Philosophical Investigations*, § 243.

fail to represent any reality without actually being intended as a falsehood. Similarly, just as Wittgenstein insists, in the second proposition here, that language only works when it mediates between minds that share a set of 'judgments' or what he sometimes calls 'criteria', so too does Chaucer show how Chauntecleer and the fox, or the summoner and the fiend, fail to communicate because they do not share the principles by which the straightforward statements they are independently making are operating.[38] And if Wittgenstein does not believe that a 'private language' is language worthy of the name, Chaucer also shows that such privacy is impossible when he makes it clear that an agent such as the Manciple cannot actually communicate with the Cook, or the crow with Phebus, or, again, the fox with Chauntecleer, or the summoner with the fiend, without dire consequences because they do not assume the same things about how their words are working. As Donald Davidson put this point (in a way that Chaucer might have particularly appreciated), language cannot function in a world filled with such a variety of agents with so many different manners and methods of speaking ('diverse folk diversely they seyde', I.3857), unless speakers employ 'principles of charity' whereby they not only assume that other persons can make sense, but they also try to inhabit their assumptions, criteria, and judgments. In the absence of such 'charity', as so often in the Language Group, it simply is not possible for words to mean.[39]

In outlining its philosophy of language, Chaucer's Language Group also presumes, above all, that language is a phenomenon that does much more than observe, reflect, or pass through the world. To the extent that it connects minds – to the extent that it succeeds in connecting agents (through principles of charity or shared criteria) – language is fundamentally *effective*. It is in this final sense that the philosophy of language on view in the Language Group is most accurately described as 'political'. This point could also be made in medieval terms, since to say that the Language Group's examination of language is 'rhetorical' is also to say that it provides and examines a kind of 'civic discourse', since this is precisely what 'rhetoric' also was in origin and in a widespread medieval understanding.[40] Chaucer himself certainly worked with texts that argued that 'eloquence' [eloquentia] was simply a 'part' [pars] of the 'system of politics' [civilis quaedam ratio],[41] and the conjunction between

38 On the term 'criteria' see Wittgenstein, *Philosophical Investigations*, §§ 164 and 580. For an analysis of this concept in Wittgenstein's thought see Stanley Cavell, *The Claim of Reason: Wittgenstein, Skepticism, Morality, and Tragedy* (Oxford: Clarendon Press, 1979), pp. 3–36 (ch. 1, 'Criteria and Judgment') and 37–48 (ch. 2, 'Criteria and Skepticism').

39 Donald Davidson, 'Three Varieties of Knowledge', pp. 205–20 in his *Subjective, Intersubjective, Objective* (Oxford: Clarendon Press, 2001), p. 211. Davidson attributes the notion to Willard Van Orman Quine, though it is less explicitly set out in his *Word and Object* (Cambridge, MA: MIT Press, 1960), but see pp. 57–61.

40 Copeland, 'Chaucer and Rhetoric', p. 135.

41 The full passage reads 'There is a scientific system of politics which includes many important departments. One of these departments – a large and important one – is eloquence based on the rules of

eloquence and politics is one that the Language Group particularly insists upon. It is clear, for example, that the lengthy description of the farm workers, dogs, cows, calves, ducks, geese and bees who chase the fox as he bears Chauntecleer off on his back constitute the 'one open reference to the great revolt' of 1381 that Chaucer makes, as he recalls 'Jackke Straw' and the shouts he and his 'meinee' uttered when they set upon London's Flemings.[42] But the deeper point here, I think, and the more modern one, is that when the widow and her daughters see the fox running off and cry 'Out! Harrow!' and 'Weilaway!/ Ha, ha, the fox!', theirs is a 'political' utterance wholly apart from either the implied or deliberate association of such 'noise' with a politically incendiary event simply because it *does* something, not only intervening in the events of the world, but changing them. Though the populace mobilized by these cries is both wholly domestic and only related by parody to any large-scale grouping of real agents, in so far as these words move thought into immediate action, they are, like the marvelously kinetic sentence in which they are set, a very precise demonstration of the power of words to 'do things'.[43] Because they are embedded in such a deeply philosophical investigation of such power this demonstration is no less consequential and far-reaching in its claims for the layered debasements (into a poor farmyard, onto animals, as no more than the rescue of a chicken) that make it funny. Indeed, as one speech act among the many that not only fill the *Canterbury Tales* but also constitute each one of them, this event in the Nun's Priest's Tale calls attention to the extent to which, as a concatenation of speech acts, all of these narratives are generally 'political' in this sense. The philosophy of language so carefully and generally explored and focused in the Language Group also shows, then, that such a politics is both most active and most broadly signifying, not where the *Canterbury Tales* is centrally or obviously concerned with some historical event or the English social world of the late fourteenth century, but rather, where it is most fully focused on the material of its own worldly interventions – on language, as an active instrument, as such.

art, which they call rhetoric' [Civilis quaedam ratio est, quae multis et magnis ex rebus constat. Eius quaedam magna et ampla pars est artificiosa eloquentia quam rhetoricam vocant], Cicero, *De inventione*, ed. and trans. H. M. Hubbell, pp. 1–345 in *Cicero in Twenty-Eight Volumes*, vol. 2 (*De inventione; De Optimo Genere Oratorum; Topica*) (Cambridge, Mass.: Harvard University Press, 1976), 1.iv.6. As Hubbell points out in a note here, this point was a 'commonplace'. On this tradition and Chaucer's relationship to it see Copeland, 'Chaucer and Rhetoric', p. 135.

42 Steven Justice, *Writing and Rebellion*, p. 207. For Justice the vision of the rebellion Chaucer conjures in these lines is a parody of Gower's representation of the rising in the *Vox clamantis* (see pp. 208–11). For accounts of the attacks on the Flemings in the rebellion see the translations of the 'Anonimalle Chronicle', Thomas Walsingham's *Historia Anglicana* and Froissart's *Chroniques* in *The Peasants' Revolt of 1381*, ed. R. B. Dobson, 2nd ed. (London: Macmillan Press, 1983; first published 1970), pp. 162, 175, and 188–9 respecitvely.

43 John Ganim also characterizes this as one of a number of scenes in which the 'noyse of the people' is represented with a political valence. See *Chaucerian Teatricality* (Princeton, NJ: Princeton University Press, 1990).

3

'Save man allone': Human Exceptionality in *Piers Plowman* and the Exemplarist Tradition

Rebecca A. Davis

> Sed ab huius uniuersalitatis regula solus homo anomala exceptione seducitur ...[1]
>
> – Alan of Lille, *De planctu Naturae*

In a central passus of *Piers Plowman*, in a vision-within-a-vision, the figure Kynde calls the Dreamer by his first name and places him at the summit of 'a mountaigne þat myddelerþe hiȝte', offering him a privileged perspective from which he might survey all of creation (B.11.324).[2] As the Dreamer understands it, he is meant to use the natural world as a repository of lessons that will lead him to love of God: 'I was fet forþ by forbisenes to knowe,/ Thorugh ech a creature kynde my creatour to louye' (B.11.325–26). Such a description aligns the Vision of Kynde with the Latin tradition of exemplarist contemplation and its authorizing metaphor of the *liber* or *speculum naturae*.[3] Rooted in

1 Alan of Lille, *De planctu Naturae*, 8.12–13, ed. Nikolaus M. Häring, *Studi medievali* 19 (1978), 833. *The Plaint of Nature*, trans. James J. Sheridan (Toronto: Pontifical Institute of Medieval Studies, 1980), p. 131: 'However, from this universal law man alone exempts himself by a nonconformist withdrawal.'

2 William Langland, *Piers Plowman: The B Text*, ed. George Kane and E. Talbot Donaldson (Berkeley and Los Angeles, 1988). Hereafter, citations of passus and line numbers are given in the text.

3 On the idea of the 'book of nature', see Ernst Robert Curtius, *European Literature and the Latin Middle Ages*, trans. Willard R. Trask, 7th ed. (Princeton: Princeton University Press, 1990), pp. 319–26, and Jesse Gellrich, *The Idea of the Book in the Middle Ages: Language Theory, Mythology, and Fiction* (Ithaca: Cornell University Press, 1985), pp. 29–50. On the 'mirror of nature', see Ritamary Bradley, 'Backgrounds of the Title Speculum in Medieval Literature', *Speculum* 29 (1954), 100–115. The connection is even more pronounced in the C-text where Kynde directs Rechelesnesse, who now takes the Dreamer's role, to look into 'the myrour of Mydelerthe' rather than placing him on a mountain of that name. This change is particularly suggestive since a *speculum*, or mirror, was a common Latin title for encyclopedic texts, which were at once the product and the tools of exemplarist endeavours.

Augustine's theory of signs in the *De doctrina Christiana*, reflected in the nature allegories of Chartres and the meditations of the Victorines, and fully systematized by Bonaventure in the thirteenth century, exemplarism expresses a Neoplatonic worldview that Marie-Dominique Chenu describes as a 'symbolist mentality'.[4] It proposes that the created world, like a book written by God, bears the imprint of its creator and that human beings have the capacity to 'read' or see spiritual lessons 'reflected' in nature. In a well-known formulation, Alan of Lille alleges that '[e]very living creature is like a book and picture and mirror to us'.[5] As a 'book' written in God's own hand, and often considered parallel to the revealed truths of scripture, the natural world provided a treasury of medieval exempla, images and phenomena that might be used to illustrate moral teachings, or, like a 'mirror', could reflect back models of good and bad behaviour to human observers.[6] If God is the exemplar, then the world itself is a great exemplum, and each of its component parts, 'ech a creature', as Langland puts it, might be viewed as individual exempla, or 'forbisenes' (B.11.325–26). But the broader philosophical and theological concept of exemplarism, as distinguished from the genre of the exemplum, posits a fundamental and universal relationship between created things and

4 Chenu, *Nature, Man, and Society in the Twelfth Century*, trans. Jerome Taylor and Lester K. Little (Chicago: University of Chicago Press, 1968), pp. 102–19. Lawrence Clopper presents a chapter on 'Langland's Exemplarism' in *Songes of Rechelesnesse: Langland and the Franciscans* (Ann Arbor: University of Michigan Press, 1997), pp. 105–44. His study does not focus on Langland's engagement with the natural world but on his Trinitarian theology and its connections to Bonaventure's exemplarist philosophy. See also Joseph S. Wittig, '*Piers Plowman* B, Passus IX–XII: Elements in the Design of the Inward Journey', *Traditio* 28 (1972), 211–80, and David Strong, 'Illumination of the Intellect: Franciscan Sermons and *Piers Plowman*', in *Speculum Sermonis: Interdisciplinary Reflections on the Medieval Sermon*, ed. Georgiana Donavin, Cary J. Nederman, and Richard Utz (Turnhout: Brepols, 2004), pp. 197–220. Both Wittig and Strong understand the Vision of Kynde, and the poem more generally, to be indebted to twelfth-century monastic discourses, including Bonaventuran exemplarism. My argument disagrees, however, with Strong's claim that '[f]rom this meeting [with Kynde], we learn that any creature, no matter how far removed from the hierarchy of humanity, capably directs the individual's mind to God' (p. 211). Ascent to knowledge of God is indeed the stated goal of the vision in B.11, but my aim in this essay is to show that it is not achieved as easily as Strong suggests.

5 Alan of Lille, *Rhythmus alter*, *PL* 210, 579A: 'Omnis mundi creatura/ Quasi liber et pictura/ Nobis est et speculum'.

6 See, for example, Hugh of St Victor's expression of this idea in *De tribus diebus*, 4.94–98, ed. Dominic Poirel, CCCM 177 (Turnhout: Brepols, 2001), p. 9: 'Vniuersus enim mundus iste sensilis quasi quidam liber est scriptus digito Dei.' On the use of natural lore as sermon exempla, and particularly that concerning animal behaviour, see John Morson, 'The English Cistercians and the Bestiary', *Bulletin of the John Rylands Library* 39 (1956), 146–70, and G. R. Owst, *Literature and the Pulpit in Medieval England*, 2nd ed. (Oxford: Oxford University Press, 1961), pp. 195–204.

7 On exempla, see Nigel F. Palmer, 'Exempla', in *Medieval Latin: An Introduction and Bibliographical Guide*, ed. F. A. C. Mantello and A. G. Rigg (Washington, D.C.: Catholic University Press, 1996), pp. 582–88, and Larry Scanlon, *Narrative, Authority, and Power: The Medieval Exemplum and the Chaucerian Tradition* (Cambridge: Cambridge University Press, 1994). Although exempla were not always used out of context, Palmer points out that the existence of exempla collections can serve to undermine the form's claims to truth: 'When the exemplum is seen in the context of a collection, the unidirectional thrust towards a particular lesson is counteracted by the wealth of diverse (and potentially contradictory) doctrine contained in the whole … Such works implicitly question the

spiritual truths, not only an incidental or rhetorically useful one.[7] As such, exemplarism offers a confident appraisal of the spiritual value of nature, but also places strict conditions on how the physical world may be apprehended and used.

At the outset, the Vision of Kynde is clearly marked as an exemplarist meditation, and its placement within the Dreamer's quest for 'kynde knowynge' highlights Langland's interest in exploring natural and experiential modes of knowledge.[8] However, as James Simpson has observed, in these central passūs of the poem, Langland's investigation of theological questions often 'subverts the literary and academic forms it apparently adopts'.[9] In this essay, I propose that the Vision of Kynde is another instance in which Langland seems to try on and then cast off a form of authoritative discourse. While the passage evokes the Latin tradition of exemplarism and related encyclopedic products, the vision finally departs from these forms by concluding not with praise of nature's creator, but with a critique of the order of nature itself. As a result, the Dreamer wakes from his inner dream angry and ashamed, the chance for spiritual enlightenment apparently lost.

Situated in a portion of the poem that has been described as 'a journey of the mind into itself', the Vision of Kynde is framed by a series of passūs in which the Dreamer meets allegorical aspects of his own psyche: Thought, Wit, Inwit, Imaginatif, and even Anima, as well as Study and Clergy, personifications of the mind's cognitive activities and the academic institutions that shape them.[10] Paradoxically, in the passus most concerned with exploring the Dreamer's inner capacities, the landscape of the human mind and soul opens into a vision of the *external* landscape of nature, the created world that Kynde

idea that an exemplum can form a compelling basis for a particular course of action: and so the literary form turns, playfully, against itself' (pp. 584–85). Similarly, Chenu remarks on the distinction between exempla and exemplarism: 'To be sure, in *exemplum* literature, as in the rhetoric taught by the *artes praedicandi* (arts of preaching), symbols were readily used as illustrations for Christian values. But in the twelfth century especially, the symbol ... was treated as an instrument capable of penetrating truth, over and beyond any brief and incidental use in mere illustration.' See Chenu, *Nature, Man, and Society*, p. 112.

8 On the association of 'kynde knowynge' and experiential knowledge see Mary Clemente Davlin, '*Kynde Knowyng* as a Major Theme in *Piers Plowman* B', *Review of English Studies* 22 (1971), 1–19; Jill Mann, 'Eating and Drinking in *Piers Plowman*', *Essays and Studies* 32 (1979), 26–43; James Simpson, 'From Reason to Affective Knowledge: Modes of Thought and Poetic Form in *Piers Plowman*', *Medium Aevum* 55 (1986), 1–23; Hugh White, *Nature and Salvation in Piers Plowman* (Cambridge: D. S. Brewer, 1988), pp. 41–59; Nicolette Zeeman, ' "Studying" in the Middle Ages – and in *Piers Plowman*', *New Medieval Literatures* 3 (1999), 185–212; and Zeeman, 'The Condition of *Kynde*', in *Medieval Literature and Historical Inquiry: Essays in Honor of Derek Pearsall*, ed. David Aers (Cambridge: D. S. Brewer, 2000), pp. 1–30.

9 Simpson, *Piers Plowman: An Introduction*, 2nd ed. (Exeter: University of Exeter Press, 2007), p. 113, and see his more detailed analysis of the poem's shifting cognitive modes in Simpson, 'From Reason to Affective Knowledge'.

10 Morton W. Bloomfield, *Piers Plowman as a Fourteenth-Century Apocalypse* (New Brunswick, NJ: Rutgers University Press, 1962), p. 64. See also Wittig, 'Inward Journey', and Simpson, 'From Reason to Affective Knowledge'.

presents for the Dreamer's observation in Passus 11. While Langland's concerns in this part of the poem are epistemological, and, as such, make vital use of academic discourses, they are also ontological, for what the Dreamer seeks in his observation of nature – but cannot yet grasp – is the human place within the larger scene.[11] Experiential knowledge, for Langland, is relational: just as Peace affirms in Passus 18 that 'no wight woot what wele is þat neuere wo suffrede', so too in Passus 11 the Dreamer is coming to know his own place in nature by regarding what he is not (B.18.206). What strikes him most in his observations is the fact of human exceptionality, not the expected superiority of human creation *imago dei*, but the impression that human beings represent a disjunction and an anomaly within an otherwise ideal scene. Like Alan of Lille's narrator before him, Langland's Will confronts the jarring disharmony of human beings within the greater harmony of created nature. The Dreamer's perception of *negative* human exceptionalism, a situation that is articulated most pointedly in Langland's comparisons of human behaviour with animal behaviour, provokes a crisis of understanding that subverts the principles of exemplarism, and the Vision of Kynde dissolves.[12]

To explore Langland's engagement with the created world as an object of knowledge, I begin with an assessment of the shifting philosophies of nature that provide a context for the Vision of Kynde in Passus 11 and the Dreamer's subsequent encounter with Imaginatif in Passus 12. In each episode, Langland draws on exemplarist discourse, not only borrowing and reshaping encyclopedic and bestiary lore, but also actively and skeptically engaging the mode of thought that produced these texts. The major obstacle to exemplarist thinking, however, is the exceptionality of human sin within the perfection of the larger order of nature, a problem that so alienates humanity from the rest of creation that the book of nature becomes illegible to human understanding. I conclude, however, with a coda that mimics Langland's own technique: for even as the Vision of Kynde dissolves with the exhaustion of exemplarist discourse, Imaginatif greets the Dreamer as he wakes from the inner dream, affirming the inadequacy of Kynde Wit but offering a way to salvage exemplarism in answer to the crisis of natural knowledge in Passus 11. Langland thus tests the value of the natural world by adopting and critiquing the discourses of nature in Passūs 11 and 12 – but in the end, his commitment to the concept of 'kynde' remains constant.[13]

11 On Langland's evocation of academic discourses in these passus, see Simpson, *Introduction*, pp. 96–98, 116–19.

12 I borrow this terminology from Laurie Shannon, whose essay I discuss in detail below. See n. 41.

13 On the systematic importance of 'kynde' in *Piers Plowman*, see Davlin, '*Kynde Knowyng* as a Major Theme'; White, *Nature and Salvation*; Anne Middleton, 'William Langland's 'Kynde Name': Authorial Signature and Social Identity in Late Fourteenth-Century England', in *Literary Practice and Social Change in Britain, 1380–1530*, ed. Lee Patterson (Berkeley, Los Angeles, and London: University of California Press, 1990), pp. 15–82; and Zeeman, 'The Condition of *Kynde*'.

The medieval sciences of nature

The exemplarist trope of 'nature as book' gives rise to actual 'books of nature' in the production of the medieval encyclopedia and related 'encyclopedic' texts, including bestiaries and other textual repositories that were given a wide range of titles in the medieval period; as Michael Twomey notes: 'Medieval books of encyclopedic proportions were called by Latin words *speculum*, *imago mundi*, *de proprietatibus rerum*, *de naturis rerum*, *elucidarium*, *compendium*, *thesaurus*, *liber floridus*, or their vernacular equivalents ... suggest[ing] a cornucopia of knowledge contained between two covers'.[14] Due to the overlapping nature of these genres, and their wide range of purposes, it is necessary to offer a definition of terms at the outset. In this essay, I use the term 'encyclopedic' to describe texts that aspire to construct inclusive visions of nature, although medieval encyclopedias certainly do often stretch beyond nature to embrace the whole gamut of human knowledge.[15] Bestiaries, which share information with encyclopedias, are 'encyclopedic' insofar as they aim to encompass the animal world and often place human beings among the orders of living creatures.[16] This essay considers animal lore both from bestiaries and from encyclopedias proper, as well as from other types of beast literature.[17] Finally, I refer to all texts that consider nature symbolically as 'exemplarist'. Encyclopedias, broadly conceived, serve as tools for the exemplarist project by

[14] Twomey, 'Towards a Reception History of Western Medieval Encyclopedias in England before 1500', in *Pre-Modern Encyclopaedic Texts: Proceedings of the Second COMERS Congress, Groningen, 1–4 July 1998*, ed. Peter Binkley (Leiden: Brill, 1997), pp. 329–62. Robert L. Fowler addresses the difficulty of defining a medieval encyclopedic genre in his essay, 'Encyclopedias: Definitions and Theoretical Problems', in *Pre-Modern Encyclopedic Texts*, ed. Binkley, pp. 3–29.

[15] Christel Meier defines eight types of medieval encyclopedias based on their function. See Meier, 'Organization of Knowledge and Encyclopaedic *Ordo*: Functions and Purposes of a Universal Literary Genre', in *Pre-Modern Encyclopaedic Texts*, ed. Binkley, pp. 103–26. The classic study of medieval systematizing is C. S. Lewis, *The Discarded Image: An Introduction to Medieval and Renaissance Literature* (Cambridge: Cambridge University Press, 1964). On the developing technologies for organizing and searching collections of knowledge, see also Mary A. and Richard K. Rouse, *Authentic Witnesses: Approaches to Medieval Texts and Manuscripts* (Notre Dame, IN: University of Notre Dame, 1991), pp. 191–255.

[16] See Dorothy Yamamoto, *The Boundaries of the Human in Medieval Literature* (Oxford: Oxford University Press, 2000), pp. 12–33. Yamamoto's introductory chapter argues that the omission of or disregard for bestiary accounts of human creation, by both medieval and modern curators, has had the unfortunate effect of ' "clos[ing] off" the Bestiary text as a straightforward catalogue of animals'. Instead, Yamamoto argues, '[w]e need to re-complicate it, to treat it as the focus for questions about the whole relationship between humans and the rest of creation' (p. 18).

[17] Two essential introductions to the development of the bestiary tradition are Florence McCulloch, *Mediaeval Latin and French Bestiaries* (Chapel Hill: University of North Carolina Press, 1960) and Willene B. Clark, ed. and trans., *A Medieval Book of Beasts* (Woodbridge: Boydell Press, 2006). See also Debra Hassig, *Medieval Bestiaries: Text, Image, Ideology* (Cambridge: Cambridge University Press, 1995) and Nona Flores, *Animals in the Middle Ages* (New York: Routledge, 2000). On the representation of animals in other genres of beast literature and their relationship to the bestiary tradition, see Jill Mann, *From Aesop to Reynard: Beast Literature in Medieval Britain* (Oxford: Oxford University Press, 2009).

rendering the variety and order of creation accessible to human understanding through observation, compilation, and classification. As these activities suggest, however, the symbolic view of nature, in which the natural world is meaningful only as a sign of higher things, was not the only way to regard nature in the Middle Ages. Instead, encyclopedic compendia fall somewhere along a spectrum of views that range from Augustinian (or Neoplatonic) to Aristotelian, two approaches that have been termed 'symbolic' and 'scientific', respectively.[18] Exemplarist undertakings are necessarily encyclopedic, in the sense that the contemplative observer must gather sensory data for symbolic interpretation, but not all encyclopedias are exemplarist, depending on their attitude toward the material they set out. The tension between these two visions of natural knowledge and the texts that they produced – from Neoplatonic allegories like Alan's *De planctu* to proto-scientific encyclopedias and moralized bestiaries – are vital contexts for understanding Langland's inquiries in Passūs 11 and 12.

In *De doctrina Christiana*, Augustine establishes a semiotics of nature based on the Neoplatonic notion that the sensible world has value only as a sign of higher things:

> So in this mortal life we are travelers away from our Lord: if we wish to return to the homeland where we can be happy we must use this world, not enjoy it, in order to discern 'the invisible attributes of God, which are understood through what has been made' or, in other words, to ascertain what is eternal and spiritual from corporeal and temporal things.[19]

The world is an object of interpretation, not a good in itself, but a means of moving on to 'invisibilia', or divine truths. Citing Romans 1.20, Augustine elaborates an exemplarist theory of the 'uses' of nature, based on biblical authority, that would remain popular throughout the medieval period.[20]

By contrast, Aristotle's teaching on nature sought to discover the inner causalities of sensible things through the observation of individual phenomena without reference to a hidden truth beyond the sensible world.[21] As Gordon Leff writes, the Aristotelian philosophy of nature is 'a non-

18 See Chenu, *Nature, Man, and Society*, pp. 102–19.

19 Augustine, *De doctrina Christiana*, 1.4.9, ed. and trans. R. P. H. Green (Oxford: Clarendon Press, 1995), pp. 16–17: '[S]ic in huius mortalitatis vita peregrinantes a domino, si redire in patriam volumus ubi beati esse possimus, utendum est hoc mundo, non fruendum, ut *invisibilia dei per ea quae facta sunt intellecta* conspiciantur, hoc est ut de corporalibus temporalibusque rebus aeterna et spiritalia capiamus.'

20 On Augustine's exemplarism, see David Knowles, *The Evolution of Medieval Thought* (Baltimore: Helicon Press, 1962), pp. 40–43.

21 On the development of a 'scientific sensibility' in relation to nature, see Brian Stock, *Myth and Science in the Twelfth Century: A Study of Bernard Silvester* (Princeton: Princeton University Press, 1972), and Chenu, *Nature, Man, and Society*.

22 Gordon Leff, *The Dissolution of the Medieval Outlook: An Essay on Intellectual and Spiritual Change in the Fourteenth Century* (New York: Harper and Row, 1976), p. 26.

transcendental interpretation of reality'.[22] It advocates study of the natural world for its own sake and on its own terms, not merely as a sign of something else. Unlike Plato, for whom the sensible world is comprised of nothing but shadows of the eternal Ideas, and unlike Neoplatonists like Augustine, for whom observation of the 'visible things' of the world is merely a prologue to higher contemplation, Aristotle placed great value on the perceptible world and the variety of its individual manifestations.

Encyclopedic texts bear the influence both of Neoplatonic symbolism, as transmitted by Augustine, and the empiricism of Aristotelian learning. From the twelfth century onwards, the study of natural philosophy was energized by the influx of Aristotelian and Arabic texts, but it was Augustine who had first called for the production of a Christian encyclopedia as an aid to biblical study, noting the impossibility of deciphering scripture without understanding its allusions to natural phenomena: 'Ignorance of things makes figurative expressions unclear when we are ignorant of the qualities of animals or stones or plants or other things mentioned in scripture for the sake of some analogy.'[23] Further, Augustine continues,

> if someone suitably qualified were interested in devoting a generous amount of time to the good of his brethren he could compile a monograph classifying and setting out all the places, animals, plants, and trees, or the stones and metals, and all the other unfamiliar kinds of objects mentioned in scripture.[24]

Although Pliny's *Naturalis historia* (c. AD 77) is considered the first Western encyclopedia, Cassiodorus's *Institutions* (c. 562) and Isidore's enormously influential *Etymologies* (c. 636) were the first major encyclopedias produced in response to the specifically Christian need that Augustine identified, and later compendia continued to declare their purposes along these lines.[25]

One such example is Bartholomaeus Anglicus's popular encyclopedic work, *De proprietatibus rerum*. His Latin text was translated into Middle English by John Trevisa at the end of the fourteenth century, and provides evidence that Augustine's exemplarist approach to nature remained current during the

23 Augustine, *De doctrina Christiana*, 2.16.59, pp. 82–85: 'Rerum autem ignorantia facit obscuras figuratas locutiones, cum ignoramus vel animantium vel lapidum vel herbarum naturas aliarumve rerum quae plerumque in scripturis similitudinis alicuius gratia ponuntur.'

24 Augustine, *De doctrina Christiana*, 2.39.141, pp. 122–23: 'si quem eorum qui possunt benignam sane operam fraternae utilitati delectet impendere, ut quoscumque terrarum locos quaeve animalia vel herbas atque arbores sive lapides vel metalla incognita speciesque quaslibet scriptura commemorat ea generatim digerens sola exposita litteris mandet'.

25 On the development of the medieval encyclopedia, see the entry for encyclopedias in the *Dictionary of the Middle Ages* 4, ed. Joseph R. Strayer (New York: Scribner, 1982–89), pp. 447–50, and Gregory G. Guzman, 'Encyclopedias', in *Medieval Latin*, ed. Mantello and Rigg, pp. 702–707.

26 Trevisa's text was complete c. 1398, but he is thought to have been working on the translation at Oxford from 1394. Even though it is unlikely that Langland ever saw Trevisa's translation, I cite Trevisa's Middle English text when referring to Bartholomaeus in this study, primarily because I seek to present a vernacular context for comparison with Langland's handling of similar topics.

period in which Langland wrote *Piers Plowman.*[26] In his prologue, Bartholomaeus explains that, by the work of the Holy Spirit, divine truths have been 'derkliche ihid and wrapped vndir liknes and fygures of propirtees of þinges of kynde and craft' because, Bartholomaeus writes, 'oure wit may not stiȝe vnto þe contemplacioun of vnseye þinges but it be ilad by consideracioun of þinges þat beþ iseye'.[27] In other words, divine truths cannot be expressed directly since immediate knowledge of such matters is beyond human cognition; therefore, scriptural texts use 'fleisschliche' figures as an aid to human understanding, so that human beings might 'stye vp' to divine knowledge through things that can be known and experienced.[28] By compiling in one place all the natures and properties of created things, the encyclopedic work constitutes an interpretive tool with which to 'unwrap' the hidden meanings of scripture.

The Latin lore and learning of these texts thus made its way into the vernacular through the production of English encyclopedias – such as Trevisa's translation of Bartholomaeus – as well as through countless instances of the borrowing and adaptation of encyclopedic material in bestiaries, lapidaries, and herbals, as well as in literary texts. Chaucer, for example, borrowed from Vincent of Beauvais' *Speculum maius* as well as from Bartholomaeus's encyclopedia.[29] Based on Langland's treatment of nature, it would seem that he knew these encyclopedias as well; it is likely that they were among the many texts that inspired his poetic investigations of the value of 'kynde'. In what follows, I suggest that Will's encounters with Kynde and Imaginatif draw broadly on the debate between the two views of nature – the 'symbolic' and the 'scientific' – and that Langland is simultaneously drawn to exemplarism's optimistic vision of natural knowledge and skeptical both of its involvement in encyclopedic looking and of its reliability as a source of spiritual truths.

Exemplarism and its limits

When the Vision of Kynde commences, the Dreamer has the opportunity to survey all of creation from his lofty perspective upon Middelerþe. His initial observations of landscape, vegetation, and animal inhabitants convey a sense of his awe at the scene before him as he emphasizes nature's variety and abundance. The Vision of Kynde is encyclopedic in its scope:

> I seiȝ þe sonne and þe see and þe sond after,

[27] John Trevisa, *On the Properties of Things: John Trevisa's translation of Bartholomaeus Anglicus, De Proprietatibus Rerum*, Prologue, lines 11–12, 18–20, ed. M. C. Seymour et al. (Oxford: Clarendon Press, 1975), p. 41.

[28] Trevisa, *On the Properties of Things*, Prologue, lines 16 and 26.

[29] On the influence of Bartholomaeus's text, see A. S. G. Edwards, 'Bartholomaeus Anglicus', *De proprietatibus rerum* and Medieval English Literature', *Archiv* 222 (1985), 121–28, and Twomey, 'Towards a Reception History', in *Pre-Modern Encyclopaedic Texts*, ed. Binkley, pp. 329–62.

> And where þat briddes and beestes by hir make þei yeden,
> Wilde wormes in wodes, and wonderful foweles
> Wiþ fleckede feþeres and of fele colours …
> And siþen I loked on þe see and so forþ on þe sterres;
> Manye selkouþes I seiȝ ben noȝt to seye nouþe.
> I seiȝ floures in þe fryth and hir faire colours
> And how among þe grene gras growed so many hewes,
> And some soure and some swete; selkouþ me þouȝte.
> Of hir kynde and hir colour to carpe it were to longe.
> (B.11.327–30, 363–68)

Sketching out the various physical realms of nature – the 'see and þe sond', the 'wodes', the 'sterres', and the 'fryth' – as well as the creatures appropriate to each elemental sphere, the Dreamer's observations convey a sense of the spaciousness and organization of the natural world. Though it does not reproduce their specificity, this passage allusively gestures toward other catalogues of nature in literary and encyclopedic texts, and even the conventionality of the Dreamer's descriptions further suggests his awe before the natural world. He protests that language is insufficient to convey the truth of what he sees: 'Manye selkouþes I seiȝ ben noȝt to seye nouþe' and 'Of hir kynde and hir colour to carpe it were to longe' (B.11.364, 368). The choice of the term 'selkouþ', meaning 'a wonder', or even 'a miracle', indicates that the Dreamer's initial reaction to the natural world remains at the level of awestruck, reverential praise, a posture required by the exemplarist method, which presupposes God's own presence in creation and sets limitations on what human knowledge might discover about nature's workings.[30]

Hugh of St Victor's exemplarist meditations on the natural world offer a useful comparison with the Dreamer's initially reverential orientation toward nature. In his twelfth-century Latin treatise *De tribus diebus*, Hugh glosses Romans 1.20, as Augustine had, to show that the wondrous, observable qualities of creation proclaim the greatness of their creator. The immensity ('inmensitas') of created things makes manifest God's power ('potentia'); their beauty ('decor') reveals his wisdom ('sapientia'); and their benefit to humankind ('utilitas') signifies his goodness ('benignitas').[31] By observing these wonderful characteristics, Hugh writes, one may not only conclude that God created the world, but also discover certain of God's own characteristics as they are 'written' into the things of creation.

In a moment of reverie, Hugh professes his amazement at the unbounded

[30] *MED* s.v. 'selcouth(e)', n. (b).

[31] Hugh of St Victor, *De tribus diebus*, 1.14–15, p. 4: 'Potentiam manifestat creaturarum inmensitas, sapientiam decor, benignitatem utilitas.' Hugh cites Rom. 1.20 in *De tribus diebus*, 1.5–6, p. 3: '*Invisibilia enim ipsius a creatura mundi per ea quae facta sunt intellecta conspiciuntur*'. The three 'invisibilia', according to Hugh's interpretation, toward which nature points us, are God's 'potentia', 'sapientia', and 'benignitas'.

quantity of created things ('Quam multa!', he exclaims), reciting element by element a catalogue of 'innumerabilia': 'How numerous! How many they are! Count the stars in the sky, grains of sand in the sea, specks of dust upon the earth, raindrops in the clouds, feathers on birds, scales on fish, hairs upon beasts, grasses in the fields, leaves and fruits upon the trees, and count the countless [numbers] of other innumerable things'.[32] Even as he anatomizes creation, Hugh remains alert to his human ignorance before God's mystery, for in naming these things 'innumerabilia', he signals his awareness of the boundaries of human knowledge. Sometimes Hugh's perception of these limitations is poignantly described, as when, in a passage that resonates with the Dreamer's desire for 'kynde knowynge', Hugh wishes that his ability to perceive the meaning of created things and to describe them to others might match his passion for appreciating them: 'If only I were able to discern these things as accurately, to recount them as adequately, as I am able ardently to love them!'[33] Nevertheless, despite the limitations of his understanding, he is inspired by the delightfulness of creation to sing out its praise, and, citing Psalm 91, invites others to join him:

> With the psalmist let us exclaim in astonishment and wonder: 'O Lord, how great are thy works! You have made all things in your wisdom; you have brought me delight, Lord, in your creation, and I shall rejoice in the work of your hands. O Lord, how great are thy works!'[34]

Hugh's meditation on nature thus demonstrates how poetic praise might legitimately issue from one's contemplation of created things when they are understood as the works ['opera'] of their divine maker. But Psalm 91 also cautions that not all observers will be able to understand what they behold in nature, for the 'foolish man' ('[v]ir insipiens') either does not perceive nature's splendour or cannot fathom its proper source and significance.[35] Later, in declaring that nature is a kind of book written by God himself ('quasi quidam liber est scriptus digito Dei'), Hugh compares those who are 'illiterate' before the book of nature with the 'illiteratus' who gazes at an 'open book' ('liber apertus') and can see but not comprehend the meaning of the characters etched upon its pages.[36] Nature then, even as an open book for all to see, nevertheless preserves

[32] Hugh of St Victor, *De tribus diebus*, 2.44–51, p. 6: 'Quam multa! Quot sunt! Numera stellas caeli, arenam maris, puluerem terrae, guttas pluuiae, pennas uolucrum, squamas piscium, pilos animalium, gramina camporum, folia uel fructus arborum, et caeterorum innumerabilium innumerabilia numera.'

[33] Hugh of St Victor, *De tribus diebus*, 4.83–84, p. 8: 'Et haec utinam ego tam possem subtiliter perspicere, tam competenter enarrare, quam possum ardenter diligere.'

[34] Hugh of St. Victor, *De tribus diebus*, 4.87–91, pp. 8–9: '[C]um psalmista stupentes et admirantes clamemus: "Quam magnificata sunt opera tua, Domine! omnia in sapientia fecisti; delectasti me, Domine, in factura tua, et in operibus manuum tuarum exultabo. Quam magnificata sunt opera tua, Domine!" '

[35] Hugh of St Victor, *De tribus diebus*, 4.92–93, p. 9: ' "Vir insipiens non cognoscet, et stultus non intelliget haec." '

[36] Hugh of St Victor, *De tribus diebus*, 4.94–102, p. 9: 'Quemadmodum autem si illiteratus quis

the secrets of God from the 'stultus et animalis homo', for though such a man may observe the figures and letters of created things, he cannot finally comprehend their true meaning. The illiterate observer of nature can only see the 'species', or outward forms, of created things, while the wise and spiritual observer not only delights in the outward beauty of God's works, but simultaneously perceives their inner significance as symbols of the creator's power, wisdom, and goodness.

Hugh's treatise on the rewards of viewing creation illustrates the exemplarist mindset at work and thus provides a useful context for Langland's Vision of Kynde. Both speakers observe nature from a similar vantage point and express an 'encyclopedic' wish to collect and analyse their observations; but Hugh's contemplation directs him to sing out the creator's praise, which issues as the *De tribus diebus* itself, while Langland's narrator appears to be the 'vir insipiens', the foolish and carnal man who is unable to 'read' nature correctly. As Imaginatif will later explain to the Dreamer, 'þow wiþ rude speche/ Lakkedest and losedest þyng þat longed noȝt to done;/ Tho hadde he [Kynde] litel liking for to lere þe moore' (B.11.420–22). The Dreamer's 'rude speche', it would seem, reveals his spiritual inadequacy before the book of nature, and so the vision ends, signalling the limits of what 'kynde' can teach him, or, from another angle, the limits of what he is prepared to learn from 'kynde'. Before we reach this point, however, Langland challenges the authority of the discourse he had initially evoked. Although the Vision of Kynde begins as an exemplarist venture, the Dreamer's observations soon lead him to fixate on an apparent flaw in the natural order – human sin – that presents a pessimistic challenge to the inherently optimistic vision of exemplarism.

Langland's beasts and the human anomaly

The Dreamer's description of the natural scene before him, general at first, becomes more exact and more critical as he moves from an awestruck appreciation of the beauty and variety of nature to observe specific details of animal behaviour. He focuses on the creatures' 'reasonable' consumption of food, reproductive habits, and domestic arrangements: 'Reson I seiȝ sooþly sewen alle beestes,/ In etynge, in drynkynge and in engendrynge of kynde' (B.11.335–36). In making a closer examination of animal behaviour, the Dreamer begins to hone in on the specifics of the scene before him, departing from the broadly wondrous account of his initial, generalized observations. In the manner of a medieval encyclopedist, the Dreamer describes the details of

apertum librum uideat, figuras aspicit, literas non cognoscit, ita stultus et animalis homo qui non percipit ea quae Dei sunt, in uisibilibus istis creaturis foris uidet speciem, sed non intelligit rationem.'

animal behaviour, including their sexual practices. He is astounded by the beasts' restraint in regard to their reproductive task:

> And after cours of concepcion noon took kepe of ooþer,
> As whan þei hadde ryde in Rotey tyme anoon reste þei after;
> Males drowen hem to males al mornyng by hemselue,
> And femelles to femelles ferded and drowe.
> Ther ne was cow ne cowkynde þat conceyued hadde
> That wolde bere after bole, ne boor after sowe;
> Boþe hors and houndes and alle oþere beestes
> Medled noȝt wiþ hir makes, saue man allone. (B.11.337–40)

As this passage reveals, the sticking point for the Dreamer is the paradox that human beings, uniquely endowed with reason, are the only creatures that do not behave reasonably in sexual matters – 'alle oþere beestes' practice sexuality with restraint, 'save man allone' (B.11.339–40). As he studies a tableau of wondrous animal behaviour, it is the particularity of human *misbehaviour* that most impresses the Dreamer. It appears, moreover, that Langland takes pains to arrange this scene to emphasize the isolation of human beings within creation.

A brief comparison of Bartholomaeus's description of the mating practices of beasts establishes how greatly Langland diverges from typical encyclopedic depictions of animal behaviour in order to highlight the disjunction presented by humankind. In describing the lustiness of bovine mating practices, Bartholomaeus invests their behaviour with rather human qualities:

> [B]oles fighten for here wyfes and he þat haþ the maystrey lepeþ on þe female; and whanne he is yfebled by moche work of lecchery þanne he þat was ouercome comeþ and fighteþ wiþ him; and he þat haþ þe maistrie lepeþ on þe female, as it were, makyng ioye of þe maistrye.[37]

Bartholomaeus anthropomorphizes the beasts in the manner typical of encyclopedic and bestiary accounts, translating their instinctual behaviour into human terms and imagining humans and animals on a single continuum. In contrast, Langland's account isolates human beings, separating humans from animals and presenting humankind as an aberration, an anomaly within the larger order of nature. Unlike the encyclopedists and the bestiarists, the Dreamer does not perceive animals as reflections of human behaviour that offer positive and negative moral examples; instead, he envisions them as part of a natural order from which human beings are divided. Humanity is an island in nature, standing out like a sore thumb, a defect, a worm in God's bliss. For amid the harmony of nature that he initially beholds with admiration, the narrator perceives that human beings alone refuse to abide by Reason's dictates:

[37] Trevisa, *On the Properties of Things*, 18.100, pp. 1251–52.

> Man and his make I myȝte se boþe.
> Pouerte and plentee, boþe pees and werre,
> Blisse and bale boþe I seiȝ at ones,
> And how men token Mede and Mercy refused. (B.11.331–34)

The Dreamer here observes a set of contraries held in balance – the good with the bad – , but the final statement jars the balance of the first three lines with a revelation of human corruption: 'man and his make' do wrong *and* refuse forgiveness. The exceptionality of human misbehaviour overwhelms the narrator and he can no longer marvel at the '[m]any selkouthes' of creation before him. As we have seen, the order, intelligence, and beauty that the Dreamer initially perceives in this vision almost succeed in leading him toward a discovery of God, who, disguised as Kynde, has authorized the vision for this very purpose. However, it is ultimately the Dreamer's inability to reconcile the human place in nature – the painful awareness of the human incongruity within an otherwise perfect scene – that brings his vision to a premature close. The Dreamer blames Reason, and by extension, the natural order itself, for failing to keep human beings out of trouble:

> Ac þat moost meued me and my mood chaunged,
> That Reson rewarded and ruled alle beestes
> Saue man and his make: many tyme me þouȝte
> No Reson hem ruled, neiþer riche ne pouere.
> Thanne I rebukede Reson … (B.11.369–73)

In these lines Langland again draws attention to the divide between human and animal creation, depicting 'man and his make' as outcasts of an otherwise unified world composed of 'alle beestes' (B.11.370–71).

The notion that human beings sit apart and at a disadvantage, both physically and morally speaking, in relation to non-human animals is a conceit with a history and a future in literary and theological texts. In Alan of Lille's *De planctu Naturae*, a suggestive context for *Piers Plowman*, the narrator marvels at Natura's garments, which depict an encyclopedic panorama of creation, including catalogues of birds, fish, and beasts of the earth.[38] In the portion of her tunic reserved for human beings, however, Alan's narrator notices an unsightly gash in the fabric: 'In this section, the tunic had suffered a rending of its parts and showed the effects of injuries and insults. In the other sections, however, the parts had sustained no injury from division or discord in the beautiful harmony of their unbroken surface.'[39] Like Langland's description of

[38] Alan of Lille, *De planctu Naturae*, 2.138–292, ed. Häring, pp. 813–19.

[39] Alan of Lille, *The Plaint of Nature*, pp. 98–99. *De planctu Naturae*, 2.234–37, ed. Häring, p. 817: 'In qua parte tunica, suarum partium passa dissidium, suarum iniuriarum contumelias demonstrabat. In reliquis tamen locis partes, eleganti continuatione concordes, nullam diuisionis in se sustinebant discordiam.'

how human greed upsets the harmonious balance of opposites in B.11.331–34, Alan also uses the categories of continuity and disruption to emphasize the human exception. Later, Natura, who is in many respects a counterpart and forerunner to Langland's Kynde, reveals that the tear in her robe is caused by human disregard for her laws; 'man alone' ('solus homo') disobeys her and produces a dislocation that mars the perfection, the 'unbroken surface', of the created world.[40] As in the Vision of Kynde, in Alan's allegory of nature, human beings are represented as an exception to the natural order and this exceptionality, at least initially, seems to pose a significant threat to human spiritual progress.

In a recent study of animals in Shakespeare, Laurie Shannon traces this same problem of human deficiency in early modern literature, usefully describing it as a rhetorical concept she calls 'negative human exceptionalism'.[41] We might place King Lear's tirade on the heath alongside Alan's and Langland's visions of human insufficiency, for in describing man as 'unaccommodated ... a poor, bare, forked animal', Lear similarly points to the exceptional status of human beings in nature. He laments the apparent injustice within creation whereby, as Shannon puts it, 'only the appropriated coats and borrowed practical knowledge of other creatures equip humankind for the world, while all other creatures are understood to arrive prepared'.[42] While Lear's concerns seem to be largely practical ones, other writers in the period expressed the human disadvantage in theological terms quite similar to those in Passus 11, where Langland formulates the problem. In the Holy Sonnets, for instance, John Donne poses the injustice this way:

> If poisonous minerals, and if that tree,
> Whose fruit threw death on else immortal us,
> If lecherous goats, if serpents envious
> Cannot be damned; alas, why should I be?
> Why should intent or reason, born in me,
> Make sins, else equal, in me more heinous?[43]

For Donne the uniquely human capacity for free will ('intent or reason, born in me') and, implicitly, the uniquely human potential for reward or punishment in the afterlife, become also a uniquely human burden. As Shannon argues, 'Man stands categorically above the beasts for Donne, to be sure; but

40 Alan of Lille, *The Plaint of Nature*, p. 143. *De planctu Naturae*, 8.12–13, ed. Häring, p. 833: 'Sed ab huius uniuersalitatis regula solus homo anomala exceptione seducitur ...'.

41 Shannon, 'The Eight Animals in Shakespeare, or, Before the Human', *PMLA* 124.2 (2009), 472–79, at p. 477.

42 Shannon, 'Eight Animals', p. 477.

43 Donne, 'Holy Sonnet 9', in *Complete English Poems*, ed. A. J. Smith (London: Penguin, 1996), lines 1–8. Shannon discusses Donne's poem in 'Poor, Bare, Forked: Animal Sovereignty, Human Negative Exceptionalism, and the Natural History of *King Lear*', *Shakespeare Quarterly* 60.2 (2009), 168–96.

his distinction is the ambivalent one of possessing a unique capacity to swerve, or fall, from type. A rational soul is "proper" to man, but it follows inevitably that the capacity for improper choice is thus his too.'[44] These explorations of the human place in the greater scheme of creation invert typical expectations of human supremacy. Along with Alan's *De planctu*, they offer a sustained tradition of inquiry in which Langland's Vision of Kynde plays an important part. Moreover, each of these examples further highlights the way in which human encounters with the animal world provoke the shock of negative human exceptionalism. In *Piers Plowman*, Will's awe before nature turns to agitation upon closer inspection of animal behaviour, particularly when he compares the animals' apparently reasonable activity to the immoderation that characterizes human life.

While Donne evokes 'lecherous goats' and 'serpents envious' to underscore the injustice of the human condition, basing his complaint on a notion that humans and animals are 'sinners' alike though not judged on equal terms, the animals that the Dreamer observes from Middelerþe are all virtuous creatures. Langland presents a sanitized and orderly vision of reproduction to establish more definitively that all animal creation, 'save man allone', operates in accord with reason and moderation. In doing so, he diverges from the encyclopedic tradition and its representation of animal sexuality. For example, in describing the diversity of behaviour found in nature, Bartholomaeus anthropomorphizes animal mating practices in a way that is reminiscent of the *Parliament of Fowls*:

> And some bestes beþ fulle cruel and redy to rees and to fight and nameliche in tyme of loue and of alle seruice of Venus. In alle bestes is appetit of loue lykynge and þanne þe males woweþ and plesiþ þe females and fighteþ for hem.[45]

As I noted above, Bartholomaeus describes how bulls copulate with pleasure and abandon, fighting with other males for the chance to 'leap' upon a female until they are 'yfebled by moche work of lechery' and then 'mak[e] ioye' of their physical and sexual triumph.[46] Langland's disinterested animals would thus seem to be at odds with those found in this influential encyclopedia, which holds that 'alle bestes' possess 'appetit of loue lykynge'. Moreover, the bestiary tradition provides further evidence that medieval impressions of animal sexuality differed greatly from the picture of moderation found in *Piers Plowman*.[47] For example, in the bestiaries, the male partridge is an 'unclean bird, for male mounts male, and lust rashly forgets gender';[48] the stag 'rages

44 Shannon, 'Poor, Bare, Forked', p. 176.

45 Trevisa, *On the Properties of Things*, 18.1, p. 1094.

46 Trevisa, *On the Properties of Things*, 18.100, pp. 1251–52.

47 Trevisa, *On the Properties of Things*, 18.1, p. 1094.

48 *A Medieval Book of Beasts*, ed. and trans. Willene B. Clark (Woodbridge: Boydell Press, 2006), p. 179: 'Avis ... immunda, nam masculus in masculum insurgit, et obliviscitur sexum libido praeceps'.

with lustful frenzy' though only at the 'appointed time of breeding';[49] the male goat is a 'wanton animal given to butting, and always burning for coitus, and, on account of lust, his eyes are always casting about';[50] the female viper, 'frenzied by lust, bites off the head of the male' and, 'whenever he feels a desire for coitus', the male viper is also said to lure eels to unnatural copulation.[51]

Although bestiaries do not shy away from graphic depictions of animal 'lust', their representation of sexuality is nevertheless quite varied, for while the animals found in these texts are not the rational and restrained creatures of Langland's vision, neither are they uniformly controlled by physical passions. Debra Hassig has shown that this variation in descriptions of sexual practices serves a useful symbolic function in the bestiaries, for sex is always tied to a moral value and determines whether the creature would serve as a 'model or antimodel' for human moral behaviour. 'What becomes obvious', Hassig writes, 'is that sex and evil go hand in hand: the more sexually involved the creature, the greater its perceived evil. As a corollary to this, freedom from sex is equated with moral virtue.'[52] To counterbalance Donne's 'lecherous goats', the bestiaries also offer chaste elephants, steadfast turtle-doves, and sexless bees.[53] While on the whole his encyclopedia highlights the pleasure that animals take in sexual encounters, even Bartholomaeus describes the behaviour of one class of creatures in terms quite similar to the Dreamer's wholesome description of the cows above:

> And briddes and foules gendrynge kepiþ couenable tyme, for in springinge tyme whanne þe generacioun comeþ inne, briddes crien and singen. Males drawen to companye of females and preyen iche oþir of loue and wowiþ by beckes and voys, and makeþ nestis and leggiþ eyren and bryngiþ forþ briddes ... But whanne þe offyce of generacioun is fulendid, þanne þey sesen of songe and departen atwynne and comeþ nouȝt togedres forto tyme of generacioun come aȝeyne.[54]

Although later Bartholomaeus seems to contradict his own depiction of restrained avian sexuality in his descriptions of 'lecherous' colvers, peacocks, and sparrows,[55] it is possible that Langland had in mind a passage such as the

49 *A Medieval Book of Beasts*, p. 135: 'Mares generis huius, cum statutum tempus venerem incitat, saeviunt rabie libininis.'

50 *A Medieval Book of Beasts*, p. 152: 'Hircus lascivum animal et petulcum, et fervens semper ad coitum, cuius oculi ob libidinem in transversum aspiciunt.'

51 *A Medieval Book of Beasts*, p. 195: 'Illa autem ex voluptate in rabiem versa, caput maris ore recepto praecidit ... Ubi coeundi cupiditatem assumpserit, muraenae maritimae notam sibi requirit copulam.'

52 Hassig, 'Sex in the Bestiaries', in *The Mark of the Beast: The Medieval Bestiary in Art, Life, and Literature*, ed. Hassig (New York: Garland, 1999), p. 73.

53 See the entries for each of these creatures in *A Medieval Book of Beasts*, pp. 127–30, 185–86, and 190–93. For discussion of the bestiaries' examples of chaste animals, including the elephant's mating habits and the 'moderate sex lives' of bestiary fish, see Hassig, 'Sex in the Bestiaries', pp. 75–77.

54 Trevisa, *On the Properties of Things*, 12.1, p. 598.

55 Trevisa, *On the Properties of Things*, 12.7, p. 615; 12.32, p. 638; and 12.33, p. 639.

one above and simply extended it to cover the behaviour of all animals. In the Vision of Kynde, there is no hint that beasts engage in sexual activity because it is pleasurable; they convene only for procreative purposes, and only during the appropriate season. As in Trevisa's translation above, they 'kepiþ couenable tyme'. Both extremes of description are anthropomorphic, for one assigns sin and lechery, while the other imputes virtue and reason.

Throughout the Vision of Kynde, the Dreamer compares the 'reasonable' behaviour of the animals to that of their human counterparts, with the animals appearing more virtuous and skilful in each case. Moving on from the sexual behaviour of beasts, the Dreamer next observes how birds appear to behave reasonably in building their homes and raising their young. For example, he notes the magpie's ingenuity when he beholds her intricately constructed nest, an avian dwelling-place so finely wrought that he doubts whether any human builder could match it: 'Ther nys wriȝte, as I wene, sholde werche hir nest to paye;/ If any Mason made a molde þerto muche wonder it were' (B.11.349–50). His considerations of the superior skill demonstrated by the magpie and the other birds' seemingly wise strategies for protecting their eggs lead the Dreamer to speculate about the source of their knowledge. 'I hadde wonder at whom and wher þe pye/ Lerned to legge þe stikkes in which she leyeþ and bredeþ', he says, later adding: 'Muche merueilled me what maister þei hadde,/ And who tauȝte hem on trees to tymbre so heiȝe/ Ther neiþer burn ne beest may hir briddes rechen' (B.11.347–48, 360–62). The wonderful proficiency of these creatures finally leads the Dreamer to the point of discovering God's role in the scene before him, just as the exemplarist method predicts. However, caught up in his concern for human waywardness, he does not recognize the implications of his inquiry: God himself is the 'maister' who teaches the animals, insofar as he has ordained creation.

The Vision of Kynde stops short of achieving its exemplarist purpose because the Dreamer is unable to assimilate the exceptionality of human 'kynde' and his own complicity in the sinfulness that is a natural consequence of the exclusively human capacity for free will. Reconciliation of this paradox can only follow patient acceptance of Kynde's provision for creation, even the possibility that suffering and sin are unavoidable facts of human experience. As Wit had first explained, Kynde is lord of 'lisse' and of 'peyne' (B.9.29); as Reason asks the Dreamer in the conclusion of the Vision of Kynde: 'Who suffreþ moore than god? … He myȝte amende in a Minute while al þat mystandeþ,/ Ac he suffreþ for som mannes goode, and so is oure bettre' (B.11.380–82). The verb 'suffer' here primarily means 'to allow', as well as 'to endure' and 'to experience pain'.[56] While God might 'amend' all that the Dreamer perceives as a fault in creation, chiefly where human beings are concerned, Reason attests that God suffers, or *allows* disorder for humankind's

56 *MED* s.v. 'sufferen', v., 8b.

own good. The proper response to recognizing an apparent injustice in nature, Reason tells the Dreamer, is not criticism, but patient acceptance. As Donne humbly, if ambiguously, concludes in his sonnet: 'But who am I, that dare dispute with thee,/ O God?'[57]

The lessons of the peacock

As is often the case in *Piers Plowman*, when one vision ends with a provisional way forward, another promptly begins, offering further insight on the subject of the previous episode from a new perspective. Here, waking from his encounter with Kynde and Reason, the Dreamer meets Imaginatif, a figure who is especially well suited to address the Dreamer's explorations of the natural world. Encyclopedias are important repositories for medieval theories of the imagination, a faculty whose intermediary position between the outer senses and the inner wits (of which it is a part) establishes its crucial role in exemplarist thinking. According to Bartholomaeus, for example, the imagination receives data from the 'vttir witte' and then processes this information by forming images and similitudes, abstract concepts by which the mind categorizes and stores impressions of the external world; furthermore, the imagination enables human beings to apprehend the 'liknes and schappis of þingis' even when they are not present, recombining collected sensory observations in order to speculate about things that have never been experienced.[58] This capacity for abstraction makes imagination a vital component of exemplarist projects, for the imagination is the means by which the human mind first begins to move from *sensibilia*, the sensible things perceived by the 'vttir witte', to higher truths that remain unknown, but which might be imagined based on sensory observations.

In furthering Will's education on the relative value of natural knowledge, Imaginatif broaches a central question in the poem's ongoing 'learning debate': whether Clergy or Kynde Wit – terms roughly equivalent to book-learning and natural capacities, respectively – better equips human beings to attain the knowledge necessary to salvation. In so doing, Imaginatif aligns the Dreamer's encyclopedic observations with pagan learning and casts doubt on natural knowledge as a means to Christian truth. The concept of Clergy

57 Donne, 'Holy Sonnet 9', lines 9–10.

58 Trevisa, *On the Properties of Things*, 3.10, p. 98. The key study of Imaginatif in the context of medieval psychological theory is A. J. Minnis, 'Langland's Ymaginatif and Late-Medieval Theories of Imagination', *Comparative Criticism* 3 (1981), 71–103. More recent studies by Mary Carruthers and Ralph Hanna have emphasized the figure's associations with elementary education and pedagogical practices. See Carruthers, 'Imaginatif, Memoria, and "The Need for Criticial Theory" in *Piers Plowman* Studies', *Yearbook of Langland Studies* 9 (1995), 103–114, and Hanna, 'Langland's Ymaginatif: Images and the Limits of Poetry', in *Images, Idolatory, and Iconoclasm in Late Medieval England*, ed. Jeremy Dimmick, James Simpson, and Nicolette Zeeman (Oxford: Oxford University Press, 2002), pp. 81–94.

implies Christian learning, revelation mediated not only through the technologies of literacy, but also through sacramental, pastoral, and other proper institutional channels. Kynde Wit, by contrast, is associated with the natural man who seeks truth by 'living and looking', as the Dreamer sets out to do in Passus 8 (B.8.57), relying on sensory observations and the power of reason, but without the revelation of Christian truth to guide him. While Clergy is 'kepere under Crist of heuene' and mediates authoritative spiritual truths to the rest of humanity, Kynde Wit merely takes its best stab at truth based on the isolated observations it scrapes together, an approach to knowledge that is described in terms strikingly similar to the Dreamer's activity in Passus 11: 'Ac kynde wit comeþ of alle kynnes siȝtes,/ Of briddes and of beestes, by tastes of truþe' (B.12.126–29). Imaginatif concedes that Clergy and Kynde Wit each have value in leading human beings toward an understanding of truth, affirming that both approaches may serve as mirrors for self-improvement and ladders leading to Christ, once again invoking the metaphors of exemplarist discourse (B.12.95–96). Nevertheless, the hierarchy remains in place, for Clergy is charged with the duty of educating those who live by Kynde Wit alone. According to Imaginatif, the search for wisdom without the guiding truths of Christianity relies on 'selkouþes' and 'diuerse siȝtes', observations of the natural world and sensory experience (B.12.131, 135). Yet while the ancient '[d]yuyneris', as Imaginatif calls them, considered their arts 'an heiȝ science', Imaginatif contends that the knowledge they laboured to obtain never saved any souls (B.12.130, 132–33). Compared with Clergy – of which 'cristes loue ... is roote' – the Kynde Wit of the pagans is but a 'trufle', merely worldly wisdom (B.12.71, 138).

Imaginatif's definition of the pagan philosophers' knowledge is thus aligned with the worldly, experiential knowledge the Dreamer seeks when earlier in the poem he announces his intention to 'lyue and loke' and 'go lerne bettre' (B.8.58). In fact, each time the Dreamer proclaims his desire for 'kynde knowyng', he associates that sort of knowledge with visual observation and personal experience akin to the 'diuerse siȝtes' and 'tastes of truþ' that define Kynde Wit (B.12.135, 129). Although the Vision of Kynde is apparently sanctioned by God himself, Imaginatif's arguments in Passus 12 now appear to devalue the activity that Kynde offers Will when he places him upon Middelerþe for the purpose of observing nature. It is important to recognize, however, that Imaginatif's critique specifically targets what Ralph Hanna calls the Dreamer's 'random, recursive, and possibly unpointed passive openness to experience'.[59] Observations of the natural world must have a guiding purpose in order to be spiritually useful.

The conclusion of Imaginatif's dialogue with the Dreamer is best understood as an answer to the problem of knowledge posed at a moment of crisis in

[59] Hanna, 'Langland's Ymaginatif', p. 83.

Passus 11. If Imaginatif explicitly condemns 'passive' observation and compilation as a method of cognition, he also shows a way to recuperate the value of natural knowledge, even though he has associated it with pagan learning and maintains its inferiority to Clergy. He indicts in specific terms the Dreamer's impetuous behaviour upon the mountain of Myddelerþe: 'And so I seye by þee þat sekest after þe whyes/ And aresonedest Reson, a rebukynge as it were,/ And willest of briddes & beestes and of hir bredyng knowe,/ Why some be alouȝ & some aloft, þi likynge it were' (B.12.217–20). In keeping with Reason's theme of 'suffrance', Imaginatif lectures the Dreamer about the inappropriate orientation of his quest for knowledge. There are some questions, Imaginatif contends, for which there are no answers, at least not in human terms. The reason that flowers wear 'colours so clere and so briȝte' and that animals behave with 'breme wittes' is beyond the reach of human understanding: 'Clergie ne kynde wit ne knew neuere þe cause,/ Ac kynde knoweþ þe cause hymself, no creature ellis' (B.12.222, 224–26). With this statement, Imaginatif reasserts God's place at the head of the natural world, reminding the Dreamer that achieving 'kynde knowynge' also means knowing Kynde, that is, recognizing God as the origin and sustainer of all created life.

Having defended the order of nature, Imaginatif again makes possible a symbolic reading of natural phenomena, including the animals that had so troubled the Dreamer in Passus 11. Observations of 'briddes and of bestes' may be spiritually useful, Imaginatif maintains, provided that they are understood as '[e]nsamples' and 'termes' (B.12.236–37). To illustrate his point, Imaginatif launches into an extended moralization of the peacock that mimics the technique of the bestiary even as some of its specific conclusions appear to veer away from established interpretations.[60] He begins with a brief resume of the peacock's physical characteristics and behavioural traits: the 'fairest fowl' but the 'foulest' breeder, the peacock is also unable to fly. The irony of the bird's glorious though useless feathers is a commonplace in bestiaries, encyclopedic descriptions, and moralized fables, which often treat the animal as an example of pride, but the detail of the peacock's unsavoury breeding habits is more difficult to trace.[61] It may derive from Bartholomaeus's description of the male peacock's aggression toward its offspring: 'þe þekok is a bride þat

[60] Imaginatif's manipulation of bestiary lore is particularly appropriate in light of Mary Carruthers' argument about the faculty's association with memory in medieval cognitive theory. The bestiary was a mnemonic text, she claims, not 'a natural history book so much as a reading-and-memory book, providing some of the "common places", the foundational blocks, of inventional mnemonics. The description of the creature is a *pictura*, and as one "paints" its picture mentally from the description in the words, maxims are attached.' See Carruthers, 'Imaginatif, Memoria, and the "Need for Critical Theory" ', p. 110. See also Beryl Rowland, 'The Art of Memory and the Bestiary', in *Beasts and Birds of the Middle Ages: The Bestiary and its Legacy*, ed. Willene B. Clark and Meredith T. McMunn (Philadelphia: University of Pennsylvania Press, 1989), pp. 12–25.

[61] See Carmen Brown, 'Bestiary Lessons on Pride and Lust', in Hassig, ed., *The Mark of the Beast*, pp. 61–62.

loueþ nouȝt his children, for þe male sechiþ out þe female and secheþ out hire eyren for to breke ham, þat he may so occupie hym þe more in his lecherye'.[62] The Dreamer's assessment of avian nesting habits had not included these details, which amount to a disclosure that the bird's behaviour is ruled by 'lecherye' and not reason; Imaginatif, however, has provided a depiction that brings the peacock down to earth, so to speak, giving it both positive and negative traits, all of which can be made to bear exemplary meaning for human observers. As soon as Imaginatif begins to sketch out these natural observations, like the bestiarist he quickly moves to fix their symbolic meaning. Providing an example of how to 'read' animals, Imaginatif explains that peacocks '[b]etokneþ riȝt riche men þat reigne here on erþe': just as the birds are borne down by the weight of their showy tail-feathers, so also the rich are hampered spiritually by their wealth and possessions (B.12.241, 249–50). In this manner, Imaginatif shows the Dreamer how natural facts can be translated into spiritual facts, making observations of nature serve a higher purpose.

Imaginatif further elaborates his description, noting that the peacock's 'flesshe is foul flessh, and his feet bothe,/ And unlovelich of leden and looth for to here' (B.12.242–43). The details of unpleasant flesh and voice are common to the bestiary tradition and can be traced to Isidore.[63] The peacock's ugly feet are not described in the bestiary tradition, but can be found in Bartholomaeus's encyclopedia, where he attributes the detail to Aristotle.[64] Continuing to translate natural observations to symbolic meaning, Imaginatif associates the peacock's ugly feet with the rich man's '[e]xecutors – false frends that fulfille noght his wille' (B.12.256–57), and he attributes this meaning to 'Avynet', the only source Imaginatif cites by name in the passage. 'Avynet' is typically understood as Avianus, the twelfth-century author of a collection of widely read Latin fables, but in fact, Avianus's fable of the peacock does not concur with the detail Imaginatif attributes to him. In the lines that follow, Imaginatif mentions an unnamed poet, presumably again 'Avynet', who 'preveth' that the peacock is esteemed only for its beautiful and valuable feathers, just as the friends of the rich only care for their wealth (B.12.259–60). In Avianus's fable of the Crane and the Peacock, the peacock mocks the crane for his comparatively lacklustre appearance. The crane takes flight in response, calling down to the flightless peacock that his vaunted plumage is nothing but useless decoration.[65] It is possible to interpret the fable as a commentary on the

62 Trevisa, *On the Properties of Things*, 12.32, p. 638.

63 See *The Etymologies of Isidore of Seville*, 12.7.48, ed. and trans. Stephen Barney et al. (Cambridge: Cambridge University Press, 2002).

64 Trevisa, *On the Properties of Things*, 12.32, p. 638.

65 See Avianus, *Fabulae Aviani*, in *Minor Latin Poets*, ed. and trans. J. Wight Duff and Arnold M. Duff, Loeb Classical Library, rev. ed., 2 vols. (London: Heinemann, 1934), 2.11–14, pp. 704–705: 'Quamvis innumerus plumas variaverit ordo,/ mersus humi semper florida terga geris:/ ast ego deformi sublimis in aera penna/ proxima sideribus numinibusque feror.'

vanity of worldly possessions, but nowhere does Avianus explicitly equate the peacock with the rich, nor does he describe the peacock's feet as 'executors', a detail that remains untraced.

Imaginatif's description of the peacock's 'foul flesshe' (B.12.242) agrees with the bestiaries' accounts of the bird's virtually inedible flesh. However, while Langland seems to emphasize the bird's uselessness, both in terms of its inability to fly and its unsuitability as meat for consumption, authoritative accounts typically associate the bird with positive qualities. The bestiary, for example, cites Martial, who in his *Epigrams* highlights the splendour of the bird's 'gleaming wings' and marvels that anyone would be so aesthetically insensitive as to hand over this glorious bird to a cook.[66] In *De civitate Dei*, Augustine also reflects on the symbolic value of the peacock's incorruptible flesh, concluding that no power but God himself might keep the dead animal's flesh from decaying, and using it as a proof from nature that the human soul might live eternally.[67] In the *Aviarium*, Hugh of Fouilloy transforms the peacock's negative traits into positive symbolic reflections of the ideal clerical teacher. The bird's incorruptible flesh symbolizes 'the minds of the teachers which neither the flame of passion burns, nor the heat of lust kindles'.[68] Further, in Hugh's account the unpleasant voice noted by bestiarists becomes the admonishing tone of the 'preacher [who] threatens sinners with the unquenchable fire of hell', and the 'eye-like forms of the tail' signify the teacher's prescience concerning 'what danger ultimately threatens each person'.[69] Despite these positive associations, however, the peacock's association with pride is not entirely absent from Hugh's interpretation; like the teacher who falls prey to flattery, he warns, the peacock will lift his tail in pride, exposing his rear end: 'thus that which is praised in the teacher's action is scorned in his pride. Therefore the peacock should carry its tail lowered, so that what the teacher does is done with humility.'[70]

It seems, therefore, that Langland's peacock is an amalgam of details drawn not only from the bestiary tradition, but from a variety of encyclopedic

66 *The Medieval Book of Beasts*, p. 188: 'Miraris quotiens gemmantes explicat alas,/ si potes hunc saevo tradere dura coco?' The bestiarist quotes Martial, *Epigrammaton libri*, 13.70 through Isidore, *Etymologiae*, 12.7.48.

67 Augustine, *The City of God against the Pagans*, 21.4, ed. R. W. Dyson (Cambridge: Cambridge University Press, 1998), pp. 1048–49.

68 Hugh of Fouilloy, *Medieval Book of Birds*, p. 249: 'Tales sunt doctorum mentes quas nec flamma cupiditatis exurit, nec calor libidinis accendit.'

69 Hugh of Fouilloy, *Medieval Book of Birds*, p. 249: 'Habet pavo vocem terribilem quando praedicator peccatoribus minatur inextinguibilem Gehennae ignem ... Quod autem quasi oculos in cauda habet, ad hoc pertinet, ut quod unusquisque doctor praevidet quod periculum in fine singulis imminet'.

70 Hugh of Fouilloy, *Medieval Book of Birds*, pp. 249–50: 'Cum autem cauda erigitur, posteriora nudantur, et sic quod laudatur in opere, deridetur in elatione. Oportet igitur ut pavo caudam submissam gerat ut quod doctor agit cum humilitate fiat.'

sources, and then layered over with invention, rather as a medieval preacher might do when mining a bestiary for sermon exempla.[71] By imitating the method of the bestiarist, Imaginatif demonstrates how natural knowledge might serve to benefit those who look at the 'diverse siȝtes' of this world (B.12.135). That Langland chooses the peacock for Imaginatif's exemplum is particularly significant. A flightless bird, the peacock is a creature that cannot 'stye up' from the earth to the heavens, as observers of nature are instructed to do in exemplarist texts; nor, with its inedible flesh, is it useful to humans. It is a creature that is purely ornamental, a thing of beauty that is simultaneously earthbound and yet without practical use. This image figures the 'carnal reader' – indeed the incorruptible peacock is nothing but durable flesh – and yet Imaginatif teaches the Dreamer how to translate even this most resistant creature into spiritual meaning.

Although Langland's vision of nature in Passus 11 is a pessimistic one that first takes the form of the optimistic exemplarist meditation and then subverts it with the crisis of negative human exceptionality, Imaginatif's answer in Passus 12 begins to delineate a way back to a confident appraisal of nature's symbolic potential. As we have seen, the Dreamer's confrontation with the animal world prompts a fearful reassessment of the human place within nature; against the backdrop of 'reasonable' animal behaviour, human beings stand out as flawed, inadequate to the task of living well and meriting salvation. Finally, in the Dreamer's encounter with Imaginatif and in subsequent passus, Langland suggests that finding the human place within the natural order is a process of interpretation, made manifest in Imaginatif's reading of the peacock, which is an interpretation in the most basic of senses. The Latin verb 'interpono' means 'to put between', 'to place among', or 'to interpose'.[72] This activity is precisely what Imaginatif models when he moralizes the peacock. While the Dreamer had only seen the bird as one of many creatures whose activities awed and perplexed him, Imaginatif offers a way of making animals meaningful in relation to human spiritual concerns. In this sense, Imaginatif completes a double interpretation, demonstrating how non-human creatures can be brought into the symbolic and spiritual realm of humankind, and re-placing the human within the larger world of creation. While the Vision of Kynde features the Dreamer's struggle to comprehend human exceptionality in nature, and a particularly *negative* impression of the burden of that exceptionality, Imaginatif's interpretation of the peacock reintegrates human and animal. This achievement is not meant to blur the traditional hierarchy that presupposes human dominion and superiority in creation, but rather to assuage the Dreamer's feelings of isolation and

[71] See Owst, *Literature and the Pulpit*, pp. 195–209.

[72] Charlton T. Lewis, *A Latin Dictionary founded on Andrews' Edition of Freund's Latin Dictionary* [= 'Lewis and Short'] (1879; repr. Oxford: Clarendon Press, 2001), s.v. 'interpono'.

helplessness when he perceives that Reason cares for 'alle beestes/ Saue man and his make' (B.11.370–71). In the coming passus, the Dreamer will continue to contend with the related problems of free will, human sin, and suffering, issues for which Imaginatif offers no answers. But Imaginatif's image of the beautiful peacock and the symbolic lessons it embodies serves to reassure the Dreamer, as well as Langland's readers, that the natural world can be both a source of aesthetic pleasure and wonder as well as a 'forbisene' of spiritual significance.

4

The Land of Cokaygne: Three Notes on the Latin Background

Peter Dronke

The Land of Cokaygne occupies a unique place in medieval English poetry. It survives only in one manuscript, London, British Library Harley 913, which most recent scholars agree was copied in Ireland, for the most part by a single hand, around 1330. The codex contains much verse and prose in Latin, and a little in French, as well as a collection of Middle English verse. The text of *Cokaygne* is not an autograph, so the poem remains hard to date with complete precision. We cannot dismiss the dating suggested by older scholars, to the second half of the thirteenth century. Attempts to date *Cokaygne* later, in the first decades of the fourteenth, have always presupposed certain historical judgments, for instance attempts to link it with other Middle English poetry in the manuscript. Yet such links seem to me improbable, not least because this poem is far more original and outstanding than any of the other English poems in the collection.

In his article of 2003, Neil Cartlidge has shown that all the historical judgments about Harley 913 made so far are only conjectures, which must be re-examined and on which no certainties have yet been reached.[1] Is this manuscript a 'friars' miscellany', as it has often been called? How many of the fifty-odd pieces it contains can safely be called Franciscan? How many can be called Irish? (Cartlidge goes into some detail about the provenance of the many Latin pieces, very few of which can be called either Franciscan or Irish with any certainty.) Was the manuscript copied at Kildare, or Waterford, or elsewhere? Is it anti-monastic – taking the side of friars against monks? Is it anti-Irish – taking the side of the English against the Irish? And, in *The Land of*

1 Neil Cartlidge, 'Festivity, Order and Community in Fourteenth-Century Ireland: The Composition of BL MS Harley 913', *The Yearbook of English Studies* 33 (2003), 33–52. Hereafter cited by page number in the text, and by item number in the notes below.

Cokaygne itself, are the lecherous epicureans in the abbey monks (e.g. Cistercians) or friars (e.g. Carmelites or Franciscans)? As Neil Cartlidge suggests:

> It may very well be that the monks mentioned in the poem are indeed monks, and not friars, but it seems to me considerably less likely that any particular order of monks is intended ... The description of the monks is vague, even casual in manner ... As an ironic celebration of misrule and disorder, expressed particularly through gluttony, idleness and incontinence, the satirical edge of *The Land of Cokaygne* clearly cuts all the regular clergy almost equally deeply; the fantasy of an ideally licentious rule is one that many medieval writers were prepared to indulge ... (pp. 41–2)

There are several poems, such as Nigel of Canterbury's Latin *Speculum stultorum* (c. 1179–87) and the Anglo-Norman *L'ordre de bel ayse* (c. 1300), which humorously project an 'ideal' order that combines all the laxities, real or imagined, of the rules of every existing order, to make them favour every kind of human weakness.[2] And in *Cokaygne*, the very fact that it evokes an abbey inhabited by *two* orders, white and grey (l. 52), is a strong hint that this abbey is likewise imaginary.

So, just as finding a precise historical context for Harley 913 remains problematic, the attempts to give *Cokaygne* a historical setting, to see it as aiming at a particular group at a particular time, reveal themselves as weak and unsatisfactory. In what follows I shall leave these aside, to attempt instead three notes that aim to give a more precise *literary* background than has been realised hitherto.

I. Traces from antiquity

In a standard edition of *The Land of Cokaygne*, G. V. Smithers, after mentioning Lucian's 'Isle of the Blest', affirms that 'In the fifth century B. C., Athenaeus quotes other such accounts by authors of Attic comedy.'[3] Later, in his notes, he claims of the rivers 'Of oile, melk, honi and wine' in *Cokaygne* (l. 46), that 'the context here shows that they derive from a Lucianesque utopia' (p. 338).

Smithers' notions of the classical tradition were hazy. Athenaeus lived not in the fifth century B.C. but eight centuries later, in the third A.D. And the four rivers in *Cokaygne* cannot 'derive from a Lucianesque utopia' – because

2 Nigel de Longchamps, *Speculum stultorum*, ed. J. H. Mozley, R. R. Raymo (Berkeley–Los Angeles: University of California Press, 1960), ll. 2413–64; *L'Ordre de Bel Ayse*, ed. I. S. T. Aspin, *Anglo-Norman Political Songs* (Oxford: Blackwell, 1953), XII.

3 *The Land of Cokaygne*, pp. 136–44 in *Early Middle English Verse and Prose*, ed. J. A. W. Bennett, G. V. Smithers, with a Glossary by Norman Davis, 2nd ed. (Oxford: Clarendon Press, 1968), IX. Smithers' responsibility for this text is stated on p. vii. For the phrases I quote here see p. 137. Hereafter quotations from this edition are cited by page number and the poem is cited by line number in the text.

neither Athenaeus nor Lucian (c. 120–180 A.D.) had reached western Europe by the early fourteenth century.

Athenaeus's only surviving work, the fragmentary *Deipnosophistae*, was brought to Venice in 1423 by Giovanni Aurispa. The manuscript (Biblioteca Marciana gr. 447) was acquired by Cardinal Bessarion and given to the city upon his death (1472). It is the basis for the few other western manuscripts that survive.[4] Manuscripts of Lucian began to arrive in Italy in the course of the fifteenth century, from 1415 onwards.[5] Chrysoloras, who came from Constantinople to Florence in 1396, began to give lessons in Greek there in 1397 and arranged for the translation of two of Lucian's dialogues (*Timon* and *Charon*) into Latin.[6] Later, Erasmus translated thirty-four of Lucian's dialogues between 1506 and 1514.[7] A search for classical antecedents of the sensual utopia of *Cokaygne* must begin with works that were accessible in Latin.

So far I know only of one, and it is a text that, as far as I can see, has lain neglected and remained virtually unknown.[8] In the second volume of *Geographi Graeci Minores* (Paris, 1861), Carl Müller edits an anonymous *Totius orbis descriptio*, composed in Antioch or Alexandria between 350 and 353 A.D., of which the Greek original is lost but two late-antique Latin versions, both of which he prints, survive. In the more complete of these two versions, we read of the Camarini, who inhabit not the Camarina on the Sicilian coast that was known to Vergil (*Aeneid* 3.701), Pliny (*N. H.* 3.89) or Claudian (*Rapt. Pros.* 2.59), but a more distant and altogether more delightful

4 *Geschichte der Textüberlieferung*, I, ed. Herbert Hunger et al. (Zürich: Atlantis Verlag, 1961), p. 303.

5 R. R. Bolgar, *The Classical Heritage and its Beneficiaries* (Cambridge: Cambridge University Press, 1954), pp. 480–1.

6 Walter Berschin, *Griechisch-lateinisches Mittelalter* (Bern–Munich: Francke, 1980), pp. 311–12.

7 Bolgar, *Classical Heritage and its Beneficiaries*, p. 441.

8 It is not mentioned, for instance, in the two more recent widely ranging books on the Cokaygne theme in western literature: Herman Pleij, *Dreaming of Cockaigne: Medieval Fantasies of the Perfect Life* (New York: Columbia University Press, 2002) (the Dutch original, *Dromen van Cocagne* [Amsterdam: Uitgeverij Prometheus] dates from 1997); and Hilário Franco Júnior, *Cocanha: A história de um país imaginário* (São Paulo: Companhia das Letras, 1998). Pleij's primary aim was to present three medieval Dutch Cokaygne texts – two in verse and one in prose – but he ventures less happily into comparative discussion. His command of Middle English is shaky – 'grene ris' (*Cokaygne* l. 8) is translated as 'green rice' (p. 166) – and Pleij's account of Boethius's celebration of 'the surpassingly happy former age' ('Felix nimium prior aetas', *Philosophiae Consolatio*, ed. L. Bieler [Corpus Christianorum XCIV (Turnhout: Brepols, 1957)], IIm5) – 'Boethius follows this description with a historical sketch of civilization slipping further and further into decline. The simplicity of the golden age was followed by a silver age …' (p. 224) – strongly suggests that he does not know *The Consolation of Philosophy* at first hand. Franco Júnior's book is distinctly more scholarly. However, his focus on the Old French '*Fabliau de Cocagne*' (ed. Veikko Väänänen, *Neuphilologische Mitteilungen* 48 [1947], 3–36) is such that it leads him to say of the English poet 'ele adaptava o original francês' (p. 165). This idea is, to say the least, implausible. The French poem shares with the English the popular *koiné* of idleness, houses made of foods, food and wine preparing themselves magically, and the sense of erotic freedom without guilt. Yet it is far less vivacious than the English, and far less specific, and at no point presents wittily sardonic pictures of clergy, monks or nuns.

spot.[9] At first it sounds like a reflection of the biblical earthly paradise, but this spot turns out still to be fully inhabited:

> They say the Camarini live in a region of the East, the land that Moses described, calling it Eden. A very great river is said to flow from there, and to be divided into four streams, whose names are Geon, Phison, Tigris and Euphrates. The people who dwell in that land are extremely upright and good – no corruption of body or spirit is found among them. If you want to know about them in more detail, it is said that they do not have our everyday bread, or food like ours, or fire such as we use, but they affirm that bread is rained down upon them each day, and a drink made of wild honey and spice …
>
> They are without government, for they can rule themselves. Just as no malignity is found among them, so they cannot have fleas or lice or bugs or anything harmful. Their clothes cannot become dirty; if that were to happen, they wait for cleaning by the sun's fire, for what burns is made better.
>
> Among them are a variety of precious stones – emeralds, pearls, jacinths, carbuncles and sapphires – in the mountains in which all these abound, as I shall explain. The stream as it flows down cuts away the mountain day and night and carries fragments of precious stones from it in the torrent. The astuteness of the inhabitants has discovered an art by which they can possess what emerges from there: making nets and casting them in the narrow parts of the stream, they can catch whatever comes down from the higher part without any difficulty.
>
> Living in such great felicity, they do not know how to work, and are not wearied by any weakness or sickness, except only for this, that their bodies do pass away. For they all die at the age of 120, and an older person never sees the death of a younger one, nor need parents lament the death of their children. When the day of death begins to draw near to each of them, they make themselves a sarcophagus bedecked with perfumes, for there are many perfumes among them. And when the last hour comes for one who is alive, then, greeting everyone and saying farewell, they place themselves in the sarcophagus, and so, with the utmost freedom from cares, they pay Nature her debt.[10]

9 *P. Vergili Maronis Opera*, ed. R. A. B. Mynors (Oxford: Oxford University Press, 1969), p. 175; Pliny, *Natural History II: Libri III–VII*, ed. and trans. H. Rackham, rev. ed. (Cambridge, MA: Harvard University Press, 1989), p. 66; Claudian, *De raptu Proserpinae*, ed. J. B. Hall (Cambridge: Cambridge University Press, 1969), p. 144.

10 *Geographi Graeci Minores*, ed. Carolus Müllerus, 2 (Paris: Firmin Didot, 1861), pp. 513–28. The passages cited here are on pp. 513–15: 'Gentes aiunt esse Camarinorum in partibus orientis, cuius terram Moyses Eden nominando descripsit; unde et fluvius maximus exire dicitur et dividi in quatuor flumina, quorum nomina sunt haec: Geon, Phison, Tigris et Euphrates. Isti autem homines qui praedictam terram inhabitant sunt valde pii et boni, apud quos nulla malitia invenitur neque corporis neque animi. Si autem aliquid vis certius discere, dicunt eos quod neque pane hoc nostro communi utantur, neque aliquo simili cibo neque igne quo nos utimur, sed panem quidem eis plui per singulos dies asserunt, et bibere de agresti melle et pipere …

Sunt autem et sine imperio, semet ipsos regentes. In quibus sicut nulla malignitas invenitur, ita neque pulices neque pediculos neque cimices aut aliquid quod est noxium habere possunt. Vestimenta eorum sordidare nesciunt; quod si contigerit, per ignem solis loturam exspectant, ardens enim melior fit.

Sunt autem apud eos lapides pretiosi et varii, hoc est smaragdi, margaritae, hyacinthi, carbunculus et sapphirus, in montibus, quibus omnes secundum hunc modum abundant. Decurrens enim

In this fabled realm, then, human beings dwell in idyllic peace and harmony. They are magically provided with delectable food and drink, and have within reach a limitless wealth of gems, from a mountain that foreshadows Scott Fitzgerald's 'diamond as big as the Ritz'.[11] Their blissful existence is free of all toil and all infirmity; they have an immensely long life and a serene death, without sorrow or fear.

Unlike the Brahmins (*Brachmanae*), whom the author mentions as living nearby, they are neither priests nor ascetics. They enjoy all the pleasures that the senses can give, *sans complexes*: their enjoyment is inseparable from their inherent goodness. There is no obvious irony in this description, and certainly it contains nothing anti-clerical and nothing salacious. We are only in some respects approaching the medieval English Land of Cokaygne.

In *Cokaygne* death is not mentioned, at least not directly. One might almost imagine that there time had been suspended; and yet we learn that the present abbot will soon have to be replaced (ll. 173–6) – by the monk who is the best sleeper in the community! Again, it is 'the yung monkes' (l. 159) who see 'the yung nunnes' (l. 152) swimming naked, and they (presumably as against the older ones) who carry the nuns off to the abbey for the sports of love.

Notwithstanding all the differences between Cokaygne and Camarina, there is one striking coincidence: where in Camarina 'neque pulices neque pediculos neque cimices aut aliquid quod est noxium habere possunt', in Cokaygne (l. 37) 'there is neither fly, flea, nor louse'. Only research into the transmission of *Totius orbis descriptio* could help to determine whether this might be more than coincidence, a possible sign of a direct debt.

II. Cucania

Among the *Carmina Burana* (222) is a brief piece, *Ego sum abbas Cucaniensis*, which is often cited in connection with the medieval vernacular Cokaygne poems, and which was set to music by Carl Orff.[12] Notwithstanding the presence

fluvius diebus ac noctibus montem abscindit et illius crusta aquarum impetu trahit. Astutia vero gentis hanc invenit artem, per quam quae inde exeunt habere possint: facientes retia et in angusta fluvii loca ponentes, ea quae de superiore parte descendunt sine ulla difficultate suscipiunt.

In tanta ergo felicitate viventes nesciunt laborare nec aliqua infirmitate aut aegritudine fatigantur, nisi hoc solum quod de corpore exeunt, sed diem obitus ante mortem habentes praecognitum; omnes enim centum annorum et viginti moriuntur, et maior minoris mortem non videt, nec parentes filios plangunt. Cum ergo unicuique illorum dies mortis coeperit propinquare, facit sibi sarcophagum ex aromatibus varium, quoniam apud eos aromata multa sunt; et cum viventi ultima venerit hora, omnes salutans omnibusque valedicens in eodem se sarcophago ponit et ita cum securitate maxima naturae debitum reddit.'

[11] *The Diamond as Big as the Ritz and Other Stories: The Stories of F. Scott Fitzgerald*, vol. 1 (Harmondsworth, Middlesex: Penguin Books, 1965).

[12] The numbering is identical in the editions of B. K. Vollmann, *Carmina Burana* (Frankfurt am Main: Deutscher Klassiker Verlag, 1987) and Bernhard Bischoff (completing the text of Otto Schumann†): *Carmina Burana* I, 3, *Die Trink- und Spielerlieder – Die geistlichen Dramen* (Heidelberg: Carl Winter, 1970).

of the name 'Cucania', the song is not in fact close to the narrative poems. It is a boasting-song (akin to the *gap* in troubadour poetry), in which the self-styled abbot proclaims that he mixes with drinkers (*cum bibulis*) in order to cheat them in playing at dice. He does this, he claims, so successfully that his dicing-partners lose their shirts to him, and leave the tavern at night railing against Fortuna (*Sors turpissima*). This Cucania carries no hint of magical festive abundance or of erotic licence. In *Cokaygne* there is no mention of dice or gambling.

While this song contains the earliest known occurrence of the name 'Cucania' in a literary text (it was composed c. 1200), there was an Italian castle named 'Cuccagna', near Treviso, which is mentioned in documents already in 1142.[13] This similarity suggests that the name must have been current in popular legend before it is recorded in the literary or learned world. Again, following up a thirteenth-century Latin reference that Bernhard Bischoff gave in his edition of *Carmina Burana* 222, I saw that the closeness of the convent of sexy nuns to the abbey of spoilt monks in the Middle English poem was probably not a spontaneous invention of the English poet but part of a wider tradition of anti-clerical satire.

The text signalled by Bischoff is once more one that scholars of the Cokaygne literature have not known. It is a letter to 'Lucia, venerable abbess of Cokaygne', composed by Henricus de Isernia. Henricus was a rhetorician born in South Italy c. 1240, educated in Naples, and later notary at the court of King Ottokar II of Bohemia (1253–78), in whose *Regesta*, a collection of his letters, still in part unpublished – official and personal letters as well as fictitious ones – is preserved. Among these last is one that begins:

> Presbiter Iohannes, dei Cupidinis gratia et ferventis libidinis incentivo sacri Ypocratici quondam imperii Cesar semper augustus, Lucie, venerabili abbatisse Cucanacensi, Chunegundi eiusdem monasterii priorisse et clericorum depredatrici omnium pergameno, ceterisque in sacri imperii consistentibus mansione, salutem et coitus assiduo studio insudare.
>
> Quoniam iam tempus venit acceptabile nostre regimini maiestatis, iam dies salutis optabilis appropinquat, in qua quelibet imperii nostri filia <procedit>, pudore postposito et reiecto moderamine castitatis, alme Veneri, cuius vicem geritis, tributum tenemini solvere incessanter.[14]

[13] Compare Arturo Graf, *Miti, leggende e superstizioni del Medio Evo*, 1 (Turin: Ermanno Loescher, 1892), p. 232. Graf's further suggestion, that the Carmen Buranum was composed between 1162 and 1164, depends on his (unfounded) assumption that these lines are by the Archpoet.

[14] *Regesta diplomatica nec non epistolaria Bohemiae et Moraviae*, Pars II, ed. Joseph Emler (Prague: Typis Gregerianis, 1882), p. 1114. In the third line of the Latin cited above Emler prints *Cacunacensi*; in the third-last, I have supplied the verb *procedit* – alternatively, *tenemini* in the last line could be emended to *tenetur*.

William of Malmesbury, *De gestis regum Anglorum* V, records an earlier, somewhat similar fantasy, which he attributes to the troubadour William of Poitiers in 1119: 'When he was building some monastic dwellings near the castle of Niort, he madly declared that he would found an abbey of concubines there, mentioning by name in his song this woman and that: whoever came from a more renowned brothel, he would establish as abbess or prioress or in one of the other offices' (Jean

[Prester John, by the grace of the god Cupid and by the incentive of burning lust ever-august Caesar of the holy, once Hippocratic (?), Empire, to Lucia, venerable abbess of Cokaygne, to Chunegundis, prioress of that same abbey and plunderess of the skin of all the clergy, and to the others that dwell in the domain of the holy Empire: greetings and work hard at the constant pursuit of intercourse!

Since the season acceptable to the rule of our majesty has now come, since the desirable day of salvation is now approaching, on which every daughter of our Empire, casting modesty aside and rejecting the rule of chastity, comes forth, you are bound to pay tribute unceasingly to bountiful Venus, whose representatives you are.]

Even without supposing a direct link, it is imaginatively but a step from Abbess Lucia's nunnery to the convent of sensual nuns described in the medieval English *Cokaygne* (ll. 147–65). That these are depicted swimming naked in a stream may owe something to the wildly amorous flower-girls in the *Roman d'Alexandre* (Branch III, sts. 164–5), who, likewise swimming naked, bring Alexander's men to an erotic death by their insatiable love-making. Another clue to the background of the English text comes from the name of the alleged author of Henricus's letter, Prester John.[15] He is the legendary, almost wholly fictitious, Nestorian priest-king of 'the three Indias', who, in an Epistle composed c. 1150 – and sent to the Byzantine Emperor Manuel Comnenos, to Emperor Frederick Barbarossa and to Pope Alexander III – vaunted his own immeasurably vast territories, in which seventy-two kings were his vassals. A number of details in this Epistle (which was extremely widely read, both in Latin and in vernacular adaptations) come remarkably close to the land of Cokagyne. Prester John rules over a land of milk and honey; there, as in *Totius orbis descriptio*, no harmful creature can exist; there is a river, full of jewels, that descends from paradise, with a fountain of youth, an island where manna rains down from heaven and people desire no other food, and where there are countless precious stones that have magic properties. It is a land of perfect harmony, no one is poor, but also – *nota bene* – no one is adulterous: 'We have no vice', Prester John proclaims. Despite the lack of any erotic fantasy in his Epistle, the land of Cokaygne was, at least in medieval Hungary, called 'the land of Prester John',[16] and I suspect that elsewhere too a *rapprochement* between the two fabled lands will have been made.

The monks in *Cokaygne*, who are evidently neither saints nor ascetics, are capable of flying – a magic power most often attributed to saints and ascetics in hagiographic legend. And their flying brings with it another sensual fantasy:

Boutière, A. H. Schutz, I.–M. Cluzel, *Biographies des troubadours*, 2nd ed. [Paris: A. G. Nizet, 1973], p. 586).

15 Gioia Zaganelli, *La lettera del Prete Gianni* (Parma: Pratiche, 1990), gives an edition of a Latin, an Anglo-Norman and an Old French version, with facing Italian translations.

16 Ferenc Tassy, 'Il paese di Cuccagna', *Acta Litteraria* 2 (1954), 369–81, at p. 378.

they refuse to fly back to the abbey 'to euensang' (l. 129) unless the abbot takes a 'maidin' and puts her across his knees, baring her 'white toute' (l. 136) and playing a drum-roll on it, thereby luring the monks to return for the pleasure of spanking her bottom too. The motif, rare in medieval poetry, of spanking as an erotic delight has a more serious analogue in Abelard's description of love-making with Heloise:

> sometimes strokes were given by love, not rage, by a grace free of anger, surpassing the softness of every balm.

In quite another register, these two lovers also had reached their *Cucania*, their paradise of sensual experiment. Abelard's text continues:

> What more shall I say? No stage of love was left out by us in our desire, and if love was able to think up anything unusual, that was added too. And inasmuch as we had experienced these joys less, the more ardently did we pursue them, and the less did they become cloying.[17]

III. Latin evidence in the Harley manuscript

Cokaygne is essentially a humorous castigation of the misdeeds of the clerical world. Its tone combines reluctant, or perhaps envious, admiration (how on earth do they get away with it?), blame (but they shouldn't be living like that!), and unbridled hyperbole (they're the greediest and most lascivious people in the world!) It is a little like seeing Berlusconi through the eyes of Italian intellectuals today. To account for the medieval English poet's outlook, it is helpful to turn to some of the Latin pieces in Harley 913.

The 'Drinkers' Mass' (inc. *Introibo ad altare Bachi*) in the manuscript, which G. V. Smithers mentioned as 'significant' for *Cokaygne* (pp. 137–8), parodies in detail the wording of a sacred mass.[18] The emphasis, however, is entirely on drinking and gambling: there is nothing of the gamut of sensual pleasures evoked in the English poem. Four other compositions contained in Harley 913 seem to me more directly relevant.

An Office of the Seven Sleepers of Ephesus[19] – who were venerated as saints

17 Abélard, *Historia calamitatum*, ed. J. Monfrin, 3rd ed. (Paris: Vrin, 1967), ll. 340–6: 'verbera quandoque dabat amor, non furor, gratia, non ira, que omnium ungentorum suavitatem transcenderent. Quid denique? Nullus a cupidis intermissus est gradus amoris, et si quid insolitum amor excogitare potuit, est additum; et quo minus ista fueramus experti gaudia, ardentius illis insistebamus, et minus in fastidium vertebantur.' I would add that in describing his love-encounter Abelard uses the double formula of 'praecisio' – 'Quid plura?' (l. 332), 'Quid denique?' (l. 342) – which he derived from Ovid, *Amores* I, 5: 'Singula quid referam?' (l. 23), 'Cetera quis nescit?' (l. 25). See *P. Ovidi Nasonis Amores*, ed. Franco Munari, 3rd ed. (Florence: La Nuova Italia, 1951), p. 11.

18 On the text see Cartlidge, 'Festivity', n. 1, no. 7. It is edited from six manuscripts in Paul Lehmann, *Die Parodie im Mittelalter*, 2nd ed. (Stuttgart: Hiersemann, 1963), pp. 233–41.

19 Cartlidge, 'Festivity', no. 6. The text is edited from Harley 913 by Hans Walther, 'Zur lateinischen Parodie des Mittelalters', *Zeitschrift für deutsches Altertum* 84 (1952–3), 265–73.

and for whose feast (27 June) a liturgical office existed – becomes in parody a series of praises of sleepiness among monks. An antiphon in rhyming octosyllabics near the close shows particular affinity with *Cokaygne*:

> Astant leti dormientes,
> tardi, pigri, somnolentes,
> lecto choro dormientes,
> anno toto negligentes,
> oscitare non valentes …
>
> [The sleepers are there joyfully,/ tardy, lazy, somnolent,/ sleepy in the handpicked choir,/ negligent the whole year round,/ unable even to yawn …]

Again, there is a prose letter from the Prince of Hell,[20] 'to all prelates of churches and clergy', joyfully proclaiming his successes in the world. 'For in the temple of Venus, your goddess, prostrate in aphrodisiac worship, you offer your votive gifts most fervently upon her altars. … The Friars Minor often refresh our stomach, for with the fat meat of lambs and the incense of rams they offer us a rich sacrifice [these last phrases, as Hans Walther noted, echo Psalm 65:15] … The Cistercians keep breathless vigil to acquire possessions, and even having piled up their riches they are oppressed by famine for more. …' The writer, evidently a Dominican, lets the Prince of Darkness 'complain' about the Dominicans: 'Only the Order of Preachers do we find less obedient to us.'

His letter is answered by 'The great monarch of the world, the Caliph of Christians, that is, the Pope'.[21] Even this initial self-description, with its vaulting claim of supreme temporal power and its Muslim title, gives the game away. This 'Pope' pretends to defend the clergy against calumny, but in trying to prove his underworld correspondent to be 'as it were a liar' (*velut falsiloquum*), he paints the accusations – the pictures of clerical lubricity, vinolence and greed – in ever more vivid detail.

Finally, the *Metra de monachis carnalibus* – a medley alternating hexameters with quotations from the Psalms – was popular in divergent versions.[22] Whilst the English version, preserved in Harley 913 and six other manuscripts, satirizes only gluttonous monastic feasting, the Continental one also includes sexual excesses:

20 Cartlidge, 'Festivity', no. 24. The text is edited in Wilhelm Wattenbach, 'Über erfundene Briefe …', *Sitzungsberichte der Königlichen Preussischen Akademie der Wissenschaften* (Berlin: Verlag der Königlichen Akademie der Wissenschaften, 1892), pp. 104–5.

21 Cartlidge, 'Festivity', no. 25. The text is also edited in Wattenbach, *Sitzungsberichte der Königlichen Preussischen Akademie der Wissenschaften*, pp. 105–16.

22 Cartlidge, 'Festivity', no. 44. A. G. Rigg, *Mittellateinisches Jahrbuch* 15 (1980), 184–92, prints 'The Three Versions', together with one rebuttal. The earlier edition, in Lehmann, *Parodie* (cit. n. 18), pp. 194–5, prints only what Rigg (pp. 184–5) calls the 'Continental Version'.

Do you want to know what the noble throng of monks is like?
'Their sound has gone forth throughout all the earth'
(Ps. 18:5; Rom. 10:18)

After Prime they go at once to raid the kitchen:
'Their throat is a wide open sepulchre'.
(Ps. 5:11; Rom. 3:13)

They hardly say their psalms and soon learn to lie with concubines
'Like horse and mule, who have no understanding ...'
(Ps. 31:9; Tob. 6:17)[23]

In the last analysis, however, Latin analogues cannot account for the individuality of the medieval English poem, or for the range of its many-sided, mischievous inventiveness. What is its point of view? Is it anticlerical satire or utopia? Is it a good-natured jest, or what Hamlet calls 'poison in jest'?

My impression is that, compared with the finest Latin satiric poets of the twelfth and early thirteenth centuries, the English poet does not show any of the moral fervour that can be found in a Walter of Châtillon or Philip the Chancellor, nor are his observations bitter or malicious, as those of Hugh Primas of Orléans often are. Among the major medieval Latin poets, he seems to me closest in outlook to the Archpoet – a generous spirit for whom criticism and sheer enjoyment are often inseparable. The Middle English poem I would see especially as the fantasy of the unprivileged in the clerical world – those who will never themselves become abbots or bishops. There are also moments when the voices of the have-nots of the wider world come through. I would see this perspective, for instance, in *Cokaygne*, lines 63–5:

All he wants a man may eat
As of right and without threat.
All is common to young and old ...[24]

And again it is the have-nots who at the close 'know' what the 'Lordinges gode and hend' (*Cokaygne* l. 183) must undergo if they wish to reach that blissful place: for seven years, a lording must first live the harshest life of the serf, wading in swine's dirt. The addition of the words 'Al anon up to the chynne' (l. 181) transforms the ordeal into a burlesque of a penance such as the desert Father Paphnutius imposed upon the courtesan Thais, whom he did not allow to move out of her own excrement.

There are some penetrating perceptions of the poem in the Marxist

23 While each hexameter is accompanied by a psalm-verse, the context in Tobias is particularly relevant here, because it makes the sexual allusion explicit: 'et suae libidini ita vacent sicut equus et mulus ...'.

24 I here cite from the attractive, lightly modernised version of J. B. Trapp, in *The Oxford Anthology of English Literature: Medieval English Literature*, ed. J. B. Trapp et al., 2nd ed. (New York–Oxford: Oxford University Press, 2002), p. 353.

interpretation offered by A. L. Morton, in *The English Utopia.* Morton sees it as 'the utopia of the hard-driven serf, the man for whom things are too difficult, for whom the getting of a bare living is a constant struggle'.[25] Such a man projects a society where there is both social justice and abundance, where everything is common to all and there is always enough to eat and drink. The poem, according to Morton, 'embodies the profoundest feelings of the masses'.[26]

While this corresponds well to certain aspects of *Cokaygne,* I would suggest that the poem's perspective is in the first instance that of the poorer, lower orders of the clergy rather than that of the serf. At the same time, behind all the merriment of his vision of Cucania, the poet-clerk has the more melancholy awareness that all this is only make-believe. The utopia in the end collapses. To provide abundance, leisure and pleasure for all, to let even the most wretched enjoy the gratified desire of the wealthiest clergy, is a hopeless prospect:

> We look before and after
> and pine for what is not:
> our sincerest laughter
> with some pain is fraught.[27]

Nonetheless in *Cokaygne,* unlike Shelley's poem, we only rarely leave the realm of laughter.

25 A. L. Morton, *The English Utopia* (London: Methuen, 1952), p. 14.

26 *English Utopia,* p. 24.

27 'To A Skylark', *The Complete Poetical Works of Percy Bysshe Shelley,* ed. T. Hutchinson (London: Oxford University Press, 1929), pp. 596–8, ll. 86–9.

5

The *Canterbury Tales* and *Gamelyn*

A. S. G. Edwards

The twenty-five manuscripts of the Middle English metrical romance *Gamelyn* make it, in numerical terms, by far the most popular extant Middle English verse romance.[1] But numbers do not convey *Gamelyn*'s appeal accurately: it occurs only in copies of Chaucer's *Canterbury Tales*; it has no wider circulation. The relationship between the romance and Chaucer's work has never been satisfactorily clarified. There is no evidence for *Gamelyn*'s date or place of origin. It has proved impossible to explain where it came from and why it was included so often with the *Canterbury Tales*. The questions it raises are obvious in nature but difficult of resolution: how does it come to survive only in manuscripts of Chaucer's work? And, given its association with Chaucer, could it actually be by Chaucer?

I

The problem of *Gamelyn* was initially addressed when it was first published in 1721 by John Urry as part of his edition of *The Works of Geoffrey Chaucer*. He had this to say about its place in the Chaucer canon:

> So many of the MSS have this Tale, that I can hardly think it could be unknown to the former Editors of this Poet's Works. Nor can I think of a Reason why they

[1] For an account of *Gamelyn* see C. Dunn, 'Romances Derived from English Legends', in *A Manual of the Writings in Middle English*, gen. ed. J. B. Severs (New Haven, CT: Connecticut Academy of Arts, Science and Letters, 1967), I, 31–33. For details of the manuscripts see J. Boffey and A. S. G. Edwards, *A New Index of Middle English Verse* (London: British Library, 2005), no. 1913. There are, in addition, two seventeenth-century copies, one in Bodleian Ashmole 1095, the other in Ashmole 45 (III); the latter seems to be a copy of a medieval witness not identifiable with any of the other surviving ones; see further A. S. G. Edwards, 'A New Text of the Canterbury Tales?' in *Studies in Late Medieval and Early Modern Renaissance Texts in Honour of John Scattergood*, ed. Anne Marie D'Arcy and Alan J. Fletcher (Dublin: Four Courts Press, 2005), pp. 121–28.

> neglected to publish it. Possibly they met only with those MSS that had not this Tale in them, and contented themselves with the Number of Tales they found in those MSS. If they had any of those MSS in which it is, I cannot give a Reason why they did not give it a Place amongst the rest, unless they doubted of its being genuine. But because I find it in so many MSS, I have no doubt of it, and therefore make it publick and call it the Fifth Tale ...[2]

Although Urry's editorial achievements have often been excoriated, he was the first editor of the *Canterbury Tales* since the sixteenth century to examine Chaucer's manuscripts and to describe those he had seen.[3] It is possible that he was the first editor to be aware of *Gamelyn*'s existence, though he doubts that this could be so. He is certainly the first to confront the issues that it raises about Chaucer's possible authorship.

His confidence that it belongs in the Chaucer canon was not to win much support. Urry's inclusion of the Tale is summarily dismissed by Thomas Tyrwhitt in his 1775 edition of the *Tales*:

> It is not be found in any of the MSS. of the first authority; and the manner, style, and versification, all prove it to have been the work of an author much inferior to Chaucer.[4]

Two later eighteenth-century editions of the *Canterbury Tales* included it, as did a single nineteenth-century one.[5] No edition of Chaucer has since.

This editorial unanimity about *Gamelyn*'s non-status within the Chaucer canon is largely reflected in the silence that surrounds any discussion of it in such modern editions of the *Canterbury Tales* as those by Robinson and the Riverside Chaucer.[6] They seem implicitly to reflect the view enunciated by Tyrwhitt. But when other scholars with an understanding of the textual traditions of the *Canterbury Tales* have discussed it they have done so in terms that seem more tentative. Over a century later after Tyrwhitt's dismissal W. W. Skeat offered a rather more complicated sense of the place of *Gamelyn* in Chaucer's canon:

> Though this tale is not by Chaucer, it belongs to his age. It is probable that he contemplated recasting it, and it would have made an admirable Yeoman's Tale ...[7]

2 *The Works of Geoffrey Chaucer* (London: Lintot, 1721), p. 36; Gamelyn is printed on pp. 37–48.

3 On Urry's edition see William L. Alderson and Arnold C. Henderson, *Chaucer and Augustan Scholarship* (Berkeley, CA: University of California Press, 1970), pp. 69–140.

4 Tyrwhitt, *The Canterbury Tales of Chaucer*, 5 vols. (London: Payne, 1775–78), IV, 145.

5 It appeared in John Bell's *The Poets of Great Britain*, 14 vols. (Edinburgh: Apollo Press, 1782), as volume 6; in volume 1 of Robert Anderson's *A Complete Edition of the Poets of England* (Edinburgh: Bell & Bradfute & J. Mundell, 1793), where it is printed after the Parson's Tale (pp. 204–17); and in Thomas Wright's edition of *The Canterbury Tales*, 3 vols. (London: Percy Society, 1847–51), I, 176–201.

6 F. N. Robinson, ed., *The Works of Geoffrey Chaucer*, 2nd ed. (Boston, MA: Houghton Mifflin, 1957); Larry D. Benson, gen. ed., *The Riverside Chaucer*, 3rd ed. (Boston, MA: Houghton Mifflin, 1987).

7 W. W. Skeat, *The Chaucer Canon* (Oxford: Clarendon Press, 1900), p. 142.

Skeat's view remained undeveloped. But it has implications that make the status of *Gamelyn* particularly unclear. He appears to assume that *Gamelyn* has some direct relationship to Chaucer ('it is probable that he contemplated recasting it') without further specification as to how or why this might be so. If Chaucer did have access to *Gamelyn* (whatever the evidence for such an assumption might be), its relationship to his canon invites further investigation.

A similar sense of Chaucer's possible connection with *Gamelyn* appears in the brief comments of Manly and Rickert, who observe that '... it was only natural that scholars should guess that Gamelyn was found in Chaucer's literary chest [for] this may be true ...'.[8] Their refusal to dismiss a possible Chaucerian attribution for *Gamelyn* remains tantalizingly undeveloped. It is only recently that the arguments for its possible canonicity have been set out in general terms by N. F. Blake:

> The internal evidence is not likely to be compelling in a poem which deliberately opts for a variety of different styles and genres. It has, however, been invoked to dismiss The Tale of Gamelyn from the canon because it is in an alliterative style which is otherwise not characteristic of Chaucer's genuine work. Although this decision is understandable, it does imply that Chaucer would never have wished to extend his range by imitating an alliterative style in a whole tale, even though he does occasionally do so within tales. The majority of scribes clearly had no problem in thinking of Chaucer as a writer of tales in this style ... If the tale were not in the alliterative style, modern scholars may have been less easily persuaded to reject it from the canon.[9]

Blake's view is limited by his conviction that *Gamelyn* is written in an 'alliterative style'. Presumably he is thinking of the seven-stress line sometimes used in alliterative verse. But in *Gamelyn* the line is not linked to any regular or indeed significant use of alliterative stress patterns, but to the regular use of rhymed couplets. There is some alliterative phrasing, of the kind parodied by Chaucer in the Tale of Sir Thopas. In view of the evident intimate grasp of romance idiom demonstrated by Chaucer in that Tale, the presence of such phrases in *Gamelyn* hardly provides a significant objection to Chaucer's authorship. At the same time, of course, these phrases do not provide any argument in favour of it. It is very improbable that any evidence of what we term stylometrics can contribute usefully to the consideration of *Gamelyn*'s canonical status, given the poem's relative brevity (902 lines) and the range of Chaucerian style.

[8] J. M. Manly and Edith Rickert, *The Text of the Canterbury Tales*, 8 vols. (Chicago, IL: University of Chicago Press, 1940), II, 172; cited henceforward as 'Manly and Rickert'.

[9] N. F. Blake, 'The Chaucer Canon: Methodological Assumptions', *Neuphilologische Mitteilungen* 90 (1989), 295–310 (308); see also Blake, 'Chaucer, Gamelyn and the Cook's Tale', *The Medieval Book and a Modern Collector: Essays in Honour of Toshiyuki Takamiya* (Cambridge: D. S. Brewer, 2004), pp. 87–98.

What the comments of Skeat, Manly and Rickert and Blake all share is a sense that they can neither explain the presence of *Gamelyn* in manuscripts of the *Canterbury Tales* nor can they wholly rule out the possibility that its presence has something to do with Chaucer. None of them feels prepared to specify the nature of that connection. In general, there does not seem to have been any broad attempt to consider the totality of the evidence of the surviving manuscripts, even though some of it has long been readily accessible through the work of William McCormick in particular, as well that of Manly and Rickert.[10] It seems worth asking whether these manuscripts can tell us anything about the relationship between the *Canterbury Tales* and *Gamelyn.* In what follows I will examine the more significant aspects of these manuscripts in order to consider the evidence they offer, evidence that has never been considered in its entirety.

II

The problem of the presence or absence of *Gamelyn* in manuscripts of the *Canterbury Tales* is inextricably involved with the incompleteness of the Cook's Tale. In the majority of the manuscripts in which *Gamelyn* occurs it is placed in relationship to that Tale, as I will discuss. And those manuscripts of the *Tales* that do not include *Gamelyn* still had to address the problem of how to handle the Cook's Tale. They do so in ways that offer some light on the presence of *Gamelyn* elsewhere.

There are twenty-nine complete or originally complete manuscripts of the *Canterbury Tales*, and two printed editions by Caxton that do not include *Gamelyn.*[11] These are:

> Aberystwyth, National Library of Wales MS Peniarth 32 (Hengwrt); Cambridge University Library (CUL) Dd. iv. 24, Gg. iv. 27; Cambridge, Trinity College R. 3. 3; Cambridge, Trinity College R. 3. 15; Holkham; Lincoln Cathedral 110; London, British Library (BL) Add. 5140, Add. 35286, Egerton 2726, Egerton 2864, Harley 7333, Harley 7335; London, Royal College of Physicians 388; Manchester, John Rylands Library Eng 113; Alnwick, Duke of Northumberland MS 455 (henceforward 'Northumberland'); Oxford, Bodleian Library Bodley 414, Bodley 686, Rawlinson 141, Rawlinson 223, Arch. Selden. B. 14; Oxford, New College

[10] William McCormick with Janet Heseltine, *The Text of the Canterbury Tales* (Oxford: Clarendon Press, 1933); henceforward cited as 'McCormick'.

[11] There are twenty-nine fifteenth-century manuscripts of the *Canterbury Tales* that are selections from it, small fragments or extracts. They will not figure in subsequent discussion; for details of nearly all of these see McCormick, pp. 535–61; a fragment of the Franklin's Tale in private hands in England is not noted there.

D. 314; Cologny-Geneva, Bodmer (*olim* Phillipps 8136); Paris, Bibliothèque Nationale, fonds anglais 39; Austin, TX, University of Texas 143; San Marino, CA, Huntington Library MS 26. C. 12 (Ellesmere); Princeton, NJ, Princeton University, Firestone Library 100 (*olim* Helmingham); Chicago, University of Chicago (*olim* McCormick); Tokyo, Takamiya 24 (*olim* Devonshire); Caxton [1476?]; Caxton [1483?]

Two of these, CUL Gg. iv. 27 and Northumberland, are physically incomplete at the point where the Cook's Tale occurs and hence provide no basis for conclusions about either *Gamelyn* and/or its relationship to the Cook's Tale. The former clearly once did include the Cook's Tale (it contains an opening rubric and a portrait of the Cook); Northumberland breaks off imperfectly partway through the Reeve's Tale.

Nearly all the manuscripts that do not include *Gamelyn*, but do include the Cook's Prologue and Tale, follow these sections with the Man of Law's Prologue and Tale. The exceptions are discussed below. A number of these manuscripts record the transition from Cook to Man of Law in various ways that seek to evade the obvious fact of the incompleteness of the Cook's Tale. Most of these note simply (with minor variations) 'Here endith the Cooke his tale and here begynnyth the Man of Lawe his prolog' (as, for example, in Oxford, New College D. 314, Princeton University Library 100, Trinity College Cambridge R. 3. 15, Tokyo, Takamiya 32, and both Caxton editions), or 'Here endith the Cookes tale and here beginneth the Lawiers prolog with his tale folwing' (Bodley Rawlinson 223) or 'Thus endeth the Cokes tale and here folowen the wordes bitwene the Hoost and the Man of Lawe' (BL Egerton 2726). Occasionally the same sense is differently rendered: 'Explicit fabula Coqui et incipit prologus (fabule) Iurisperiti' (BL Add. 5140, Manchester, Rylands Eng. 113); 'Finitur fabula Coci Incipit Prologus Legisperiti' (Austin, University of Texas 143). Two others, Lincoln Cathedral 110 and Trinity College Cambridge R. 3. 3, similarly provide no indication of the incompleteness of the Cook's Tale but do not offer any transition to the Man of Law.

These solutions to the problem of the unfinished Cook's Tale simply deny that the Tale is incomplete. Bodleian Bodley 414, BL Add. 35286, Harley 7335, Holkham (where the Reeve's Tale is followed by the Second Nun's Tale), Paris, and Bodmer adopt a variant of this strategy and omit the Cook's Tale entirely, ending Fragment I at the Reeve's Tale. In several of these manuscripts this omission seems to be part of a larger pragmatics of compilation designed to eliminate evidence of incompleteness. Both Bodley 414 and Bodmer also omit the link to the Man of Law's Tale that would normally follow the Cook's Tale and also do not include the incomplete Squire's Tale while Paris 'deliberately omits the Squire's ... Tale'.[12] The pattern is not, however, invariable (both

12 McCormick, p. 379.

Harley 7335 and Holkham leave blank spaces at the end of the Squire's Tale in the expectation of an ending becoming available), although the general trend is clear.

The majority of these manuscripts are later ones in the textual history of the *Canterbury Tales.* The economy of their solutions to the question of the Cook's Tale can be contrasted with some slightly earlier manuscripts that insist on drawing attention to its incompleteness in their rubrics: 'Chaunces made no moor of the Cookis tale Heer bigynneth the prolog of the Sergeantes tale of Lawe' (BL Egerton 2864); 'of this tale Chauncier made namore Nowe this eondith here the Cookes tale and nexste folowyng begynnethe the prologe of the Man of Lawes tale' (BL Harley 7333:); 'of this Cookes tale makith Chauncer no more Here endith the Cookes tale The prohemye of the Manne of Lawes tale' (Royal College of Physicians 388). These are doubtless vestiges of earlier stages in the textual history of the *Canterbury Tales* that were less inclined to smooth over anomalies of content.

Rather surprisingly, only a couple of manuscripts attempt to paper over the cracks by solutions that involved creating new text. Both Chicago, University Library 564 and Bodleian Rawlinson 141 insert a brief conclusion to the Cook's Tale:

> And thus with hordam and briberie
> Together þei vsed tyl hanged hye
> For who so euel byeth shal make a sory sale
> And þus I make an ende to my tale[13]

Some other manuscripts reposition the Cook's Tale in the larger narrative sequence. BL Add. 35286 moves the Reeve's-Cook link and the Cook's Tale to close to the end of the sequence of tales, placing them between the Second Nun's Tale and the Prologue to the Canon's Yeoman's Tale. Bodleian Arch. Selden. B. 14, puts this link before the Clerk's Tale. It is hard to pronounce confidently on the extent to which such relocations have any relationship to the question of the Cook's Tale's incompleteness. One might speculate, for example, that in BL Add. 35286 the shift might have prompted by a wish to defer the inclusion of the Cook's Tale for as long as possible in the (unfulfilled) hope that additional copy to complete it would emerge.

The earlier manuscripts sometimes reveal a scribal sense that a more complex strategy is necessary to account for the incompleteness of the received text of the Cook's Tale, one that is linked to a seemingly confident expectation that, while the available material was incomplete at the moment of transcription, there were grounds for believing more material would become available. CUL Dd. iv. 24 ends part way down a verso leaf, the rest of which is left blank.

[13] Printed in McCormick, pp. 328, 426–27.

At the top of the recto of the next leaf is the heading 'Hic desinit fabula Coci et incipit prologus Legisperiti.' Possibly the scribe felt, for a while at least, that he might expect some text to fill the gap.[14]

Stephen Partridge has shown how Bodleian Bodley 686 combines aspects of different strategies employed elsewhere, copying the opening lines of the Cook's Tale to the bottom of fol. 54v, while placing on the following leaf (fol. 55) 'an expanded and revised version' of the last part of the Tale together with an ending.[15] Quite possibly, as Partridge suggests, there was an interval between these phases of transcription, and they reflect a combination of distinct 'scribal practises': leaving a blank space initially on fol. 55 and subsequently filling that space to present the Tale as complete.[16]

Other early manuscripts leave a clearer sense of the problematics of incompleteness in the Cook's Tale. Hengwrt, probably the earliest surviving manuscript of the *Canterbury Tales*, does not situate the Cook's Tale before the Man of Law's Tale. Here the concluding rubric reads: 'Of this Cokes tale maked Chaucer na more Here bigynneth the prologe of the tale of the Wyfe of Bathe (fol. 57v)'. But the rest of the leaf is left blank and it seems that a gathering now lost (signed 'j') was originally included at this point. While Hengwrt's rubric obviously identifies the Cook's Tale as incomplete, its scribe seems initially to have expected something would become available to fill the gap.[17] The uncertainty about the overall availability of copy indicates Hengwrt's preliminary role in the assembling and ordering of those materials that form the *Canterbury Tales.*

Ellesmere, which is generally held to have been copied by the same scribe as Hengwrt, also seems to indicate that more text was to come after the existing Cook's Tale to complete it in some way.[18] It signals the incompleteness of the Tale by leaving blank both the rest of the verso on which it concludes (fol. 57v) and the whole of the following leaf. The Prologue to the Man of Law's Tale

14 Blake suggests that *Gamelyn* was not included in Dd. iv. 24 because it lacked a link to the preceding Tale: 'That other manuscripts in the a group were prepared to include Gamelyn if the necessary links were provided is suggested by the blanks which occur in some manuscripts after CkT' (N. F. Blake, *The Textual Tradition of the Canterbury Tales* [London: Edward Arnold, 1985], p. 124). It is not clear which manuscripts he is thinking of. Not all the manuscripts that do include *Gamelyn* have any link. And, as I will show, a number only have a transitional couplet; hence 'links' did not need to be extensive.

15 Printed in McCormick, pp. 40–41.

16 'Minding the Gaps: Interpreting the Manuscript Evidence of the Cook's Tale and the Squire's Tale', *The English Medieval Book: Studies in Memory of Jeremy Griffiths*, ed. A. S. G. Edwards, Vincent Gillespie and Ralph Hanna (London: British Library, 2000), pp. 51–86 (57–58).

17 This rubric is added in the margin. Cf. the comments of Manly and Rickert: 'It was only later that [the scribe] learned that no more of CkT could be found; for his remark, "Of this Cokes Tale maked Chaucer na moore" is written, not in the ink of Section A, but in that of Section D' (I, 274).

18 On this scribe see A. I. Doyle and M. B. Parkes, 'The Production of Copies of the *Canterbury Tales* and the *Confessio Amantis* in the Early Fifteenth Century', *Medieval Scribes, Manuscripts and Libraries: Essays Presented to N. R. Ker*, ed. M. B. Parkes and A. G. Watson (London: Scolar Press, 1977), pp. 163–210, especially pp. 170–74.

starts at the top of a new leaf. Clearly the extent of this gap indicates the expectation of quite substantial material to come.

In general, the treatment of the Cook's Tale's incompleteness in the later manuscripts follows different forms of a predictable strategy: in each case the indications of an imperfect form are carefully concealed. The evidence of Hengwrt and Ellesmere points in a different direction, suggesting that, early in the textual tradition of the work, at a time when a regular sequence for the *Canterbury Tales* was still being established, there was an expectation that something was likely to follow to complete the Cook's Tale.

III

There are twenty-five manuscripts of the *Canterbury Tales* that include *Gamelyn*:

> Cambridge, CUL Ii. 3. 26, Mm. 2. 5; Cambridge, Fitzwilliam Museum McClean 181; Glasgow University Hunterian U. 1. 1; Lichfield Cathedral 29; London, BL Egerton 2863, Harley 1758, Harley 7334, Lansdowne 851, Royal 17 D XV, Royal 18 C II, Sloane 1685, Sloane 1686; Oxford, Bodleian Barlow 20, Hatton donat. 1, Laud misc. 600, Laud misc. 739, Rawlinson poet 149; Oxford, Christ Church 152; Oxford, Corpus Christi College 198; Oxford, Trinity College 49; Petworth; New York, Pierpont Morgan Library M 249; Philadelphia, Rosenbach Foundation 1084; Tokyo, Takamiya 32 (*olim* Delamere)

The great majority of these manuscripts situate *Gamelyn* immediately after the Cook's Tale. (The only exceptions are Rawlinson poet 149 and the Rosenbach manuscript, both of which are physically imperfect and disordered, and Hatton donat. 1, where *Gamelyn* occurs after the Man of Law's Tale, and before the Squire's Tale.)[19] *Gamelyn* is generally followed by the Prologue to the Man of Law's Tale although in four manuscripts (CUL Mm. 2. 5; Petworth; Glasgow; and Rosenbach) it is followed by the Shipman's Tale; and in four others (Oxford, Trinity College 49; Laud misc. 600; Rawlinson poet 149; and Christ Church 152) it is followed by the Wife of Bath's Prologue and Tale.

Thirteen of the manuscripts that include *Gamelyn* link it to the Cook's Tale by a transitional couplet that reads (with minor variations):

> But herof I wolle passe as now
> And of ȝong Gamelyn I wil telle ȝow[20]

[19] In Rawlinson poet 149, the Cook's Tale is lacking and *Gamelyn* begins imperfectly; the Merchant's Tale follows. The Rosenbach manuscript is both imperfect and disordered; *Gamelyn* follows the Knight's Tale as currently constituted. See further McCormick, pp. 224–25.

[20] I quote the version in Barlow 20.

These are: Cambridge, CUL Ii. 3. 26, Mm. 2. 5; Cambridge, Fitzwilliam Museum McClean 181; Glasgow; Lichfield Cathedral 29; London, BL Egerton 2863, Royal 18 C. II, Sloane 1685; Oxford, Bodleian Barlow 20, Hatton donat. 1, Laud misc. 739; Petworth; and New York, Pierpont Morgan M 249.[21]

Most of the manuscripts emphasize by their running titles the perceived canonicity of *Gamelyn*, designating it '(The) Cook' or 'The Cokes tale', sometimes buttressing such designations by rubrics that identify it as the Cook's Tale. Occasionally manuscripts do identify *Gamelyn* as 'Gamelyn' in their running titles, not specifying a relationship to the Cook's Tale (for example Sloane 1686 and Takamiya 32). Other manuscripts offer a divided view: for example, in Lichfield 29 and Rawlinson poet 149 the running titles vary, sometimes readings 'The Cook' sometimes 'Gamelyn.'

The uncertainty as to how *Gamelyn* relates to the Cook's Tale is also reflected in some of the manuscript rubrics. Takamiya 32 is unique in refusing to ascribe *Gamelyn* anywhere to the Cook; its rubrics are consistent with its running titles; they read 'Explicit the cokis tale | here beegynnyht Gamelyn' (fol. 45rb) and finally 'Explicit Gamelyn' (fol. 51ra). Rawlinson poet 149 similarly has a rubric consistent with its running titles; it reads before the start of *Gamelyn* 'Here begynneþ þe Cokes tale. Gamelyn' (fol. 62v); Sloane 1686 reads 'The tale of Gamelyn tolde be the Cooke' (fol. 71) and reinforces this at its finish: 'Here endith the Cookes tale of Gamelyn' (fol. 86v); Egerton 2863 has the same reading (fol. 37); Lichfield's opening rubric is 'The tale of ȝonge Gamelyn' (fol. 57), but it concludes 'Thus endeth þe Cokes Tale' (fol. 69). Petworth has a marginal heading at the start of *Gamelyn* 'þe tale of yonge Gamelyne'; Oxford, Trinity College 49 has 'Incipit ffabula de Gamelyn' (fol. 60v) and 'Explicit fabula de Gamelyn' (fol. 73). Occasionally, as with Glasgow, a rubric seeks to explain the relationship between the two tales more clearly; it reads 'The tale of yong Gamelyn tolde by the Coke of London' (fol. 24ra). The running titles and rubrics of Harley 7334 and Royal 18 C. II will be discussed below.

The majority of the other manuscripts confirm *Gamelyn* as the Cook's Tale in their explicits, as in BL Harley 1758 (which lacks the beginning) 'Here endith the Cokis tale'; BL Lansdowne 851: 'Explicit fabula Coci'; Bodleian Hatton 1: 'Here endeth the Cokes tale of the Prentise of London'; Pierpont Morgan Library 249, Bodleian Rawlinson poet 149 and Rosenbach Foundation 1084: 'Here endeth the Cokes tale'. Two manuscripts, Christ Church and CUL Ii. 3. 26, treat the original, incomplete Cook's Tale as the prologue to the tale proper (i.e. *Gamelyn*): 'Here begynnyth the prologe of the Coke of London ... Here begynneth the Cokes tale'. BL Royal 17 D XV is the only manuscript to identify *Gamelyn* as a second tale told by the Cook: 'Here endeth the tale of the Coke and folowyth another tale of the same Cooke' (fol. 66v).

21 It was probably also in BL Harley 1758; see McCormick, p. 190n.

Some manuscripts make greater efforts to accommodate *Gamelyn* into the Canterbury Tales sequence by a combination of rubrics, decoration and text. For example, BL Lansdowne 851, one of the earliest complete manuscripts of the *Tales*, produced to a high standard in London, goes to considerable lengths to establish its canonical status. Throughout it gives as the rubricated running title for *Gamelyn* 'þe coke'; the start of *Gamelyn* is not signalled by a separate heading, but, in common with the beginning of other tales it has a large (8-line) illuminated initial on fol. 54v and a demi-vinet border (both these decorative features also occur at the start of the Cook's Tale on fol. 53); and the transition from Cook's Tale to *Gamelyn* is handled deftly. The final line of the Cook's Tale is the last line on fol. 54r; this unique transitional passage appears at the top of fol. 54v:

> Fye þerone it is so foule I wil nowe tell no forþere
> For schame of þe harlotrie þat seweþ after
> A velany it were þare of more to spell
> Bot of a knyhte and his sounes my tale I forþe tell
> And þerefore listeneþ and herkneþ þis tale ariht[22]

Another very early manuscript, BL Harley 7334, offers further insight into the early accommodation of *Gamelyn* into the *Canterbury Tales.* Here the Cook's Tale ends at the bottom of fol. 58v with two lines untypically written as one to preserve the regular 38-line format for verse texts in this part of the manuscript. These lines read: 'And þus þe ioly prentys had his leue | Now let hym ryot al þe night or leue'. *Gamelyn* then follows at the beginning of fol. 59; its beginning is marked by a demi-vinet border and a six-line illuminated initial. In this manuscript these are characteristically the markers of the beginning of a new Tale or a new textual division; for example, the Cook's Prologue, fol. 57v, and start of his Tale proper, fol. 58, are both indicated in such ways.

Gamelyn occupies twelve complete leaves, fols. 59–70v; it ends twenty-seven lines down fol. 70v, the rest of which is left blank. The Man of Law's Prologue starts a new leaf, fol. 71. It begins partway through gathering 'h' which runs from fol. 57 to fol. 64v and continues through all of gathering 'i' which has only six leaves, fols. 65–70 (rather than the standard eight). The running titles for *Gamelyn* generally read 'The kookes' (verso) | 'Tale' (recto). This physical evidence suggests clearly that *Gamelyn* was available to the scribe of Harley 7334 as a distinct codicological unit sufficiently far in advance of transcription for him to plan for its relatively seamless inclusion into the *Canterbury Tales* sequence. The only small glitches in the design were the slight space overrun at the point of the transitional couplet on fol. 58v (where two lines are written as one) and the small amount of space on fol. 70v.

There are some vestiges of the process of including *Gamelyn* that suggest a

22 Printed in McCormick, p. 274.

degree of confusion or uncertainty as to the relationship between *Gamelyn* and the Cook's Tale. A very early cursive hand has written at the bottom of fol. 58v (the end of the Cook's Tale): 'Icy commencera le | fable de Gamelyn'. This same hand has also written at several points above the running title 'The ȝong gamelyn' (fols. 62, 66, 69) and once 'The gamelyn' (fol. 59). It is hard to be sure whether these are notes made during the compilation of the manuscript to aid in its assemblage, or made subsequently by an early reader as guidance for his/her reading, but the notations above the running title seem to suggest the latter.

The manner of the placement of *Gamelyn* in Harley 7334 corresponds in important respects to the way the Tale is placed in BL Royal 18 C. II. Here the rubricated heading to the Prologue to the Cook's Tale on fol. 56v is followed by a similar heading at the start of the Tale on fol. 57, both accompanied by gilded and painted four-line initials with gold studded spray work. The Cook's Tale ends at the bottom of fol. 57v with the usual transitional couplet: 'But here of I wil passe as now | And of ȝong Gamelyne I wil telle ȝow'. Then *Gamelyn* starts at the very top of fol. 58 and continues until ten lines from the bottom of fol. 67v. The Prologue to the Man of Law's Tale begins immediately, in contrast to Harley 7334, where blank space is left after the end of *Gamelyn* on fol. 70v, before the Prologue to the Man of Law's Tale at the top of a new leaf, fol. 71. In BL Royal 18 C. II the rubricated running title throughout *Gamelyn* is 'The Cooke' on both verso and recto. And at the start of *Gamelyn*, in the outer margin, is a note in an early cursive hand 'the tale of ȝonge gamlyn'. This stage in the compilation of Royal 18 C. II suggests a further step in the smoothing out of the integration of *Gamelyn* into the narrative sequence.

Other manuscripts also deftly fit *Gamelyn* into the larger sequence of the *Canterbury Tales.* In Bodleian Barlow 20 the Cook's Tale concludes at the very bottom of fol. 52 with the usual transitional couplet. *Gamelyn* begins at the top of fol. 53 and concludes at the very bottom of fol. 64v with the rubric: 'here endith þe Cokes tale and here bygynneth | þe prolog of þe man of law.' Throughout both the Cook's Tale and *Gamelyn* the running title is 'The Coke' (on both recto and verso). Lichfield 29, on the other hand, seems to reflect the transcription of a textual unit in which the Cook's Tale and *Gamelyn* were already combined. The Reeve's Tale ends at the bottom of fol. 56 with 'explicit fabula'. The Prologue to the Cook's Tale begins at the top of fol. 56v; the Tale itself begins near the top of fol. 57 with a demi-vinet border and five-line illuminated initial and merges into *Gamelyn* with the transitional couplet (on fol. 57v) followed by the heading 'The tale of ȝonge Gamelyn', which is marked by a four-line painted initial. The running title is generally 'The Cook' (on both recto and verso), but occasionally (on fols. 65, 66v, 67v, 68) this title is followed by the words 'Of Gamelyn.'

In Bodleian Laud misc. 600, there is some indication at the end of *Gamelyn* that the poem was transmitted as part of a larger textual unit. The Prologue to the Cook's Tale begins partway down fol. 61 with the rubric 'The prolog of þe Coke' – words that are repeated in the running title. There is no completed heading for the start of the Cook's Tale itself, only an initial 'H' (fol. 61v). On fol. 62v there is the rubric 'Here begynneþ þe cokes tale. Gamelyn', with a four-line illuminated initial and a border in the inner margin. The text of *Gamelyn* ends at the very bottom of fol. 75v with the rubric 'Here begynneþ þe prolog of þe wif of Bathe'. The running titles (which occur on the rectos only) reflect a divided sense of what the work is to be termed: those on fols. 62–67 read 'þe coke'; those on fols. 68–75 read 'Gamelyn'. In this respect, the change in running title reflects the evidence of early manuscripts that combine the seamless integration of *Gamelyn* into the larger narrative sequence with a degree of uncertainty about title and hence (possibly) about the relationship of tale to teller.

Other manuscripts seek to make this integration of *Gamelyn* into the larger sequence of tales even more seamless. New York, Pierpont Morgan 249 concludes the Reeve's Tale at the bottom of fol. 60v: 'Explicit fabula &c. And in the next leaf bygynneth the prologe of the Cook &c'. The Cook's Prologue begins at the top of fol. 61, followed by the Tale itself on fol. 61v and the transitional couplet on fol. 62 followed by only a simple four-line painted initial to mark the start of *Gamelyn*. The running title throughout is 'The Cook' (on both recto and verso). In Cambridge, Fitzwilliam Museum McClean 181, the Prologue begins at the very top of fol. 64 and the Tale itself at the very top of fol. 64v. The transitional couplet comes on fol. 65 and *Gamelyn* ends at the very bottom of fol. 77. The Prologue to the Man of Law's Tale starts at the top of fol. 77v. Throughout *Gamelyn* the running title, on rectos only, is 'The Cokes Tale' (often cropped). In BL Harley 1758, an early manuscript with high production values, the final line of the Reeve's Tale is the first on fol. 45v. After a 22-line break the Prologue to the Cook's Tale is marked by a nine-line illuminated initial and demi-vinet border. After this a leaf has been lost and *Gamelyn* begins imperfectly and ends near the bottom of fol. 55, the rest of which is left blank. The running title throughout is 'The Cookis Tale' on both recto and verso. In CUL Mm. 2. 5, the concluding fit is even neater. *Gamelyn* ends at the bottom of fol. 58v and the Shipman's Tale begins at the top of fol. 59.

One manuscript, Oxford, Christ Church 152, is particularly interesting because it contains more accretions to the *Tales* that are either manifestly or arguably spurious than any other manuscript. It is late, probably third quarter of the fifteenth century, and is unusual in including a 'Plowman's Tale' (Hoccleve's Miracle of the Virgin, fols. 228–31), Lydgate's continuation of the *Canterbury Tales*, his *Siege of Thebes* (fols. 291–350), as well as *Gamelyn*. It also has a tale sequence not found elsewhere.[23] It has recently been convincingly argued, on codicological evidence, that 'the source materials for the Tale of

[23] See further McCormick, pp. 77–84.

Gamelyn were available at the same time as those used for a canonical part of the poem' and that it may have been a part of the original design of the *Canterbury Tales* in this manuscript.[24]

IV

Very few of the manuscripts of the *Canterbury Tales* that include *Gamelyn* have left indications that they felt that its authenticity was in doubt. Only one manuscript, Tokyo, Takamiya 32, seems to distance the tale from Chaucer's work. The rest either make it part of the Cook's Tale through a transitional couplet or other verse transitions or see it as part of the Tale, to which the earlier (indisputably Chaucerian) part is some form of preamble. Only one manuscript, Royal 17 D XV, presents it as a second distinct tale.

But some of the manuscripts, particularly early ones, seem to indicate a measure of uncertainty about its inclusion in the *Canterbury Tales* sequence by intermittently varying its running title and occasional rubrics from 'The Cook's Tale' to 'Gamelyn' or 'The tale of ȝonge Gamelyn'. Such uncertainty may be, at least in part, the consequence of comparison of exemplars by stationers or scribes, not all of which included *Gamelyn*. It is possible that, in some of the manuscripts that did include *Gamelyn*, this uncertainty came about because the poem was not initially available as part of the exemplar but only came to hand subsequently. It has been suggested that this belated discovery occurred in the case of the Christ Church and Harley 7334 manuscripts, both of which complete the copying of *Gamelyn* in anomalous shorter quires.[25]

In its totality the evidence seems to suggest that whether *Gamelyn* was included in the *Canterbury Tales* sequence depended chiefly on a single factor: exemplar availability. Both of the earliest manuscripts, Hengwrt and Ellesmere, reveal the unfulfilled expectation of such availability, for which they had planned. It is clearly the case that Hengwrt reflects a tentative and incomplete representation of the text of the *Canterbury Tales* that was reordered and enlarged in Ellesmere. Neither manuscript could complete the Cook's Tale, but their layouts clearly indicate that their scribes expected they would be able to do so. The unpredictable availability of the rest of the Cook's Tale does not, of course signify that they were necessarily waiting for *Gamelyn*, but the idea is not implausible. Certainly *Gamelyn* entered the orbit of the *Canterbury Tales* very early in the textual tradition of Chaucer's work. Its appearance in such manuscripts as Lansdowne 851, Harley 7334 and Petworth (among others) makes that sufficiently clear. And these (and other) manuscripts that did

24 Jacob Thaisen, 'The Merchant, the Squire and Gamelyn in the Christ Church Chaucer Manuscript', *Notes & Queries*, n.s. 55 (2008), 265–69.

25 See further Partridge, 'Minding the Gaps', pp. 56–57, 58–60.

include it have left few indications that they doubted the work was by Chaucer, either as a part of the Cook's Tale or as another tale told by Chaucer. The strongest indication of uncertainty is the intermittent disposition in some early manuscripts to give it the title 'The tale of young Gamelyn'. This alternative title may reflect some doubt about the proper status of *Gamelyn* in the form it became initially available, when it may not have been titled 'The Cook's Tale'.

Such doubts may recall the recent debate about the canonicity of the Canon's Yeoman's Tale, which is not included in Hengwrt. At the very least such debates remind us that the state of the *Canterbury Tales* on Chaucer's death was messy. Some of the individual tales had clearly circulated separately, some of them before the *Canterbury Tales* was conceived. These included the Knight's and Second Nun's tales and (probably) some version of the Wife of Bath's Tale. Complicating matters further, other tales are 'contextless'; like *Gamelyn,* these tales reveal no obvious relationship between tale and teller. If there seems no compelling reason to assign *Gamelyn* to the Cook, there are other similarly arbitrary assignments of pilgrims to tales, as in the Shipman's Tale, originally intended for the Wife of Bath and assigned to its subsequent teller for no clear reason.

But in spite of the demonstrable incompleteness of Chaucer's design and the seeming operation of arbitrary forces in the manuscript shaping(s) of the *Canterbury Tales,* it still seems more reasonable to assume that *Gamelyn* had some connection with Chaucer than to assume that early scribes or editors decided to incorporate it into the framework of the *Canterbury Tales* on wholly whimsical grounds. Other spurious interpolations like the Tale of Beryn or the two different Plowman's tales are late and unique. *Gamelyn* is so frequently and exclusively associated with Chaucer's work from an early stage in its textual transmission as to suggest a general confidence that it had something to do with him. Especially since there was an obvious alternative, one adopted by a number of manuscripts, that of simple omission of the incomplete Cook's Prologue and Tale which together amount in total to only 97 lines (I.4325–4422), the briefest of the Canterbury Tales. Hence the option of leaving it out would have few implications for casting off copy for the rest of the manuscript.

The evidence suggests that it is necessary to assume that those close in time to the production of manuscripts of the *Canterbury Tales* (a) did not believe that the received text of the Cook's Tale represented its completed form and (b) felt there was some relationship between *Gamelyn* and Chaucer. The different strategies of both those early manuscripts that did not include it, like Hengwrt and Ellesmere, and those that did, like Lansdowne 851 and Harley 7334, seem to confirm these assumptions.

Few admirers of Chaucer will find pleasure in considering the possibility that the clunking verse of *Gamelyn* could have anything to do with him. It is, of course, possible that Chaucer may have owned a copy of it that was found among his papers and erroneously believed to be his own work. But such an hypothesis would not readily account for its inclusion in the *Canterbury Tales* as part of the Cook's Tale. It is ultimately the extent and exclusivity of the association of *Gamelyn* with Chaucer that cannot be readily ignored, just as it cannot be comfortably explained.

If the chief objection to any association of *Gamelyn* with Chaucer is shaped by aesthetic considerations, characterized by an implicit assumption that Chaucer could not have written a work that falls so far short of our sense of his genius, it will remain easy to ignore *Gamelyn*'s claims to a place in the Chaucer canon. For the student of Chaucer's manuscripts, however, the evidence points in a different direction and suggests that *Gamelyn* was probably intended to be included as part of the *Canterbury Tales* from an early stage in the textual history of the work. Whether the controlling intention to include it was Chaucer's own or that of his putative literary executors is a question that invites further consideration.[26]

[26] I am very grateful to Maura Nolan and Chris Cannon for their patient efforts to improve my argument. My debt to Jill Mann is beyond words.

6

The Cheerful Science: Nicholas Oresme, Home Economics, and Literary Dissemination

Elizabeth B. Edwards

In 1371, Nicholas Oresme, scholar, academic, councillor of Charles V and later Bishop of Lisieux, completed a translation and commentary in French on the Pseudo-Aristotelian *Livre Yconomique*, and one on Aristotle's *Politics*, companion works to his earlier commentary on the *Ethics*. Produced under the aegis of a publication program of Charles V, Oresme's commentaries are remarkable for many reasons. Both text and gloss are in French, in a striking departure from the usual scholastic context of such works, and they thus introduce many neologisms and new terms for concepts. They are found in deluxe manuscripts, with wonderful programs of illustration, as befitting royal commissions.[1] Oresme's glosses are designed for a different reader than academic commentaries, because they aim at forming an educative program in the public good. But the best reason for calling attention to them is for their originality and charm. For example, in speaking of the proper deportment of married couples, Oresme's gloss surprises and delights by its etymological literalism (where 'T' is text and 'G' is gloss):

> T. Car en tel apparat que ont le homme et la femme qui sunt ensemble par marriage, tel aournement ne differe en rien des parlers que l'en seult faire es tragedies.
> G. C'est a dire que tel excés de cointise est leaide chose et deshoneste, aussi comme sunt les paroles de tragedies. Ou selon une autre exposition, tele chose donne Acheson de parler en mal, aussi comme l'en parle es tragedies. Ce sunt dicties et rimes de choses villaines et deshonestes. Et est dit de tragos en grec, que est bouc ou beste puante; car en signe des ordes paroles et diffamees que l'en disoit en teles rimes, l'en donnoit un bouc.

1 These have been vividly analyzed in Claire Richter Sherman, *Imagining Aristotle* (Berkeley: University of California Press, 1995).

> [T. For the outward adornment of the couple may be no different from the speeches commonly associated with tragedies.
> G. That is to say that such an excess of affectation is ugly and unseemly, like the words used in tragedies. Or according to another commentator, such a thing gives opportunity for evil tongues, such as one hears in tragedy. Tragedies are ditties and rimes about base and improper things. And the word is derived from *tragos* in Greek, meaning goat or stinking animal, because to symbolize the filthy words and scandal of these rimes, a goat was sacrificed.][2]

Oresme is certainly misled by his commentator, and shows a worse understanding of what tragedy is than Chaucer or Philippe de Mézières; moreover, the error here is probably due to learning itself, that is to the correct knowledge of the etymological goat lurking in the word 'tragedy'. It may be a little unfair to be delighted by this inadvertent comedy on the subject of tragedy by a commentator as conscientious and accurate as Oresme, except that the tragic matters he speaks of will recur later in this essay. Late medieval Aristotelianism produced widely disseminated habits of thought, and I will suggest that Aristotelian thinking gone wrong produces comedies (or, as Oresme here calls them, tragedies).

The dissemination of scholarly work is often difficult to track, but in the case of these translations we have a most concrete instance of an aim towards such cultural dispersal, which usually takes place in less explicit ways. The circumstances of the production of these works in the particular milieu of the court of Charles V, and the evidence of the care with which their publication was handled, mark them as part of an initiative in public intellectualism, a concerted effort to educate and edify public officials and counsellors.[3] There is significant evidence of the importance placed by the King on this initiative.[4] As Susan Babbitt writes of the *Politiques*, Oresme's commentary 'is informed by a belief that Aristotle could do some service to Valois France'.[5] In the present essay, I will consider Oresme's fascinating texts on home economics, mainly the *Yconomique* and to some extent the *Politiques* and *Ethiques*, as well as his earlier work on financial economics (*De moneta*), in relation to the possible relevance of such commentary to literature. For while economics is the science of the household, literature also has the particular, if unscientific, project of representing the household and its sexual and financial arrangements. Moreover, the literature which does so best could also be considered to be at the

2 Nicholas Oresme, *Le Livre de Yconomique d'Aristote*, ed. Albert Douglas Menut, *Transactions of the American Philosophical Society* 47 (1957), 785–847 at p. 817. All subsequent paranthetical citations are to this edition. English translations are by Menut.

3 Susan M. Babbit, 'Oresme's *Livre de Politiques* and the France of Charles V', *Proceeding of the American Philological Society* 75 (1985), 30.

4 Evidence such as the King's letters can be found in Albert Douglas Menut, 'Introduction' to Nicholas Oresme, *Le Livre de Ethiques d'Aristote*, ed. Albert Douglas Menut (New York: Stechert, 1940), p. 16.

5 Babbit, 'Oresme's *Livre de Politiques*', p. 32.

bottom of the hierarchy of genres, should one exist, just as 'economics' is of sciences. I will therefore conclude with some consideration of the possible effects of Aristotelian habits of thought for the *fabliau*, followed by more direct evidence of the reception of Oresme's work by Eustache Deschamps. Aristotle himself is rarely found in the scholarship on the medieval marriage debate, quite possibly because he did not write much about it; in contrast, pseudo-Aristotle's treatise not only provides an important intervention on the subject, but amplifies the significance of marriage in his *Politics* and *Ethics*.[6] Deschamps was plainly reading or remembering the *Yconomique*. It seems likely that marriage was one of the topics, like astrology, debated in the circle of Charles V, with entries coming from such generically diverse places as Oresme's Aristotle commentaries, Deschamps *Miroir de Mariage* and de Mézière's *Livre de la sacrament de marriage*.[7] Oresme's thought about home economics is of great interest in its own right, as I hope to show, while also tracking the dissemination and reception of apparently recondite academic writing, revealing the influence of commentary on Aristotle in the debate on marriage. And beyond Deschamps … Chaucer?

This enquiry is inspired by the work of Jill Mann in two ways, one general and one particular. First, it has been characteristic of her work to relate the writings of the learned world (scholastic and clerical) to the writings in vernacular literature. Second, it was in her seminal essay 'Language, Truth and Value in *Sir Gawain and the Green Knight*' that I first encountered the scholarly commentaries on Aristotle of the fourteenth-century French academic, Jean Buridan, and so was led to his student Nicholas Oresme, whose work made intriguing advances in the economic questions so central to the literature of the period. Oresme's Aristotle commentaries in particular mark just such an interface between the worlds of academics, public intellectuals, and poets that Mann has so consistently and persuasively illuminated.

Economics, home and elsewhere

Oresme is commonly held to be the first 'economist' in the modern sense of the word, a title awarded for his treatise on money, *De moneta*, a heartfelt argument against the debasement of currency.[8] He is so considered exactly because he severed the specific question of the debasement of money from the context

6 H. A. Kelly spends only four pages on the Aristotelean's contribution in *Love and Marriage in the Age of Chaucer* (Ithaca: Cornell University Press, 1975), pp. 281–85.

7 Joan Cadden establishes the debate about astrology: 'Charles V, Nicle Oresme and Christine de Pizan: Unities and Uses of Knowledge in Fourteenth-Century France', in *Texts and Contexts in Ancient and Medieval Science: Studies on the Occasion of John E. Murdoch's Seventieth Birthday*, ed. Edith Sylla and Michael McVaugh (Leiden: Brill, 1997), pp. 208–45.

8 Oresme is also famous for accomplishments in an astonishing variety of fields including mathematics, physics and music theory. For biographical information, see Sherman, *Imagining Aristotle*, pp. 6–22.

of scholarly commentaries on Aristotle, whose theory of money dominated the period. André Lapidus writes: 'Not until the publication of Oresme's *Treatise on Money* in the mid-fourteenth century was the subject noteworthy enough to constitute the matter of a single essay that was not explicitly structured by a reflection on Aristotle's work.'[9] Odd Langholm, a noted historian of Aristotelianism in medieval economics, describes Oresme's treatise as 'shining forth amidst the financial barbarism of the Middle Ages'.[10] But if the work is economic in the modern sense of the word, it is less evidently so in the medieval sense. *Economy*, in this period, means the science or body of knowledge about household management: 'maison est ce de quoi traicte yconomique' (p. 807G) [Economics treats of the household]. It is located among the most remote and earthbound positions in the hieracrchies of science; for example, Kilwardby's schema in *De ortu scientarum* places it last in the order, with monastics and politics, as branches of ethics, itself a branch of operative science, itself a branch of the science of human things. It is thus very distant from the higher sciences on which Oresme's reputation is largely built – apparently in a branch conceptually parallel to tailoring.[11] It is customary to stress the difference between the modern definitions of 'economy' as a science of national and personal finances and the collective social wealth, and the medieval understanding, as if these were in sharp opposition. Albert Menut, for example, writes of the *Yconomique*: 'we shall be concerned with the unadulterated etymological economies … family economy or more precisely the regulation and orderly administration of a family household or estate'.[12] He goes on to suggest works that would be about the 'economy' in medieval terms would now be described otherwise, for instance *Le Livre de chevalier de la Tour-Landry*, a conduct book, or Walter of Henley's *Husbandry*, which considers the nuts and bolts of estate management. But the insistence that *economy* has a narrow medieval meaning effaces the vital connection between *home* economics and *financial* economics as we now understand the term. Thus in the first chapter of Book I of the *Ethiques*, Aristotle states flatly that 'richesces sont la fin de yconomie' [wealth is the end of economics] a point which Oresme glosses more fully as follows:

> Yconomie est art de gouverner un hostel et les appatenances pour acquerir richesces. Et ceste fin est pour autre fin, c'est assavoir, pour bien user d'icelles.[13]
>
> [Economics is the art of managing a household and what belongs to it in order to

9 André Lapidus, 'Metal, Money and the Prince: John Buridan and Nicolas Oresme after Thomas Aquinas', *History of Political Economy* 29.1 (1997), 21–53, p. 22.

10 Odd Langholm, *Wealth and Money in the Aristotelian Tradition* (Oslo: Universitetsforlaget, 1983), p. 13.

11 Kilwardby's scheme, as reconstructed graphically by Weisheipl, is found in Birgit van den Hoven, *Work in Ancient and Medieval Thought* (Amsterdam: J. C. Geiben, 1996), p. 193 n. 114.

12 'Introduction', *Yconomique*, p. 785.

13 Oresme, *Le Livre de Ethiques d'Aristote*, ed. Menut, p. 104 T and G.

acquire riches. And this end is for another end, that is to say, to use these things well.]

Oresme's account of home economics follows that of the Aristotelian tradition in understanding the domestic sphere as the *proper* place for financial life, as the locus for the exercise of the 'art of acquisition' (to give one of the translations of the difficult term 'chrematistic' from the *Politics*).[14] Therefore, the theory of money and exchange in *Politics* is found in, and is subordinate to, the discussion of the household, which is the first subject of the work. The household is a fundamental unit of political life, intermediate between the *polis* and the individual; but it is *the* branch expressly concerned with financial theory and practice. There are of course *improper* financial dealings; for instance, Aristotle concedes that there are those who have wrongly taken the point of the arts of acquisition to be the accumulation of currency, instead of the precondition for the flourishing of the household. That is, they have mistaken the means for the end. But the household is in accord with natural productivity, and most properly 'l'acquisition de teles richeces naturelez appartient a yconomique' [the acquisition of such natural riches belongs to economic science].[15] Medieval Aristotelian economics are, therefore, always about libidinal economies, economies of sexuality; their very situation within the household decrees that this will be so.

Langholm has repeatedly stressed that, for the medieval period, financial economics is a branch of ethics and politics, and discussions of it are wound around and largely inextricable from ethical questions.[16] Aristotle's other discussion of money is found in Book Five of the *Nichomachean Ethics*, which treats of the virtue of justice. The foremost principle of Aristotle's ethics is that of the virtue as a mean between two vices; virtues are acquired by habit in the pursuit of the good life, which leads to friendship and happiness. Courage, for example, is a mean between cowardice and foolhardiness. There are indeed particular virtues concerned with money: liberality and magnificence. Justice, however, is the one virtue that is not a mean between vices (i.e. it is not a mean between injustice and hyper-justice, because there is no excess to justice) but it is nevertheless a mean. 'Chose juste est moienne entre aucun gaaing et aucun damage' [a just act is the mean between a certain gain and a certain loss].[17] Because justice is, for Aristotle, primarily a matter of the proper distribution of goods (whether proportionally or arithmetically distributed), money matters are entirely subsumed by ethics. Oresme's commitment to the ethics of the

14 Aristotle, *The Politics of Aristotle* I.8–11, ed. Ernest Barker (Oxford: Clarendon Press, 1946; repr. 1973). See Barker's note 'E' on 'chrematistic' (p. 22).

15 Nicholas Oresme, *Le Livre de Politiques d'Aristote*, ed. Albert Douglas Menut, *Transactions of the American Philosophical Society*, n.s. 67 (1970) p. 64T. All subsequent citations of *Politiques* are to this edition.

16 Odd Langholm, *Price and Value in the Aristotelian Tradition* (Oslo: Universitetsforlaget, 1983), p. 12; *Wealth and Money in the Aristotelian Tradition*, ch. 2.

17 Oresme, *Ethiques*, p. 291T.

virtuous mean will become clear in later discussion, for he is deeply Aristotelian in his conceptual structure. The household has the task of acquiring riches, financial activity is a branch of justice, therefore the household is an ethical unit concerning itself with virtue, the proper direction of eros, the tempering of greed, prodigality, and lust, and the yoking of human affect to material and cultural productivity. This conception of economics can be described as a 'cheerful science', in stark contrast with the moral bleakness of Ricardo's 'dreary science'.

Given the embeddedness of medieval financial economics within Aristotelian commentaries, it is then indeed striking that Oresme wrote a free-standing tract on money. But if this earns him modern renown, he deserves also to be noted for, at a later date, taking the material of his *De moneta* and *putting it back* into the structure of commentary on Aristotle which was its original inspiration and which supplies the holistic frame of a more synthetic thinking.[18] My consideration of the *De moneta* considers it rather in the light of its interconnectedness with other, older 'economics'.

Money

Oresme's *De moneta* is an argument against the debasement of the currency and a direct intervention in public policy. Written in 1355 or thereabout, it is a response to the frequent debasements of the previous decades, which in turn contributed to the political circumstances of the Jacquerie, and to the scandal of King Jean's devastatingly huge ransom bill. Following Book 5 of the *Ethics*, Oresme argues that money was invented as a means of commensurability, to make it possible to compare the value of unlike things; in addition, it has the convenience of portability. Money is both a medium and a measure for exchange in the community; it is a medium because it goes between people for the purpose of exchange; it is a measure with which to compare different goods. It is also a means to an end: exchange. Indeed, it is the basis of community, the condition of its possibility, and it is therefore necessarily the community which owns the money, though the ruler mints it and guarantees its value. Oresme, like Buridan, is a speciesist: he believes the gold and silver species of which coin is made give real value to money.[19] Devaluation thus includes three evils: it destroys the medium of exchange for the community; it changes that which has the aim of remaining the same as a measure; and it cheats on the natural value of gold and silver. Devaluation, for Oresme, is worse than usury, which is at least consensual; as a fraudulent act of tyranny, devaluation should

[18] Oresme's glosses in *Politiques*, Book 1, and *Ethiques*, Book 5, not only refer to the treatise on money but reproduce the content and even provide schematic charts of the system.

[19] For a comparison with the influential theory of Aquinas, who was not a speciesist, see Lapidus, 'Metal, Money and the Prince', p. 23 and *passim*.

be termed, Oresme thinks, 'robbery with violence or fraudulent extortion' [uiolentia predacio uel exaccio fraudulenta].[20]

Beginning with the familiar theory of money from the *Politics* and the *Nichomachean Ethics*, Oresme derives the theory of a Prince whose task is the disposition of the good of the community. Only the community can decide on a debasement of the currency, since it, and not the Prince, owns it; therefore, there must be some body or council which mediates between Prince and community. This account maps out an interesting position in political economy, but the relation of the *De moneta* to domestic economy is found rather in its theory of nature, especially in the argument about proper generation which underlies the claims both about money and about the household and its *yconomique*.

The most proper form of generation is that of natural fecundity, of seed bearing fruit. As the *De moneta* has it:

> Although all injustice is in a way contrary to nature, yet to make a profit from altering the coinage is specifically an unnatural act of injustice. For it is natural for certain natural riches to multiply, like grains of corn, 'which' says Ovid, 'when sown, the field with ample interest repays.' But it is monstrous and unnatural that an unfruitful thing should bear. ...[21]

This Aristotelian argument was widely known and oft-repeated in relation to usury;[22] it is an argument Oresme adapts to debasement of coinage, and it also arises in relation to the vexing question of profit itself. As Joel Kaye frames the debate: 'Was it licit to re-sell something for more than one had paid for it? If so, where did this *superabundantia* – this superadded value – come from?'[23] Suspicion attends any kind of profit, and the entire tradition reflects Aristotle's own fiscal conservativism and dislike of merchants. The central points of commentators such as Aquinas, Henry of Ghent, Walter Burley, Buridan, Oresme and others are well-known to historians of economics: money is a medium of exchange and a mean or measure. What it measures is *indigentia* or human need. It cannot breed for two reasons: because it is meant to be a stable and consistent unit of measure, and because the species metal it is made of is not capable of breeding. Human labour might add value to the thing bought or sold, thus allowing for small profits, but on the whole, no other increase (or decrease) in value should be possible. This analysis of breeding returns to the

20 Oresme, *The De moneta of Nicholas Oresme and English Mint Documents*, ed. and trans. Charles Johnson (London: Thomas Nelson, 1956), pp. 27–28.

21 'Quamquis omnis inusticia sit quodammodo contra naturam, uerumptamen accipere lucrum ex mutacione monete est quodam speciali modo iniustum innaturale. Naturale enim est quibusdam naturalibus diuiciis se multiplicare, sicut cerealia grana "que sata cum multo fenore reddit ager" ut ait Ouidius, sed monstruosum est et contra naturam quod infecunda pariat' (Oresme, *De moneta*, p. 25).

22 See Odd Langholm, *The Aristotelian Analysis of Usury* (Oslo: Universitetsforlaget, 1984), esp. ch. 3.

23 Joel Kaye, *Economy and Nature in the Fourteenth Century: Money, Market Exchange and the Emergence of Scientific Thought* (Cambridge: Cambridge University Press, 1998), p. 139.

household, conceived of throughout the *Politics* and the *Yconomique* as agricultural, as the unit of engagement with the natural productivity of the earth, gathering natural riches:

> G. Car si comme il appert par ... *Politiques*, des possessions ou recheces les unes sunt natureles, si comme sunt les fruis de la terre; et les autres artificieles, si comme or et argent et teles choses. (810)
>
> [For as shown in ... the *Politics* certain goods or riches are natural, such as the fruits of the soil; others are artificial, like gold and silver and such.]

Not only are gold and silver artificial because produced by toil, they are also, as specie, produced by art. Money is, then, a clever and artificial thing, made up by men as a portable exchange value. Artificial things cannot grow and breed; plant a bed, and it will not sprout into another bed, as Aristotle has it in his *Physics*. Thus money is unlike natural riches.

The household is the unit of human association that concerns itself with providing the material conditions for human flourishing, which are preconditions for political life: 'Car il est certain que quant les gens ne pevent avoir ceste chose la communité est dissolute et deffaicte' (808T) [For it is certain that when people cannot have these basic necessities for good living the bond of civil unity is destroyed]. The *Yconomique* concedes that violence and predation (seizure) sometimes have a place in the arts of acquisition, but its primary paradigm of acquisition is agriculture:

> T. ... car a toutes choses leur nourissement est et vient naturelement de leur mere. Et pour ce dondonques vient nourissement a homme de la terre. (810)
>
> [for the sustenance of all things is naturally derived from the mother. And therefore man receives his sustenance from the earth.]

Oresme glosses this claim at some length with citations of Ovid, Vergil and scripture, ending:

> G. ... Et donques, aussi comme l'enfant est nourri du lait de sa mere, nature humaine est nourrie des fruis de la terre et est chose naturele. (810)
>
> [Therefore, just as the child is nourished on its mother's milk, so mankind is nourished by the earth and this is a natural thing.]

The questions about usury, profit and the breeding of money are more amply addressed by others and so this brief synopsis is presented in order to make two points.[24] First, the entire Aristotelian tradition, in its very insistence on the true nature of money, tacitly admits that money can, and does, defeat nature at every point. It breeds, it produces profits, it is accumulated for its own sake. This behaviour is not impeded at all by the fact that money ought

24 See, for example, Langholm, *Usury*, Lapidus 'Metal, Money and the Prince', and Kaye, *Economy and Nature*.

not to reproduce itself. The investigation of why money goes against its own nature, and in what circumstances it does so, forms a substantial part of Oresme's commentaries. To give just one brief example: people may mistake the means for the end, and substitute the accumulation of currency for real economic productivity, resulting in hoarding. The reasons people hoard are in part because of anxiety about future livelihood, and in part because in taking money as an end, rather than as the means to the end of exchange, they have subjected it to the infinite desire that attends ends: 'avarice est semblable a ydropsie, car tant plus boit l'idropique, tant a plus soif' [avarice is like hydropsie, for the more the hydroptic drinks, the more he thirsts].[25] The very language used about money as means, medium, and measure invokes the Aristotelian sense of the virtues; and the financial vices are as important as the virtues in elucidating the topic.

The second direction concerns the language about sex and family which suffuses the discussion of financial economics. The argument about the breeding of money not only relies on the agricultural parallel of the generative seed, but also often directly evoke sexual reproduction. William of Moerbeke's glosses on the *Politics*, for example, brings out the sense in which the Greek word for interest, *tokos*, means 'offspring' – that which resembles the parent.[26] Langholm, like others, understands the language about breeding as metaphorical, implying that financial generation is merely comparable to sexual reproduction. But the medieval, Aristotelian, economic theory is directly tied to Aristotelian natural science, sharing the theory of natural generation. The connections to sexuality in economic theory are therefore not figural; when money strays from nature, it becomes linked to 'unnatural' sexuality. The passage quoted above from *De moneta* deploys a language of *preter naturam*, *contra naturam*, and a vocabulary of the monstrous, which plainly evoke medieval discourse about sodomy. Dante, in *Inferno* XVII, describes the usurers in the desert of the burning sands, scratching like dogs, and links them explicitly to their neighbours, the sodomites. They are placed in the circle of the violent, whose conceptual subdivisions are the violent against God (blasphemers) against nature (suicides and sodomites) and against art (usurers). The early Dante commentator Gelli remarked on the aptness of this congruence between sodomites and usurers, because the sodomites make what is naturally fertile sterile, and the usurers make what is naturally sterile fertile.[27] In Oresme's texts, over and against the linguistic thread about sterility and unnature is set the language of burgeoning and nurturing, the maternal earth, and the productive seed, which is also the basis of the family. This

25 Oresme, *Le Livre de Politiques d'Aristote*, ed. Menut, p. 65G.

26 Langholm, *Usury*, p. 56.

27 'Commentary', in Dante Alighieri, *Inferno*, trans. Dorothy L. Sayers (Harmondsworth, Middlesex: Penguin, 1981), p. 178.

understanding of reproduction is, therefore, not an analogy or a metaphor, but the basic principle of Aristotelian economic thinking.

The comedy of love and marriage

Although we know now that the text that Oresme translates as *Le Livre de Yconomique d'Aristote* was not written by Aristotle (it was 'mistakenly introduced into the Aristotelian corpus in the twelfth century, by Averroes'),[28] it was certainly canonical in Oresme's day.[29] Its *pseudo* status means it is now not much considered; moreover, it is a short text which reiterates many points more substantially addressed in the *Politics* and the *Ethics*. But only here are the inner workings of marriage described, and their discussion attributed to the greatest of authorities. It is therefore important to recover what medieval thinkers understood the Philosopher to have contributed to the question of marriage. The *Yconomique* describes the proper deployment of the art of acquisition, the relation between husband and wife (including the sexual), the treatment of children, the management of servants and slaves (including a précis of Aristotle's theory of natural servitude), the arrangement of the house and the proper divisions of labour, and so on to bookkeeping and storage facilities. Marriage is given very prominent treatment; the entire second book of the treatise is devoted to the subject. As Sherman writes, it is 'a contribution to the companionate theory of marriage'.[30]

Not only is marriage important as the social form for natural generation, it is also the basic building block of political life. For the sense in which the household is generative is not only in relation to the human species, but also of the polis itself; and such generation is fundamentally economic in the modern sense because it has to do with providing the material necessities for 'bien vivre'. Moreover, the bond between husband and wife is political, by Aristotle's definition; it is indeed the most basic political bond, unlike the bond between father and son, which is monarchial. Marriage is political in that it has its basis in consent and agreement to be governed, though it differs from other forms of political life in that the wife will never rule.[31]

The household has recently been given prominence as a 'rich conceptual topic' by D. Vance Smith in *Arts of Possession* (a title taken from Aristotle), which shows the political centrality of the household.[32] The intertwining of

28 See Sherman, *Imagining Aristotle*, p. 280.

29 For the complicated textual history of his exemplar, descended from an Arabico-Latin version, and the 1267 Latin translation of William of Moerbeke, see 'Introduction', *Yconomique*, ed. Menut, p. 787.

30 Sherman, *Imagining Aristotle*, p. 289.

31 J. M. Blythe, 'Family, Government and the Medieval Aristotelians', *History of Political Thought* 10 (1989), 3.

32 Smith, *Arts of Possession: The Middle English Household Imaginary* (Minneapolis: University of Minnesota Press, 2003), p. xiv. The 'arts of possession' are just what I have called 'arts of

public policy with home economics can be seen, for example, in William of Pagula's *Speculum regis Edward III*, a work about the evils of royal purveyance that locates the King's political troubles exactly in 'the mismanagement of his household'.[33] Smith writes that 'most of the discussions of economic moderation in the Middle Ages concern either royal or aristocratic subjects', a claim supported by the context of Oresme's work. But at the centre of the *Yconomique* is an ideal of the small household – a man, his wife, an ox. This household is complete because the category of the wife includes the idea of children, and the category of the ox includes all servants and slaves and animals of the household (809G). The wonderful illuminations of the royal manuscripts of the *Yconomique* show the man plowing (with horses, not oxen) while his wife sits inside with a spindle and a baby; the clothing in the miniatures reflects a 'middle- or upper-class household' even though the activities represented would seem to belong to prosperous peasantry.[34] The images in the royal manuscripts are important testimony because, as Claire Richter Sherman establishes beyond a reasonable doubt, Oresme was directly involved in the illustration program. Like the images, the text presents a modest household, characterized by industry, prudence, and friendly familial relations, all resting on a direct connection to the generative earth and its natural riches.

Indeed it seems there was an ideological investment in the modest and thrifty household just where it would seem least apt, in the royal court. For if Charles V had been alarmed by the outrages of the poor in the Jacquerie (who were motivated partly by the devaluations of the currency), he was also alarmed by the power of the magnates; these two groups represent the dangers of the 'democrats' and the 'oligarchs' in Aristotle's scheme of bad governments. Charles surrounded himself with bourgeois counsellors, famous for their thrift and financial prudence, policies in which Oresme no doubt had a large influence. These are the low-born fiscally conservative advisors whom Deschamps refers to as the 'old councillors' who, in his time, had been succeeded by an equally thrifty group including Deschamps himself. These were the advisors pilloried by the King's brothers as 'marmosets' – that is to say, as gargoyles or grotesques.[35] Evidence of the councillors' ideas might be found in many of his poems of advice to the Prince, such as Balade 940 with its refrain 'Restraingnon; si ferons que saige' [Let us exercise restraint; we will

acquisition'; the apparent discrepancy is resolved in Oresme's language: 'il s'ensuit que la possessive par quoy homme aquert teles choses pour necessité de vie humaine est naturale' [it follows that the art of possession by which man acquires those goods necessary for human life is natural] (*Politiques*, p. 62G). This art is contrasted with 'pecuniative' trade.

33 Cary J. Nederman, 'The Monarch and Marketplace: Economic Policy and Royal Finance in Willian of Pagula's *Speculum regis Edwardi III*', *History of Political Economy* 33 (2001), 62.

34 Sherman, *Imagining Aristotle*, p. 301.

35 Barbara W. Tuchman, *A Distant Mirror: The Calamitous 14th Century* (New York: Knopf, 1978), p. 345.

indeed be wise to do so].[36] In this struggle between aristocratic grandeur and fiscal responsibility, the small holding and companiate marriage had an ideological value in the great household of the king.

Certainly Oresme, heavily committed to the notion of the mean, believed that citizens should be of average wealth. A miniature from the *Politiques* shows *policie* as a mean between 'povres gens' and 'riches gens';[37] the middle class itself, then, emerges as a kind of virtue. As Oresme has it in the *Politiques*,

> G. Car a bien vivre et a bonne sustenance de nature ne convient pas trop de choses car, si comme dit Seneque: Paucis natura content est. Nature est contente de peu choses ...[38]
>
> [G. Because living well and according to the good sustenance of nature does not require many things, as Seneca said: Paucis natura content est. Nature is content with little.]

The fundamental economic paradigm of generation and natural riches also accounts for the prominence of marriage in the *Yconomique.* The pseudo-Aristotelian main text gives marriage considerable attention, but Oresme's glosses greatly amplify this interest. His glosses often run fifty lines to four lines of text, providing cross-references by chapter and book to all the work of Aristotle, larding in biblical support, other authorities, and his own commentary, as well as identifying where he thinks the text is corrupt. The central argument begins with the subject of natural generation. The bond between man and woman is natural because generation cannot be accomplished singly. Humans, like animals, have a duty to the life of the species. Offspring are the payment of the 'l'aministrement de nature' (813T) [the debt to nature]. But generative nature is not a sufficient explanation of either the bond between husband and wife or between parent and child, because human activity also has another purpose – not merely in order to live, but to live well. Put another way, generation is both the cause and the end, or *telos*, of animal life, but the *telos* of human life is friendship, association and political life. Thus children are not only for 'continuation des especes' (814T) [maintenance of the species] but for a super-added value, translated by Oresme as 'profit' – this profit, which emerges in a hyper-economy beyond that of natural generation, is the social bond, which results in the support and maintenance of the parents in their old age. The language here, of debt, payment and profit, is again *not* metaphorical, referring to some independent financial system, but forms an intrinsic part of the sexual-family economy.

36 Eustache Deschamps, *Oeuvres Complètes de Eustache Deschamps*, 11 vols., ed. Marquis de Queux de Sainte-Hilaire (Paris: Firmin Didot, 1878–1903), vol. 5 *Balades*, pp. 153–55. Poems from this edition will be cited hereafter by *balade*, page and line numbers. English translations are my own.

37 Reproduced in Sherman, *Imagining Aristotle*, pp. 227–28.

38 Oresme, *Le Livre de Politiques d'Aristote*, ed. Menut, p. 119.

In the case of marriage as well, natural, generative, sexuality is superceded by social sexuality. I will quote Oresme at length, in order to preserve the flavour of his commentary.

> G. [Husbands and wives live together] selon vertu en amisté de marriage, laquelle comprent toutes les causes et especes de amisté, si comme il appert par le .xvii.[e] chapitre de le .viii.[e] D'*Ethiques.* Car elle a en soi bien utile et bien delectation; ce est assavoir, charnele et vertueuse ou sensitive et intellective. Item, ceste amisté est singuliere, car elle est entre un seul et une seule … .Item, encor appert parce que nature mist delectation de couple charnel es bestes tant seulement pour cause et afin de generation; mes elle mist es gens tele delectation pour la cause desus dicte et pour acrestre et coninuer et garder amisté entre homme et femme. Et de ce est signe ce que dit Plinius; que nulle femelle depuis que elle a conceu et est prenante ne appete tel couple charnel fors tant seulement femme. Item, la plus grande unite est cause de plus grand amisté. (813)

> [G. [Husbands and wives live together] virtuously as in married friendship, which includes all the causes and kinds of friendship as stated in the *Ethics* VIII, 17. For this friendship comprises at once the good of usefulness, the good of pleasure and the good of virtue and double enjoyment – that is, both the carnal and the virtuous or the sensual and intellectual pleasures. This friendship exists between two individuals only … This is clear from the fact that nature granted carnal pleasures to the animals only for the purpose of reproduction; but it accorded the human species this pleasure not only for reproduction of its kind but also to enhance the friendship between man and woman. This is implied in Pliny's statement that no female, after she has become pregnant, seeks sexual union except woman only. And this greater unity is a cause of greater friendship.]

Human sexuality then has an abundance, a superfluity which is expressed so strikingly in the woman's desire for sex even when pregnant. It is in excess to the need for reproduction. Sociality, or friendship, emerges as a supplement to merely generative nature. The friendship is of course somewhat one-sided; by no means are men and women equal, but because their bond is political, it is also rational and deliberative.

One name for this supplemental character of sexual abundance might be love; and Oresme waxes poetical on the subject:

> G. il avient souvent que .ii. jennes gens, homme et femme, aiment l'un l'autre en especial par election et plaisance de cuer et de amour qui est oveques usage de raison, combien que aucune fois elle ne soit pas selon droite raison. Et selon ce, Ovide fist un livre de art de tele amor, laquele ne est pas entre les bestes mues …
> T. Item, en communication de masle et de femelle generalement apparoissent plus les aides que il funt et oevrent ensemble.
> G. Si comme nous veons de aucuns oiseaux qui s'entreaident a faire leur niz et a nourrir leur petis oyselés. (812)

> [G. it often happens that two young people, man and woman, love each other by

> special choice from a feeling of joy in their hearts, with a love that is accompanied by reason, even though it may sometimes happen to be without correct reason. Accordingly Ovid wrote a book on the art of this kind of love, which does not exist between dumb animals …
> T. When man and woman live together one observes how frequently they assist each other and cooperate and work together.
> G. Just as we notice that certain birds help each other in building their nest and in feeding their little ones.]

Thus, the theory of marriage in the *Yconomique* is comic: men and women come together with a feeling of joy in their hearts, nest together like little birds, divide their labour according to their natural capacities in a way that seems to Oresme similar to the harmony produced by properly proportioned musical tones (815G), and have sex when they do not need to, simply as the icing on the cake of friendship. This economics of marriage is comedy in the sense of the *Divine Comedy*: a cheerful science of rational, balanced, unified living which has as its end the happiness of friendship and good living, the accumulation of necessaries and the joy of sex.

There is, then, a rigorous logic to the total economic theory, consistent from the husband and wife and their ox to recommendations about royal policy on the devaluation of currency. Generative nature is the most fundamental economic fact. Understanding this nature means understanding that hard cold money cannot breed and therefore should not. What can breed, should breed – crops, animals, and humans. The first, primal form of human association, husband and wife, in itself encapsulates both the end of nature and the more properly human end of association in the polis. The household founded on husband, and wife (and ox), just because it is sexually natural itself and manages other natural generation (crops, children, animals, slaves) has the task of acquisition and possession of property; it is the proper domain of financial economics. The interdependence of such households requires a medium of exchange, money; the prosperity of the household is the goal of economics, not the proliferation of money.

Lurking beside this wonderfully comic vision is the spectre of everything that can go wrong with it. The 'filthy words and scandals' of Oresme's domestic tragedies attend the very description of domestic bliss. The reason they do so is exactly because of the most basic Aristotelian conceptual structure of the *Ethics*, *Politics*, and the *Yconomique*, that of the virtue as a mean between two extremes. We see the concept most vividly in the miniatures that adorn the manuscripts of the royal library: 'Liberalité' flanked by 'Prodigalité' and 'Avarice'; 'Attemprance' by 'Desattemprance' and 'Insensibilité', and so on. Two unprecedented miniatures in manuscripts of the *Ethiques* illustrate virtue as a abstract concept; that is, rather than showing a specific virtue and its vices, 'Virtue' herself stands at the centre. In one version she is flanked by two handmaidens, 'Bonne Volenté' and 'Cognoissance': to her right is a grotesque giant labeled 'Vice', 'Exces', and to her left a dwarfish figure, 'Vice' or

Figure 1. The Hague, Rijksmuseum Meermanno-Westreenianum, MW 10 d 1, fol. 24v. Reproduced with the permision of the Nationale Binliotheek van Nederland.

'Deffaute' (see Figure 1).[39] 'Excess', also commonly called 'Superhabundance' in the text, and 'Defect' are contorted and grimacing, looking away from the beautiful mean. These extremes are not the negation of the virtue, and are not evils in themselves; rather these grotesque exaggerations attend the mean as surely as her own handmaidens. Since the virtue is part of a continuum, in order to know what the virtuous mean is, one must know the vices. Aristotelian ethics provides a very different model than that of a Christian ethics of sin and evil, transcendence and salvation, and given the scholastic prestige of the Philosopher, that model was very widely known. We might say that Christian ethics are a vertical system, moving up and down from Heaven to Hell, but Aristotelian ethics are a horizontal system. Understanding that both systems coexist at the same time, even though they sometimes contradict each other, is vital to understanding the *mentalité* of the era, and its representations.

The notion of the mean pervades Oresme's thinking; 'Excess' and 'Defect', the giant and the dwarf, also attend of all the recommendations for a happy household in the *Yconomique*. A husband should not be too indifferent or too harsh; a wife should not be too familiar (like a courtesan), nor too fearful with her husband; servants should be treated neither too leniently nor too harshly. The giant and dwarf are especially in attendance in sexual matters:

[39] The Hague, Rijksmuseum Meermanno-Westreenianum, MS 10 d 1, fol. 24v. The other illustration, from Brussels, Bibliothèque Royale Albert Ier, MS 9505–06, fol. 24 is reproduced in Sherman, *Imagining Aristotle*, fig. 11a, and in Smith, *Arts of Possession*, p. 162.

> T. Item, quant est de cognoistre sa femme charnelment, le mari doit faire qu'elle ne ait pas de ce deffaute et ne doit pas tant de ce faire qu'elle ne se peut contenir se il avenoit que le mari fust aussi comme un de ceulz qui sunt absens.
> ... G. Car se il estoit de ce trop abstinent, la femme pourroit traire soy vers un autre. Et se ou commencement il frequentoit mout tele chose, quant après ... la femme avroit acoustumé tele chose ne se pourroit contenir. (816)
>
> [T. With respect to sexual intercourse with his wife, the husband should see that she has no lack of it; but he must not indulge her so that she cannot contain herself when it happens that he has to abstain or to be absent from home.
> ... G. For if he were too abstemious in this matter, his wife might be attracted to another man. And if he were too demanding at the beginning of their marriage, then later ... the wife, being accustomed to frequent indulgence, would be unable to contain herself.]

Thus, female sexual desire must be made temperate by habit. Too much excitement, and sexuality overflows the proper boundary of the household. Likewise in the case of superabundance of *male* sexual activity; Oresme criticises the scattering of the paternal seed which produces illegitimate children, which he oddly glosses 'si comme funt les Sodomites' (836G) [as the sodomites do]. This gloss suggests that natural generation, if outside the household, is a kind of sterility, because, as he subsequently remarks, illegitimate children undermine the household's mission to acquire, preserve and enhance riches. The notion of excess is particularly problematic for sexuality because, as we have already seen, one kind of excess in sexual desire is necessary to promote the friendship of husband and wife; but this surplus cannot become too excessive, or it swells into vice.

Aristotlian horizontal ethics seem to permit both play and perspective in the system. It can be difficult to tell at which point a virtue might tip over into the monstrous or dwarfish figures of excess or default (into satire and parody). This instability is particularly evident when it comes to women. In a long gloss on the subject, advocating, of course, a middle way in the treatment of wives, Oresme likens the characters of some women to twisted sticks, and others to straight sticks. Even after soaking, some of the twisted sticks will 'retournent tantost et sunt tortueuses et boisteuses' [revert to their twisted and tortuous original shape]. Thus some women then are naturally grotesque or evil, some good – but Oresme despairs of knowing which are which, for 'a nature et condition de femme est tres fort a cognoistre et aucune fois se varie occultement d'une maniere en autre' (837G) [the nature and character of a woman are very difficult to know and sometimes they vary secretly from one state to another]. The two handmaidens of virtue in the miniature, 'Bonne Volenté' and 'Cognoissance' should be what determine the mean. But we have already seen in the passage above (812G) that the joyful heart may will *outside* the dictates of right reason; and we may reflect on the specious chains of reasoning employed by Chaucer's uxorious Chanticleer or by the loathsome January in the Merchant's Tale, those comic characters who do not know that they have become vices.

What Oresme's texts and their illustrations suggest is that the Aristotelian system itself produces the deviations, excesses, and deformities to either side of the mean. Indeed while Oresme represents the self-conscious dissemination of such thought, its presumptions implicitly characterize literary genres like fabliau with its endless concern with the circulation of money, extraordinary profits and unnatural acts. Aristotle's theoretical structure of means produces concrete analogues in literature, which is the ordinary domain of representations of the household. The abstract Aristotelian figures of excess and defect are translated into a series of literary types and tropes that are the mainstay of the comic (or, as Oresme would say, tragic) stories found in the genres of fabliau and satire such as Chaucer's Merchant's or Shipman's Tale and Deschamps' *Miroir de Mariage* – types such as the old husband, the libidinous wife, the miserly husband and the spendthrift wife, and tropes such as the breeding of money.

Envoy: Oresme to Deschamps

There is at least one more concrete testimony to the dissemination of the *Yconomique*. Eustache Deschamps writes:

> Car nulle vraie policie
> N'est sanz marriage assevie
> Ne hostel; et bien le verras
> En Ethiques, quant tu vourras,
> Et Pollitiques d'Aristote
> Qui plus a plain ce nous denote
>
> [For there can be no true policy or household without marriage. And this will you see well, if you like, in the *Ethics* and *Politics* of Aristotle, which show us this fully.][40]

These lines are from the introductory passages of the *Miroir de Mariage*, that famously misogynist text which by no means espouses the view the passage proposes, that marriage is essential to *policie*; indeed, the lines are part of the argument of the false friends, particularly 'Faintis' [Fantasy], to 'Franc Vouloir' [Free Will], the central character of the poem. The passage continues with a thirty-line account of the thrifty, competent, soft-spoken, modestly dressed wife, who governs and manages the indoor household. This woman appears nowhere in the two texts the poet mentions; but she is fully there in the *Yconomique*. The parallels between the two texts are sufficient to establish that Deschamps knew the work and was deliberately evoking it (see my Appendix).

[40] Deschamps, *Oeuvres Complètes*, vol. 9, *Le Miroir de Mariage*, pp. 10–11, lines 211–215. Hereafter the *Miroir* will be cited from this edition by line number. Translations are my own.

His portrait of the ideal wife is only vaguely Aristotelian in terms of the texts he names, while it is *precisely* pseudo-Aristotelian in the terms of the *Yconomique*; this is the text that provides an Aristotelian ideal of wifely conduct.[41] Whether Deschamps knew Oresme's translation is unprovable; he had himself been to university and is obviously not at a loss for a learned reference. It is possible he knew the Latin versions directly. But not only is he the target audience for the publication project – a member of the next generation of royal counsellors and himself a proponent of public and political discourse – but he is also known to have used Oresme's *Livre de Divinacions* in his own *Demonstrations contre Sortileges*.[42]

But Deschamps is not receiving the wisdom of the Philosopher in quite the way envisioned in Oresme's translation work. That earnest and edifying work is immediately undermined by its context as a speech from Faintis. The ideal wife comes from fantasyland; she is a construct of the four deceitful 'friends' who consistently offer Franc Vouloir the rosiest glosses on marriage and other affairs. Franc Vouloir soon turns from this pleasant dream to what he has actually heard about marriage, and there we find the entrance of the 'giant and the dwarf', in the catalogue of the excesses and defects that constitute the archive of misogyny. The *Miroir* implies that there is no mean or measure in marriage, only the extremes of January and May. Deschamps' satire here overturns solemn philosophical forays into the public good.

Deschamps is not, however, always in the grip of the cankered muse. His own poetry produces overwhelming evidence that Aristotle and the notion of the mean were always in mind, often occurring as sage counsel about both marriage and politics.[43] To take just one example, *Balade* 996 (pp. 248–49) reverses the satire of the *Miroir* by suggesting the middle way – marriage to a wife neither too young or too old, neither too grand or too humble, and advises:

> Prengne femme qui sache gouverner …
> Si se fait bon ou moyen ordonner :
> Sage zest cilz qui ainsy se marie (4–16)
>
> [Take a wife who knows how to manage (a household) … He does himself good who arranges the medium way: Wise is he who marries thus.]

The woman who knows how to manage a household in accordance with the

41 Michelle Stoneburner briefly considers the reference to Aristotle in a general way in '*Le Miroir de marriage*: Misunderstood Misogyny', in *Eustache Deschamps: French Courtier Poet*, ed. Deborah M. Sinnreich-Levi (New York: AMS Press, 1998), p. 149. Laura Kendrick also notices Deschamps' Aristotelianism, but attributes it to his reading of Brunetto Latini's summary. See her 'Rhetoric and the Rise of Public Poetry: The Career of Eustache Deschamps', *Studies in Philology* 80 (1983), p. 4.

42 G. W. Coopland, *Nicole Oresme and the Astrologers* (Cambridge, Mass.: Harvard University Press, 1952), pp. 8–9.

43 For a few examples see *Balades* 916 (pp. 117–18), 940 (pp. 153–55), 952 (pp. 171–73), 970 (pp. 205–07) and 992 (pp. 242–43).

mean; perhaps it is still fantasy speaking. But it is certainly an Aristotelian fantasy.

Conclusions

The pervasiveness of Aristotle's thought in the Middle Ages is widely acknowledged, but perhaps not fully understood in areas that are apparently remote from its academic context, such as literature. The *pseudo* status of the *Yconomique* has undoubtedly impeded consideration of the full medieval understanding of Aristotle on marriage. In this essay I have tracked one instance of the dissemination of that thought, as presented by a thinker whose work is also, as I hope I have demonstrated, of independent interest. Oresme's holistic economic theory includes both financial matters and household matters and shows us that these are essentially related: that the economy of love and marriage is based on the same principles as the economy of money. I have also suggested that the characteristic Aristotelian conceptualization of the mean, in both virtuous and economic practice, can be seen as enabling a comic structure, because of the attendant dwarves of defect and giants of excess. Such comedy inadvertently creeps into Oresme's work, and self-consciously into Deschamps'. This theory of comedy may not be that of Aristotle's treatise on comedy; but, perhaps fortunately for me, that work is lost.[44]

44 A version of this paper was presented as the keynote address to the Atlantic Medieval Association in Antigonish, 2009. I would like to thank the association, and Simon Gaunt and Calum Agnew, for their help with the final version.

Appendix

Correspondences between *Le Miroir de Mariage* 221–251
and *Le Livre Yconomique.*

Homs doit par dehors ordonner, 221
Femme doit dedenz gouverner:
Elle est si doulce en sa parole,
Son mari sert, baise et acole,
Et fait, quant il est a martire, 225
Qu'elle le puisse getter d'ire.
S'il a griefté, celle le garde,
Et piteusement le resgarde,
Et mainte foiz par sa douçour
Le retrait de mortel langour; 230
Elle gouverne son hostel
Et son bestail d'autre costel;
Elle est guettant, saige et apperte,
Et voit que rien ne voist a perte;
Elle veille sur ses sergens; 235
Elle scet restraindre ses gens,
Quant mestiers est, et eslargir;
Elle se scet taire et souffrir,
Espargnier scet et avoir soing
Pour le despendre a un besoing: 240
Ce ne fait pas mesgnie estrange,
Qui vuide l'escrin et la grange
Et ne pense fors de rober,
De po faire et de temps passer.
Matin lieve et se couche tart, 245
Car son cuer et sa pensée art
Tousjours a son gouvernement.
Eureux, se Salemon ne ment,
Et cilz qui treuve bonne fame!
Il puisera de corps et d'ame 250
Joye devers Nostre Seigneur.

[The husband should command outdoors 221
The wife ought to govern within
She is very sweet in her speech,
She serves her husband, humbly and meekly,
And so manages, when he is persecuted, 225

That she enables him to cast anger away.
If he has sorrows, she takes care of him,
And treats him sympathetically,
And often by her sweetness
Keeps him from mortal decline; 230
She manages his household
And his beasts outside;
She is watchful, wise and clever,
And sees to it that nothing is wasted;
She keeps an eye on their retainers; 235
She knows how to retain her servants,
When necessary, and when to let them go;
She can keep quiet and wait patiently,
She knows how to save and to have a care
For the necessary expenditures: 240
She does not do for hordes of strangers,
Who empty the money-box and the barn,
And think nothing of robbing,
Or of idleness and wasting time.
She is early to rise and late to bed, 245
For her heart and her thought are
Always on her domestic duties.
Unless Solomon lies, happy
Is he who finds this good wife!
He will draw joy from body and soul 250
Towards our Lord.]

While some of the parallels could be generic to any picture of the good wife, and none of them except the first provides exact parallels in language, together I believe the following correspondences between the *Miroir* and *Le Livre Yconomique* demonstrate that Deschamps is referring directly and precisely to the *Yconomique*:

Miroir 213–14; Deschamps invokes *Politics*; *Yconomique* is found as a short addendum to *Politiques* in manuscripts and early printed versions of Oresme's translations.

Miroir 221–22; *Yconomique* 815T, repeated at 822G: 'T. Et afin que l'en quere et prepare les choses qui sunt dehors le hostel, ce est le mari; et que l'autre salve et garde celles qui sunt dedens' [And in order that the husband may prepare and look after the outdoor work of the homestead while the wife attends to and watches over the indoor work].

Miroir 232, 'son bestial' and 243, 'la grange' indicate the agricultural small-holding scene of *Yconomique* (811G).

Miroir 223–24, 'Elle est si doulce …'; 'T. Et qu'elle die toujours tres bonnes paroles et lui face service et obedience en chose avenantes' (829); [She must always speak kindly and be obedient and helpful in all good and proper things …].

Miroir 226–30, 'S'il a griefté …'; on the wife's duty of kindliness to her husband when he has adversity, see *Yconomique* 829 T and G and 831: 'T. … mes en adversité ne veulent communiquer femmes fors celles qui sunt tres bonnes. G. Et qui aiment leur maris de bonne amour' [T. … but only the best of women are willing to share in adversity. G. And those who love their husbands with true affection].

Miroir 235ff; on the duty of both husband and wife to manage their servants and be watchful see *Yconomique* 824.

Miroir 238; *Yconomique* 829T: 'Et se elle seuffre et porte pacienment … elle gouvernera legierement la maison …' [If she endures and bears her lot patiently … she will manage her household easily].

Miroir 239–40; *Yconomique* 827G: '… elle doit garder et dispenser les choses de l'ostel au bon plaisir de son mari et a ses amis. Et pource que femme est naturelment tenante, elle fait les despens plus modestement …' [she should watch over and spend the household goods according to her husband's pleasure and that of his friends. And since woman is naturally parsimonious, she spends more moderately …].

Miroir 241–44; *Yconomique* 827G: 'Se elle souffroit hommes estrange entrer et converser a l'oste, ses voisines en parleroient en mal' [If she were to permit strange men to enter and live in the house, her female neighbours would spread a scandal]. More generally on both the husband and wife's duty to preserve goods, *Yconomique* 823T.

Miroir 245; 'il convient pour les seigneurs ester premierement levés … et dormir les desreniers' (824T) [the masters must be first to rise and last to go to sleep] with Oresme's gloss 'Et je cuide que par les seigneurs il entende le mari et la femme' (823G).

7

The Poetics of Catastrophe: Ovidian Allusion in Gower's *Vox Clamantis*[1]

Maura Nolan

The lion's share of critical attention for the *Vox Clamantis* has come from medievalists interested in Gower's outraged response to the Rising of 1381 in Book I (known as the *Visio*), particularly his indictment of the peasants in a vicious beast allegory.[2] But beast allegory is not the only genre at work in the *Visio*. It is also a Boethian account of the relation between self and society, individual and community, dramatized in part by a dialogue between the narrator and Wisdom and cast as a story of exile.[3] These latter aspects of the

1 It would not have been possible for me to write this essay without Jill Mann. I had the good fortune of being Jill Mann's junior colleague for five years and I have had the marvelous experience of being her friend for the past twelve. No one is more generous than Jill. Over the years, she has read everything I have written with an acute eye for detail (for which she is famous), but also with her unerring sense of the stakes of an argument. Jill has perfect pitch when reading literary texts or literary criticism and she is a genius at balancing large and small claims in proper proportion. She knows exactly when modesty is required and when boldness is appropriate. Jill's criticism is always accompanied by specific instructions for revision, which often are rooted in her own unsung labours: to help her friends, I have known her to reread multi-volume poems, make special trips to the library, transcribe passages from manuscripts, translate Latin (or another one of the many languages in which she is expert), and come home to serve her guests an elegant dinner at the end of the day. This essay is a small attempt to pay homage to Jill and to thank her for lessons in literary criticism and in life. Jill may be small in stature, but she is one of the giants on whose shoulders we all stand.

2 Based on his analysis of the manuscripts, Macaulay suggested that Books 2–7 of the *Vox* were composed first, and the *Visio* added later, in response to the events of 1381 (G. C. Macaulay, ed., *The Complete Works of John Gower: the Latin Works*, vol. 4 (Oxford: Clarendon Press, 1902), p. xxxi). One manuscript, Oxford, Bodleian Library MS Laud 719, omits the *Visio* almost entirely, leaving only the Prologue and first chapter, which do not address the Rising; the remaining books are then numbered 1–6, with Book 1 identified as what is usually Book 2. John Fisher, *John Gower: Moral Philosopher and Friend of Chaucer* (New York: New York University Press, 1964), p. 103, notes as well that the shortest book in the *Vox* is Book 2, at 630 lines, suggesting strongly that Gower originally intended it to be the prologue to the work.

3 Macaulay, *Gower: Latin Works*, vol. 4, Book I, lines 1527–28; subsequent references will be in the text by book and line number. Throughout the text, I have reformatted the verses to reflect the fact that Gower is writing in elegiac distichs, hexameter followed by pentameter, by indenting the

poem foreground the narrator's emotional response to the catastrophe of the Rising, and thereby produce a structural tension between the representation of individual feelings and the representation of the social whole (embodied by the use of allegory). Gower's use of the conflicting genres of beast allegory and Boethian complaint makes visible the foundational tension between authority and experience, those medieval categories imagined by the Wife of Bath as gendered modes of knowledge. In the *Visio*, authority and experience can be described as forms of relation to the world. The former is based on detachment, on viewing the world through predetermined categories dictated by social hierarchies; the latter is fundamentally a mode of attachment, which depends on the notion that the subjective experience of the individual – of multiple individuals – constitutes the matter out of which both social relations and the aesthetic are formed. Attachment reveals itself through passion, through the expression of emotions like fear, sorrow, anger or joy, and through the senses, those mechanisms by which human beings experience the world and its sights, sounds, tastes, smells, and touches. This opposition between detachment and attachment is made manifest in the *Visio* by the uneasy relation between the prophetic persona adopted by the narrator and those several moments at which he abandons the prophetic voice to engage in passionate self-disclosure.

Gower tells readers in the Prologue that 'Qui magis inspiciet opus istud, tempus et instans,/ Inveniet toto carmine dulce nichil' [One who looks further into this work and into the present time will find nothing consoling in the whole poem] (I.41–42). Despite his gloomy assessment of the *Visio*, filled with 'nothing consoling', Gower establishes here the proper reading practice for the text, 'looking further'. What the reader finds upon looking further is the key to understanding the opposition between detachment and attachment that structures the text: hidden in plain sight is a pervasive counter-text created by repeated allusions to Ovid.[4] Even a cursory familiarity with Ovid lends to the verse of the *Visio* a familiar sound; Gower appropriates phrases, lines, and passages from his predecessor and embeds them in a new context, thereby forging links between his own verses and a variety of Ovid's works.[5] Even as

pentameter line. I have also silently substituted *v* for Macaulay's *u* where appropriate. Translations throughout are modified versions of Stockton's translation of the *Vox*; see Eric Stockton, *The Major Latin Works of John Gower* (Seattle: University of Washington Press, 1962). I have made a number of changes to Stockton's translations for accuracy and felicity, guided, as always, by Jill Mann.

4 For Gower's use of allusion in his Latin works, see A. G. Rigg and Edward Moore, 'The Latin Works: Politics, Lament and Praise', in *A Companion to Gower*, ed. Siân Echard (Cambridge: D. S. Brewer, 2004), pp. 153–64, p. 155.

5 Various critics have identified Gower's allusions to Ovid in the *Vox Clamantis*, each building on the work of his predecessors. In the notes to his edition, Macaulay listed a long series of these allusions; Stockton added to this foundation in the notes to his translation with a number of new references. The most thorough account of Gower's allusions to Ovid, with many references that do not appear in Macaulay or Stockton, can be found in Frederick Crittenden Mish, 'The Influence of Ovid on John Gower's *Vox Clamantis*' (Ph.D. dissertation, University of Minnesota, 1973). See also Maria

they yield new meanings in the new textual environment of the *Visio*, however, Ovid's words continue to evoke their original significances and to gesture to their original contexts, a phenomenon that creates a kind of 'perforated' text with a distinctively layered structure. Allusions to Ovid puncture the surface of the poem, producing openings in the text through which readers can access Ovid's verse in all of its complexity and multivalence. This Ovidian counter-text makes available an alternative way of seeing – a new kind of vision – revealing a space in which different rules apply and different freedoms are available to poets. The practice of allusion thus allows Gower to posit a counterfactual mode that fundamentally changes the vision of poetic artifice and its place in the world offered in the remainder of the *Vox*.[6]

Before I turn to Gower's direct engagement with Ovid, let me first illustrate the opposition between authority and experience, prophecy and self-disclosure, that structures the *Visio* from the start. At the very beginning of the Prologue, the narrator describes his writing practice in overwrought terms:

> Quos mea terra dedit casus nouitatis adibo,
> Nam pius est patrie facta referre labor.
> Quod michi flere licet scribam lacrimabile tempus,
> Sic quod in exemplum posteritatis eat.
> Flebilis ut noster status est, ita flebile Carmen,
> Materie scripto conueniente sue.
> Omne quod est huius operis lacrimabile, lector
> Scriptum de lacrimis censeat esse meis:
> Penna madet lacrimis hec me scribente profusis,
> Dumque feror studiis, cor tremit atque manus.
> Scribere cumque volo, michi pondere pressa laboris
> Est manus et vires subtrahit inde timor.
> Qui magis inspiciet opus istud, tempus et instans,
> Inveniet toto carmine dulce nichil. (Prol., lines 29–42)

> [I shall enter into the recent misfortunes that my country has exhibited, for it is a worthy labor to report the deeds of one's native land. I will write

Wickert, *Studies in John Gower*, trans. Robert J. Meindl (Washington, DC: University Press of America, 1981). Yoshiko Kobayashi reads Gower's allusions to Ovid in relation to the Roman poet's discourse of exile, arguing that Gower positions himself as a poet-prophet at the end of the *Visio*. See 'The Voice of an Exile: John Gower's *Vox Clamantis*', in *Through a Classical Eye: Transcultural and Transhistorical Visions in Medieval English, Italian, and Latin Literature in Honour of Winthrop Wetherbee*, ed. Andrew Galloway and R. F. Yeager (Toronto: University of Toronto Press, 2009), pp. 339–62. Other discussions of Gower's use of sources in the *Visio* include Malte Urban, 'Past and Present: Gower's Use of Old Books in *Vox Clamantis*', in *John Gower: Manuscripts, Readers, Contexts*, ed. Malte Urban (Turnhout: Brepols, 2009), pp. 159–80, and Eve Salisbury, 'Remembering Origins: Gower's Monstrous Body Poetic', in *Re-Visioning Gower*, ed. R. F. Yeager (Asheville, NC: Pegasus Press, 1998), pp. 159–84.

6 Gower's vision of Latin poetics underwent a significant change over the course of his career, as David Carlson has shown, moving from the 'more readily apprehensible' style that characterizes the *Vox* to his 'ornate, late mannerism'. See Carlson, 'A Rhyme Distribution Chronology of John Gower's Latin Poetry', *Studies in Philology* 104 (2007), 15–55, pp. 47–49.

> about the woeful time which it is permitted me to lament, and which may in this way go forth as an example for posterity. Just as our condition is mournful, so the poem is mournful, the writing being in accord with its subject matter. The reader may judge everything of this book which is tearful to have been written with my own tears. As I write these things my pen grows wet with profuse weeping, and while I am carried forward by my zeal, my heart and hand tremble. And when I wish to write, my hand is burdened by the weight of the task, and anxiety takes away its strength. One who looks further into this work and into the present time will find nothing consoling in the whole poem].

The tear-saturated text ('flebile carmen') is married to its sorrowful content; form and meaning are united by the mournful poet, for whom weeping and writing have merged to become a singular act of self-expression. This fusion of author and text blurs the distinction between history and the self, so much so that the narrator, the times, and the work are all described with versions of the same word: 'scriptum de *lacrimis* esse meis' [to have been written with my tears]; 'penna madet *lacrimis* profusis' [the pen grows wet with profuse tears]; '*lacrimabile* tempus' [tearful time]; 'omne quod est huius operis *lacrimabile*' [everything of this book which is tearful]. These introductory lines not only insist upon the relevance of the narrator's subjective response to the crisis, but they also construct the *Visio* as a mode of attachment to the world, as a text whose relation to history is created by its author's passionate investment in events, their causes, and their effects. When the text is defined in this way, the emotional condition of the author – his tearful state of sorrow – becomes the subjective quality that links history ('lacrimabile tempus') to its representation (the book is literally written with 'lacrimis', tears). This connection will become, for Gower, a paradigm for the proper relation of a poet to the world and to his community. It is a relation dependent upon what philosophers of mind now call 'qualia', the qualitative or subjective aspects of experience, defined by Frank Jackson as 'certain properties of certain mental states [that] ... are such that their possession or absence makes no difference to the physical world'.[7] For Gower, qualia – which he represents through the figure of the narrator – exist in tension with authority, which transforms individual experience into detached and objective structures of order. These structures include the social model of the three estates (familiar from all three of Gower's major works) and the more fundamental distinction in the *Visio* between civilized humanity and beasts. As I will show, the *Visio* increasingly incorporates qualia

[7] To be clear, I am using the term 'qualia' in its most general sense; it has been the subject of exhaustive debate in recent years among philosophers of mind, cognitive scientists, and others who study consciousness. The quotation comes from Frank Jackson, 'Epiphenomenal Qualia', *Philosophical Quarterly* 32 (1982), 127–36, p. 133; see also Edmond Wright, ed., *The Case for Qualia* (Cambridge, MA: MIT Press, 2008), and for a different view, see Daniel Dennett, *Consciousness Explained* (New York: Back Bay Books, 1992).

through its allusions to Ovid, moving toward a notion of poetics as a mode of attachment that can remake the world by fostering harmony between the individual and the group. This relation is created by the shared experience of qualia, those emotions and sense-impressions made visible by the figure of the narrator, who is less an individual subject than a nodal point for the revelation of experience. This notion of poetics coexists with the satirical, detached mode usually associated with Gower's French and Latin works, which take the form of estates satire and aggressively impose standards and structures on the world. But it is in the *Visio* that Gower most explicitly contrasts the two modes, using his Ovidian counter-text as a way of exploring the parameters of the 'poetics of attachment' that will flower in his English work. His prophetic voice (the *vox clamantis*) is not the only voice heard in the *Visio*; the text is divided between authoritative pronouncement and subjective lament, between Gower's desire to assert order and his wish to articulate the experience of attachment to the world as events unfold in a disordered and uncontrolled way. In one sense, Gower lays claim to social hierarchy; he stigmatizes the peasantry as bestial madmen and thereby ventriloquizes the voice of earthly power, a voice that insists upon its own detachment from events and thus its own agency. In another way, however, Gower's choice of the first person binds him only to describe his narrator's *experience* of the Rising, not the historical reasons for its occurrence (such as taxation). Human experience, of course, is notoriously unreliable, unreasonable, and sentimental; by associating the *Visio* with experience, Gower implies that emotion, rather than reason, is the force guiding his hand as he writes. The *Visio*'s intense engagement with Ovid opens up its seemingly vitriolic and moralizing argument, producing a discourse of emotion and changeability (including both joy and sorrow) that implicitly counters its dark portrait of England in 1381. I argue here that Gower's allusions provide him with an aesthetic discourse through which he can explore modes of attachment to the world, such as grief, passion, melancholy, love, and pain – those qualia that poetry can translate into shared experience as a way of forging social bonds.

R. F. Yeager has shown that this technique of taking lines dramatically out of context and remaking them with a new theme and as part of a new narrative (known as *cento* and common in classical poetry) was favored by Gower in the *Vox*, in which 'approximately one-third … contains splicings from other sources, altered very slightly … and put to serve a meaning wholly new'.[8] In Chapter 16 alone, for example, Gower uses lines from Ovid's *Ars Amatoria*, *Ex Ponto*, *Fasti*, *Heroides*, *Remedia Amoris*, and *Tristia* – and from nine out of the fifteen books making up the *Metamorphoses* (two, three, four, seven, eight, nine, thirteen, fourteen, and fifteen). I begin my discussion of *cento* in the *Visio*

[8] R. F. Yeager, 'Did Gower Write *Cento*?' in *John Gower: Recent Readings*, ed. R. F. Yeager, pp. 113–32, p. 119.

just prior to a crucial turning point in Chapter 16, when the narrative shifts from allegory to first-person dream vision. Once Gower has finished his animal allegory, compared London to Troy, narrated various rebel atrocities and indicted Wat Tyler, he turns back to the suffering Boethian self introduced in the Prologue. This narrative shift is coupled with intensified borrowings from Ovid, so much so that a counter-narrative of attachment emerges that suggests poetic alternatives to the harsh prophetic mode of discourse with which Gower has represented the catastrophe of the Rising. These alternatives are not always utopian – though sometimes they paint an idealized picture – but they do always produce a tension between the supposedly 'real' events of history and the fantastical imaginary worlds created by Ovid. As I will argue, the *Visio* sheds new light on Gower's understanding of the place of poetry in the world as he seeks out workable models for his own socio-poetic practice. In particular, he gestures to the figure of Arion toward the end of the text, presaging his embrace of an Arionic voice in the *Confessio Amantis.* Coupled with the optimism that Arion produces, however, is Gower's recognition that his own quest for a transformative poetic voice – one that can effect changes in both history and individuals – shares crucial characteristics with the peasant voices he condemns: an interest in autonomy and intimacy with power. In the *Visio*, these characteristics are summoned into being by the Ovidian allusions that constantly murmur underneath the surface of the main text, and it is that murmuring counter-text that structures my reading here.

Beasts and human beings: Ovidian anti-allegory

As readers have long recognized, Gower dehumanizes the rebels of 1381, imagining them as animals incapable of speech, driven by base desires to produce a 'clangor':[9]

> Sepius exclamant monstrorum vocibus altis,
>   Atque modis variis dant variare tonos ...
> Ecce rudis clangor, sonus altus, fedaque rixa,
>   Vox ita terribilis non fuit ulla prius. (I:797–98, 815–16)
>
> [Time and time again they cried out with the deep voices of monsters and they kept making various noises in various ways ... Behold the loud din, the deep roar, the savage brawling – no sound was ever so terrible before.]

[9] A critic whose work is representative of the position that Gower is motivated by class privilege and hostility toward the peasants is David Aers, who has written a number of articles on the *Vox Clamantis*: see '*Vox populi* and the Literature of 1381', in *The Cambridge History of Middle English Literature*, ed. David Wallace (Cambridge: Cambridge University Press, 1999), pp. 432–53; 'Reflections on Gower as *Sapiens* in Ethics and Politics', in *Re-Visioning Gower*, ed. R. F. Yeager (Asheville, NC: Pegasus Press, 1998), pp. 185–201; 'Representations of the "Third Estate": Social Conflict and its Milieu around 1381', *Southern Review* 16 (1983), 335–49.

He sums up his view of the rebels in an apostrophe: 'O furor insane, gens rustica, plebs violenta' [O mad folly, boorish race, violent people] (I:1133). But the values that the *Vox* assumes – that peasants deserve their lot, that nobles were wronged in the Rising, that justice must be done – are altered and shifted, made to seem amorphous and troubled by the allusions to Ovid found throughout the *Visio*, which frequently function as challenging undercurrents to its surface narrative, an alternate universe beneath the surface of the rhetoric. It should come as no surprise that this undercurrent becomes more prominent as Gower shifts gears and begins to move toward the personal complaint of Chapter 16 and beyond. As he describes the laments of the nobility, Gower links their fear to Ovid's account of Pythagoras in *Metamorphoses* XV:

> 'Fer, precor,' inquit, 'opem, nostroque medere timori
>   Egraque sors abeat, o deus!' omnis ait.
> Rusticus ingenuis, 'Stat magna potencia nobis,'
>   Dixerat, 'et vester ammodo cesset honor.'
> *O genus attonitum gelide formidine mortis,*
>   Quam variata tibi sors dedit ista mali!
> Est in thesauris abscondita causa supremis,
>   Cur ruit ingenuos tanta procella viros. (I:1289–96; emphasis added)
>
> [Every man said, 'O God, give us help, I pray, and relieve our fear, and let our wretched fortune now depart.' The peasant said to the nobles, 'We have great power, and from this time on there will be an end of respect for you.' *O people stunned by the fear of chill death*, how fickle a fate placed such evil things upon you! There is a reason hidden in the vaults above as to why such a great storm overwhelmed the nobles.]

This passage relies on the speech of Pythagoras near the end of the *Metamorphoses*, specifically on Ovid's line, 'O genus attonitum gelidae formidine mortis' [O race of men, stunned with the fear of chill death] (XV:153). In this speech, Pythagoras propounds his theory of mutability and metempsychosis, the idea that souls merely move from body to body rather than dying. 'Variata sors' is every man's condition, in Pythagoras's system; he conceives of transformation as consolation for death, a way of continuing life beyond the loss of the body. His vision of the world celebrates life in all of its forms, animal and human, and provides a counter to Gower's stark division between beasts and men. For example, just prior to the doctrine of metempsychosis, we find a long discussion of vegetarianism, in which Pythagoras condemns the practice of animal sacrifice:

> Longius inde nefas abiit, et prima putatur
> hostia sus meruisse mori quia semina pando
> eruerit rostro spemque interceperit anni;
> vite caper morsa Bacchi mactandus ad aras
> ducitur ultoris: nocuit sua culpa duobus!

quid meruistis oves, placidum pecus inque tuendos
natum homines, pleno quae fertis in ubere nectar,
mollia quae nobis vestras velamina lanas
praebetis vitaque magis quam morte iuvatis?
quid meruere boves, animal sine fraude dolisque,
innocuum, simplex, natum tolerare labores?
(*Metamorphoses* XV:111–121)

[Further impiety grew out of that, and it is thought that the sow was first condemned to death as a sacrifical victim because with her broad snout she had rooted up the planted seeds and cut off the season's promised crop. The goat is held fit for sacrifice at the avenging altars because he had browsed the grape-vines. These two suffered because of their own offences! But, ye sheep, what did you ever do to merit death, a peaceful flock, born for man's service, who bring us sweet milk to drink in your full udders, who give us your wool for soft clothing, and who help more by your life than by your death? What have the oxen done, those faithful, guileless beasts, harmless and simple, born to a life of toil?]

This list of innocent farmyard animals – the sow, the goat, the sheep, the oxen – inevitably recalls Gower's beast allegory, in which the servants of nobles are transformed into the servants of men, beasts 'in tuendos natum homines', born for men's service.[10] It is a list that creates an inverted mirror of the *Visio*, hinged upon the *cento* that connects Chapter 15 of Gower's work to Book 15 of Ovid's *Metamorphoses*: 'O genus attonitum gelide formidine mortis' (*Vox* I:1293; *Metamorphoses* XV:153) [O people stunned by the fear of chill death]. Indeed, Gower himself returns to beasts in the very next lines of Chapter 15, describing how 'Vidi nam catulos minimos agitare leonem,/ Nec loca tuta sibi tunc leopardus habet:/ Aspera grex ovium pastori cornua tendunt' [I saw the smallest whelps frighten the lion, and the leopard found no quarters safe for him then. The flock of sheep pointed its sharp horns at the shepherd] (I:1301–1303). The tension between Gower's representation of domestic beasts who attack their masters (or weak beasts who attack stronger beasts), and the Pythagorean vision of beasts being exploited and tormented by human beings captures in miniature the relationship Gower constructs between his text and its Ovidian intertext; repeatedly, the surface meaning of the *Visio* is countered by an alternative, often more utopian, image of social relations. These alternative images testify to the transformative power of Gower's poetics of attachment, demonstrating that poetry itself has the capacity to remake the world in a positive way. It is the sharing of qualia that enables such transformation.[11]

10 Although the sow and the goat are 'guilty', their crimes consist only of behaving like animals, eating seeds and grapes; they could not have understood prohibitions against eating certain kinds of food, and thus their punishments are out of proportion to their crimes.

11 The idea that Gower promotes poetry as an agent of change in the world illustrates an important difference between his understanding of subjective and qualitative experience and that of

Shortly after his allusion to Pythagoras, in Chapter 16, Gower foregrounds the figure of the narrator, who indulges in first-person Boethian complaint and engages with Wisdom in a Boethian dialogue. It begins with Wisdom's exhortation to patience:

> 'Siste, precor, lacrimas et pacienter age.
> Sic tibi fata volunt non crimina, crede set illud
> Quo deus offensus te reparando vocat.
> Non merito penam pateris set numinis iram:
> Ne timeas, finem nam dolor omnis habet.'
> Talibus exemplis aliis quoque rebus vt essem
> Absque metu paciens sepe Sophia monet;
> Conscia mensque michi fuerat, culpe licet expers,
> Spes tamen ambigue nulla salutis adest.
> *Non fuerant artes tanti que numinis iram*
> A me tollentes tempora leta ferunt. (I:1546–56)
>
> ['Cease your tears, I pray, and be patient. The fates, not your crimes, will matter thus for you. But believe that this is the means by which an offended God calls on you to make reparation. You are not suffering this torment as due punishment, you are suffering the wrath of heaven. Do not be afraid, for every sorrow has an end.' Through such precepts and through other means Wisdom warned me repeatedly that I should be patient without fear. But granted that I was free from personal blame, my mind was uneasy – although it was free from guilt, yet there was no hope of a precarious safety. *There were no means of removing the wrath of such a mighty God* from me and bringing back happy times.]

This passage is punctuated by lines from Ovid's *Fasti* and his *Metamorphoses* that put intense pressure on the poetic choices that have led the narrator to the point of breakdown, and thus to the dialogue with Wisdom.[12] I will focus here on the line Gower appropriates from the *Metamorphoses*, 'Non fuerant artes tanti que numinis iram' [There were no means of removing the wrath of such a mighty God] (I:1555), which forges a connection between the beast allegory in the earlier portion of the *Visio* and the inward-turning discourse of Chapters 16–21, and thus resists the split in the narrative – and the narrator – that appears when Wisdom is introduced.

In *Metamorphoses* II, this line refers to Ocyroe, daughter of the Centaur, who has exploited the gift of prophecy in order to tell the future of her father and his foster child. Having done so, she immediately regrets her action and

contemporary philosophers of mind: as Jackson's definition of qualia (cited above) illustrates, these qualities are thought by many scholars to have no effect on the physical world and to be essentially impossible to share between persons.

12 The references to the *Fasti* include: *Vox* I:1546, from *Fasti* I:479–480; *Vox* I:1549, from *Fasti* I.483; *Vox* I:1548, from *Fasti* I.482; *Vox* I:1553–54, from *Fasti* I:485. See Ovid, *Fasti*, trans. James G. Frazer and revised by G. P. Goold (Cambridge, MA: Harvard University Press, 1996). Subsequent references to the *Fasti* will be in the text by book and line number.

cries out, 'Non fuerant artes tanti quae numinis iram/ contraxere mihi' [Not worth the cost were those arts which have brought down the wrath of heaven upon me] (II:659). Ocyroe's transgression is prophecy – a crime that resonates strikingly with Gower's initial insistence that the *Visio* is a prophetic text.[13] His very first line reads: 'Scripture veteris capiunt exempla futuri' [Writings of the past contain fit examples for the future] (I:1); further, Daniel and Joseph are cited as models, 'Ex Daniele patet quid sompnia significarunt,/ Nec fuit in sompnis visio vana Ioseph' [What dreams have meant is clear from Daniel, and Joseph's vision in his sleep was not meaningless] (I:7–8). Readers are asked to imagine both that the narrator is being given a vision of the future (though they know the events have already happened) and that this prophecy is designed to prevent such future happenings. But as Ocyroe's punishment reveals, prophecy is a serious business, one that can seem to the gods like transgression, like an attempt to usurp the prerogatives of divinity. Ocyroe's cry, then, her lament about the 'numinis iram' [wrath of the gods] has dark implications for prophets, and indeed, dark implications for Gower himself. This sense of foreboding is reinforced in the very next lines in *Metamorphoses* II, when Ocyroe's punishment is revealed:

> 'iam mihi subduci facies humana videtur,
> iam cibus herba placet, iam latis currere campis
> impetus est: in equam cognataque corpora vertor.
> tota tamen quare? pater est mihi nempe biformis.'
> talia dicenti pars est extrema querellae
> intellecta parum confusaque verba fuerunt;
> mox nec verba quidem nec equae sonus ille videtur
> sed simulantis equam, parvoque in tempore certos
> edidit hinnitus et bracchia movit in herbas.
> tum digiti coeunt et quinos alligat ungues
> perpetuo cornu levis ungula, crescit et oris
> et colli spatium, longae pars maxima pallae
> cauda fit, utque vagi crines per colla iacebant,
> in dextras abiere iubas, pariterque novata est
> et vox et facies; nomen quoque monstra dedere.
> (*Metamorphoses* II:661–75)

> ['Now my human shape seems to be passing. Now grass pleases as food; now I am eager to race around the broad pastures. I am turning into a mare, my kindred shape. But why completely? Surely my father is half human?' Even while she spoke, the last part of her complaint became scarce understood and her words were all confused. Soon they seemed neither words nor yet the sound of a mare, but as of one trying to imitate a

[13] For an important discussion of the role of prophecy in Gower's work, see Russell Peck, 'John Gower and the Book of Daniel', in *John Gower: Recent Readings*, ed. R. F. Yeager (Kalamazoo, MI: Medieval Institute Publications, 1989), p. 167.

> mare. At last she clearly whinnied and her arms became legs and moved along the ground. Her fingers drew together and one continuous light hoof of horn bound together the five nails of her hand. Her mouth enlarged, her neck was extended, the train of her gown became a tail; and her locks as they lay roaming over her neck were become a mane on the right side. Now was she changed alike in voice and feature; and this new wonder gave her a new name as well].

Ocyroe is transformed into a mare – changed, that is, into a barnyard animal, much as Gower transformed English peasants into asses, oxen, swine, dogs, cats, foxes, domestic birds and owls, flies and frogs. And just as the peasants' sinfulness lay in their desire to exceed their stations, to turn the world upside down and to live as lords, so too Ocyroe transgressed by acting like a god in disclosing the secrets of the future. What, then, of Gower himself? Our narrator has gone to great lengths to establish himself as a prophetic figure, a 'vox clamantis in deserto'; here, when he finds himself at his lowest ebb, he uses the words of Ocyroe to describe his plight to Wisdom, 'Non fuerant artes tanti qui numinis iram/ A me tollentes tempora leta ferunt' [There were no means of removing the wrath of such a mighty God from me and bringing back happy times]. It is no coincidence that the meaning of 'artes' is the signification on which Gower's alteration ultimately rests: in Ovid, 'artes' means 'arts of foreknowledge', while for Gower, the word means 'arts of removing the wrath of God'. Gower's 'artes' clearly are designed to recall Ocyroe's 'artes'; together with the allusion to Pythagoras, the story of Ocyroe suggests that the dream of the peasants-as-animals is potentially reflexive: the narrator, as a type of Ocyroe, can be transformed into an animal for his presumption in prophesying. Coupled with Pythagoras's oration, in which beasts are imagined as victims of human cruelty, the allusion to Ocyroe fundamentally alters Gower's beast allegory by invoking a world in which its central division between the animal and the human becomes fragile, subject to transformation and change. Pythagoras's utopia, in which beasts are recognized as creatures of nature akin to humans, is based on his doctrine of change and mutability, of fertility and fecundity, of the cycle of life and death. It dissolves the rigid hierarchies that Gower invokes when he aligns peasants with beasts and nobles with their masters. Paradoxically, Gower also negates the distinction between animals and human beings when he labels the rebels vicious beasts – but he does so as a way of redefining the human as 'non-rebellious subjects and nobles', thus reinforcing social hierarchy by excluding rebellious peasants from humanity itself.

The sheer boldness of this redefinition is perhaps what lies behind the anxiety aroused by Ocyroe; only God should have the power to define the human, and Gower's appropriation of that power through the *Visio*'s 'prophecy' of past events inevitably resembles Ocyroe's transgression. Indeed, her punishment literalizes Gower's allegorical metamorphosis of peasants into beasts: the power of the gods physically transforms a human being into an actual mare. Pythagoras reminds Gower of the responsibilities of the powerful to the disempowered; he insists that beasts do not deserve human cruelty and that animals and humans together take part in the cycle of life and death. Ocyroe's example suggests that poetry can transgress, can – by using its transformative capacity – unwisely rival the power of gods to make and unmake the world. Both of these references to Ovid put strain on the surface of Gower's *Visio*, exerting a powerful undertow that draws the reader – and Gower himself – away from the hierarchies and the violence of history, and forces a confrontation between the persona of the narrator-as-victim and his own culpability. This powerful force operates in both negative and positive guises: negatively, by showing Gower his own transgression and his own potential animality, and positively, by imagining a world in which the cycle of life and death proceeds naturally and peacefully – a world of change, but a world of delight in transformation and harmony amid variation. The potential for poetry to mimic this latter world – not merely to represent it, but also to enact its transformative capacity – is a potential that derives from the perforated text of the *Visio*, which opens onto and thus shares Ovid's vivid renderings of the subjective and qualitative experience of Pythagoras and Ocyroe. The sufferings of the sow and the goat; the sweetness of sheep's milk, the fullness of their udders, the softness of their wool, the faithfulness of the oxen, combined with Ocyroe's newfound taste for grass and her desire to race around the pastures, the sound of her partial whinnies and the feeling in her arms as they become legs and move along the ground: these are all forms of experience in which Ovid invites readers to participate. When Gower appropriates lines from Ovid, he also imports that notion of participation, so that the *Visio* shares in the sensory experiences realized by the *Metamorphoses*. Poetry becomes, at moments like these, an aesthetic practice neatly opposed to prophecy, one based on attachment and participation rather than on an authority that enforces order from above. At the same time, it is important to recognize that Gower, like his friend Chaucer, is never content with binary distinctions between good and evil or positive and negative; prophecy is never entirely detached, nor is participation an unalloyed good; after all, the violence of the peasants came about as a result of shared passion. It is clear, however, that Gower's hopeful vision of a world based on love requires the poetics of attachment and participation that he finds embedded in the poetry of Ovid – particularly, as I will show in the next section, in the figure of Arion, the harper who creates peace through song.

Arion and the poetics of harmony

The plot of the remainder of Book 1 is simple. The narrator climbs aboard a ship filled with nobles, and immediately finds himself in the midst of a terrible storm. He spends over a hundred lines describing the storm, many of which are drawn from *Metamorphoses* XI and its description of the bad weather that killed Ceyx in the story of Ceyx and Alcione, and makes the allegorical link between the Tower of London and the fictional ship explicit. Throughout the storm, the narrator and the nobles frantically pray to God for relief from the gales and gusts; at last the 'graculus' or 'Jay' – Wat Tyler, the rebel leader – is killed, and with this sacrifice God is appeased (though the narrator professes uncertainty about the causal link between Tyler's execution and the calming of the storm). A celestial voice speaks and proclaims 'Adhuc modicum restat michi tempus, et ecce/ Differo iudicium cum pietate meum' [Now the time is fitting for me, and behold, I proclaim my judgment with mercy] (I:1891–92). The narrator floats aboard the rudderless, storm-damaged ship until he comes to shore on the Island of Brut and is devastated to learn that he has arrived at a contentious and war-torn land. The same celestial voice intervenes and tells him not to waste time feeling sorrow, but rather to write down everything he has seen in his dream. The narrator concludes by announcing that the peasants are once again in chains, and by vowing to record the events of the dream so that 'every man of the future will find a moral' [in quibus exemplum quisque futurus habet!] (I:2144).

As this plot unfolds, long passages are devoted to the narrator's laments, thoughts, and messages from God. In this section, I focus on a key passage in the *Visio* in which the narrator's identity is linked to Gower's role as a poet, and in which an allusion to Ovid offers shared experience as a counter to the prophetic voice that dominates the beast allegory. The allusion appears in Gower's description of the narrator's thoughts during the storm that afflicted the ship of London:

> Nimirum quod ego, dum talia ferre putabam,
>   Territus in sompnis et timefactus eram:
> Ductus in ambiguis dixi quam sepe periclis,
>   *Quod michi naue mea tucius equor erat* ...   (*Vox* I:1771–74)
>
> [There was no doubt that I was terrified and alarmed in my dreams, as I thought that I suffered such things. Led so often into uncertain dangers, I declared *that the sea was safer for me than my ship.*]

The final line in this passage is taken from Ovid's *Fasti*: 'at tibi nave tua tutius aequor erat' [But the sea, in truth, was safer for you than your ship] (II: 98). Ovid's line comes from his calendar of Roman festivals, in which he uses the second person briefly to address one of the honorees: Arion, who sings and plays music. In this story, Arion escapes from a ship of enemies by leaping on the back of a dolphin, paying for his passage by playing his lyre. Ovid's remark that 'The sea was safer than your ship' reveals the intimacy of Arion's relationship to the natural world, to which he is linked by his singing and playing, skills that cross the boundary between the human and the animal to create a currency acceptable to both. When Gower appropriates Ovid's address to Arion and shapes it to fit himself, he takes up both roles: like Ovid, he comments on the safety of the sea; like Arion, he 'sings and plays' by composing verse. This echo of Arion in the *Visio* presages Gower's adoption of the Ovidian figure as his central symbol of the poet's role in relation to the world in the *Confessio Amantis*, where Arion appears as an exemplar of poetry's power to create harmony and peace. In the *Visio*, Gower's narrator is provoked by the uncertainty and danger of events – the storm at sea, or the Rising – to claim that, like Arion, he will be safer in the sea. There is a crucial difference between Arion and the narrator, however. Arion found himself on a ship filled with enemies; Gower's narrator is on a ship with other refugees from the violence of the peasants, presumably members of his own class, all of whom are under attack. This difference strongly suggests that what Gower found imitable in Arion's predicament aboard ship was the idea of a separation between the poet and his community, a poetic space disengaged from the social group from which he can 'sing and play' and produce peace for all.[14] What stands in his way, at this point in the *Visio*, is his own profound sense of guilt – a culpability that can only be addressed by forging an Arionic poetics capable of transforming the violence of 1381 into stability and peace. Rather than addressing social classes or groups, however, this poetics will offer to readers a participatory relationship, one in which the poet's experience is shared in order to create points of connection between the narratorial 'I' and individual readers. The qualia of individual experience become an experience of mutuality that creates community even as it enables self-reflection and self-discovery. The poetics of Arion thus turns away from the detached voice of authority that excoriated the rebels and affirmed social hierarchies, in order to embrace forms of attachment: peace, harmony, community, love. That is not to say that Gower abandons authority or social order, but rather that he turns from the imperative to the interrogative voice – from the tyrannical voice that transformed peasants into beasts to the questioning voice that faces its own culpability – out of dissatisfaction with the capacity of the former to represent fully the complexities of the self and the world.

It would be difficult to over-emphasize the importance of Arion for Gower's poetics, though the figure is usually associated with the *Confessio Amantis*.[15] Several critics have written extensively about Arion, including R. F. Yeager, Ann Astell, and Frank Grady, each of whom describes how Gower

14 Gower will elaborate this poetic role – as insider and outsider – throughout the *Confessio Amantis*; as John Ganim has noted, 'An insider both born and made, he assumes a position of outsider – just barely outside – in his own 'lond'. See John Ganim, 'Gower, Liminality, and the Politics of Space', *Exemplaria* 19 (2007), 90–116, p. 113. Eve Salisbury makes a similar point in 'Remembering Origins', noting that portraits of the poet as an archer in two of the manuscripts of the *Vox* (British Library, Cotton Tiberius MS A.iv and Oxford, Bodleian Library MS Laud 719) show Gower assuming 'a marginal stance in relation to the three estates; he stands outside the world in a proximate position' (p. 176).

15 Frank Grady notes the link between the *Vox* and the *Fasti* at the end of Book One in his 'Gower's Boat, Richard's Barge, and the True Story of the *Confessio Amantis*: Text and Gloss', *Texas Studies in Literature and Language* 44 (2002), 1–15, p. 14, n. 22.

came to invoke Arion as an image of the peacemaking poet and as an alternative to the prophetic 'vox clamantis in deserto' of the *Vox*.[16] Russell Peck has suggested that when Arion appears at the end of the Prologue to the *Confessio*, the image is deliberately set against Nebuchadnezzar's dream from Daniel as a way of countering degeneration with regeneration, the notion of the world's gradual collapse with an ideal of worldly creativity.[17] Thus, we find the prophetic voice of the *Vox* being supplanted by a new voice of harmony and unity – a voice associated by most critics with the vernacularity of the *Confessio* and with Gower's attempt to forge an English poetic mode of social commentary and peacemaking. Finding an echo of the Arion story in the *Visio* runs counter to all expectations, given Gower's strongly articulated prophetic voice and his seemingly brutal satire of current events. But Gower is deeply ambivalent about the prophetic voice in the *Visio*, an ambivalence hidden beneath the surface of the text in his allusions to figures like Ocyroe, transformed into a beast for daring to prophesy. In particular, near the end of the poem he subtly gestures toward the power of song to create peace and order – countering apocalyptic, terrifying pronouncements with creative and pleasurable playing and singing.

This allusion to Arion assumes significance as a back-formation from the *Confessio Amantis*, the poem in which Gower calls on Arion as the ideal exemplar of a new poetics.[18] In this model, poetry becomes a social and aesthetic practice that produces unity, cohesion, harmony, and love. It is a model that explicitly diverges from the poetics found in the *Vox Clamantis*:

> Bot wolde God that now were on
> An other such as Arion,
> Which hadde an harpe of such temprure,

16 R. F. Yeager, *John Gower's Poetic: The Search for a New Arion*, Publications of the John Gower Society II (Cambridge: D. S. Brewer, 1990); Ann Astell, *Political Allegory in Late Medieval England* (Ithaca: Cornell University Press, 1999). Yeager argues that Arion was a figure of the poet as peacemaker for Gower, a figure that would bring 'harmony inclusive and cosmic' in a poetry 'capable, like Arion's harping, of reinstating a near Edenic innocence and goodwill in a world striated both naturally and socially' (p. 244). Astell argues that Gower uses the story from Ovid's *Fasti* to allegorize the poet's relationship with Richard II (p. 81).

17 Russell Peck, *Kingship and Common Profit in Gower's 'Confessio Amantis'* (Carbondale and Edwardsville: Southern Illinois University Press, 1978), p. 22.

18 Scholars are largely agreed that the *Confessio Amantis* postdates the *Visio* (and the *Vox Clamantis* as a whole) by a number of years. Macaulay discusses the dating of the *Vox* in the preface to his edition (*Gower: the Latin Works*, pp. xxx–xxxii), coming to the conclusion that it was finished shortly after the Rising of 1381. His account of the dating of the *Confessio Amantis* appears in the preface to *The Complete Works of John Gower: the English Works*, vols. 2 and 3 (Oxford: Clarendon Press, 1901), vol. 2, pp. xxi–xxviii, and concludes that the first recension of the poem was finished in 1390. I have quoted the *Confessio Amantis* from this edition, and cite it in the text by book and line numbers. A very useful summary of the scholarly consensus regarding the dating of Gower's works can be found in the introduction to *John Gower, Confessio Amantis*, vol. 1, ed. Russell Peck with Latin translations by Andrew Galloway (Kalamazoo: Medieval Institute Publications, 2000; 2nd edition, 2006), which concludes with a 'Chronology of Gower's Life and Works', p. 38.

And therto of so good mesure
He song, that he the bestes wilde
Made of his note tame and milde,
The hind in pes with the leoun,
The wolf in pes with the moltoun,
The hare in pees stod with the hound;
And every man upon this ground
Which Arion that time herde,
Als wel the lord as the schepherde,
He broghte hem alle in good acord;
So that the comun with the lord,
And lord with the comun also,
He sette in love both tuo
And putte awey malencolie.
That was a lusti melodie,
Whan every man with other low; (*Confessio Amantis*, Prol., 1053–71)

No reader of the *Visio* can mistake Gower's reference here. He is turning away from the political poetry of the *Vox*, with its satirical and critical voice, and seeking a new Arionic poetics of harmony and love. In direct contrast to the *Visio*'s warring and rebellious creatures, he imagines animals at peace: in the *Vox*, the 'minim[i] catul[i]' agitate the lion and the sheep point their horns at their shepherds ('Aspera grex ovium pastori cornua tendunt') (I:1301, 1303), while in the *Confessio* he describes 'The hind in pes with the leoun/ The wolf in pes with the moltoun' (Prol., 1059–60). In the *Vox*, lords and commons are engaged in combat to the death, but in Arion's world they exist in 'good acord' – a far different scenario from the resolution of the *Visio*, in which the peasants are bound in chains ('Sic cum rusticitas fuerat religata cathenis') (I:2093) but lurk, hoping for a chance to destroy the aristocracy ('Semper ad interitum nam rusticus insidiatur,/ Si genus ingenuum subdere forte queat') (I:2099–2100).

A crucial question remains about this back-formation I am labeling an 'Arionic' poetics and the extent to which Gower can be understood in the *Visio* to be groping his way toward a poetry that heals divisions without enslaving those who challenge the established order. The Prologue to the *Confessio* would seem to suggest that the harmony created by Arion's song includes the entire social and animal world, beasts, commons, and lords. Earlier I suggested that Gower alluded to Ovid's Pythagorean vision of a world driven by change and mutability, fertility and fecundity, as a way of articulating an alternative to the nightmarish world of rebellion and counter-rebellion he describes. Arion functions in much the same way. Gower's allusion opens up the another possibility for forging attachments to the world and in the world, both politically and individually, through love of others and a commitment to peace. At the same time, however, as the Ocyroe episode shows, Ovidian allusion can carry with it dark intimations of danger. It is not a coincidence that the figure of Ocyroe is drawn from the *Metamorphoses*; metamorphosis is itself a double-edged sword, sometimes leading to freedom (for Philomela, for example) and sometimes to tragedy (for Actaeon, transformed into a stag and eaten by his own dogs). What Gower sought in Ovid, that is, was not only a 'private, passionate realm' (to use James Simpson's words), but also a realm in which the authority of prophecy could be made open to experience, a realm of flexible signification that could free the 'I' – the first-person – from the constraints of the forms that comprise the *Visio*: the Boethian complaint and the beast allegory.[19] Once that 'I' emerges from behind the prophetic scrim that characterizes the early parts of the *Visio*, it is free to move on to the *Confessio Amantis* and to the complex consideration of human motivation and desire that characterizes the later text.

When the *Visio* comes to an end, Gower reaches an impasse. He must describe the end of the Rising, maintain the dream vision fiction, and praise God, while also gesturing toward the new kind of writing that his Ovidian allusions have evoked. He manages these tasks by turning to a standard trope of the dream vision: it appears that his narrator awakens and proposes to write down the visions he has seen:

> Set quia tunc variis tumidis iactabar in undis,
>   Que mea mens hausit, iam resoluta vomet.
> Me licet unda maris rapuit, mea numina laudo,
>   *Fluctibus ingenium non cecidisse meum.*
> Dum mea mens memor est, scribens memoranda notabit,
>   In specie sompni que vigilando quasi
> Concepi pavidus, nec dum tamen inde quietus
>   Persto, set absconso singula corde fero.
> *Non dedimus sompno quas sompnus postulat horas,*
>   Tale licet sompnis fingo videre malum.
> O vigiles sompni, per quos michi visio nulla
>   Sompniferi generis set vigilantis erat!
> O vigiles sompni, qui sompnia vera tulistis,
>   In quibus exemplum quisque futurus habet!
> O vigiles sompni, quorum sentencia scriptis
>   Ammodo difficilis est recitanda meis!
> Ut michi vox alias que vidi scribere iussit,
>   Amplius ex toto corde vacare volo:
> Quod solet esse michi vetus hoc opus ammodo cedat,
>   Sit prior et *cura cura* repulsa nova. (*Vox* I:2131–50; emphasis added)

[But since I was tossed this way and that on the billowing waves, my mind, now resolute, will utter what it drank in. Although the ocean's billow seized me, I praised God *that my spirit did not succumb to the floods.* While my mind remembers them, I will note down in writing, in the form of a

[19] James Simpson, *Sciences and the Self in Medieval Poetry: Alan of Lille's 'Anticlaudianus' & John Gower's 'Confessio Amantis'* (Cambridge: Cambridge University Press, 1995), p. 289.

dream, the memorable things which I perceived with fear when I was awake. For because of them I am not yet at peace, but suffer them all secretly in my heart. *In this dream I did not give to sleep the hours which sleep requires*, although I do imagine seeing this calamity in my dreams. O wakeful sleep, in which I had a vision not of a sleep-inducing nature, but a watchful one! O wakeful sleep, you which brought on real dreams in which every man of the future will find a moral! O wakeful sleep, whose difficult meaning my writings must now tell! Because a voice ordered me to write the things I saw at other times, I wish with all my heart to be free to devote myself (to this). Let the task of long standing which is wontedly mine now yield, and let my former care be banished by this new one.]

On the most literal level, it is difficult to understand the meaning of these lines. It is not clear if the narrator experienced a dream or a waking vision; it is hard to tell what the 'former care' or the 'task of long standing' might be; it is unclear whether the narrator is within or outside the dream while uttering these lines. There are two possible clues to unraveling the mystery of Gower's conclusion; two of the lines in the passage above are from Ovid's *Tristia* and *Ex Ponto*, and their context sheds some light on the meaning of these last lines:

Ipse ego nunc miror tantis animique marisque
Fluctibus ingenium non cecidisse meum.
Seu stupor huic studio siue est insania nomen,
Omnis ab hac cura cura leuata mea est. (*Tristia* I.xi.9–12)

[I marvel myself my skill didn't fail me
In such a turmoil of seas and feelings,
Whether numbness or madness is the name for such efforts,
All my troubles were eased by these troubles.]

Cum dedimus somno quas corpus postulat horas,
Quo ponam uigilans tempora longa modo? (*Ex Ponto* I.v.47–48)

[When I've granted the time my body needs for sleep
How should I spend the long hours of wakefulness?]

In both of these passages, Ovid is describing the problem of writing while in exile; in the first case, he is recounting his attempts to write while on a ship, traveling to Tomis, while in the second, he is explaining why he writes while in a barbarian land. This kind of writing is far removed from the *Amores* or *Remedia Amoris*; writing has become essential to survival even though it is fundamentally useless. As he states in *Ex Ponto* I.v, 'Cum bene quaesieris quid agam, magis utile nil est/ artibus his quae nil utilitatis habent' [When you've thought deeply about what I should do,/ you'll find nothing more useful than this useless art] (lines 53–54). Ovid's art has become useful *for itself*; as he explains in the *Tristia*, 'Omnis ab hac cura cura leuata mea est' [All my troubles were eased by these troubles] (I.x.12). Poetry here functions as relief from care in a bitter and hostile world – and it is this formulation, with its repetition of 'care' ('cura cura') that Gower imports into the final line of the *Visio*, 'Sit prior et *cura cura* repulsa nova'. With this reference to the *Tristia*, the ultimate meaning of Gower's final verses begins to emerge. Ovid means that the 'care' of being on a ship in fear is banished by the 'care' he takes with his verse. Gower argues that his 'former care' [prior cura] will be erased by his 'nova cura' – the production of the *Visio*, the new task of his narrator. But what is his 'prior cura'? Temporally, of course, these lines do not make sense: the text of the *Visio* is ending, even as the narrator proposes to write it in the future. One possibility is that Gower's 'prior cura' is simply the fearful Rising itself, which can be processed and tamed by the act of writing poetry; after all, though the peasants are in chains, Gower still imagines them wanting to overthrow their masters. Certainly, this vision of poetry as a kind of historical curative has a long tradition; Ovid himself views his verse in this way in the passages above. But it is also the case that Gower had finished Books 2–7 of the *Vox* just prior to writing the *Visio*.[20] I would suggest that the 'prior cura' from which Gower seeks the 'ocia' [leisure] demanded by the celestial voice (I:2043), rendered here as 'vacare' [to have leisure; to be free to devote oneself to something] (I:2148), is both the trauma of the Rising and the 'cura' of constructing the *Vox*.[21] As an estates satire, Books 2–7 of the *Vox* are fundamentally structured by the kind of detached poetic mode with which Gower grapples in the *Visio*; the genre is designed to bring order to chaotic social conditions, both by imposing a system of hierarchy and by demanding that readers conform to a set of social prescriptions. When Gower refers to his 'prior cura', he is in part identifying his own use of the estates satire genre – and thus of the mode of detachment it requires – as a kind of care, a troublesome labor he wishes to leave behind.

As Gower comes to the end of writing the *Visio*, a work in which he has stretched the boundaries of Latin verse to their limits by constructing the perforated text I have described, he begins to look forward to a new kind of writing.[22] It is the poetics of Arion that he will turn to next, in the *Confessio Amantis*, a text in which he embraces the vernacular and eschews the prophetic. The formal structure of the *Visio*, with its Latin surface narrative overlaying a teeming, contradictory, passionate and fertile subtext from Ovid, is turned inside-out in the *Confessio*.[23] There, the complexity of the subtext is

20 See Macaulay, *Gower: Latin Works*, vol. 4, p. xxxi and note 1 above.

21 See Charlton T. Lewis and Charles Short, eds., *Latin Dictionary Founded on Andrew's Edition of Freund's Latin Dictionary* (Oxford: Oxford University Press, 1956), s.v. 'vaco', II.2.a.

22 Siân Echard discusses the relationship of Gower's Latin poetry, especially the *Vox Clamantis*, to his English poetry in very useful terms as an 'accumulation' rather than an 'evolution'. See her 'Gower's 'bokes of Latin': Language, Politics, and Poetry', *Studies in the Age of Chaucer* 25 (2003), 123–56, p. 156.

23 As John Ganim describes the shift from the *Vox* to the *Confessio*, 'Metaphors that carry a certain set of loaded political associations elsewhere in Gower, such as in the *Mirour de l'Omme* and the *Vox Clamantis*, are employed for personal, even passionately romantic purposes in the *Confessio Amantis*.' See 'Gower, Liminality, and the Politics of Space', p. 105.

brought to the surface and the resulting verse displays features like emotion, contradiction, and contingency in a strategically controlled framework, as a dialogue between Amans and Genius. This combination of order with disorder, detachment with attachment, lies at the heart of Gower's poetics. It is made manifest, for example, in the way that Gower frames the *Confessio* with Latin verses and glosses, creating a tension between Latin authority and vernacular plasticity. This poetics enables Gower to embrace the unpredictability of the vernacular, even as he constructs a text (the *Confessio*) designed to produce authoritative commentary on matters of love. By the time that the *Confessio* comes to an end, Gower has forged a workable discourse that combines the authority of public speech with the transformative capacity of vernacular poetry. The nexus he creates between the individual and the public, or the individual and history, is held together by the narration of individual lives: the self-disclosure of Amans, the 'cura' of the narrator in the *Visio*, the self-recognition of 'John Gower' at the end of the *Confessio Amantis*. Gower does not imagine that the self constitutes an inviolable entity set apart from the randomness of history and the brutality of politics. Rather, he sets out to produce a kind of art that depends on disclosure as a means of mortaring the bonds between individuals on which the social world depends.

Disclosure, in its verbal form in Middle English (*disclosen*), means 'to expose, reveal' and 'make known, show forth'; it comes from the French *desclore* and ultimately the Latin *disclaudere*, to open.[24] It is the opposite of closure, 'the act of closing or shutting; a bringing to a conclusion' – in other words, what readers might expect to find at the end of the *Visio*.[25] Instead, the poem ends with the ambiguous 'double care', seemingly poised between the detached poetics of the estates satire and the poetics of disclosure heralded by Arion. 'Disclosure' is the fully formed version of the poetics of attachment that I have described, in which qualia, or subjective experience, provide a means of creating shared participation in the world. It is inimical to closure – to shutting up, closing down, to reaching tidy conclusions and to the assertion of static hierarchies. In the *Visio*, Ovid functions as an emblem of such disclosure; Ovidian allusions open up the possibility of embracing transformation and change at the level of both personal history and the history of the realm. The *Confessio* is the work in which Gower most fully articulated those possibilities, and the self-disclosure appearing at its end, when Amans is revealed to be 'John Gower', is the central element of that new poetics. Retrospectively, then, it becomes clear that the *Visio* is perhaps the most experimental text that Gower wrote about poetry – the testing-ground for his theories about art – and it is no coincidence that Gower should forge his poetics in the crucible of rebellion and destruction. The Rising, too, is a kind of disclosure; it is a form of

24 *MED*, s.v. 'disclosen', 2; for the etymology, see the *OED*, s.v. 'disclose'.
25 *OED*, s.v. 'closure', 5a, 8a.

resistance to the closure embodied in social hierarchy and repression. It revealed possibilities; it exposed injustices; it opened closed doors and disclosed emblems of power within. Gower's poetics of disclosure is called into being by the demands of the peasants for self-determination; his narrator is created by the crisis the rebels brought about. Their demands were shocking – not least, Gower suggests, because self-determination was the obsession of clerks and poets. Gower understood that the threat of the Rising went far beyond the destruction of buildings and the burning of documents. He knew that the *clamor* of the peasants was hardly different from his own *clamans*, that he, like Ocyroe and the peasants, was vulnerable to being transformed into a beast for presumption.[26] In turning to self-disclosure as a means of negotiating the relationship between detachment and attachment, history and experience, Gower recognized that his attempt to forge a poetic voice capable of both individual transformation and social reform was a distant cousin of peasant claims to autonomy and freedom – and this realization, more than any other, constitutes the double care that still oppresses him at the *Visio*'s end.

26 Steven Justice makes this point in his *Writing and Rebellion: England in 1381* (Berkeley: University of California Press, 1994): 'the *clamans* of the poem's title resembles too much the *clamor* the animals make' (p. 216).

8

Preaching with the Hands: Carthusian Book Production and the *Speculum devotorum*[1]

Paul J. Patterson

When the University of Notre Dame purchased at auction a copy of the *Speculum devotorum*, or *Mirror to Devout People*, from the private collection of the Foyle family in 2000, they made available an invaluable record of the Carthusian/Syon axis of textual production and exchange. The manuscript contains three works: the *Speculum devotorum*, a fifteenth-century Middle English devotional work written for a sister at the Birgittine Syon Abbey by an anonymous Carthusian at Sheen; the *O Intemerata*, a Latin prayer to Mary and John the Evangelist; and the *Book of the Craft of Dying*, a Middle English work in the *ars moriendi* tradition. The sources used in the *Speculum* suggest a complex system of literary exchange between the Carthusians on the royal manor of Sheen and the Birgittines who resided across the River Thames. Further, an initial on the opening folio of the manuscript displays the impaled arms of two families, the Scropes and the Chaworths, which suggests that the distribution of texts between the Sheen Charterhouse and Syon Abbey extended beyond their cloistered walls to lay readers.

Jill Mann, having taken up an endowed chair at the University of Notre Dame in 1999, played an important role in acquiring the *Speculum* manuscript by encouraging the University to begin adding examples of Middle English

[1] I am grateful to Christopher Cannon, Vincent Gillespie, Graham Hammill, Jesse Lander, and Maura Nolan for their careful readings of earlier drafts. Shannon Gayk added invaluable comments near the completion of this chapter. Attendees at a University of Pennsylvania Medieval/Renaissance Seminar, for whom I presented this article, gave invaluable feedback. A Shallek Dissertation Award from the Medieval Academy of America and the Richard III Society of America along with a Zahm Travel Grant from the University of Notre Dame made possible much of the research presented here. I am most grateful to Jill Mann. Her careful attention to detail, patient reading of drafts, and rigorous criticism made her an ideal director and her genuine care for her students and colleagues makes her a cherished friend.

manuscripts to its already impressive medieval and early book collections. In 2001 an inaugural conference for Jill Mann and Michael Lapidge entitled 'Medieval Manuscripts at Notre Dame' was held, at which many of the papers addressed textual and cultural issues found in the newly acquired Notre Dame MS 67. Those essays that focussed on the *Speculum*, now collected in a volume edited by Jill Mann and Maura Nolan, argued for a reassessment of the role of Carthusians in the dissemination of devotional writing in fifteenth-century England.[2] This reconsideration of Carthusian interventions in vernacular writing revises our estimation of the number of texts written for a lay audience by Carthusian monks, while providing evidence for the significant role played by the brethren at Syon Abbey in distributing to the laity religious texts written by Carthusians for professional religious.

In his contribution to the edited volume, Vincent Gillespie argues that Carthusian devotional texts written in the years following the supremely confident *Mirror of the Blessed Life of Jesus Christ* (c. 1409 by the Carthusian Nicholas Love) reveal a diminishing confidence and heightened anxiety about reader access. Fifteenth-century Carthusian texts became more narrowly focussed on a clerical readership, rather than on the lay audience addressed by Love. Those texts that did become available outside religious circles primarily made their way into the hands of a select group of aristocratic and wealthy lay readers through the outward ministry of the Syon brethren, who were charged with preaching regularly to the laity. As a result, texts like the *Speculum devotorum* were written for the use of the Syon community by Carthusians, but possibly overseen by the Syon brethren. They were then made available to an exclusive circle of aristocratic lay readers through Syon.[3]

This movement from closed work to open exchange by way of Syon Abbey is a result of the close relationship between the two houses. From their inception, the Charterhouse of Jesus of Bethlehem at Sheen and the Abbey of Saint Saviour, BVM, and Saint Birgitta at Syon were considered a double foundation and a unified project.[4] The Sheen Charterhouse, founded in 1415, was located closest to the royal manor house on the Surrey bank of the River Thames, essentially placing it at the center of the nexus of religious houses located on the royal manor. Syon Abbey, a double monastery, was founded

2 The volume is *The Text in the Community: Essays on Medieval Works, Manuscripts, Authors, and Readers*, ed. Jill Mann and Maura Nolan (Notre Dame, IN: University of Notre Dame Press, 2006).

3 See Vincent Gillespie, 'The Haunted Text: Reflections in *A Mirror to Devout People*', in *The Text in the Community*, pp. 129–72. Gillespie reprinted this article in 2008 with some additional material as 'The Haunted Text: Reflections in *The Mirror to Deuout People*', in *Medieval Texts in Context*, ed. Graham D. Caie and Denis Renevey (New York: Routledge, 2008), pp. 136–66.

4 See Jeremy Catto, 'Religious Change under Henry V', in *Henry V: Practice of Kingship* (Oxford: Oxford University Press, 1986), p. 106 and see Neil Beckett, 'St. Bridget, Henry V, and Syon Abbey', in *Studies in St. Brigitta and the Brigittine Order*, ed. James Hogg, Analecta Cartusiana 35:19 (Salzburg: Institut für Anglistik und Amerikanistik; Lewiston, NY: Edwin Mellen Press, 1993), 2:126.

later in the spring of 1415, at a short distance from Sheen, at Twickenham, on the Middlesex bank.[5] Both the men and the women had separate libraries, though no record exists of the sisters' library.[6] Following Syon's move from Twickenham to Isleworth sometime in the early winter of 1431, the new abbey was located almost directly across the Thames from Sheen.

In this essay I argue that the close relationship between Syon and Sheen, particularly the writing of devotional works by Carthusians for the spiritual guidance of the sisters at Syon, initiated the production of a number of important Middle English devotional texts in the early fifteenth century. More than any other work originating within the Syon/Sheen textual nexus, the *Speculum devotorum* and the use of its sources reveal that the Carthusians, in their efforts to minister effectively to the sisters at Syon, were drawing on the resources of the Syon brethren's library and the broader networks of textual exchange in England. In the first section of this essay, I suggest that in addition to the resources at Syon Abbey, the Carthusians had available to them an established network of textual exchange that existed among the Charterhouses in England. These strands of book production and preservation reveal the complexity and devotion of the Carthusians' efforts to fulfill their founder's mandate to preach with their hands by writing, translating, copying, and preserving works of devotional literature.[7] The books produced at the Sheen Charterhouse suggest that the Carthusians took a major role in mentoring the sisters at Syon Abbey during the institutions' early years. This mentoring relationship indicates a close affiliation between the two houses that seems likely to have led to a sharing of resources. It is through the exchange of textual resources that the Carthusians were able to produce vernacular religious works for the female readers at Syon Abbey. In the final section of the essay, I examine the works of three female authors, Saint Birgitta of Sweden, Catherine of Siena, and Mechtild of Hackeborn, whom the *Speculum* author describes as 'approved

5 Syon Abbey was arranged as a double monastery, consisting of sixty nuns and twenty-five brethren, made up of twelve priests, four deacons and eight lay brethren, led by a confessor-general who had supremacy over the spiritualities of both houses but was otherwise subordinate to the abbess. The men were separated from the sisters, with the priests taking services, preaching sermons, and seeing to the sisters' devotional and educational needs, while the lay brothers were responsible for attending to the needs of the entire monastery. The standard account of Syon Abbey remains G. J. Aungier, *The History and Antiquities of Syon Monastery, the Parish of Isleworth and the Chapelry of Hounslow* (London: J. B. Nichols, 1840) as well as M. B. Tait, 'The Brigittine Monastery of Syon (Middlesex) with Special Reference to its Monastic Uses' (unpublished D.Phil. thesis, Oxford, 1975).

6 Christopher de Hamel, *Syon Abbey: The Library of the Bridgettine Nuns and their Peregrinations after the Reformation*, Roxburghe Club (Otley: Roxburghe Club, 1991). See also Vincent Gillespie, ed., *Syon Abbey*, Corpus of British Medieval Library Catalogues 9 (London: The British Library in association with The British Academy, 2001), which supersedes Mary Bateson, ed., *Catalogue of the Library of Syon Monastery, Isleworth* (Cambridge: Cambridge University Press, 1898). See also, David N. Bell, *What Nuns Read: Books and Libraries in Medieval English Nunneries* (Kalamazoo: Cistercian Publications, 1995).

7 See Jessica Brantley, *Reading in the Wilderness: Private Devotion and Public Performance in Late Medieval England* (Chicago: University of Chicago Press, 2007), pp. 48–49.

women', and discuss the role they play as major sources in the *Speculum devotorum*.[8] The works of the three female authors act as a guide for the female reader, thus creating a text directed to a female audience, while also providing the strongest evidence for the exchange of textual resources between Syon Abbey and the Carthusian monastery at Sheen.

Textual exchange between Syon and Sheen

The close proximity of Syon Abbey and the Sheen Charterhouse allowed for an exchange of books that benefited the libraries of both houses and made possible the creation of texts, such as the *Speculum devotorum*, which were designed to instruct and mentor the sisters at Syon Abbey. Surviving manuscripts point to the fact that the majority of the texts written and translated at the Sheen Charterhouse were for the sisters at Syon Abbey. In the first fifty years of Syon's foundation, the only substantial works that can be attributed to a Syon author are the *Myroure of Oure Ladye* and *The Orcherd of Syon*. Both the *Myroure* and the *Orcherd* are directed to the sisters at Syon and, as Vincent Gillespie points out, there are no texts in the brethren's library catalogue that are assigned Syon authorship.[9] There are, however, many works for the sisters at Syon that originated within the Sheen Charterhouse. William Darker (d. 1513), a well-known Sheen scribe, wrote one of the first English translations of the *Imitatio Christi* (Glasgow University Library, Hunter MS 136) for the abbess of Syon, Elizabeth Gibbs (1497–1518). Another manuscript (Cambridge University Library, MS Ff.6.33) written by Darker and containing a copy of *The Rewyll of Seynt Sauioure*, the Middle English version of Birgitta's rules for her order, was also intended for a Syon audience.[10] The important Latin compilation of contemplative works titled the *Speculum spiritualium* is attributed to 'Adam monachus Cartusiensis' by William Betson in his index to the Syon brethren's library catalogue. Further, the entry describing the copy at M.60–1 in the catalogue identifies the preceding rubrics as 'ex compilacione dompni Henrici Domus Cartusiensis de Bethleem monachi', or the Sheen Charterhouse.[11] Due to the detailed records of the Syon brethren's library and the lack of records of books in English Carthusian libraries, nearly all evidence of textual exchange shows the one-way transmission of books from Sheen into Syon. It seems likely, though, that if Carthusians were mentoring the Syon

8 Elizabeth of Hungary (Töss in the *Speculum*) appears in the final chapter. Unlike the other 'approued women', Elizabeth's writings are not referenced in the *Speculum* and her *vita* appears to be a direct translation from the *Legenda aurea*.

9 Gillespie, 'The Haunted Text' (2008), p. 140.

10 Ann M. Hutchison, 'Devotional Reading in the Monastery and in the Household', in *De Cella in Seculum: Religious and Secular Life and Devotion in Late Medieval England*, ed. Michael G. Sargent (Cambridge: D. S. Brewer, 1989), p. 216.

11 Gillespie, 'Haunted Text' (2008), p. 160, n. 19.

nuns through devotional writing and writing texts for use at Syon, then the Syon brethren would allow the Carthusians to use their extensive library. If this type of borrowing existed, it would indicate a relationship between the two houses that featured a fluid exchange of texts for the use of Carthusian monks to facilitate the creation of devotional works to guide the Syon sisters.

The *Speculum devotorum*'s sources further suggest that Syon and Sheen were supporting each other in the creation of vernacular religious texts. As the Carthusians took on the task of mentoring the sisters of Syon through the written word, the Syon brethren made the books in their library available to the Carthusians. Early in the Preface, the author of the *Speculum* addresses the choices he made in selecting his sources:

> Forthermore, gostely sustre, ȝe shall vnderstonde þat þe grounde of þe booke folowyng is þe gospell and þe doctores þerapoun. And specyally I haue folowed in þis werke two doctores, of þe whiche one is comonly called þe Maistre of þe Stories, and his booke [fol. 3r] in Englissh þe *Scole Story*; that other maistre, Nicholas of Lyre, the whiche was a worthi doctor of diuinite and glosed all þe Bible as to þe leterale vnderstondyng. And þerfore I take these two doctores moste specially as to þis werke, ffor þei gone moste nerest to þe story and to þe letterale vnderstondyng of ony doctores þat I haue redde. Noghtwythstondyng, I haue broght in other doctores in diuers places, as to morall vertues, and also some reuelaciouns of approued women (Preface, lines 102–114).[12]

Since both Syon Abbey and the Sheen Charterhouse held numerous copies of the Bible and major patristic sources, access for the *Speculum* author to the 'gospel and þe doctores þerapoun' most likely meant using the resources at Sheen. However, the scarcity of information concerning the holdings of the Sheen library make it difficult to know if the *Speculum* author had access to other sources.

In addition to the sources he mentions in the Preface – Peter Comestor's (the Master of Stories) *Historia scholastica*, Nicholas of Lyre's *Postilla litteralis*, and the 'approued women' – he also draws on standard post-patristic sources with the intent of intructing the female reader in her spiritual journey. The pseudo-Bonaventuran *Meditationes vitae Christi* is central to the narrative formation of the *Speculum*. The author specifies the importance of the *Meditationes* when he says in his Preface that he nearly gave up on writing the *Speculum* because 'Boneauenture, a cardynale and a worthi clerk, made a booke of þe same matier, þe which is called Vita Cristi' (Preface, lines 20–21). Throughout his account of Christ's life, the *Speculum* author repeatedly turns to the *Meditationes* for details and explanations to support his narrative. Heinrich Suso's *Horologium sapientiae*, on the other hand, appears briefly in the

12 All quotations from the *Speculum devotorum* are taken from my unpublished dissertation, 'Mirror to Devout People (Speculum Devotorum): An Edition with Commentary' (Ph.D. dissertation, University of Notre Dame, 2007). Chapter and line numbers will be cited in the text.

Preface, with three separate quotations woven together to support the author's assertion that the 'diligent thynkyng of our Lordis manhode is a trewe waye withouten disceyte to vertues and gostely knowyng and trewe l[o]uyng of God and swetnesse in grace to a deuoute soule þat kan deuoutely and diligently occupye hym þerin' (Preface, lines 63–66). As Rebecca Selman points out, the *Speculum* author translates Suso's work with a female reader in mind when he changes many of the masculine pronouns in the Latin *Horologium* into feminine pronouns in English.[13] Jacobus de Voragine's *Legenda aurea* and John Hildesheim's *Historia trium regum* (*Three Kings of Cologne*) both play a central role in the *Speculum*'s narrative as the author uses them frequently to illustrate points about female spirituality. In the eighth chapter of the *Speculum*, which deals with the Purification of Mary, the *Three Kings of Cologne* is used to describe the location to which Mary went for her purification. However, the author primarily relies on the *Legenda aurea*'s account of Mary's purification to shape his own account. He ends the chapter with the story of the noblewoman who, during the celebration of the feast, sees a vision of Saint Lawrence, Saint Vincent, and Christ himself.[14] In addition to the purification passages, the author relies on the *Legenda aurea* to provide evidence for Mary's perpetual virginity, to relate details of Octavian's census of the people of Syria, and within a discussion of the conversation between John the Evangelist and Mary at the Crucifixion. He also occasionally mistakes the *Legenda* for other works, at one point attributing passages from the *Legenda* to Saint Bernard (Chapter 6, lines 68–73). Walter Hilton's *Scale of Perfection* and the *Miracles of the Virgin* are also used one time each by the *Speculum* author to add detail to the discussion in the narrative.[15] All of the works discussed here, which comprise all but three of the post-patristic sources used in the *Speculum*, were in the Syon library prior to 1450. Since the *Speculum* was written between 1430 and 1450, it is possible that the *Speculum* author had access to all of these works through Syon. The three post-patristic authors not available at Syon were Bede, Adam the Carthusian, and Peter Damian. The *Infancy Gospel*, most likely *The Gospel of Pseudo-Matthew*, does not appear in the book lists of either house. It may have been stored with the Bibles and therefore kept on a separate list, which makes it possible that both Syon and Sheen had a copy of the work. The books at Sheen that did survive the dissolution may have existed in many copies. In the final chapter of the *Speculum*, the sermons attributed to Bede are a mixture of Peter Damian's sermons and Bede's sermons. There is no record of the sermons of Bede or Peter Damian in either Syon or Sheen, but these are

[13] Rebecca Selman, 'Spirituality and Sex Change: *Horologium sapientiae* and *Speculum devotorum*', in *Writing Religious Women: Female Spiritual and Textual Practices in Late Medieval England*, ed. Denis Reveney and Christiania Whitehead (Toronto: University of Toronto Press, 2000), pp. 61–79.

[14] Jacobus de Voragine, *Legenda aurea*, ed. Giovanni Paolo Maggioni, SISMEL, 2 vols. (Tavarnuzze/Florence: Edizioni del Galluzzo, 1998), vol. 1, pp. 249–51.

[15] For a list of the sources available at Syon Abbey, see the Appendix.

works that may have been available in one of the many *florilegia* that collected numerous works together in one volume. This leaves few gaps to be filled by Carthusian libraries and again suggests that the proximity of Sheen and Syon allowed for a textual exchange that fulfilled the needs of both houses by providing Syon with vernacular texts of devotional instruction and the Carthusians with access to the resources needed to write these guides.

While it seems likely that the Carthusians were drawing on Syon's resources to write books for Syon, it is possible they had access to the libraries of other religious houses. If one assumes that the Sheen Carthusians had use of the Syon library as well as access to a system of book exchange among Carthusian monasteries, in which manuscripts could be supplied from the House of the Salutation in London to the other houses when those books were needed, then a brief survey of relevant books in Charterhouses other than Sheen is warranted. The library at the London House of the Salutation acted as the head library of the Order in England and other houses were dependent on its library for their supply of books. Extant lists of books sent from the London Charterhouse to other houses suggest that the Carthusians took the opportunity to send manuscripts for copying when monks transferred from London to another house.[16] The Sheen Charterhouse's proximity to London possibly gave it greater access to the library at the House of Salutation than Charterhouses in the further reaches of England. Ease of access to the House of Salutation adds another dimension to the textual production and exchange between Syon and Sheen. Not only does it offer an alternative resource for the sources of the *Speculum*, but it also suggests the variety of resources that was available to both houses. It is likely that works coming into the Sheen library from the London trade network eventually found their way into Syon's library as well.

The existing records of books from the London Charterhouse indicate that it contained some copies of sources that appear in the pages of the *Speculum*. Three copies of Hilton's *Scale* were located at London. The first two are in Middle English: Cambridge University Library, MS Ee.4.30, dating to the early- to mid-fifteenth century and British Library, MS Harley 6579, which is tentatively dated to the early- to mid-fifteenth century. On the first leaf of the Cambridge manuscript is written a common indication of ownership: 'Liber domus matris Dei Ordinis Cartusiensis prope Londonias'. The final Hilton manuscript is untraced, but was owned in the eighteenth century by a John Murray. The library at London also contained two Latin copies of Mechtild's *Liber specialis gratiae*, one of which is now Cambridge University Library, MS Ff.1.19; the other is untraced. These books are dated to 1492 and 1513, respectively, which is far too late to be of use to the author of the *Speculum*

[16] E. M. Thompson, *The Carthusian Order in England* (London: Society for Promoting Christian Knowledge, 1930), p. 324.

devotorum.[17] Some of the lists of manuscripts that recorded what books were sent out from the London community to other Carthusian houses exist and they give evidence of a book trade that allowed monks to transfer books to other communities.[18] It is certain that manuscripts circulated among the eleven English Carthusian monasteries in England at the time the *Speculum* was written, but it is nearly impossible to know what books were located at each institution and how exactly, if at all, the author gained access to them.[19]

Further complicating the textual exchange between Syon and Sheen is the possibility that the reclusory at Sheen played a role in providing sources to the Carthusian monks. One of the earliest recluses at Sheen was John Dygoun, who was admitted in 1435 and took up residence in the cell personally founded by Henry V. As a recluse, Dygoun was not a member of either Sheen or Syon, but prior to his taking up residence in the reclusory, he played a prominent role in English religious life. After taking a degree at Oxford and being ordained in 1406, he held numerous positions in the Church, including serving as rector of the London church of St Andrew, Holborn. Dygoun also owned a number of manuscripts, of which he bequeathed seven to Magdalene College, Oxford, upon his death. Among these manuscripts was the earliest extant copy of the *De imitatione Christi*, the transcription of which Dygoun completed in 1438 (Oxford, Magdalen College, MS lat. 93). Dygoun's interest in more popular forms of religious writing is apparent in a copy of theological tractates and sermons containing the writings of Richard Rolle (Oxford, St John's College, MS 77). He also owned a copy of Birgitta's *Revelaciones beate Brigitte* (Oxford, Magdalen College, MS lat. 77), a central source in the *Speculum devotorum*. Both of these manuscripts date to the early- to mid-fifteenth century, as do other works in Dygoun's library, many of which mirror those in the library at Syon.[20] If the monks at Sheen and the brethren at Syon had access to the personal libraries of John Dygoun and later recluses, then it is possible that they had an accessible and regularly updated library of privately owned books available for their use.[21]

17 See J. Ware, *Catalogus librorum manuscriptorum in bibliotheca Iacobi Waraei equitis aur. Catalogus* (Dublin: Robert Hughes, 1648).

18 Thompson, *The Carthusian Order*, pp. 324–26. Thompson provides an undated list of books of the House of Salutation in London that were carried away by Dan John Spalding when he returned to the Charterhouse at Hull.

19 Thompson, *The Carthusian Order*, p. 316. The most complete listing of books available at Sheen is to be found in Ker, *Medieval Libraries* and Watson's *Supplement* to it.

20 See Gillespie, ed., *Syon Abbey*, p. 575.

21 For John Dygoun's life and books, see Ralph Hanna, 'John Dygon, Fifth Recluse of Sheen: His Career, Books, and Acquaintance', in *Imagining Books*, ed. John Thompson and Ryan Kelly (Turnhout: Brepols, 2006), pp. 127–41, and 'Producing Magdalen College MS lat. 93', *Yearbook of English Studies* 33, Medieval and Early Modern Miscellanies and Anthologies (2003), 142–55. See also A. B. Emden, *A Biographical Register of the University of Oxford to 1500*, 3 vols. (Oxford: Clarendon Press, 1957–59) vol. 1, pp. 615–16. See also, Roger Lovatt, 'The Imitation of Christ in Late Medieval England', *Transactions of the Royal Historical Society*, 5th ser. 18 (1968), 97–121.

Along with the works available to the Carthusians from each of the resources discussed above, there were also sources available in the Sheen Charterhouse. The few records that do exist of the library at the Sheen Charterhouse reveal some additional sources for the *Speculum devotorum*. Of the manuscripts that did survive, one in particular that was housed at Sheen contains a work not listed in the collection of Syon Abbey: Dublin, Trinity College, MS 281 contains Adam the Carthusian's sermon on St John the Evangelist's Day along with works by Augustine, Richard Rolle, and a number of other religious treatises. Adam's sermon makes up much of the section in the final chapter of the *Speculum* that deals with St John the Evangelist and the privileges accorded to him. Along with this manuscript, there are a number of books in the Sheen library that overlap with the sources held at Syon. These manuscripts consist of three copies of Walter Hilton's *Scale of Perfection* (Cambridge, Trinity College, MS 354; Philadelphia, Rosenbach Foundation, Inc. H491 [pr. bk]; Oxford, Bodleian Library, MS Latin theology, e.26), all of which date from between 1474 to 1494, with the exception of the Oxford copy, which has been dated to the first half of the fifteenth century with a likely date of 1440.[22] Since the *Speculum* dates to between 1430 and 1450, it is possible that the author used Sheen's earlier copy of the *Scale* as a source. Sheen also held a copy of Nicholas Love's *Mirror of the Blessed Life of Jesus Christ* (Glasgow University Library, MS Hunterian 77) dating from 1474 to 1475, a copy of Nicholas of Lyre (Cambridge, Emmanuel College, MS 241), which dates to 1474, and a copy of John Chrysostom (Chandlers Cross, Mr W. L. Wood) which dates to 1496. Clearly, the *Speculum* author did not have access to any of these books while composing his work, since their date places them well after the early- to mid-fifteenth-century date of the *Speculum*'s composition. Many of these texts were printed, however, which suggests that Sheen may have owned earlier manuscript copies. The diversity of texts passing through the cells at Syon and Sheen could only have added to the rich exchange of textual resources between the two religious centers as the close relationship between each house allowed them to share the works they received from the complex networks of textual exchange in England.

Approved women and the Sheen–Syon connection

The writings of the approved women, Saint Birgitta of Sweden, Saint Catherine of Siena, and Saint Mechtild of Hackeborn, benefited from these networks of textual exchange and frequently circulated in a number of devotional works associated with Syon and Sheen. In the remainder of this essay, I will focus on the three female authors used by the *Speculum devotorum* and

22 See O. Pächt and J. J. G. Alexander, *Illuminated Manuscripts in the Bodleian Library* (Oxford: Clarendon Press, 1973). The manuscript is number 935, plate LXXXIX.

how they function in relation to the author's focus on female readers. Each of the female authors plays a central role within the larger network of textual exchange at Syon and Sheen. Many of the works in which they appear, including the *Speculum*, originated within Sheen and Syon. The three female authors are used by the *Speculum* to guide the reader through her spiritual journey by giving examples of how to properly discern visions, to pray, and to meditate on the Passion of Christ. Their presence within the *Speculum* also provides evidence of the Carthusians' role in the active transmission of Continental mystical writings to England during the late fourteenth and early fifteenth centuries. Within a decade of the founding of Syon Abbey, English translations of the works by Birgitta, Catherine of Siena, and Mechtild of Hackeborn, possibly translated by Syon brethren, appeared in English.[23] Shortly after these English translations, the Carthusians in England included them in numerous devotional texts. The connection of these women's writings to Syon Abbey and their use within the devotional works by Carthusians makes them an important element in coming to a deeper understanding of the production and circulation of religious texts in late medieval England and the textual connections between Syon and Sheen.

Many of the Carthusian texts that incorporate the three approved women were guides for religious, which is also true for the *Speculum devotorum*. In the opening lines of the *Speculum*, the anonymous Carthusian author suggests a mentoring relationship between monks at the Carthusian monastery at Sheen and the sisters at Syon Abbey. The *Speculum* author alludes to this relationship with a promise to write a life of Christ for a 'gostly syster' that he made when the two 'spake laste togyderys'. Carthusians' strict adherence to an ascetic and cloistered lifestyle suggests that the two probably never spoke together; however, in the early years of the establishment of Syon Abbey and the Sheen Charterhouse, when the *Speculum devotorum* was written and both institutions were solidifying their identities, it is not surprising that a more open relationship of mentoring and textual exchange resulted in the Sheen Carthusians providing some form of advising to the sisters situated across the River Thames. Carthusians placed an emphasis on withdrawing into the spiritual desert of the soul to avoid temptation while also recognizing the need for pastoral care within their own charterhouse, which was orchestrated by the prior of each individual house.[24] This care rarely extended beyond the charterhouse, but it appears that the proximity of Syon and Sheen resulted in some exceptions.[25] When the author of the *Speculum*, in a moment of doubt

23 Hope Emily Allen discusses this possibility in the introduction to *The Book of Margery Kempe*, ed. Sanford Brown Meech and Hope Emily Allen, Early English Text Society, o.s. 212 (Oxford: Oxford University Press, 1940), p. lxvi.

24 See Brantley, *Reading*, pp. 79–119.

25 At least one other mentoring relationship connected to Syon and Sheen existed between James Grenehalgh, a monk of Sheen, and Joanna Sewell, a nun at Syon. Grenehalgh took on the role of adviser to Sewell and, on her profession into Syon on 28 April 1500, presented her with a copy of

about his intended project, asked 'counseill of spyrituell and goode men and, most in specyall, leue of my Pryoure' (Preface, lines 23–25), he received a response that suggested a willingness to offer guidance to the sisters at Syon Abbey: 'And I trowe I tolde hym what meved me, and he charetably conforted me to perfourme hit with such wordes as come to his mynde for þe tyme' (Preface, lines 28–30). Encouraged by his prior, the *Speculum* author offers more than the meditation on the Passion that he originally promised: 'Bot I doo yow to wytt that by counseill I haue putte to mykyll more þan I behette yow' (Preface, lines 26–27). The prior's reply and the author's enthusiasm about expanding the scope of his project suggest that the mentoring of Syon sisters through the written word was an important aspect of the relationship between Sheen and Syon.

It is not surprising, then, that the *Speculum* relies on Birgitta more than any of the other approved women for a text intended to act as a guide to a sister of her order. Her work was immensely popular in England and both Syon and Sheen owned copies of her writings. Birgitta first gained notice in England in 1348 when she wrote to the kings of France and England in support of Edward III's right to both kingdoms. Following her death in 1373, her popularity began to grow in England and by the early fifteenth century she was especially revered among many of the wealthy laity. In 1406, Henry Fitzhugh, after attending the wedding of Philippa, Henry IV's daughter, in Sweden, offered his estate at Cherry Hinton for a Birgittine abbey. Birgitta's revelations were an important part of English devotional life, due in large part to extracts of her work that circulated, often in badly translated and inaccurate versions, through numerous miscellanies. It appears that many of the miscellanies were in circulation before the founding of Syon Abbey.[26] However, it was a Syon brother who translated her life into English and her connections to both Sheen and Syon were established in the initial years of the two houses.[27] Since the life of Birgitta was translated at Syon, it is likely that the copies of Birgitta's works at Sheen were copied from manuscripts at Syon.

The author of the *Speculum* draws on Birgitta's *Revelaciones* to guide the reader through the events of Christ's life and to provide details concerning Christ's childhood. This information is available only through Mary's accounts of her son, as given to Birgitta in a series of visions. The *Revelaciones* are first used in the *Speculum* to give the reader detailed descriptions of the

Wynkyn de Worde's 1494 printed edition of Walter Hilton's *Scale of Perfection* to which he had added annotations. He also wrote numerous comments to Sewell that appear in other books and correspondence. The correspondence continued until Grenehalgh was eventually removed from Sheen in 1507 or 1508. See Michael Sargent, *James Grenehalgh as Textual Critic*, 2 vols., Analecta Cartusiana 85 (Salzburg: Institut für Anglistik und Amerikanistik, 1984).

26 See Roger Ellis, ' "Flores ad Fabricandam … Coronam": An Investigation of the Revelations of St. Bridget of Sweden in Fifteenth-Century England', *Medium Aevum* 51 (1982), 163–86.

27 Roger Ellis, ed., *Liber Celestis*, Early English Text Society, o.s. 291 (Oxford: Oxford University Press, 1987), p. xvi.

Nativity and Mary's ease in giving birth to Christ. Mary is described as 'a perfite ensample and a trewe myrour of perfeccioun to all wymmen, as our Lorde Ihesu to all men' (Chapter 4, lines 51–52), which encourages the female reader's imitation of Mary's behavior. The birth is told entirely from Saint Birgitta's perspective, who receives her vision through the eyes of Mary; as the *Speculum* author writes, 'our Lady shewede [Christ's birth] by reuelacioun full feire to Seinte Brigette' (Chapter 5, line 69). This powerful use of Mary's vision allows the reader to experience the birth and later the Passion through the eyes of the perfect example on whom she is meant to base all of her actions.

The most important use of Birgitta's *Revelaciones* occurs in the twenty-second chapter of the *Speculum* when the Crucifixion is described in detail. Birgitta's account vividly portrays the dying Christ and provides a focal point on which the reader can meditate in order to experience the Savior's suffering. Small details gain significance and allow for an increasing intensification of the reality of Christ's suffering. The reader is repeatedly told to 'beholden' as Christ's body is broken with painful detail. It is clear that the *Speculum* author translates carefully selected passages from Birgitta's Latin work to enhance the effect of each word used to describe the Crucifixion. He encourages the reader to experience Christ's suffering through Birgitta's own, highly personalized account:

> Bot she telleth it in hir owne persone as she seeghe it, þe whiche I tourne it into þe fourme of meditacioun, not goynge, by þe grace of God, fro þe menynge of hir wordes. Nowe þan beholdeth with þe forseide holy lady howe þe foreside tourmentours fixeth and maketh faste strongly þe crosse in þe forseide hole, with trees myghtyly ysmyte þeraboute with a betill, þat it myghte stonde þe faster and not falle. (Chapter 22, lines 43–49)

The continual encouragement to meditate on Birgitta's detailed descriptions allows the author to assert a level of authority by going beyond the scriptures and providing a brutal account of what occurred at Golgotha:

> And þan beholdeth howe þei drawen downe all þe body by þe crosse and putten þat one legge vppon þat other, and þan þei ioynede þe two fete togidre. And when mykell þei streynede oute þo gloriouse members strongely in þe crosse þat all þe veynes and senewes tobreste. And when þis was done, þei putte þe crowene of thorne þat þei hadde taken fro his hede when he was crucyfiede vppon his hede aȝene, þe whiche so strongely prikkede his reuerente hede þat his eyne were fillede anone with blode flowynge and his eres were stoppede and his face and his berde were as it hadde be keuerede and depte with þat rede blode. And anone þo crucyfyours and knyghtes mevede awey violentely all þo tables þat were aboute þe crosse, and þan þe crosse bode alone and our Lorde crucifyede þeron.
>
> (Chapter 22, lines 61–73)

The fidelity to source material and the command to pay close attention – 'Nowe þan beholdeth' – focusses the attention of the reader in order to bring about the proper meditative experience. As the passage continues, Birgitta's vision of Mary allows the reader to experience the sorrow of a mother:

> After þis thenketh howe our Lady was there presente and seeghe all þis done, and þerfore thenketh inwardly howe grete sorowe it was to hir to see hir suete sone and Lorde in so mykyll peyne and dispite. And þan beholdeth howe she wepeth and wayleth and falleth downe to þe erthe for sorowe as halfe dede.
> (Chapter 22, lines 75–79)

Through the command to 'thenketh' and 'beholdeth', Birgitta's vivid account gives the reader access to Christ's Passion and allows for the necessary affective response. The fact that the Passion is presented through the writings of Birgitta, the founder of the order to which Syon belongs, adds particular weight to these passages. A sister at the Abbey of Saint Saviour, BVM, and Saint Birgitta at Syon Abbey, who is reading the writings of the founder of her order on Mary, for whom her house is named, would feel a strong connection to this account of the Passion. It is no surprise that both Syon and Sheen owned copies of the popular and influential writings of Birgitta and that these works circulated between the two houses.

The second of the 'approued women', Mechtild of Hackeborn, was also familiar to the English Carthusian reader and her work existed in the library of Syon and in a number of Carthusian manuscripts. The origins of the translation of Mechtild's work into English is unknown, but in the introduction to her edition of Mechtild's Middle English *Booke of Gostlye Grace*, Theresa Halligan argues that Flemish Carthusians who were transferred to Sheen when it was founded in 1414 brought Mechtild's work with them. Mechtild's *Liber specialis gratiae* was popular in the Low Countries and the Carthusians regularly imported and translated Latin devotional works to England. The *Booke of Gostlye Grace* has close ties to Syon and Sheen, likely through the Carthusians, and offers another example of a text of Carthusian origin that made its way into the library at Syon.[28]

Mechtild's work appears in a short passage found in Chapter 29 of the *Speculum*, which deals with the resurrection and first (apocryphal) appearance of Christ. It reads:

> And at þis gloriouse Resurreccioun yhe may thenke þer was a grete multitude of aungels, for it is conteynede in a reuelacioun of Seynte Maute þat hir semede she seeghe suche a multitude of aungels aboute þe sepulcre þat fro þe erth to þe skye þei wente aboute our Lorde as it hadde be a walle. (lines 27–30)

The passage relates Mechtild's vision of a wall of angels filling the sky following Christ's resurrection and is taken from the Middle English translation of her *Liber specialis gratiae*, titled *The Booke of Gostlye Grace* in its English form.[29]

28 *The Booke of Gostlye Grace of Mechtild of Hackeborn*, ed. Theresa A. Halligan (Toronto: Pontifical Institute of Medieval Studies, 1979), pp. 47–59.

29 Halligan, *The Booke of Gostlye Grace*, p. 181, lines 2–6.

Mechtild (St Maude or St Maute, as she is called in many Middle English translations, including the *Speculum*) was a popular figure in late medieval England and her work was frequently excerpted in devotional texts, often with links to Syon Abbey. Along with the *Speculum*, Mechtild's *Booke* also appears in *The Myroure of Oure Ladye.* The *Myroure* contains an English translation of the Birgittine Breviary, Hours, Masses, and Offices, along with an account, written in Latin by Birgitta's confessor Master Peter, explaining how the Birgittine service was revealed to her by an angel. It is uncertain when the *Myroure* was written, since the only surviving copy is a manuscript dating to the late fifteenth or early sixteenth century. It is likely, however, that it was originally composed between 1420 and 1448.[30] The *Myroure* contains two excerpts from Mechtild's *Booke*: one to inform readers that they can miss confession before Mass or divine service with a legitimate reason and the second to recommend the reading of the prayers Christ gave to Mechtild.[31] Much of the *Myroure* is concerned with instructing the sisters at Syon on the proper way to read for devotional purposes, calling the devout reading of holy books 'one of the partes of contemplacyon'.[32] The reliance on 'St Maude' as an example of proper prayer, and the existence of seven copies of her work in the Syon library, suggest her work was a regular part of the reading program for the sisters and possibly brethren at Syon. Of the seven copies of her work at Syon, three of the books are sixteenth-century printed editions, but the other four are manuscripts that contain Mechtild's work in varying stages of completion. Three manuscripts are in Latin, of which only one contains a complete copy of the *Liber*; however, the fourth manuscript, titled *Reuelaciones beate Matildis in anglico*, contains the entire English translation of the *Liber.*[33] Similarly to Birgitta's works, Mechtild's *Liber* and its Middle English translation have close ties to the Birgittines and Carthusians.

The work of the final approved woman, Catherine of Siena, also circulated within numerous devotional compilations alongside the writings of Birgitta and Mechtild. It appears that Catherine's work made its way into England through the Syon brethren rather than through the Carthusians. The *Dialogo* was completed by Catherine in 1378, two years before her death, and was widely circulated. Twenty-five Italian and sixteen Latin manuscripts survive from the time immediately following her death. Since the two earliest manuscripts containing the Middle English translation of the *Dialogo* – the *Orcherd of Syon*, in British Library, MS Harley 3432 and Cambridge, St John's College,

30 *Myroure*, pp. vii–viii and Hutchison, 'Devotional Reading', p. 220.

31 Rosalynn Voaden, 'The Company She Keeps: Mechtild of Hackeborn in Late-Medieval Devotional Compilations', in *Prophets Abroad: The Reception of Continental Holy Women in Late-Medieval England*, ed. Rosalynn Voaden (Cambridge : D. S. Brewer, 1996), pp. 54–55; Halligan, *The Booke of Gostlye Grace*, p. 50.

32 *Myroure*, p. 65.

33 Vincent Gillespie, ed., *Syon Abbey*, pp. 226, 236, 239, 251, 252, 255, 258.

MS C 24 – date to the early fifteenth century, and the Middle English 'Preface' of Catherine's work addresses the 'Religyous modir & deuoute sustren clepid & chosen bisily to laboure at the hous of Syon', it is likely that the *Orcherd* was prepared sometime early in Syon's existence, perhaps between the founding of the abbey in 1415 and its first professions made in 1420.[34] This early date reveals that Syon was actively collecting contemporary religious works that were directed toward women at its founding. Since no record exists of a copy of Catherine's works in Sheen, it is assumed that it was translated by one of the brethren at Syon.

In the *Speculum devotorum*, Catherine's *Dialogo* is used to guide the reader in the proper discernment of visions by instructing 'howe a man or a woman myght knowe a gode visione from ane euyle and when reuelaciouns or visiones bene of [God] or of þe ennemy' (Chapter 3, lines 86–87). A lengthy quotation from Catherine's work provides the reader with the knowledge to distinguish God-given visions (in which initial bitterness becomes sweet) from visions from the devil, which begin with sweetness and end with dread: 'Þe vision of þe ennemy [which] hath þe contrary, for he ȝeueth in þe begynnynge as it semeth a manere of gladnes, sikernes, or suetnesse, bot alwaye by processe drede and bitternesse growen contynualy in þe mynde of hym or hir þat seeth' (Chapter 3, lines 99–102). The advice is fairly standard and gives the reader direction in preparation for the forthcoming visions of Saint Birgitta. However, the choice of Catherine as an authority to discuss the discernment of visions is an important one. Firstly, the topic of *discretio spirituum* traditionally fell to men in the Middle Ages.[35] Allowing Catherine authority within a predominantly masculine domain makes the *Speculum devotorum* especially accessible to female readers; in contrast, texts that instruct through masculine perspectives tend to present a form of *imitatio Christi* and discussions of visions attuned to male sensibilities. By including the passages from Catherine's *Dialogo*, the *Speculum* author enables an audience of women to engage with a female mystic's imitation of Christ, which, as Karma Lochrie has shown, could be quite different from masculine *imitatio Christi.*[36] Catherine's instruction on the proper discernment of visions prepares the reader for Birgitta's highly affective visions of Christ's life, while the vision of Mechtild enhances the *Speculum*'s account of the Resurrection. The manuscripts in which the works of these three female authors are contained also provide ample evidence of a rich exchange of resources between the Carthusians at Sheen and their neighbors at Syon.

34 *The Orcherd of Syon*, ed. Phyllis Hodgson and Gabriel M. Liegey, Early English Text Society, o.s. 258 (Oxford: Oxford University Press, 1966), pp. vi–vii, 1–2.

35 See Rosalynn Voaden, *God's Words, Women's Voices: The Discernment of Spirits in the Writings of Late-Medieval Women Visionaries* (York: York Medieval Press, 1999), p. 48 and Selman, 'Spirituality and Sex Change', p. 71.

36 Karma Lochrie, *Margery Kempe and Translations of the Flesh* (Philadelphia: University of Pennsylvania Press, 1991), p. 16, discusses the difficulty faced by women imitating the suffering of Christ's masculine body.

In the initial years following the founding of Syon and Sheen, the two houses relied on each other for textual resources and spiritual guidance. The lack of records for the Sheen library makes it difficult to know from which house different works derived; however, the sources found in the *Speculum devotorum* suggest a mentoring practice in which the Carthusians, relying on the resources in Syon's library, wrote devotional works for the community at Syon. Once in Syon's library, as Vincent Gillespie has suggested, many of these works made their way into the hands of a select group of laity. Such a transmission from Syon to lay readers certainly occurred in the case of Notre Dame MS 67, which, as noted above, was owned by the Scrope family. Through the exchange of texts and spiritual advice between the Carthusians and Birgittines at the Sheen royal manor, the combination of the libraries of the two houses became a powerful resource for the translation and preservation of devotional writing at a time in England when there was a great demand for orthodox, approved works of religious writing.

Appendix

This list includes books containing the *Speculum devotorum*'s post-patristic sources and the works of the 'approued women' that were available in the library of the brethren at Syon Abbey between 1410 and 1450.[1] Each work is accompanied by its corresponding class-mark from the brethren's library.

Post-Patristic authors at Syon Abbey

Iohannis de Caulibus, *Meditactiones vitae Christi*:
    M.6: SSI.739
    M.7: SSI.740
    erased at M.76: SS2.142
Peter Comestor, *Historia scholastica*:
    E17: SSI.323a, with Richard of Saint-Victor
    erased at E.52: SS2.91
Heinrich Suso, *Horologium sapientiae*:
    O.3: SSI.945f
Nicholas of Lyre, *Postilla litteralis*:
    E.28–9: SSI.334–5
    erased copies in SS2
Jacobus de Voragine, *Legenda aurea*:
    M.9: SSI.742
John of Hildesheim, *Historia trium regum* [*Three Kings of Cologne*]:
    M.15: SSI.748m–n
    M17: SSI.750g, in English
Walter Hilton, *The Scale of Perfection*:
    M.24: SSI.757b–c, in English
    erased at M.26: SS2.127a
    M.110: SS2.147
    Latin translation by Thomas Fishlake is at M.25: SS1.758
Miracles of the Virgin (the contents of these collections varied greatly):
    O.39: SSI.981d

Approved women at Syon

Birgitta of Sweden, *Revelaciones*:
    M.64: SSI.797, now London, British Library, MS Harley 612, s.xv[1]
    M.65: SSI.798, M.66: SSI.799

[1] This list is extracted from a list originally compiled by Vincent Gillespie in 'Haunted Text' (2008), pp. 171–72, n. 62.

Mechtild of Hackeborn, *Liber specialis gratiae*:
 M.47: SSI.780
 M.94: SSI.827g
 M.98: SSI.831, *The Booke of Gostlye Grace* (English translation of *Liber*)
Catherine of Siena:
 M.71: SSI.804g

9

The Necessity of Difference: The Speech of Peace and the Doctrine of Contraries in Langland's *Piers Plowman*

Derek Pearsall

In Passus XX of the C-Text of William Langland's *Piers Plowman* (B XVIII), the Four Daughters of God gather and debate the Incarnation, its meaning and its consequences.[1] The debate has its roots in Psalm 84.10–11 (AV 85.10–11): 'Surely his salvation is near to them that fear him, that glory may dwell in our land. Mercy and truth have met each other, justice and peace have kissed.'[2] From these verses, with the help of a reference to 'God's daughters' in Isaiah 43.6, 'bring my sons from afar and my daughters from the end of the earth' (in the context, those who bear witness to God's name), biblical commentators of the twelfth century constructed a narrative scene in which four young women meet and, after some debate of the idea of Atonement, embrace and kiss. The new narrative was well adapted to a time of doctrinal change when Atonement theology began to stress the reconciliation of God and man through mercy rather than the legal problem of the justice of the devil's claim to rights over man. The most important agents in the development of the debate are Hugh of St Victor and St Bernard of Clairvaux, in his sermon on the Annunciation.[3] The debate, because of its dramatic effectiveness and theological boldness, became widely popular. The most successful line of transmission was through the pseudo-Bonaventuran *Meditationes vitae Christi*, and the most influential

1 There is an extensive literature on the debate of the Four Daughters. An excellent analysis of the tradition is given by Kari Sajavaara in the introduction to his edition of *The Middle English Translations of Robert Grosseteste's Chateau d'Amour*, Mémoires de la Société Néophilologique de Helsinki 32 (Helsinki: Société Néophilologique, 1967), pp. 54–90.

2 In the Vulgate: 'Verumtamen prope timentes eum salutare ipsius,/ Ut inhabet gloria in terra nostra. Misericordia et veritas obviaverunt sibi; justitia et pax osculatae sunt.'

3 Hugh of St Victor, *Miscellanea: Liber II* (*Annotationes … in Psalmos*), cap. lxiii (J.-P. Migne, *Patrologiae cursus completus, series latina*, 221 vols. [Paris, 1844–64], 177, cols. 623–25); St Bernard, *Patrologia Latina* 183, cols. 383–90.

early vernacular work was *Le Chasteau d'Amour* of Robert Grosseteste, translated into English as *The Castle of Love.*[4]

In Langland, the debate acts as a prelude to the Harrowing of Hell and the arguments about the Atonement between the devils that precede the Harrowing and the speech of Christ that performs and concludes it. Mercy and Peace argue for the Atonement as a form of compensatory sacrifice, a life for a life, a death for a death, guile defeated by guile, Peace adding her special illustrations through contraries (which will be discussed in detail later) and through the legal analogy of 'maynprise' (C XX 188).[5] Christ stands bail for man, and accepts the ultimate responsibility of a bailor, that is, to give his own life.[6] Truth and Righteousness, meanwhile, are unanimous in their insistence that there is no release from hell. After the debate of the Four Daughters, there is a brief interlude in which 'Book' calls upon the witness of the elements to confirm that Christ came to save man and to destroy sin. When the light announces Christ's presence before the gates of hell, an urgent debate breaks out among the devils which ends when Christ arrives and answers the devils' objections (and those of the sterner sisters) with scrupulous care, item by item. It was never decreed that man's punishment should be for ever; Lucifer's deceit makes God's use of guile (the disguising of Christ as an ordinary man) a legal and just response; it is justice not *maistrie* (C XX 299) that inspires his actions; the Atonement is a legally binding process of compensatory sacrifice – a life for a life, a death for a death, so that what was lost through a tree should be redeemed through a tree. The basic argument, to which Langland adds his own special delight in the poetry of verbal play and antithesis, is that first formulated by Paul: 'Christ offered for all time a single sacrifice for sins' (Heb. 10.12), 'an expiation by his blood' (Rom. 3.25).

The debate of the Four Daughters is usually set in the court of heaven as part of the discussion of whether man should be redeemed, a discussion that ends with Christ volunteering himself as the necessary sacrifice. The debate thus makes a kind of prologue to the Incarnation, as in the fifteenth-century poem of *The Court of Sapience*, which contains perhaps the most richly dramatic representation of the debate. Less often, the debate takes place at the moment of 'particular' judgment as the soul leaves the body at death

4 See Sajavaara, ed., *Middle English Translations of the Chateau d'Amour.*

5 The C-Text is quoted from George Russell and George Kane, eds., *Piers Plowman: The C Version* (London: Athlone Press, 1997), and the B-Text from George Kane and E. Talbot Donaldson, eds., *Piers Plowman: The B Version* (London: Athlone Press, 1975). Reference is also made to A. V. C. Schmidt, ed., *Piers Plowman: A Parallel-Text Edition*, 2 vols., Vol. I, *Text* (London: Longman, 1995), Vol. II, *Introduction, Notes and Glossary* (Kalamazoo, Michigan: Medieval Institute Publications, 2008).

6 See Anna Baldwin, *The Theme of Government in Piers Plowman*, Piers Plowman Studies 1 (Cambridge: D. S. Brewer, 1981), p. 65. Baldwin gives an excellent account of the historical background to the legal analogies that Langland uses and alludes to. It should be stressed, though, that these analogies are used primarily for dramatic purposes, and do not *explain* Langland's view of the Atonement.

(distinguished from the 'general' judgment at Doomsday), as in the *Pélerinage de l'Ame*, an allegorical poem by Guillaume de Deguileville (fl. 1330–1360), the second part of a trilogy possibly known to Langland, and in the fifteenth-century morality play of *The Castle of Perseverance*.[7] In their different ways, the one general, the other particular, these are the obvious places, theologically, for the debate. Langland is alone, it appears, in placing the scene at the moment when, before the gates of hell, a strange light first announces the coming of the crucified Christ. The unusual placement of the debate may owe something to the *Gospel of Nicodemus*, where the two sons of Symeon are released from death and hell by Christ so that they may witness the Harrowing of Hell, thus fulfilling the prophecy made by their father, 'the just and devout man' of Luke 2.25, that Christ would bring 'a light for revelation to the Gentiles' (Luke 2.32).[8] Langland makes it a moment of high drama and excitement, as the dreamer watches events unfold in a live enactment, as if for the first time, of the momentous meaning of the Redemption.[9]

The debate is first of all between Mercy and Truth, the first two to arrive at the place where the dreamer stands watching. Mercy argues that the purpose of the Incarnation is so that God can take human form and assume the burden of man's sins and so atone for them and bring about man's redemption. Truth is scornful of this explanation:

> 'That thow tellest,' quod treuthe, 'is bote a tale of walterot!' (C XX 145)

Man sinned, she says, through his own free will, fell, and was condemned to eternal perdition. Mercy puts forward the familiar explanation of the legal working of the Atonement: the devil caused man to sin through trickery and

7 The three *Pélerinages* are edited by J. J. Stürzinger (London: Roxburghe Club, 1893, 1895, 1897). For Langland's possible knowledge of Deguileville, see Dorothy L. Owen, *Piers Plowman: A Comparison with some Earlier and Contemporary French Allegories* (London: University of London Press, 1912). *The Castle of Perseverance* is edited by Mark Eccles, in *The Macro Plays*, Early English Text Society 262 (London: Oxford University Press, 1969).

8 The *Gospel of Nicodemus* forms the second part of the Latin *Descensus Christi ad Inferos*, edited by Constantin von Tischendorf, *Evangelia Apocrypha*, 2nd ed. (Leipzig: Avenarius and Mendelssohn, 1976). There are several Middle English translations, prose and verse, of both the *Gospel of Nicodemus* and of the *Harrowing of Hell* independently, most of them still unedited: see *A Manual of the Writings in Middle English 1050–1500*, ed. J. Burke Severs, Vol. II, chapter V.6, 'Legends of Jesus and Mary', by Frances A. Foster (Hamden, CT: Connecticut Academy of Arts and Sciences, 1970), pp. 448–49. The most recent edition of a Middle English translation is that of C. W. Marx, *'The Devils' Parliament' and 'The Harrowing of Hell and Destruction of Jerusalem'*, Middle English Texts 25 (Heidelberg: Universitätsverlag C. Winter, 1993), though the description there of the revelation to Simeon's sons, 'Lentyk and Kareyn' (133–294), was not used by Langland. Versions of the story, in both Latin and English, had a great influence on the English mystery plays as well as upon Langland, who also made use of the widely known version of the story of the Harrowing of Hell in the *Legenda aurea*, chap. 54.

9 John Burrow, in *Langland's Fictions* (Oxford: Clarendon Press, 1993), pp. 62–64, gives other examples of this characteristically Langlandian kind of narrative, in which the dreamer acts as an eye-witness.

now, just as one venom drives out another, the tricker is to be tricked with a trick:

> *Ars ut Artem falleret.* (C XX 165a)

God came into earth as a sinless man and the devil, who failed to recognise him, was deceived into having him killed, thus breaking the terms of his contract with God and bringing about the abrogation of 'the devil's rights'. Langland makes little substantive use of the theology of the devil's rights, and, though he keeps some of the sensational paraphernalia, such as the story of the deception of the devil, he is less interested in the devil's claim over man than in the reconciliation of man with God.[10] He draws not so much on scholastic theology as on the vernacular *Gospel of Nicodemus*, the Middle English *Harrowing of Hell*, and the English translation of Grosseteste's *Chasteau d'Amour*. His own theology of the Atonement is highly eclectic and at times inconsistent.[11]

At this point, Peace and Righteousness join the other two, Peace dressed in her finest array and strolling gaily along ('pleiynge', C XX 171). She says that she already has letters from Jesus to confirm that man is to be forgiven and all those in hell are to be let out. Righteousness ridicules her:

> 'Rauest thow?' quod rihtwisnesse, 'or thow art riht dronke!' (C XX 193)

She restates forcibly the argument for justice: man sinned through the will of the flesh and in defiance of God's command and of his own God-given gift of reason and must pay the penalty of perpetual pain:

> 'For hit is boteles bale, the bite that they eten.' (C XX 207)

Peace now puts forward an unusual argument, which is the subject of the present essay, concerning God's purpose in the Incarnation. She sets it out deliberately as if arguing a case, not making a hopeful petition, which is why the emendation 'preue' for 'preye' in the first line is so important.[12] The whole passage (C XX 208–38) is quoted here:[13]

[10] See C. W. Marx, *The Devil's Rights and the Redemption in the Literature of Medieval England* (Cambridge: D. S. Brewer, 1995), p. 113. Marx offers a valuable history of the theology of the Atonement, with special reference to the idea of the Devil's Rights.

[11] See Richard Firth Green, *A Crisis of Truth: Literature and Law in Ricardian England* (Philadelphia: University of Pennsylvania Press, 1999), p. 361.

[12] Schmidt's preference for 'preye' is interesting. In every way, 'preue' is the more appropriate word in the context, it has sufficient manuscript support, and it is accepted by the Athlone Press editors for both B and C: 'preye' is a feeble substitute and a classic *lectio facilior*. Schmidt's motive for accepting 'preye' may have to do with his generally strict adherence to his copy-text, but it may also be that, since he finds Peace's arguments theologically unacceptable, he wishes to deny her the freedom to say that she *proves* them. There is a possibility that C records the same hesitation on the part of the scribe of the C archetype or even on the part of Langland, who may in his revision have been hesitant about unnecessary challenges to the reader (compare the archetypal reading for *modicum*, 225).

Footnote 13 appears on page 156

'And y shal pre[u]e,' quod pees, 'here payne moet haue ende
And wo into wele moet wende at þe laste.
For hadde they wist of no wo, wele hadde thay nat knowen; 210
For no wiht woet what wele is þat neuere wo soffrede
Ne what is hoet hunger þat hadde neuere defaute.
Ho couthe kyndeliche whit colour descreue
Yf all þe world were whit or swan-whit all thynges?
Yf no nyht ne were no man, [as] y leue, 215
Sholde ywyte witterly what day is to mene.
Ne hadde god ysoffred of som oþer then hymsulue
He hadde nat wist witterly where deth were sour or swete.
For sholde neuere riȝt riche man þat lyueth in rest and hele
Ywyte what wo is ne were þe deth of kynde. 220
So god þat bigan al of his gode wille
Bycam man of a mayde mankynde to saue
And soffred to be sold to se þe sorwe of deynge,
The which vnknytteth alle care and comsyng is of reste.
For til [*modicum*] mete with vs, y may hit wel avowe, 225
Ne woet no wyht, as y wene, what is ynow to mene.
Forthy god, of his goednesse, þe furste [gome] Adam,
Sette hym in solace and in souereyne merthe
And sethe he soffrede hym synne sorwe to fele,
To wyte what wele [was], kyndeliche to knowe [hit]. 230
And aftur god auntred hymsulue and toek Adames kynde
To wyte what he hath soffred in thre sundry places,
Bothe in heuene and in erthe, and now to helle he thenketh
To wyte what al wo is þat woet of alle ioye:
Omnia probate; quod bonum est tenete.
So hit shal fare bi this folk: here folye and here synne 235
Shal lere hem what l[angour] is and lisse withouten ende.
For woet no wiht what werre is þer [þat] pees regneth
Ne what is witterliche wele til welaway hym teche.'

The argument rests on two points, each of which is reiterated in turn (210–30, 231–38). The purpose of the Fall, says Peace, was to give man experience of sorrow so that he could properly understand happiness and well-being, for knowledge of things is made complete only by knowledge of their contraries: who could understand happiness without the experience of unhappiness, or hunger without plenty, or whiteness if the whole world were white, or day without the experience of night?[14] So God gave man perfect happiness in Eden

[13] Substantive emendations of the copy-text (Huntington MS HM 143) by Russell and Kane are as follows: 208. preue] *from a single C-MS (and so B); all other C-MSS* preye. 225. modicum] *so B; all C-MSS* moreyne. 227. gome] *two C-MSS (so B); X and rest* man. languor] *so B; all C-MSS* loue. 237. Schmidt (*Parallel-Text Edition*) accepts only the emendation at 227.

[14] Langland used a variant of the 'white/ not white' analogy in B X 442–3, in a passage not taken up in C: 'And wherby wiste men which [is] whit if alle þyng blak were,/ And who were a good man but if

so that he could fully appreciate the nature of sorrow after the Fall. God too had to experience mankind's suffering so that he could fully understand the sorrow of death, just as a rich man would know only happiness were it not for the certainty of death. She then repeats the twofold argument in other words: God took the risk ('auntred hymsulue') of becoming man so that he could know what man had suffered in heaven, earth, and now in hell. Likewise, she concludes, the folk in limbo have, through their folly and sin, been given the experience of suffering and will now truly appreciate happiness and love, just as war teaches us the joy of peace.

The support given to the argument by the theory of contraries – that things can only be fully known through their contraries – draws on a commonplace topos in medieval writing. The theory is explained in detail in the *De consolatione Philosophiae* of Boethius and in the portion of the *Roman de la Rose* by Jean de Meun. In the former, Philosophy argues thus from contraries in Book III, metre 1:

> Dulcior est apium mage labor,
> si malus ora prius sapor edat.
> Gratius astra nitent ubi notus
> desinit imbriferos dare sonas. (5–8)[15]
>
> [The tongue that first has tasted bitter food
> Finds honey that the bees have won more sweet;
> And stars shine out more pleasing to the eye
> When from the south the rain winged wind has dropped.]

Thus true good, she goes on, is recognised when false good has been seen for what it is. At the beginning of prose 2 of Book IV, Philosophy puts the argument in a more philosophical way:

> Primum igitur, inquit, bonis semper adesse potentiam, malos cunctis uiribus esse desertos agnoscas licebit quorum quidem alterum demonstratur ex altero.
> (*Consolatio*, IV.prose ii.2)
>
> ['First then', she said, 'that the good are always strong and the wicked always bereft of all power, these are facts that you will be able to see, the one being proved by the other'.] (Watts, translation, p. 118)

Since good and bad are contraries, she goes on, the weakness of the one is made clear by understanding the strength of the other. In the *Roman de la Rose*, the Lover is advised to enjoy as many women as possible, for only thus

þer were som sherewe'. Peace again uses contraries – sun after showers, love and peace after strife – to celebrate the final reconciliation of the sisters at C XX 452–8. The Latin she quotes (XX 451ab) derives from the *Liber parabolarum* of Alanus de Insulis (*Patrologia Latina* 210, cols. 581–82).

15 Boethius, *De consolatione Philosophiae*, ed. Adrianus a Forti Scuto [Adrian Fortescue] (London: Burns Oates & Washbourne, 1925). The translation is that of V. E. Watts, *Boethius, The Consolation of Philosophy* (Harmondsworth: Penguin, 1969).

will he become a true connoisseur, just as one needs to know what tastes bad before one can appreciate really good food, to know shame in order to know what honour means, to learn comfort through discomfort, pleasure through pain. This is the way with all contraries: the one explains the other:

> Ainsi va des contreres choses,
> les unes sunt des autres gloses. (21543–44)[16]

To understand something properly one needs to have experience of its opposite. The same sets of analogies are used by Pandarus in *Troilus and Criseyde* (iii.637–48) to persuade Troilus that only by bitter suffering can he know the full sweetness of love, just as white can only be known by black, and honour by shame:

> By his contrarie is every thing declared. (i.637)[17]

Pandarus offers some further *ad hoc* consolations of doubtful efficacy, arguing that wise men are warned by the example of fools (like himself) and that someone who has been so unsuccessful in love is bound to give good advice to a lover. Lydgate picks up Chaucer's use of the topos in his *Temple of Glass* (391–416), where Venus comforts the love-lorn lady with the thought that joy is always the end of pain, and further that joy can only be known by the experience of pain, as the sweetness of sugar cannot be known without the taste of bitterness, or light without darkness, or 'wirship withoute some debate'.[18] Other allusions to the topos are numerous (Alanus de Insulis has already been cited), and of course the concept of understanding through contraries is at the foundation of modern linguistic philosophy and structural linguistics.[19]

The only medieval writer to offer more than a hint of a larger philosophical dimension to the doctrine of contraries is Boethius. In all other cases, the imagery of the contrasting experience of contraries is always of the sharpening of sensation towards full appreciation (and therefore towards a kind of 'knowledge'), not of the deepening of moral or intellectual awareness. There may be a hint of that Boethian awareness in Peace's speech, but it is slight, and

16 *Le Roman de la Rose*, by Guillaume de Lorris and Jean de Meun, ed. Félix Lecoy, Les Classiques français du Moyen Age, 3 vols. (Paris: Librairie Honoré Champion, 1965–70).

17 *The Riverside Chaucer*, ed. L. D. Benson (Boston: Houghton Mifflin, 1987).

18 *The Temple of Glass*, 399, in the edition by John Norton-Smith, *John Lydgate: Poems* (Oxford: Clarendon Press, 1966), with excellent notes, p. 185.

19 'We only know anything by knowing it as distinguished from something else: all consciousness is of difference … a thing is only seen to be what it is, by contrast with what it is not' (John Stuart Mill, *An Examination of Sir William Hamilton's Philosophy* [1865], in *Collected Works*, ed. J. M. Robson, Vol. IX [Toronto: University of Toronto Press, 1979], p. 4); 'In language there are only differences … and no positive terms. Whether we take the signification or the signal, the language includes neither ideas nor sounds existing prior to the linguistic system, but only conceptual and phonic differences arising out of that system' (Ferdinand de Saussure, *Course in General Linguistics* [first published in French, 1916], trans. Roy Harris [London: Duckworth, 1983], p. 118).

the sequences of examples of knowledge by contraries that she gives would be little more than a medieval commonplace were it not applied to the insufficient nature of God's knowledge, which in respect of the medieval tradition of contraries seems outrageous.

These two arguments that Peace makes – that the Fall was fortunate in that it enabled man to learn of sorrow by experience, and that God profited in the same way though the Incarnation, and the support given to both by the theory of contraries – are unprecedented in the context of discussion of the Atonement.[20] Schmidt calls the idea that God needed 'first-hand knowledge of suffering and death' 'somewhat surprising', and finds knowledge by contraries, though persuasive in 'the sensory domain', 'doubtful' in the moral.[21] Peace's arguments do seem rather naïve, especially in appearing to assume that God needed to know anything, or that he lacked any kind of knowledge, or that he was anything other than omniscient. Such an assumption, for the Fathers, is absurd. Peter Lombard declares that 'God's knowledge, like his essence, cannot change, enlarge, or diminish. ... God cannot know more than he knows, for that would be a self-contradiction.'[22] Aquinas explains the self-contradiction briskly: 'It should not be granted that God can know more than he does know: because that statement would imply that first he did not know, and then he did know.'[23] Furthermore, for Peace to suggest that God needed the experience of being human in order to appreciate the full nature of sin and death is to place a limit on his absolute omnipotence, which is also a self-contradiction.

The absurdity of attributing limits to God's knowledge in discussion of the Incarnation does not usually arise, since a clear distinction is always made between God and the Incarnate Son, and between what God might know in his omniscience and what God might have allowed himself to need to know in his incarnate self as a man, a distinction that Langland elsewhere makes clear. Jesus had to be schooled in *lechecraeft* (C XVIII 137) before he could fulfil his mission of healing and had to 'conne mony sleythes' in order to make his way as a leader (C XVIII 201). Christ in his manhood had to learn what it is to be human, or, as Aers puts it, 'The creator in his Incarnation is obliged to learn creaturely limitation', citing further a line earlier in B (XVI 215) which is revised out in C: 'creatour weex creature to knowe what was boþe'.[24]

20 The argument, 'that God allowed humanity to sin in order that he might know sorrow and better appreciate good, and God himself took on human nature in order to know suffering', is, says Marx (*Devil's Rights*, p. 104), 'without precedent in other versions of the debate'.

21 Schmidt, *Parallel-Text Edition* (see note 5, above), Notes, p. 691.

22 Marcia L. Colish, *Peter Lombard*, 2 vols. (Leiden: E. J. Brill, 1994), I, 288.

23 St Thomas Aquinas, *Summa Theologica*, Blackfriars translation (Cambridge: Blackfriars, 1964), 1 q. 14, art. 15. 'Non debet concedi quod Deus possit plura scire quam sciat, quia haec propositio implicat quod ante nesciverit, et postea sciat' (*Summa Theologica*, in the Parma edition of the *Opera Omnia*, Vol. I [1852], p. 69).

24 See David Aers, *Piers Plowman and Christian Theology* (London: Edward Arnold, 1975), p. 109. See also Daniel M. Murtaugh, *Piers Plowman and the Image of God* (Gainesville: University Presses of

Bernard, in his *Tractatus de gradibus humilitatis et superbiae*, addresses himself to the further question, How can Christ, in his joint being with God in the Trinity, not already know what he is supposed to have to learn? He answers that Christ chose to suffer that he might know feeling for those who suffer, and to be made poor and needy that he might learn to feel compassion, so that, as it is written, 'he learned obedience through what he suffered' (Heb. 5.8), he might thereby learn mercy.[25] It is not that he learnt something that he did not know, for he had known it from all eternity; but what he had always known he now learnt by experience in human time.

Peace also seems by implication to deny the doctrine of the 'impassibility' of God, that is, that God cannot suffer as human beings suffer, and that even in his incarnate being he retains this impassibility: Christ suffered in his humanity, as has already been explained, but not in his Godhead. Langland had earlier made this quite clear in his description of Christ being clad for his joust with Death in the plate-armour of Piers Plowman:

> '*Liberum dei Arbitrium* for loue hath vndertake
> That this iesus of his gentrice shal iouste in Pers Armes,
> In his helm and in his haberion, *humana natura*;
> That Crist be nat yknowe for *consumm[a]tus deus*,
> In [Pers paltok] the [plouhman] this prikiare shal ryde
> For no d[yn]t shal hym dere as *in deitate patris*.' (C XX 20–25)

It was further explained, in discussion of the Incarnation, that Christ could fully suffer as a man though not as God, since as a man he had 'emptied himself' of his divinity. Christ, 'though he was in the form of God, did not count equality with God a thing to be grasped, but emptied himself, taking the form of a servant, being born in the likeness of men' (Philippians 2.6–7).[26] Through his self-emptying (*kenosis*), Christ becomes 'a slave to death'.[27] However, Langland is not careful to ensure that Peace makes the vital distinction between the suffering of God and the suffering of Christ (note that 'of', in C XX 217, 'Ne hadde god ysoffred of som oþer then hymsulue', means 'at the

Florida, 1978), p. 120 ('Christ, by taking on a human nature capable of suffering, was learning how to cure His suffering, fallen human creatures'); Samuel A. Overstreet, 'Langland's Elusive Plowman', *Traditio* 45 (1989–90), 257–341 ('He had to assume the frailty of human nature in order to accomplish redemption', p. 312).

25 '... qui pati voluit, ut compati sciret; miser fieri, ut misereri disceret, ut quomodo de ipso scriptum est: *Didicit ex his quae passus est obedientiam*, ita et misericordiam disceret. Non quod ante misereri nesciret, cuius misericordia ab aeterno, et usque in aeternum; sed, quod natura sciebat ab aeterno, temporali didicit experimento' (cap. iii.7, *Patrologia Latina* 182, col. 945, explained further in cap. iii.12, *Patrologia Latina* 182, col. 948).

26 For 'servant', 'slave' is offered as an alternative translation of the Greek (and superior in the context) in the *Revised Standard Version of the The Holy Bible: New Testament* (London: Nelson, 1946), p. 181.

27 Schmidt, *Parallel-Text Edition*, Notes, p. 691. For *kenosis*, and especially its connection with impassibility, see Nicholas Watson, 'Conceptions of the Word: The Mother Tongue and the Incarnation of God', *New Medieval Literatures* 1 (1997), 85–124 (see pp. 86–9).

hands of' rather than 'in the person of'). It might be argued that Peace's apparently unorthodox account of God's omniscience takes advantage of a familiar ambiguity in the word 'God'. 'God' can be used to refer to God incarnate in Christ as well as 'God', and is so used in passages immediately preceding Peace's speech (77, 135, 187, 196, etc.), but it is clear in the context of that speech that the knowledge of sorrow and pain through experience of contraries was not, according to Peace, merely something that Christ had to learn (like the physician's art) but something God, in planning the Incarnation, wanted to *find out*:

> And aftur god auntred hymsulue and toek Adames kynde
> To wyte what he hath soffred in thre sundry places. (231–32)

It could be said, in extenuation of the oddities that have been pointed out in Peace's discourse, that Langland's theology is not that of a schoolman: it is eclectic and sometimes apparently inconsistent. There are human and dramatic values that he is more pressingly conscious of than the dogmatic precision of theology. Whether these concessions are sufficient to explain or make sense of the unusual nature of Peace's argument is doubtful. One conclusion might be that Peace is an 'unreliable witness'. If this seems an unlikely role for a daughter of God, it might not be trivial to point out that Langland, whether through deliberate intention or inadvertence, never actually mentions that the four sisters are daughters so well-born. Be that as it may, it is not unusual for characters in Langland with respectable-sounding names and pedigrees to say things that are dubious. Imaginatyf, for instance, offers some very doubtful arguments for the benefits of learning (e.g. C XIV 129) and is a little fanciful and capricious in his analogies and metaphors.[28] Patience also, surely with an elevated rank in the hierarchy of witness, argues for the benefits that poverty offers in the combat with the deadly sins (C XVI 44–99) with a pragmatism that verges on the immoral or even the comic (e.g. C XVI 84).[29] Perhaps Peace is another such Langlandian character, offering fanciful arguments for her optimistic view of the redemption, and occasionally wandering from the point. The line alluding to the consoling stoic view of the welcome peacefulness of death,

> The which vnknytteth alle care and comsyng is of reste (224)

seems quite inappropriate in the midst of the concern with the sorrow of dying, even for someone called 'Peace'. To make a distinction between the

[28] See Ralph Hanna, 'Langland's Ymaginatif: Images and the Limits of Poetry', in *Images, Idolatry and Iconoclasm in Late Medieval England: Textuality and the Visual Image*, ed. Jeremy Dimmick, James Simpson and Nicolette Zeeman (Oxford: Oxford University Press, 2002), pp. 81–94.

[29] David Aers, in *Sanctifying Signs: Making Christian Tradition in Late Medieval England* (Notre Dame: University of Notre Dame Press, 2004), pp. 129–31, argues that Poverty's acquiescence in the oppressions of real poverty marks him out as a Franciscan apologist.

sorrow of dying and the satisfaction of being dead is likewise completely out of place in the context of a debate about sin and salvation.

It must be admitted that finding characters in a fiction 'unreliable' is a practice with some doubtful antecedents. There is always the danger that identifying inadequate witnesses will be an opportunity for the critic to find his or her own opinions miraculously intact among the wreckage he or she has made of the poem's sense. But perhaps Peace's peculiar arguments should be understood as part of her role in an allegorical debate. It is part of the character of the debate, and of debate in general, that it is envisioned as taking place between characters who do not know everything and who all have their own axes to grind. Peace argues from what she knows, and by her name and presumed nature has a prime interest in looking for conciliatory explanations and reconciliation, even if truth has to be a little compromised to achieve it. Peace's optimistic quest for a peaceful outcome turns out, though not for the reasons she advances, to be the right one: it is apt that she should take a leading role in the singing and celebrations that end the scene (C XX 451), for it is she who anticipates, early on, this celebratory singing and dancing (C XX 183), and it is appropriate to her gay strolling nature and love of merry-making that she should be optimistic in looking for comfortable prospects and in seeking the peaceful reconciliation of difficulties. Beyond that, the function of Peace's speech as an element in a continuing and unfinished debate would fit the nature of a poem that delights in the rehearsal of arguments and opinions which only find their full fruition of truth in Christ or his surrogates, the metamorphosed Piers Plowman and the Good Samaritan.

Furthermore, it is not only a debate: it is an allegorical debate, and the nature of allegory, simply put, is that it clarifies and explains the abstract in terms of the sensory. In the richest and most satisfying forms of allegory, the two are not equated but have a mutually reinforcing metaphorical correlation, as Jill Mann explains in the best brief account of allegory that I know.[30] This is why there is always room for literal-minded commentators to complain about the literal absurdity of allegory. What has been analysed here in the speech of Peace is literally a kind of absurdity, even heresy, but judged by its effectiveness as drama and as a dramatic demonstration of the closeness of God and man (which is more important, and less absurd, than any respect that might be paid to the devil's rights), it is fully in the finest spirit of allegory. Within such an allegory, it is impossible to subject the statements of the characters to the strict analysis that might be appropriate if we were being presented with a series of propositions. It is the rhetorical and imaginative quality of the arguments that gives them their greatest effectiveness, not their logical force: the imagery of the Christ-knight; the pleasing outrageousness of the idea that God might use

30 Jill Mann, *Langland and Allegory*, The Morton W. Bloomfield Lectures in Medieval English Literature 2 (Kalamazoo, MI: Medieval Institute Publications, 1992), p. 14.

tricks to combat the devil, so that guile may defeat guile; the dramatic antitheses, not much more sophisticated, theologically, than the *lex talionis*, of one tree destroying the power of another, of one unlawful seizure cancelling another, of one body standing bail for another body. All is finally resolved in a symbolic dance, with everyone holding hands. Debates are rarely meant to arrive at 'the right answer'. The participants do their best, according to their lights, and then someone else decides, whether Nicholas of Guildford or God. The singing and dancing are as poetically satisfactory a conclusion to the debate of the four daughters as any that could be imagined.

In some respects, this might seem a satisfactory solution to the puzzle I have been mulling over. But it ends by belittling and even ignoring what Langland actually says in the speech of Peace. This speech is strikingly original and memorable, and it places a marked and characteristically Langlandian emphasis on the humanity and human experience of Christ. Throughout the poem Langland has emphasised that Jesus came to bring the gospel to ordinary men and women, not to an elect. The first annunciation was to common shepherds, 'lewede men' (C XIV 96, 101), and the first appearance after the resurrection was to an ordinary sinful woman, Mary Magdalen (C VII 137). Jesus was humbly born and appears to men most familiarly in the guise of a poor man:

> Forthy lerne we t[he] lawe of loue as oure lord tauhte
> And pore peple fayle we nat while eny peny vs lasteth,
> For in here likenesse oure lord lome hath be yknowe. (C XII 120–22)

Langland's emphasis on the 'humanity' of Christ is not the devotion to Christ's body and wounds and to the suffering of Christ in his human flesh that now tends to be dominant in accounts of later medieval spirituality. With this kind of 'affective devotion' Langland's poetry has little affinity, and his account of the Crucifixion in B XVIII/ C XX pays little attention to the details of Christ's bodily suffering.[31] The contrast with the characteristic emphases of affective devotion, as they are amply demonstrated in a contemporary work of wide dissemination and enormous influence, the pseudo-Bonaventuran *Meditationes vitae Christi*, is striking. Nor is it bodily suffering as such that Peace focuses upon, but rather the suffering of being human, of sin and of death. It is these experiences that God wished to know about and why he came down to earth. In this sense, the arguments of Peace are a further confirmation of the centrality of human experience in Langland's poem, the experience of sinning, suffering, striving.

If we look again at the patristic sources for the doctrine of impassibility, and attend to the detail of the language that is used, a striking fact emerges. They do

[31] See David Aers, 'Christ's Humanity and *Piers Plowman*: Contexts and Political Implications', *Yearbook of Langland Studies* 8 (1994), 107–25 (see pp. 109–10, 121).

not talk about the incapacity of God to feel bodily suffering, but of the impossibility for God of feeling compassion. For Anselm, an authoritative early source for the doctrine, to say that God is 'impassible' means that he cannot suffer or undergo anything, cannot be acted upon by anything else; he simply acts. One of the things that he cannot feel, or feel for, is the suffering of others. In chapter 8 of the *Proslogion*, Anselm asks how God can be both merciful and impassible:

> Sed et misericors simul et impassibilis quomodo es? Nam si es impassibilis, non compateris; si non compateris, non est tibi miserum cor ex compassione miseri, quod est esse misericordem.[32]
>
> [But how can you be both merciful and impassible? For if you are impassible, you feel no compassion, nor is your heart sorrowful out of compassion with the sorrowful, which is what being merciful is.]

He explains that God is merciful according to our way of looking at things but not according to his way:

> Es [misericors] quippe secundum nostrum sensum, et non es secundum tuum. Etenim cum tu respicis nos miseros, nos sentimus misericordis effectum, tu non sentis affectum.[33]
>
> [In fact you are merciful according to our way of seeing things and not according to your way. For when you look upon us in our misery, we feel the effect of your mercy, where you do not experience the feeling.]

The reason for denying God the capacity to feel for the suffering of others is of course that a vulnerability to influences outside himself would deny his immutability and omnipotence, which permit no feeling of grief and sorrow: his mercy must be the product of a magisterial and unfeeling pity.[34]

> Non est possibile Deum extra suam naturalem conditionem aliqualiter trahi, cum sit omnino immutabilis ... tristitia et dolor, ex ipsa sui ratione, in Deo esse non possunt.
>
> [It is not possible for God to suffer in any way that is not part of his natural being, for he is altogether immutable ... sadness and sorrow, because of his very nature, cannot exist in God.]

So Aquinas, in the *Summa contra Gentiles*.[35]

32 St Anselm's *Proslogion*, ed. and trans. M. J. Charlesworth (Oxford: Clarendon Press, 1965), p. 125.

33 Anselm, *Proslogion*, ed. and trans. Charlesworth, p. 125.

34 The word 'pity' is understood here to be properly distinct from 'compassion', though the distinction is often obscured. The word 'compassion' began to be used in the fourteenth century, most characteristically of the compassion of Jesus on the cross and his mother for each other (*MED*, s.v. 'compassioun', 1). Later it came to be used, partly because of the influence of the collocation 'have compassion upon' (contrast 'moved with compassion'), as a synonym for 'pity', where there tends to be some sense of the feeling of a superior for an inferior (*MED*, s.v. 'compassioun', 2; *OED*, s.v. 'compassion', 2). It is in this latter sense that I use the word in the text.

35 I.lxxxix, in *Opera Omnia*, Parma edition, Vol. V (1852), p. 60.

If we look more closely at the words of Peace's speech, it is clear that she is talking about this kind of impassibility in God not as an attribute of divinity but as a lack. She does not say that God wishes to experience pain for its own sake, but that he wishes to find out what pain and sorrow are like for men and so feel compassion, and through that save mankind. His desire was to overcome his impassibility, and share with man that compassion or fellow-feeling that the Good Samaritan had identified as that human attribute the denial or refusal of which is a denial or refusal of being truly human. It is this *vnkyndenesse*, this 'unnaturalness' or denial of one's human nature, that quenches the grace of the holy ghost:

> Be vnkynde to thyn emcristene and al that thow canst bidde,
> Dele and do penaunce day and nyht euere
> And purchase al the pardoun of Pampilon and of Rome
> And indulgences ynowe, and be ingrate to thy kynde,
> The holy goest hereth the nat ne helpeth the, be thow certeyne.
> For vnkyndenesse quencheth hym that he can nat shine
> Ne brenne ne blase clere for blowynge of vnkyndenesse. (C XIX 220–26)

> Thus is vnkyndenesse the contrarie that quencheth, as hit were,
> The grace of the holy goest, godes owene kynde. (XIX 255–56)

This is not the leech-craft that Christ has to learn so that he can fulfil his task, but the highest potential of human nature, as it is represented in Piers Plowman, the power to feel for others as oneself.

Finally, it may be that Peace's language of contraries not only challenges orthodoxy but actually enriches her argument. God, in the blankness of his omniscience, in which of course compassion is 'known', as everything is known, in eternity, needs the 'purchase' of experience of an opposite in order to learn what man's sorrow truly is and to share it with him – and perhaps something more:

> God needed humanity to fall so that *both* could understand *kyndeliche* the reality of suffering and pain: in part, that is, so that God, by becoming less than himself, might understand his own fullness.[36]

Langland is not vitally concerned with the bodily suffering of Christ, but with the reconciliation of man and God through a mutual acknowledgement of fellowship in compassion.

36 Watson, 'Conceptions of the Word', p. 117.

10

Chaucer's *Complaint unto Pity* and the Insights of Allegory

Ad Putter

One of the many things I remember Jill Mann saying to me is: 'If close reading is so easy, then why is so little of it any good?' Her point was that intelligent literary criticism is not as simple as it seems. In the case of Middle English literature, it requires, above all, a sympathetic understanding of the values dear to medieval writers together with an appreciation of the possibilities of literary modes and genres that are no longer current. Jill Man's own criticism always achieves that inwardness with the things that mattered to poets, including their chosen forms. This essay in her honour is deeply indebted to the style and substance of her work, particularly to her discussion of pity in Geoffrey Chaucer and of personification allegory in William Langland. Drawing on both these discussions, I would like to attempt a close reading of one of Chaucer's shorter poems, *The Complaint unto Pity*. I hope to show that Chaucer used personification allegory perceptively in this poem, and said something that is both interesting and true about the virtue of pity.

Fortunately, *The Complaint unto Pity* has not produced a daunting tradition of critical commentary, so there is no received opinion to contend with – except perhaps the opinion (summarised in *The Riverside Chaucer*) that 'it is artificial and therefore must have been written when Chaucer was still learning his craft; it is derivative, although no exact source has been found'.[1] This opinion need not detain us for very long. 'Writing poetry', wrote Elizabeth

1 Laila Z. Gross, in *The Riverside Chaucer*, gen. ed. Larry D. Benson (Boston: Houghton Mifflin, 1987), p. 1077. All quotations from Chaucer are taken from this edition. Gross's appraisal echoes that of Wolfgang Clemen in his *Chaucer's Early Poetry*, trans. C. A. M. Sym (London: Methuen, 1963), p. 173. The penetrating recent discussions of the poem by James Simpson, in *Oxford English Literary History, II. 1350–1547: Reform and Cultural Revolution* (Oxford: Oxford University Press, 2002), pp. 128–30, and A.C. Spearing, in *Textual Subjectivity: The Encoding of Subjectivity in Medieval Narratives and Lyrics* (Oxford: Oxford University Press, 2005), pp. 198–210, should help to restore confidence in the poem's quality.

Bishop, 'is an unnatural act',[2] so we should not be disappointed to find 'artificiality' in a poem – especially one written in a demanding verse form, the rhyme royal stanza (which Chaucer actually adopted *after* he had learned his craft) and in the mode of an allegorical story. Personification allegory is and has always been an unusually artificial genre. Its point of departure is a figure of speech, its essence, in Maureen Quilligan's words, the 'self-reflexive tension between the literal and the metaphorical';[3] and the twists and turns of an allegorical story tend to draw attention to the flexibility of words, the multiplicity of their senses and associations. Allegory is thus proudly 'artificial', aware of its own artifice, and I suspect that the real reason why Chaucer's *Complaint unto Pity* has not been well liked is the modern prejudice against allegory *per se*. With regard to the charge that the poem is derivative, I fail to see how it answers the case when no close analogues, let alone a source, have ever been found. It is true that the poem gives expression to ideas and sentiments that are highly conventional, but conventions come *naturally* to us in situations that are recurrent and familiar. The scenario of *The Complaint unto Pity* is obviously one of these situations: that of a frustrated lover who is hopelessly devoted to an unsympathetic lady.

By way of an introduction to the conventions that applied to that situation in Middle English literature, I would like to look briefly at an early fifteenth-century lover's complaint, *A Sovereign Mistress*. Although the lyric is not allegorical, it exemplifies the standard motifs and tropes that form the basis of Chaucer's allegory. The poem begins as follows:

> Myn worldy Ioy, vpon me rewe,
> And mercyles let me noȝt pace;
> For life or deth I wyll yow sewe,
> Þough I in yow neuer fynde grace.
> Lete pite daunger out off your herte race. [**race:** tear]
> And mercy cruelte remewe.
> O bounteous lady, femenygne off face
> Rewe on my peynys, þat am so trewe … (*A Sovereign Mistress*, 1–8)[4]

In accord with complaints of this genre, the lover suffers physically for love of his lady; she is not only beautiful outside ('femenygne off face') but also virtuous within ('bounteous'), and so should therefore appreciate the fact that he is 'trewe'; but if his steadfast devotion to her is to be rewarded, he needs her 'pity' and 'mercy' to repel 'cruelty' and 'daunger'.

2 The quotation is the title given to a fragmentary piece by Elizabeth Bishop, posthumously published in *Edgar Allan Poe and the Juke-Box: Uncollected Poems, Drafts, and Fragments*, ed. Alice Quinn (New York: Farrar, Straus and Giroux, 2006).

3 Maureen Quilligan, *The Language of Allegory: Defining the Genre* (Ithaca: Cornell University Press, 1979), p. 64.

4 Rossell Hope Robbins, ed., *Secular Lyrics of the XIVth and XVth Centuries* (Oxford: Clarendon Press, 1952), no. 140.

The centrality of 'pity' will be evident from the range of words used to express it: the verb 'rewe' and the nouns 'pity', 'grace', and 'mercy', the latter also present negatively in 'mercyles'. This conception of pity as the sentiment on which the lover's chances hinge condenses a great deal of traditional wisdom. As the association of pity with 'grace' indicates,[5] the inspiration behind this conception is theological. Man cannot achieve salvation by virtue of his own merits, because salvation depends not just on his own deeds but also on God's grace, his mercy. Such are our shortcomings that we can only beg God for compassion. So Jonah (in the poem *Patience*) prays:

> 'Þou schal releue me, renk, whil þy ryȝt slepeȝ
> Þurȝ myȝt of þy mercy þat mukel is to tryste.' (323–4)[6]

'Right', i.e. the law of just deserts, gets us nowhere with a creator whose standards of justice are infinitely superior, so we must hope that God's 'right' will be permitted to sleep while his 'mercy' comes to our rescue.[7] The theological background clarifies the point that showing pity is not like settling an IOU, fulfilling an obligation arising from the justness of some moral claim, but rather an emotional response to the painful recognition that this claim, for all its worth, must always fall short of what is required in view of the claimant's essential inadequacy. Vis-à-vis God, this inadequacy will not go away, however hard we struggle to raise ourselves to his standards; it is an insurmountable obstacle that can only be lifted if God deigns to lower himself to our level. In medieval love poetry, this idea, along with many other theological notions,[8] is transferred to the idealised lady (or occasionally the man), who is the object of distant desire. Her excellence is such that the lover cannot hope to win her simply by his own merits or his unwavering devotion (his 'truth'), but only by hoping for the lady's gratuitous renunciation of her superiority. As another

5 As Douglas Gray has remarked, there is a 'hint of theological undertones in the association of *pite* with grace'. See his 'Chaucer and "Pite" ', in *J. R. R. Tolkien, Scholar and Storyteller: Essays in Memoriam*, ed. Mary Salu and Robert T. Farrell (Ithaca: Cornell University Press, 1979), pp. 173–203 (p. 178).

6 *Patience*, ed. J. J. Anderson (Manchester: Manchester University Press, 1969). I translate: 'You shall come to the rescue of me, your man, while your justice sleeps, through the power of your mercy, which is greatly to be trusted.' Anderson's assumption that *renk* refers to God is mistaken: the relationship between Jonah and God is consistently presented in this poem as a quasi-feudal relationship, in which Jonah is God's *renk* ('man'; see also lines 351, 431, 490).

7 The conflict between *right* ('justice') and *mercy* is a topos of medieval literature (see, for example, *Pearl*, ed. E. V. Gordon [Oxford: Clarendon Press, 1953], lines 669–72) and the subject of a contemporary debate poem, 'Mercy and Right', ed. J. Bazire, *Leeds Studies in English* 16 (1985), 259–71.

8 For other examples of such transference see Alcuin Blamires, 'The "Religion of Love" in Chaucer's *Troilus and Criseyde* and Medieval Visual Art', in *Word and Visual Imagination: Studies in the Interaction of English Literature and the Visual Arts*, ed. Karl Joseph Höltgen, Peter M. Daly and Wolfgang Lottes (Erlangen: Universitätsbund Erlangen-Nürnberg, 1988), pp. 11–31, and Elizabeth Archibald, 'Chaucer's Lovers in Metaphorical Heaven', in *Envisaging Heaven in the Middle Ages*, ed. Carolyn Muessig and Ad Putter (London: Routledge, 2006), pp. 222–36.

Middle English love complaint puts it in its concluding line, 'Saue vpon mercy I can noȝt complayne' (*A Pitiless Mistress*, line 37).[9] Pity is the lover's only ground for appeal because compassion brings about a kind of symbolic levelling – which is why pity often finds expression in acts of raising, e.g. lifting a grovelling suppliant back on his feet, or acts of lowering, as when Theseus in Chaucer's Knight's Tale (I.952–3) jumps down from his horse '[w]ith herte pitous' to place himself on an equal footing with the Theban widows – a moment which (in Jill Mann's words) illustrates 'dramatically the levelling of conqueror with victims'.[10]

The *Complaint unto Pity* can be placed against the same background of thought and feeling, but Chaucer takes its figures of speech more seriously than other Middle English poets. The entire allegory is based on a series of metaphors that are merely implied in the lyrics I have cited. Since the lover 'can noȝt complayne ... save upon mercy', Chaucer's *Complaint* becomes, quite literally, a petition to Pity. The dormant metaphor implicit in the notion that pity can 'remove' cruelty is brought to life in Chaucer's allegorical fiction that 'Pity' has been ousted from her rightful place by 'Cruelty' and should take immediate action to recover her position. And last but not least, the idea that the lover needs to find grace produces the story of a lover who sets out on a mission to 'find' Pity only to 'find' her dead. The fundamental device of the allegory, the troping of inner experience as outer discovery, owes much to the richness of the verb 'to find', with its double sense of experiencing within and discovering without. We shall return to that point later.

As all good allegorists do, Chaucer begins by teasing out the figurative potential of words:

> Pite, that I have sought so yore agoo
> With herte soore and ful of besy peyne,
> That in this world was never wight so woo
> Withoute deth – and yf I shal not feyne,
> My purpos was to Pite to compleyne
> Upon the crueltee and tirannye
> Of Love, that for my trouthe doth me dye.
>
> And when that I, be lengthe of certeyne yeres,
> Had evere in oon a tyme sought to speke,
> To Pitee ran I al bespreynt with teres,
> To prayen hir on Cruelte me awreke.
> But er I myghte with any word outbreke
> Or tellen any of my peynes smerte,
> I fond hir ded, and buried in an herte.
>
> Adoun I fel when that I saugh the herse,
> Ded as a ston while that the swogh me laste;

[9] *Secular Lyrics*, ed. Robbins, no. 139.

[10] Jill Mann, *Feminizing Chaucer* (Cambridge: D. S. Brewer, 2002), p. 135.

But up I roos wyth colour ful dyverse
And pitously on hir myn eyen I caste,
And ner the corps I gan to presen faste,
And for the soule I shop me for to preye.
I was but lorn, ther was no more to seye. (1–21)

One of the pleasures of reading allegorical fictions is trying to sort out where personification begins and ends. As Jill Mann has shown, in medieval poems these pleasures are heightened by the absence of a system of capitalisation that discriminates between common and proper names.[11] 'Pity' is potentially a personification from the outset, since the poem begins with an address to pity, who is apostrophised as if she were a person. Personification is also potentially present in the statement that the lover has 'sought' pity for a very long time ('seek' means 'try to obtain' but also 'try to find somebody'). But the latent allegory only becomes fully explicit after Chaucer's knowing use of the sincerity topos, 'yf I shall not feyne', which ushers in the 'feigned' story of a lover who one day sets out to 'find' Pity in order to complain about love's cruelty and disregard for his 'truth'. For understandable reasons, the *Riverside Chaucer* does not capitalise any of the nouns at lines 6–7 except for Love, but Cruelty and Truth both resurface as personifications later on in the poem (see lines 11, 74). Since Pity is the 'coroune of vertues alle' (58), but unforthcoming in the lover's case, she is appropriately allegorised as a grand and unapproachable lady. This conceit gives added point to the lines 'When that I, be lengthe of certeyn yeres/ Had evere in oon *a tyme* sought to speke'. It is sometimes assumed that 'a tyme' goes with the adverbial construction 'Ever in oon', as if the whole phrase meant 'continually',[12] but I think that the operative sense of 'tyme' is 'an occasion', or, more precisely, 'a point in time used for an appointment'.[13] To illustrate this sense, the *MED* cites, for instance, the following extract from the *Rolls of Parliament* (Henry IV, November 1411): 'William Gascoine ... shalle come to the forsaid place ... atte such a resonable tyme as it likyth the forsaid lord the Roos to assigne.'[14] This sense of 'time' and the larger cultural context of feudal service are very relevant to *The Complaint*, for the lover's relationship to Pity is modelled on that of a servant to a great lord. To gain an audience with such powerful people, you need to be granted an appointment. The lover has often sought one, but to no avail; and since pity obviously does not 'run' in his lady's heart,[15] he finally despairs and 'runs' to her.

[11] The implications of this fact are beautifully developed in her *Langland and Allegory*, Morton Bloomfield Lectures on Medieval English Literature (Kalamazoo: Medieval Institute Publications, Western Michigan University, 1992).

[12] See, e.g., Simpson, *Reform and Cultural Revolution*, p. 129.

[13] See *The Middle English Dictionary* [*MED*], ed. Hans Kurath et al. (Ann Arbor: University of Michigan, 1954–), s.v. 'time' n. 9(a).

[14] The citation is from the recent edition by C. Given-Wilson et al., *The Parliament Rolls of Medieval England*, on-line at http://www.sd-editions.com/PROME/.

[15] I allude of course to Chaucer's favourite saying 'pitee renneth soone in gentil herte' (Knight's Tale,

This sequence leads to the first of a number of twists in the allegorical fiction: Pity is found 'dead and buried in' a heart. In the allegorical scheme of things, it is odd to be asked to imagine a lady being buried in a heart, but poets who take metaphors seriously also tend to be more aware that metaphors is all they are. Langland was another such poet, and it is worth comparing Chaucer's momentary suspension of allegorical belief with Langland's abandonment of the allegorical pilgrimage to Truth in *Piers Plowman*.[16] This allegory starts off with Will wanting to find Truth. Piers Plowman gives elaborate directions on how to get to Truth – in a mode of allegory that is deliberately threadbare:

> 'And so boweth forth by a brook, "Beth-buxom-of-speche",
> Forto ye fynden a ford, "Youre-fadres-honoureth":
> *Honora patrem et matrem* ...' (V.566–7)[17]

Since there is no 'way' to truth other than doing what God commands, Langland makes sure we notice that the route is nothing more than a transfiguration of the Ten Commandments. And the allegorical story of a pilgrimage is then dropped almost completely when Piers promises that, at the end of this 'way', 'Thou shalt see in thiselve Truth sitte in thyn herte' (V.606). In Chaucer as in Langland, these 'deconstructive' moments draw our attention to the fact that the illusions of allegory are ultimately conjured by the interplay of different senses of the same words ('seeking truth', 'finding pity'). Because this interplay is an inescapable fact of ordinary language – metaphor being, in I. A. Richards's words, 'the omnipresent principle of language'[18] – it follows that an irreducible residue of figurative language remains even when particular conceits have been abandoned. Truth, even when it is no longer a Saint, still 'sits' in your heart, and pity, even when it is no longer a grand dame, still lies 'dead and buried in' a heart.

I would like to take the comparison between *The Complaint* and *Piers Plowman* one step further by adding that in both these poems the allegory develops in quirky ways that follow the happy accidents of wordplay. For instance, in Langland the allegorical fiction of Christ 'jousting' with Satan is ignited by a pun on the words 'joust' and 'just' (Jesus, a *justice* sone ... sholde ... *juste* therfore' (XVI.92–5).[19] In *The Complaint*, the allegorical story is similarly put back on track by a pun:

I.1761, Merchant's Tale, IV.1986, Squire's Tale, IV.479, and Prologue to the *Legend of Good Women* (F 503; G 491).

16 This paragraph owes much to J. A. Burrow, 'The Action of Langland's Second Vision', *Essays in Criticism* 15 (1965), 247–68, repr. in *Style and Symbolism in Piers Plowman: A Modern Critical Anthology*, ed. Robert J. Blanch (Knoxville: University of Tennessee Press, 1969), pp. 209–27.

17 References to *Piers Plowman* are to *The Vision of Piers Plowman: A Complete Edition of the B-text*, ed. A. V. C. Schmidt, 2nd ed. (London: J. M. Dent, 1995).

18 I. A. Richards, *The Philosophy of Rhetoric* (New York: Oxford University Press, 1965), p. 92.

19 Quilligan, *Allegory*, p. 73.

> I found hir ded and buried in an *herte.*
>
> Adoun I fel when that I saugh the *herse* …

The shift from 'herte' to 'herse' reanimates the allegory and allows it to develop in a new direction, since the hearse sets the scene for an occasion of public mourning. Pity's body lies in state, and the lover responds appropriately. He prepares to say a prayer for the soul, now pointedly separated from the 'corps' (19), and '*pitously* on hir [i.e. Pity] myn eyen I caste'. The *lover's* pity, in other words, is *not* dead, but, in accordance with the solemn state occasion in which we now find ourselves, his personal complaint becomes a universal lament, as if for the death of a great queen who has left her people defenceless:

> Thus am I slayn sith that Pite is ded;
> Allas, that day, that euer hyt schulde falle.
> What maner man dar now hold up his hed?
> To whom shal any sorwful herte calle?
> Now Cruelte hath cast to slee us alle,
> In ydel hope, folk redeless of peyne,
> Syth she is ded, to whom shul we compleyne? (22–8)

'I' no longer speaks for himself but for 'us alle'.

One might thus expect the 'I' to figure from now on as a representative of all lovers, as a kind of Amans, but Chaucer deliberately raises these expectations to make us share the surprise that awaits the lover as the story continues:

> But yet encreseth me this wonder newe,
> That no wight woot that she is ded, but I –
> So many men as in her tyme hir knewe –
> And yet she dyed not so sodeynly,
> For I have sought hir ever ful besely
> Sith first I hadde wit or mannes mynde,
> But she was ded er that I koude hir fynde. (29–35)

The allegorical situation has here become bizarrely surreal. Although Pity's corpse is ceremoniously displayed, the protagonist seems to be the only person who knows she is dead. The apparent absurdity in the allegorical situation can only be resolved if we appreciate that pity here functions simultaneously as a person (Pity) and as an abstract quality (pity). And it is by exposing Pity's double life as proper noun and common noun that Chaucer forces us to return to the realities of life that the allegory is trying to absorb.[20] Most men do not find their ladies' pity dead. The line 'So many men as in her tyme hir knewe' hints that there are plenty of men who had pity from their ladies (perhaps even

[20] I am indebted here to Jill Mann's argument in *Langland and Allegory* (as cited above, n. 11) that *Piers Plowman* requires the same kind of double reading: we are asked to respond to his personifications both as people and as the common nouns which they represent.

from the lover's lady[21]). 'Pity' may therefore *logically* be 'dead' to one person and 'alive' to others. Indeed, do we not know for certain that 'pity' is 'dead' to us precisely because we have noticed it is 'alive' for others? The apparent inconsistency in the allegorical situation manages to glimpse this uncomfortable truth.

The surreal weirdness of the allegorical situation only deepens when the lover tries to think it through. Perhaps, he wonders, she died suddenly – in which case he might just be the first to find out. But no, since he has been trying to get in touch with Pity since reaching manhood without ever getting anywhere, she must have been dead for a good while. The lover's struggle to make sense of his situation exposes the tragic irony in the lover's declaration that Pity 'was ded er that I koude hir fynde'. In the allegorical story, this means that Lady Pity died before he could reach her, but of course the sad reality is that for this lover at least pity was always already 'dead'. For all his years of devotion he never actually 'found' (i.e. experienced) pity at all.

This contradiction between the allegorical fiction and the plain factforeshadows the remarkable twist at the end of the 'Bill of Complaint'. In this Bill, purportedly written *before* the lover finds Pity dead, the lover already speaks of her as 'dead':

> Sith ye be ded – allas that hyt is soo –
> Thus for your deth I may wel wepe and pleyne
> With herte sore and ful of besy peyne. (117–19)

Many critics have argued that these final lines cannot be part of the Bill itself,[22] but there is no *explicit* to indicate that the Bill ends at line 116, and the continued use of the second person implies that the address within the Bill carries on uninterrupted. The truth of the matter is that *The Complaint* does not seem to mind 'inconsistency',[23] and an altogether more interesting interpretation of these lines has recently been provided by James Simpson, who sees them as symptomatic of the lover's hopelessness:

21 This is how Spearing interprets the line: 'on the level of the allegory this allusion to [the lady's] generosity becomes a more explicit and indecorous jab at her promiscuity: many men 'knew' Lady Pity, perhaps in the most bodily sense, in her time' (*Textual Subjectivity*, p. 206). But the allegory is not as explicit as Spearing argues, for 'her tyme' more probably means '*their* time' rather than '*her* time'. In the text of *The Complaint* (based on the Fairfax manuscript), *her* (their) and *hir* (her) are distinguished, although that distinction is not always consistently maintained in the manuscript as a whole: see F. Wyld, *Die sprachlichen Eigentümlichkeiten der wichtigeren Chaucer-Handschriften* (Vienna: W. Braumüller, 1915), p. 274. Future editors who read the line as Spearing does might consider emending *her* to *hir* in this line.

22 See, e.g., John Norton-Smith, *Geoffrey Chaucer* (London: Routledge & K. Paul, 1974), pp. 22–3, and Charles Nolan, 'Structural Sophistication in "The Complaint Unto Pity" ', *Chaucer Review* 13 (1979), 363–72.

23 Spearing makes a similar point in *Textual Subjectivity*, and argues that 'the final "inconsistency" by which he mentions her death in a petition written before he knew of it is in fact part of the wit arising from Chaucer's grasp of the internal contradictions of personification-allegory. 'Pity' is both the lady's pity and Lady Pity; if on one level the lady has so little pity that she does not care "whether I flete or synke" (110), on another that must mean that Pity is dead' (p. 209).

> The document ends with an affirmation of what the impulse of its composition had originally denied (i.e. Pity's death) . . . Narrative falters in this situation, since all the resources of narrative are defeated. The sequence of time is itself destroyed, since everything must always remain as it is. The poem gestures towards narrative sequence along the lines of '*first* I found Pity dead, and *then* I read out the bill I had written before I knew of her death'; but the Complaint reveals that Pity's death underwrites the entire text as its premiss. The temporal stasis is underlined by the identity of the last line with the second.[24]

The conflict between sequence and stasis, narrative and lyric utterance, can be read as a deliberate tension, according to Simpson. I would add to his observation that this tension is already present in the different senses of 'I fond hir ded' and is resolved in ordinary language and experience. 'Finding', as Chaucer's wordplay reminds us, has two basic senses that are relevant here, one dynamic ('to come upon, to discover') – a sense that presupposes a particular time and place and suits narrative (as in 'one day I found her dead') – and the other static ('to feel, experience, consider') – a sense that suits lyric utterance (as in 'I found her pitiless'). In the latter sense 'find' is what grammarians call a 'stative' verb.[25] The same 'dynamic' and 'stative' senses are present in the adjective 'dead'. Literally, in the sense of 'inanimate', the adjective is obviously stative, but figuratively (as in 'The dede sleepe', Miller's Tale, I.3643), the adjective can denote a temporary condition of inertia or unresponsiveness. In Chaucer's poem, the lover 'finds pity dead' in both these senses, stative and dynamic, and the interplay between the two says something very true about how we do 'find out' such things as the lover does. Lack of pity is discovered in a moment of unresponsiveness, but as such moments of 'deadness' mount up we realise that they were signs, not of emotional reserve, but rather of an emotional void. Like Chaucer's lover, we may thus find ('discover') that pity was dead, stillborn, long before we found ('experienced') her dead (unresponsive).

In the stanzas that follow, the people surrounding the hearse figure the lady's virtues:

> Aboute hir herse there stoden lustely,
> Withouten any woo as thoughte me,
> Bounte parfyt, wel armed and richely,
> And fresshe Beaute, Lust, and Jolyte,
> Assured Maner, Youthe, and Honeste,
> Wisdom, Estaat, Drede, and Governauance,
> Confedered both by bonde and alliaunce.

24 Simpson, *Reform and Cultural Revolution*, pp. 128–9. See also V. J. Scattergood's interpretation of the final lines, as revealing 'the trapped mind of the speaker, enclosed in its powerlessness': Alastair Minnis, V. J. Scattergood and J. J. Smith, *Oxford Guide to Chaucer: The Shorter Poems* (Oxford: Oxford University Press, 1995), p. 469.

25 On stative and dynamic verbs and adjectives see Randolph Quirk and Sidney Greenbaum, *A University Grammar of English* (London: Longman, 1973), 2.8, 3.35 and 5.19.

A compleynt had I, writen in myn hond,
For to have put to Pite as a bille;
But when I al this companye ther fond,
That rather wolden al my cause spille
Then do me helpe, I held my pleynte stille,
For to that folk, withouten any fayle,
Withoute Pitee, ther may no bille availe.

Then leve I al these vertues, sauf Pite,
Kepynge the corps as ye have herd me seyn,
Confedered alle by bond of Cruelte
And ben assented when I shal be sleyn. (36–53)

The great C. S. Lewis thought that this showed 'the use of personification at its lowest level – the most faint and frigid result of the popularity of allegory. Not only do the allegorical figures fail to interact, as in true allegory; they even fail to be pictorial: they *become* a mere catalogue' (italics mine).[26] The question is whether Chaucer ever tried to pretend otherwise, whether it would not be fairer to say that a catalogue is all this *is* and was ever meant to be. I think myself that Chaucer expected his readers to recognise this as a conventional list of the lady's qualities, a rhetorical *notatio* thinly disguised as allegory.[27] The obvious comparison is with Langland's equally transparent allegorization of the route to Truth, which 'becomes a mere catalogue' of the Ten Commandments because that is what it is and what Langland wanted it to be. As in Langland, so in Chaucer, the lack of a 'pictorial' element contributes positively to the transparency of the allegory. Those attributes that Chaucer does give to the virtues are purely iconic. Beauty is 'fressche' (with the final -*e* of the weak inflection, since the grammar obeys the fictional postulate that nouns are proper names[28]), 'Maner' is 'Assured', and 'Bounté' is 'well armed and richely'. This description of Bounty has baffled critics;[29] I would suggest that Chaucer was alive to the different senses of the word 'bounty', which in Middle English, as in the original Old French, meant (a) 'goodness, virtue', and (b) 'knightly prowess, strength, valor, chivalry'.[30] The epithet 'wel armed and richely' fits 'bounty' in that latter sense. With regard to Lewis's criticism that Chaucer's personifications fail to 'interact', it must be said in Chaucer's defence that abstractions obviously cannot 'interact' with each other as people do. Even

26 C. S. Lewis, *The Allegory of Love* (New York: Oxford University Press, 1958), p. 167.

27 In rhetoric, *notatio* is the term for a description of a person's character (Cicero, *Rhetorica ad Herrenium*, Book IV). As shown by Norton-Smith (*Geoffrey Chaucer*, p. 18), this figure is conventionally found in secular complaints.

28 Attributive adjectives modifying proper names normally take final *e*. See David Burnley, 'Inflexion in Chaucer's Adjectives', *Neuphilologische Mitteilungen* 83 (1982), 169–77.

29 *Riverside Chaucer*, p. 1078: 'it is not clear why "Bounte" should be "wel armed" '.

30 See *MED* s.v. 'bountē' n. 1(a) and (b). The second sense, 'prowess', comes to the fore in the description of Hercules ('What for his strength and for his heigh bountee'), in Chaucer's Monk's Tale, VII.2114).

when poets do show them 'interacting' in the way that Lewis likes (say, in a 'battle' between virtues and vices), the real interest of the action lies in the specification of *relationships*. In *The Complaint unto Pity*, these relationships are very intelligently indicated. Since 'Pity' is the presiding virtue, central to all others, the other virtues are ranged *around* her, 'aboute the herse', but, although *and* because pity is dead, they are inevitably 'Withouten any woo' (37). Moreover, since without pity, all other virtues are useless to the lover ('Eke what availeth Maner and Gentilesse/ Withoute yow, benygne creature', 78–9), they are also, now that Pity is dead, ranged *against* the lover, who, as the only non-personified character in the poem, stands isolated and helpless against their combined force.[31] And, finally, since the lady's cruelty will kill the lover in the end ('Though ye me sle by Cruelte your foo', 114), Cruelty is imagined as the mastermind behind an evil plot, a 'confederacy' that naturally includes the lady's virtues, who keep the lover 'hooked' on his heartless lady and so aid and abet Cruelty in plotting his death. Together they have connived ('ben assented to') *when* (not *if*) he will die. As will be clear from this paraphrase, 'confedered' and 'ben assented to' are rather more sinister than *The Riverside Chaucer* would suggest.[32] The imagined situation is that of an assassination plot against a hapless servant by a clique of household retainers, and it is perhaps not surprising to find a parallel in John Skelton's terrifying *Bowge of Court*, where the 'I' (personified as Dread) similarly finds (or imagines) himself the target of a murderous conspiracy:

> And as he rounded thus in myne ere
> Of fals collusyoun *confetryd* by *assente*,
> Me thoughte I see lewde felawes here and there
> Came for to slee me of mortall entente. (526–9)[33]

Chaucer's perfectly coherent presentation of virtues as hostile adversaries leads to some wonderfully paradoxical lines in which the lover 'leaves' her virtues:

> Then leve I al these vertues, sauf Pite,
> Kepynge the corps as ye have herd me seyn …
> … For to my *foes* my bille I dar not schewe
> Th'effect of which saith thus, in wordes fewe. (50–56)

31 Bruce Holsinger gets at this when he writes: '[M]uch of the poem's gloomy narrative tension results from the subjective isolation of the speaker over against a formidable company of other allegorical figures (none of them mourning).' See his chapter 'Lyrics and Short Poems', in *The Yale Companion to Chaucer*, ed. Seth Lerer (New Haven: Yale University Press, 2006), pp. 179–221 (p. 205).

32 The *Riverside Chaucer* glosses 'confedered' as 'confederated, joined together' and 'ben assented' as 'are agreed' (in the general glossary).

33 J. V. Scattergood, ed., *John Skelton: The Complete English Poems* (Harmondsworth, Middlesex: Penguin Books, 1983).

Chaucer's reference to these personifications first as 'virtues' and then as 'foes' is a contradiction that immediately sparks illumination. Supreme beauty, goodness, etc., are, of course, great virtues in a lady, but, when you love such a lady and cannot hope to match her in these departments, these same fine qualities can (in Tennyson's memorable phrase) 'shadow an angry distance',[34] since they put her out of your reach, make her unattainable. In the allegory, therefore, these virtues are figured not so much as 'allegorical mourners'[35] – for they stand 'lustely,/ Withouten any woo as thoghte me', 36–7) – but as *guards* who are 'Kepyng the corps' (51) and so prevent the lover from reaching Pity. Another nice touch in this passage is its double vision of the 'virtues' as both 'people' and as a rhetorical commonplace. The announcement that the speaker will 'leave' them 'guarding the corpse' brings them alive as persons, but the logical impossibility of 'leaving' them but not Pity herself ('sauf Pite'), when they are supposed to surround her, makes us appreciate that what is really being left behind is a topic, a list of virtues, rather than a group of people,[36] and that from this catalogue of virtues pity is excepted ('sauf Pite') because it is a virtue that the lady does not possess.

This self-reflexive artificiality culminates in the final 'Bill of Complaint'. As Charles Nolan and others have shown,[37] this 'bill' is modelled on legal documents (a 'bill' being 'a written petition or complaint, used to initiate an action at law'[38]): after a salutation (57–63), the petitioner describes his grievance and then prays for redress. The combination of the legal and amatory discourse has been thought 'problematical',[39] but that may not be a fair criticism. The legalistic 'bill' follows neatly from the preceding story: the lover's intention was always to 'compleyne' to Pity (line 5); for that purpose he brought with him a 'compleynt' written in his own hand, which he meant to present to Pity as a bill ('For to have put to Pite as a bille', 44); since he found Pity dead he keeps his 'pleynte' (47) to himself, because his enemies would sooner 'al my cause spille' (46) than help him. As these snippets from the poem show, the legal tone is set from the start: 'compleynt' and 'pleinte' are legal terms ('a lawsuit, legal

34 Tennyson uses the phrase to describe the agonistic effect that noble ideals can have on someone who despairs about ever being able to live up to them: *Balin and Balan*, line 231, in *Idylls of the King*, ed. J. M. Gray (Harmondsworth: Middlesex: Penguin Books, 1996).

35 Spearing, *Textual Subjectivity*, p. 202.

36 I was alerted to his point by Norton-Smith's choice of the variant reading 'Then leue [we] all [þees] virtues, sauf Pite', in *Geoffrey Chaucer*, p. 22. I hope it is clear that I do not share his preference for this reading, let alone his view that 'this transitional passage ... seems terribly crude'.

37 Nolan, 'Structural Sophistication'. See also Holsinger, 'Lyrics', who comments on 'sheweth' (p. 212, n. 46), and Spearing, *Textual Subjectivity*, who notes that the inversion of subject ('Youre servaunt') and indirect object ('unto your rial excellence') in lines 59–60 follows the convention (proper to formal salutations to a superior) 'that the recipient's name should precede the sender's' (p. 201).

38 I cite the definition of the word by John A. Alford, *Piers Plowman: A Glossary of Legal Diction* (Cambridge: D. S. Brewer, 1988), s.v. 'bille'.

39 Nolan, 'Structural Sophistication', p. 363.

complaint, accusation'[40]), as are the phrases 'put (up) a bill'[41] and 'spill my cause' ('undermine my legal case').[42] We may like to think that love and law do not mix, but they do in our everyday language (e.g. 'suitor') and also in the poem's title 'A Complaint unto Pity' (given in the majority of manuscripts as 'A Complaint of Pity').[43] The whole direction of the allegorical story is anticipated in the title word, for, as it turns out, 'Complaint' names not only what the poem 'really' is (a lover's complaint) but also what it 'fictionally' becomes, i.e. a 'complaynt' (54) presented to Pity. The surprise that an amatory 'complaint' should issue in a legal 'complaint' is therefore based on impeccable linguistic logic.

Like most medieval lawsuits, the one instigated by the lover takes the form of a property dispute, and it is couched in the customary terms of property law:

> Hit stondeth thus: your contraire, Crueltee,
> Allyed is ayenst your regalye ...
> Under colour of womanly Beaute –
> For men schulde not, lo, knowe hir tirannye,
> And hath depryued yow now of your place
> That hyghte 'Beaute apertenant to Grace.'
>
> For kyndely by your herytage ryght
> Ye ben annexed ever unto Bounte;
> And verrayly ye oughte do youre myght
> To helpe Trouthe in his adversyte.
> Ye be also the corowne of Beaute,
> And certes if ye wanten in these tweyne,
> The world is lore; ther is no more to seyne. (64–77)

Chaucer leaves us a great deal to unpack in this mini-allegory. Since 'Pity' is the 'crown' of all virtues, the conspiracy against her by Cruelty and her allies is an offence against her royal authority ('regalye').[44] Cruelty is Pity's 'contraire' (in the double sense of 'opposite' and 'opponent'), charged with having wrongly taken over a 'place' belonging to Pity, namely 'Beaute apertenant to Grace'. To get into this place without being recognised as the tyrant she really is, she has gone 'under colour of Womanly Beauty'. This, too, has legal overtones, for

40 Alford, *Glossary*, s.v. 'pleinte'.

41 See *Piers Plowman* B IV.47, 'And thanne com Pees into parlement and putte up a bille'.

42 Alford, *Glossary*, s.v. 'cause'. 'Spill' had, besides the general meaning 'destroy', a specific application to breaking or invalidating a law, subverting a case or message by misrepresenting it (see *MED* s.v. 'spillen', v. 5).

43 The title is found in manuscripts of both the α- and ß-branches of the stemma, and so has a good claim to represent the archetype. See *Riverside Chaucer*, ed. Benson, p. 1186.

44 Spearing thinks that Chaucer gave Pity royal rank (for the first time in the stanza at the exact middle of the poem, lines 57–63) in order to mark the 'sovereign mid point' of his poem. Whatever one thinks of this argument, it is not really the case 'that there was no requirement that Pity should be given royal rank' (*Textual Subjectivity*, pp. 199–200). As the 'coroune of vertues alle', 'pity' is the *sovereign* virtue, and so is aptly allegorised as a queen.

'under colour' was used with reference to the pretence under which criminal deception was carried out (see *Liber Albus*, 368: 'Certain persons … do daily exert themselves to maintain the false abominable contract of usury, trading under cover and colour [*desouz le coverture et colour*] of good and lawful trading').[45] The charge implies that the lady's beauty, which was once the natural expression of her grace, has become a false mask for her cruelty. The *Riverside Chaucer*, which sheds more darkness than light on these lines, glosses 'apertenant' as 'suitable, properly belonging to' but it is important to note that the term is legal. It derives from 'appurtenance', the technical word for a piece of property that belongs 'to another thing more worthy as principal, and which passes in possession with it, as a right of way or other easement of land; an outhouse, barn, garden, etc. belonging to a house or messuage'.[46] This precise sense matters not only because of its legal register but also because it sharpens the sense. Pity's residence is the kind of Beauty that 'belongs to' Grace in the way a minor property 'belongs to' principal one. True beauty is, as it were, an 'outhouse' of grace. Or rather, this *was* the status of Beauty, for now that Cruelty has usurped Pity's place the old name has ceased to be valid. The past tense in 'Thy place … that *hyghte* "Beaute appertenant to Grace" ' is significant.

Chaucer's legalistic manner of speaking continues with 'annexed', which again has a technical sense in law (where it is used of properties or lands that belong to an estate).[47] Pity, claims the petitioner, is separate from but legally bound up with Bounty, and since Bounty (the lady's innate goodness) values Truth, Pity ought to help Truth in his adversity ('Trouthe' being of course a personification of the lover's steadfast loyalty, an animation of the 'trouthe' averred by the lover at line 7). Because Pity is also the quality that ennobles Beauty (i.e. it is Beauty's 'crown'), it would be disastrous if Pity 'wanted in these tweyne'. *The Riverside Chaucer* assumes that 'these tweyn' refers to Truth and Beauty, but 'these two' are surely 'Beaute' and 'Bounte'. Linked as they are by sound and sense (as outer and inner beauty), Chaucer consistently couples them in his works;[48] they are, to his mind, exactly the virtues that need to be tempered by pity to make the lady less forbidding to the lover.

Chaucer's meaning may become clearer if we look at a simpler expression of the same idea in *The Book of the Duchess*. In that poem, the Black Knight describes how he finally plucked up the courage to declare his love to Blanche

45 Cited in Alford, *Glossary*, s.v. 'colour'.

46 Alford, *Glossary*, s.v. 'appurtenaunce'.

47 See *MED* s.v. 'annexen' v. 1. Citations there include the following (from a will): 'I woll þat þere be founde a perpetuell chaunterie … with cottages annexid þerto'.

48 See, e.g., *A Balade of Complaint*, lines 5–7: '[God] That Bounte made, and Beaute list to grave/ In your persone, and bad hem both in-fere/ Ever t'awayte, and ay be wher ye were'.

when he considered that her supreme beauty and bounty made it likely that she would also possess the virtue of pity, on which his fate depended:

> 'So at the laste, soth to sayne,
> I bethoghte me that Nature
> Ne formed never in creature
> So moche beaute, trewely,
> And bounte, wythoute mercy.
> In hope of that, my tale I tolde …
> I seyde "Mercy"!' and no more.' (1194–9, 1219)

There exists a natural connection between Beauty and Bounty on the one hand, and Pity on the other, and to have the first two without the last would make a lady a freak of nature. In Chaucer's *Complaint* this train of thought is appropriately developed in legal diction. Pity is inherently, 'by heritage', annexed to Bounty, and 'Beauty' is her ancestral dwelling place. She should therefore be present in both (for a lady born bounteous and beautiful must also have been born pitiful). Pity ought therefore to assert her birthright against her enemy Cruelty: if she continues to be absent from Bounty and Beauty, the natural order would come to an end: 'The world is lore; ther is no more to seyne'.

The lover has in fact much to more to say, and there is much more to be said about that, too, but I will let his *topos* prompt my brief conclusion. The qualities I have tried to highlight in my reading of the poem, its intelligent attention to its own method of proceeding, to polysemy and *paranomasia* as the driving forces of its fiction, are unlikely to endear it to those who find it 'artificial'. Fortunately for them, *The Complaint unto Pity* is unrepresentative of Chaucer's art. Chaucer is usually a storyteller who does not allow narrative to be sabotaged by self-referential involvement. *The Complaint to Pity*, however, reveals an unexpected side of Chaucer's talent, his gift for allegory. Because wordplay and puns make allegory possible in the first place, the self-reflexiveness of *The Complaint* is entirely natural. Indeed, the 'deconstructive moments' in *The Complaint*, those moments in which the narrative falters or no longer adds up, really do not so much derail the allegorical story as focus attention on its mechanics, on the double meanings that form the story's two tracks, and on the switch words that straddle them. As Maureen Quilligan has pointed out (in her critique of Burrow's reading of the pilgrimage allegory in *Piers Plowman*), this short-circuiting of the narrative is not a deviation from true allegory but a distillation of its essence.

This is not to say that the pursuit of self-reflexiveness makes an allegorical poem worthwhile in and of itself. There is nothing to be gained from a poem that turns obsessively on the multiple senses of its words unless these senses are connected meaningfully by a poet, connected, that is, in a way that recovers some of the reasons why our ancestors thought it wise to entrust different meanings to the same word in the first place. *The Complaint of Pity* manages, I think, to do just that. There is something about this allegory, particularly in the fluidities of its movements from dynamic to stative 'finding', that returns us to life as well as words. The same is true of Pity's double life in this poem as a 'person' (who lives and dies) and a quality (which can be 'dead' to some but alive to others). Since personification allegory works by turning qualities into people, abstract nouns into proper nouns, this double life similarly draws attention to the mechanics of the genre. Yet these mechanics, too, have a basis in ordinary life, where virtues such as 'pity' are inevitably instantiated in an individual person. In Jill Mann's words, allegory's 'linguistic ambivalence reflects an ambivalence in life, where an abstract principle will always be merged into the texture of lived experience'.[49]

Perhaps the most valuable insight to be gained from Jill Mann's observations – this one included – is that the alien and 'artificial' aspects of medieval poems are much more 'normal' than we first imagined, for the simple reason that the 'normal' operations of life are stranger than they seem. To read *The Complaint unto Pity* in the spirit of this insight is to discover in the strange non-sequiturs of Chaucer's allegory the entanglements of ordinary words and experiences.

49 Mann, *Langland and Allegory*, p. 8.

11

Amor in claustro

† Paul Gerhard Schmidt

Denis Diderot's novel *La religieuse*, the story of a nun struggling to be released from her monastic vows, is one of the most embittered monastic satires of the Enlightenment. In this novel Diderot, whose point of departure was a public trial in 1758, took the view that the monastic life is incompatible with human nature and indeed with Christianity itself. He demonstrated this through the sufferings of his unfortunate heroine in three separate nunneries. She was only able finally to escape from the unnatural monastic life with the help of a priest. Alessandro Manzoni's novel *Monaca di Monza*, in effect the germ of his great *Promessi sposi*, also treats the unbearable living conditions of a nun in a convent. This work, too, developed from reports of a public trial. The reports paint a truly horrific picture. They speak of murder and of the seduction of several nuns by the lover of the mother superior, who bore him two children. The novels of Diderot and Manzoni paint a depressing picture of the lies and rape which characterize the monastic experience in the modern period, an experience in which only dissoluteness and licence appear to have the upper hand. But is familiarity with these novels, and with reading the *facetiae* ('comic anecdotes') and novellas of the Italian Renaissance, an appropriate basis on which to judge the relations between the sexes in monasteries of the Middle Ages?[1] It is well known that novels obey their own laws.

Monastic life in the Middle Ages was defined by strict laws and rules. Anyone who took monastic vows was bound to chastity, poverty and obedience. Monks and nuns were obliged to renounce sexual activity, personal

[1] Anyone who writes an article for Jill on the position of women in the Middle Ages runs the risk of carrying coals to Newcastle. For other readers I would mention that Boccaccio and Chaucer marked a turning point in the hitherto negative perception of women, who were reckoned as *confusio hominis*. For stories about love in the cloister, in which *inter alia* a supposed deaf-mute cuckolds God, see Giovanni Boccaccio, *Decameron*, ed. Vittore Branca (Florence: Felice Le Monnier, 1965), pp. 318–27 (3.1) and 1030–4 (9.2).

property and individual volition.[2] It was not given to everyone to conform unreservedly to these rules. Despite the monastic rules, there were transgressions – secret possession of money and other valuables, sexual relationships – and it happened in no few cases that a monk or a nun left the monastery to which he or she ought to have belonged for the entire span of their life. There are no reliable statistics on the number of infractions of these rules.[3] It was not in the interest of any monastic house to publicize occurrences of this sort, which were ascribed to the influence of the devil. Monastic chronicles record events of a very different kind, such as the election of a new abbot or abbess, visits of royalty or bishops to the monastery; they mention building-works, unusual changes in the weather, crop-yields, famine, prodigies and marvels, fires and other catastrophes as well as deaths. But, as a rule, they pass over in silence cases of apostasy, shocking love-affairs, pregnancies or even births within the monastic precincts. Medieval sources only mention scandals of this sort if a swift punishment or a shameful death befell the guilty party, or if through divine agency it led to a conversion of the repentant sinner and her re-admission the monastery. But in general it is the case that we possess no precise information concerning the frequency of violations of the rules and are thrown back on speculations, which of course differ widely according to the viewpoint of the modern observer.

In the early modern period the sources of information are considerably better. Someone who wishes, for example, to obtain information concerning the broken vows of Venetian nuns in the sixteenth century can find numerous reports of non-monastic origin preserved in the Archivio di Stato in Venice, as the richly detailed study of Mary Laven has shown.[4] It is not possible to provide for the medieval period a comparable analysis of broken vows based on the same sort of sources. One can, however, point to underlying patterns of

2 On life in the nunnery, see Michel Parisse, *Les nonnes au moyen âge* (Le Puy: C. Bonneton, 1983), and Norbert Ohler, *Mönche und Nonnen im Mittelalter* (Düsseldorf: Patmos, 2008). On love poetry composed by women religious, see two studies by Peter Dronke: *Medieval Latin and the Rise of European Love-Lyric* (Oxford: Clarendon Press, 1968), and 'Pseudo-Ovid, *Facetus*, and the Arts of Love', *Mittellateinisches Jahrbuch* 11 (1976), 126–31. A reproduction of a medieval drawing of a monk and a nun in the act of making love (from London, British Library, Additional MS 10294, fol. 1r), is found in Anna-Maria Gruia, 'Sex on the Stove', *Medium Aevum Quotidianum* 55 (2007), 19–58, at 38.

3 On the number of runaways in England (based on the evidence of episcopal registers), see F. Donald Logan, *Runaway Religious in Medieval England, c. 1240–1540* (Cambridge: Cambridge University Press, 1996), esp. pp. 66–96, with examples of women apostates at pp. 83–9. Still indispensable is the study by Eileen Power, *Medieval English Nunneries* (Cambridge: Cambridge University Press, 1922), esp. pp. 436–74 ('The old daunce'). There is a fascinating study of sexual malpractice by nuns at thirteenth-century Zamora (in Spain) by Peter Linehan, *The Ladies of Zamora* (Manchester: Manchester University Press, 1977).

4 Mary Laven, *Virgins of Venice. Enclosed Lives and Broken Vows in the Renaissance Convent* (London: Viking, 2002); see also Werner Paravicini, 'Un amour malheureux au XVe siècle: Pierre de Hagenbach et la dame de Remiremont', *Journal des Savants* (2006), 105–81.

thought and motivation in certain medieval texts, which led to the recording of a particular scandal.

Typical in this respect are two stories which the Cistercian author Caesarius of Heisterbach included in his *Dialogus miraculorum* in the third decade of the thirteenth century.[5] The first occurs in ch. 103 of the fourth book, and bears the title *De sanctimoniali in Anglia, quae a suo provisore tentata est* ('The nun in England who was tempted by her confessor'). Caesarius names no authority for this anecdote, as he does on many other occasions. Nor does he name the English monastery in which the incident is alleged to have taken place; he does not mention the monastic order, nor even the name of the nun and her confessor. The confessor is described as an impressive person of great attractiveness, so brimming with health and *joie de vivre* that one would not take him to be celibate or a religious at all. This *descriptio pulchritudinis* of a man has a disturbing effect on the modern reader, because it suggests that the combination of piety and dazzling appearance is highly unusual, as if no religious ought to have rosy cheeks and flashing eyes. A young nun from the nunnery entrusted to him is so infatuated with this handsome confessor, that she puts aside all inhibitions and confesses her love to him. The man, as devout as he is good looking, rejects her advances. He reminds her that she is the *sponsa Christi* and that God would punish her if by chance he should commit this sin with her. His second counter-argument concerns the loss of his good reputation. A sexual relationship could not be hidden from others and would damage the reputation of the participants. But his grounds for rejection count for nothing with the love-crazed nun, who threatens him with suicide if he won't accede to her request. So under compulsion he agrees to a tryst, but insists, against her inclination, that it take place in daylight and not in the depths of night. At the secret meeting in the cloister garden he requests that she examine his body closely before their love-making begins. When he undresses, a hair shirt becomes visible beneath his splendid outer garment, which covers up a blackened body afflicted with scabies and crawling with maggots, which his ascetic devotions made unmistakable. This sight so shocked the nun that she immediately turned pale with horror, then blushed red with shame, and threw herself on the ground in front of him, begging his forgiveness. From this moment on, she was cured of her profane love. The nameless, devout confessor embodies a well-known allegorical figure, namely the World-as-Woman, which from the front offers a seductive and attractive appearance, but whose back reveals all the signs of rottenness and decay.[6] It is for this reason that the story in the *Dialogus miraculorum* is not localized and the names of the nun and her confessor are not supplied.

5 Caesarius of Heisterbach, *Dialogus miraculorum*, ed. J. Strange (Cologne: J. M. Heberle, 1851), I, pp. 273–4.

6 See Wolfgang Stammler, *Frau Welt: Eine mittelalterliche Allegorie* (Freiburg [Switzerland]: Universitätsverlag, 1959).

The second example from Caesarius immediately precedes the story of the nun and her confessor.[7] Ch. 102 of Book IV has the title *De nobili castellana, quae stimulum carnis in aqua restrinxit* ('Concerning the noble châtelaine, who quenched the promptings of the flesh in water'). Here, too, any localization is lacking, and no names are given, but Caesarius ascribes his account of this event to an informant whom he calls a *sacerdos religiosus.* The protagonist is a noble matron. One day she is possessed by the spirit of sexual desire. She is seized with inner restlessness, feels an all-consuming fire, and begins to look for an object for her passion. Since she is all alone in the castle, there being no one else present but the porter, she seeks to extinguish her burning desire with him. But, like the steward in the adjacent story, the porter is a devout man. So he rejects her unambiguous request and reminds her of God's commandment and her good reputation, which she would lose if she were to get involved with him. The rejected noblewoman thereupon leaves the castle and rushes to the nearby river – not in order to end her life there, but to extinguish her burning desire in the cool water. God Himself had prompted this thought in her. The ice-cold water fulfils its function as a cure for love-longing. Freed from the sensation of wicked desire, she returns to the castle and thanks the porter for his steadfast refusal. The cold water has so chastened her that she would not now be willing to do for a thousand silver marks what she had requested from him a short while before. Caesarius concludes this *exemplum* with a simile. God in His goodness behaves like a loving mother, who allows her own child to run about in the vicinity of a dangerous fire, but if the child wants to run into the fire, it will be held back and preserved from harm.

It is a common feature of both episodes that in each case the woman is driven by sexual desire and wishes to transgress divine commandment and human morality. It is she who takes the initiative. The message is clear: since the days of the first human couple, the weaker sex succumbs to the promptings and temptations of the devil. Men on the other hand are, in the view of Caesarius and his contemporaries, the embodiment of discipline, morality and unshakeable belief. The steward who chastizes himself reminds us, with his otherwise carefully concealed and ill-treated body, of the transience of all beauty and of death. Furthermore, insofar as he prohibits the young nun to speak to a third party about his hair shirt, he behaves like a future saint. The porter of the second episode, who is from a lower social class, is certainly not a saint in disguise, but he nonetheless conducts himself as a devout Christian, one who feels bound by God's commandment. The rescue of the sinner here follows from the direct intervention of God, Who recommends to the matron the bath in cold water as the antidote to sinful conduct. This means of salvation is a well-known and established feature of many saints' Lives: in order to

[7] Caesarius, *Dialogus miraculorum*, I, pp. 272–3.

destroy sexual desire, a saint will throw himself into thorns, nettles or even into ice-cold waters. In this way he escapes the heat of hell's flames.

The typically misogynistic attitude of Caesarius can be illustrated from many other examples. One case may be mentioned, in which Caesarius speaks of his own experience. It concerns one Richwin from Cologne, who entered the Cistercian abbey of Heisterbach as a novice.[8] The devil, who grieves at any entry into a monastery, makes use of a woman (again following his customary procedure), in order to divert Richwin from his purpose. He has a canoness of the nunnery of St Caecilia in Cologne, who is in love with Richwin, write a letter to the novice. In the letter she advises him against the monastic life, and urges him to apostasy. She announces similar plans of her own, for she offers him her hand and the prospect of her immense fortune. This alluring offer plunges Richwin into great inner distress. On one hand, wealth and sensual love attract him, on the other hand the admonitions and pleas of his monastic brethren hold him back. In a dramatic struggle with the devil Richwin finally gains the victory. He decides in favour of the monastic life and makes his profession. The alliance between the canoness and the devil was not powerful enough to dissuade the novice from the decision he had formerly taken. As he later explained (at least according to Caesarius), he never regretted his decision. The temptation, which had once nearly broken his heart, now seemed to him like a speck of dust on his outer garment which did not touch him inwardly.

Such quasi-stereotypical *exempla* pale into insignificance when compared to the spectacular incident which took place in the Gilbertine double house of Watton in 1160.[9] The case of the nun of Watton received masterly literary expression at the hands of the Cistercian monk Aelred of Rievaulx. The case is so well known to English-speaking medievalists that it is not necessary here to repeat more than the most important details. The protagonist is an unnamed young nun who at the age of four was taken into the convent, where she frequently made herself conspicuous by her undisciplined behaviour. When several men were staying in the convent (during the day-time) to attend to building-works, she fell in love with a canon. According to Aelred's account, the rapprochement of the couple – in which the devil naturally had a hand – followed step by step the rules of medieval love treatises. The initiative comes from the young man, who thereby incurs the greater blame because he is the

8 Caesarius, *Dialogus miraculorum*, I, pp. 260–1.

9 See Giles Constable, 'Aelred of Rievaulx and the Nun of Watton: An Episode in the Early History of the Gilbertine Order', in his *Monks, Hermits and Crusaders in Medieval Europe* (London: Variorum Reprints, 1988), pp. 205–26, and P. G. Schmidt, 'Die Nonnne von Watton: Amor illicitus, Apostasia, Miraculum', in *Studien zur Geschichte des Mittelalters. Jürgen Petersohn zum 65. Geburtstag*, ed. Matthias Thumser, Annegret Wenz-Haubfleisch and Peter Wiegand (Stuttgart: Theiss, 2000), pp. 122–8. The text of the miracle is found in J.-P. Migne, *Patrologiae cursus completus, series latina*, 221 vols. (Paris, 1844–64), 195, cols. 789–96.

driving force. Contrary to the usual tendency in other such accounts, the young woman is more victim than culprit. The nightly encounters of the two lovers do not go unnoticed, and they have inevitable consequences. The other nuns discover that she is pregnant and they engage in long discussions about how scandal is to be avoided and the fallen nun is to be punished. Thanks to her willingness to co-operate, her fellow-sinner (i.e. the canon) is lured into an ambush. In fact the intention was simply to beat the outsmarted man as a cure for his sexual drive, but the situation gets out of hand and turns into a scene of horror. The grim nuns behave like Furies and compel the young woman to castrate – with her own hands – the father of her as yet unborn child. Then she is chained up in the monastic prison and closely guarded. There is a fear that she will give birth to twins. One morning it is observed that the pregnancy has come to an end; in spite of careful searches there is no trace of the fruits of the womb in the tiny prison cell. A physical examination of the prisoner leads to the conclusion that no birth has taken place. She herself speaks of nocturnal visions in the course of which two women took the baby away from her. When her foot-fetters come undone, the community of Watton is at a loss. Aelred, who is brought in as an authority, sees in the puzzling course of events a miracle. God's mercy must be seen as greater than her guilt, and more powerful than all the efforts of the devil to bring a convent into disrepute! The good reputation of the monastery is preserved; the fate of the nun, on the other hand, is irrelevant. The miracle, which occurred in a place which for centuries had been distinguished for its holiness, is decisive.

If a love affair took place in a monastery, nothing was feared more than public opinion. In his Life of Abbess Lioba,[10] Rudolf of Fulda recorded a typical incident. He tells of a hushed-up birth and the disposal of the newborn infant in a river near the monastery. By chance the body is found by a woman of the village when she goes to fetch water. Instantly an angry crowd of people assumes that the monastery is involved, and that a nun has given birth and murdered her baby. It is supposed, reasonably enough, that a sexual liaison between two religious has taken place. The reproaches and prejudices are expressed in so menacing a form that Lioba is compelled to put all her effort into trying to identify the culprit. A nun who, with the abbess's permission, has been visiting her relatives, is called back to the monastery. All the sisters are closely questioned, but without result. With processions and petitions Lioba appeals to Christ: *Rex virginum, libera nos ab hac infamia* ('O King of virgins, release us from this disgrace'). Influenced by this scenario, a crippled woman, who begged for her livelihood at the monastery doors, broke down and confessed that she was the mother of the murdered child. Lioba, who in after-life would be considered a saint, was able to overcome the devil through her

10 Rudolfus Fuldensis, *Vita Leobae Abbatissae Biscofesheimensis*, ch. 12, in Monumenta Germaniae Historica, Scriptores XV/1 (Hanover, 1887), pp. 126–7.

belief and trust in God, and thus to preserve the good reputation of her monastery when it was under hostile attack: so runs the conclusion of this Carolingian anecdote. A male or female saint is defamed, but in the end establishes his or her innocence. The question of the veracity of the reported events pales before such testimony.

If in spite of all controls and supervision a nun or even an abbess should have a love affair and become pregnant, the monastic sources as a rule pass over such events in silence. However, miracle narratives and fictional texts eagerly concern themselves with such sensational events, particularly when scandal is avoided by means of a miracle. Thus several *exempla*-collections treat of a pregnant abbess whom the Virgin Mary is said to have assisted at the secret birth.[11] The newborn baby is suckled by a female deer, after Christ Himself has baptized it. The message of the *exemplum* is unmistakable: whoever feels remorse for his own sins and promises improvement, experiences the mercy and protection of Heaven. In the twelfth and thirteenth centuries, when the cult of the Virgin reached its apogee, it is almost invariably the Virgin Mary, without the assistance of the Trinity, who mercifully comes to the aid of female sinners.

In another version of the same motif the pregnant abbess is denounced to the relevant bishop by her own nuns.[12] She confesses to him and repents. He stipulates that the child be handed over to a hermit, who brings it up to be an exemplary Christian. The illegitimate child, once grown up, will later even become the bishop's successor; in other words, the disturbed order of things is conspicuously returned to normal. This *exemplum*, which was not fixed in any textual form, was so widely disseminated and well known, that when John of Garland incorporated it into his collection of Marian legends under the heading *De abbatissa quam Beata Virgo liberavit ab infamia* ('Concerning the abbess whom the Blessed Virgin freed from disgrace'), he needed only a few verses to record his version of the familiar motif.[13]

The aforementioned denunciation of the pregnant abbess by the nuns of her own convent – whether factual or fictional is not important – reveals something of the tensions to which the cloistered life must often have given rise. The mortuary roll (*rotulus*) of Mathilde, the daughter of William the Conqueror who died in 1143 as abbess of Caen, provides us with an unusual example of the accusation of an abbess. In the parchment roll, alongside the notice of her death, are entered the names of no fewer than 253 persons and institutions, who offer their condolences in verse and prose. Mostly these

11 Frederic C. Tubach, *Index exemplorum. A Handbook of Medieval Religious Tales* (Helsinki: Suomalainen Tiedeakatemia, 1969), p. 9 (no. 2).

12 Tubach, *Index exemplorum*, p. 9 (no. 4).

13 Johannes de Garlandia, *Stella maris*, ed. E. F. Wilson (Cambridge, MA: Wellesley College and the Mediaeval Academy of America, 1946), pp. 93–4 and 156–7.

consist of a prayer for the soul of the dead abbess, or praise of her holiness and virtue. An exception is the entry of an unnamed nun in the border of the roll. She used the obituary notice for an embittered poem about her own fate. In her eyes all abbesses deserved their death, because they incarcerated nuns who were rumoured to have had sexual relations. It is entry no. 217 in the *rotulus*:

Titulus sancti Juliani monacharum

Abbatissae debent mori,
Quae subjectas nos amori
Claudi jubent culpa gravi,
Quod tormentum jam temptavi.
Loco clausa sub obscuro,
Diu vixi pane duro.
Hujus poenae fuit causa,
Quod amare dicor ausa.[14]

Is this a rhetorical exercise, or do we have here a genuine personal testimony? Did a nun, wrongly suspected, really wish to recall the time of her imprisonment on dry bread, and to protest yet again her innocence? How did it happen that, of all things, she should have been authorized by her monastery to undertake responsibility for their entry in the *rotulus*? Was she the only person fluent in Latin in her convent? Could she be certain that the administration of her house would not see her entry, or would not understand it? Did she want the protestation of her innocence and the lament about her imprisonment to reach her own convent, the neighbouring monasteries, and all readers of the *rotulus*?

Nuns often had the reputation of using every possible opportunity to engage in amorous liaisons. Naturally the sources for this rumour usually come from men, and were probably also addressed to men. Andreas Capellanus dedicated an entire chapter of his book *De amore* to the love of nuns.[15] In this chapter he explains how even he himself was once almost seduced by a nun. Only at the very last moment did he succeed in escaping from her deadly snares. From this experience he is able to boast that he knows all the means to overcome the insanity of love. But how easily would those nuns fall into sin, who were less knowledgeable than he about the art of love! And so he warns his friend Walter to avoid at all costs any encounter with a nun.

14 Léopold Delisle, *Rouleaux des morts du IXe au XVe siècle* (Paris: Mme. Ve. J. Renouard, 1866), pp. 276–7: 'Superscription of the nuns of Saint-Julien. Abbesses ought to die – the ones who order those of us enslaved to love to be locked up as for a grave sin. I once experienced this torment: enclosed in a dark place, I lived for a long time on hard bread. The cause of this punishment was that I am said to have been in love.'

15 Andreas Capellanus, *De amore*, I. 8, ed. E. Trojel (repr. Munich: Eidos, 1964), pp. 221–4 (*De amore monacharum*).

The nun as a cleric-devouring incarnation of evil: this is an ineradicable cliché. Thus a verse dialogue transmitted in many manuscripts describes the seduction-technique of a black nun. The cleric, whose opposition the nun is trying to break down by ever new arguments, proves to be resistant. Under no circumstances does he wish to commit a sin with a bride of Christ, to intrude into a holy union as an adulterer, and to make God jealous by putting, as it were, the horns of a cuckold on his Maker.

M(onacha): Te mihi meque tibi genus, aetas et decor aequat:
Cur non ergo sumus sic in amore pares?
C(lericus): Non hac veste places aliis nec vestis ametur:
Quae nigra sunt fugio, candida semper amo.
M(onacha): Si sim veste nigra, niveam tamen aspice carnem.
Quae nigra sunt fugias, candida crura petas.
C(lericus): Nupsisti Christo, quem non offendere fas est:
Hoc velum sponsam te notat esse Dei.
M(onacha): Deponam velum, deponam caetera quaeque:
Ibit ad lectum nuda puella tuum.
C(lericus): Si velo careas, tamen altera non potes esse:
Vestibus ablatis non mea culpa minor.
M(onacha): Culpa quidem, sed culpa levis tamen ipsa fatetur
Hoc fore peccatum, sed veniale tamen.
C(lericus): Uxorem violare viri grave crimen habetur.
Sed gravius sponsam te violare Dei.
M(onacha): Cum non sit rectum, vicini frangere lectum,
Plus reor esse reum, zelotypare Deum.[16]

This dialogue expresses once again the male conviction that woman is a shameless creature. For even as a member of a religious order, she succumbs to

[16] Hermann Hagen, *Carmina medii aevi maximam partem inedita* (Bern: G. Frobenius, 1887), pp. 206–7. In my view the last two verses should not be assigned to the nun, but rather to the cleric. Further manuscripts of the poem are listed in Hans Walther, *Das Streitgedicht in der lateinischen Literatur des Mittelalters*, mit einem Vorwort, Nachträgen und Registern von Paul Gerhard Schmidt (Hildesheim: G. Olms, 1984).
Nun: You and I are matched in terms of birth, age and beauty: why, then, are we not partners in love?
Cleric: You do not please others with this habit, nor is your habit adored: I flee from things which are black, but I always love things which are white.
Nun: I may be black in my habit, but look at my white flesh: flee things which are black if you want, but seek out my white thighs.
Cleric: You are married to Christ, Whom it is not lawful to offend: this veil indicates that you are the bride of God.
Nun: I'll take off the veil, I'll take off all my other clothes: a naked girl will go to your bed.
Cleric: Even if you haven't got your veil, you can't nevertheless be different: my guilt is not the less because you've taken your clothes off.
Nun: Guilt, certainly, but the light guilt confesses that this is a sin, but a venial one.
Cleric: It is reckoned a serious crime to violate the wife of a man: but even more serious to violate you, the bride of God.
Nun: Although it is not right to violate the bed of a neighbour, I think it a greater sin to arouse God's jealousy.

her sexual drive and her desire. An ineradicable medieval prejudice is being expressed here. In the background of such expressions one seems always to hear the *basso continuo*: 'Naturam expelles furca, tamen usque recurret'.[17] She is, and remains, first and foremost a woman, even when she wears the habit of a nun.

Contrary examples are few and far between. Only rarely is a man cast in the role of someone who has abandoned his vow of chastity. In addition, only a few historical sources describe bishops having affairs with concubines or nuns: but only in brief allusions. A cautionary tale about the life and death of a sinful cleric is contained in the *exemplum* (transmitted in many versions) of Udo, allegedly the archbishop of Magdeburg.[18] This – surely fictional – bishop is supposed to have had a scandalous love affair with the abbess of the convent of Lilienthal. Despite three nocturnal warnings delivered by a voice from the other world – *fac finem ludo, quia lusisti satis Udo* ('put an end to your game, because you've played around enough, Udo') – he did not abandon his way of life, for which he eventually received his well-deserved punishment. In one version of the *exemplum* he is tortured on a fiery bed and afterwards toppled into hell; in another he is condemned by Christ's judgement in a nocturnal trial which takes place in the cathedral of Magdeburg, and beheaded by an executioner. Up until the nineteenth century one could be shown the place of his execution on a slab of red-coloured marble, in front of the high altar in Magdeburg Cathedral. Udo's *exemplum horribile* confirmed and strengthened the conviction, widely current among the laity during the Middle Ages, that even high-ranking clerics were not free of sin and that an affair with an abbess was particularly detestable behaviour, which brought with it a merciless punishment. Through stories of this sort public opinion clearly distanced itself from infringements of the laws of chastity and the breaking of monastic vows.

The didactic *exempla*, aimed at inculcating discipline, naturally provide only a very limited glimpse of reality. They help to influence popular perception and opinion and are to this extent valuable evidence of the spiritual ethos of the time. Compared to the vast numbers in which they survive, one can count the few authentic accounts of love affairs on the fingers of one hand. Without doubt the so-called 'Söflingen Love-Letters', which have been transmitted in their original form, are authentic.[19] These are letters which were found in 1484 during the reform of the convent of Poor Clares at Söflingen near Ulm, and were confiscated under notarial supervision. There are fifty-five letters, the majority of which are addressed to the sisters of Söflingen by

[17] Horace, *Epistulae* I. x. 24: 'You will drive away nature with a pitch-fork, but it will always come back' in *Q. Horati Flacci Carmina*, ed. Friedrich Vollmer (Leipzig: Teubner, 1912), p. 269.

[18] Nigel F. Palmer, 'Udo von Magdeburg', *Die deutsche Literatur des Mittelalters: Verfasserlexikon* (Berlin and New York: de Gruyter, 1995), IX, 1213–20.

[19] Helga Schüppert, 'Söflinger Briefe und Lieder', in *Die deutsche Literatur des Mittelalters*, IX, pp. 13–16.

Franciscans and various non-resident women belonging to the house. In many cases the letters concern day-to-day events, cloister intrigues, and business matters. A few, however, use such distinctly amorous language that it is difficult to evaluate them. According to the standpoint of the modern observer, they have been interpreted as letters of courtship, as love letters, or as evidence of spiritual friendship.[20]

A further authentic collection of love letters has been edited recently by Werner Paravicini. Among these are found letters by a canoness – not certainly identifiable – from Remiremont, to the local governor Peter of Hagenbach, executed in 1474.[21] The collection contains eleven letters in French, which provide a glimpse of a highly emotional love affair. The canoness speaks unreservedly about her suffering and desire to be united permanently with her beloved. But Peter of Hagenbach decided against the unidentified authoress of the letters and married another woman.

The fate of nuns who escaped from the convent tended not to interest the authors of medieval texts. If it happened that an escaped nun married her spiritual adviser, who had supported her during her escape or had persuaded her to it, such a case was, as far as I know, never mentioned. In the early sixteenth century, escape from monasteries was almost a daily occurrence, so frequently did it happen. Under the terms of the new dispensation, marriage between a former nun and a former monk was no rarity. The tradition of the Protestant parsonage derives from the marriage of the Cistercian nun Katherine of Bora, who had fled from the convent of Nimbschen, to the former Augustinian canon Martin Luther. The two of them embody *amor coniugalis extra claustrum.*

20 See Max Miller, *Die Söflinger Briefe und das Klarissenkloster Söflingen bei Ulm a. D. im Spätmittelalter* (Würzburg and Aumühle: [Konrad] Triltsch [Verlag], 1940); Marc Müntz, 'Freundschaften und Feindschaften in einem spätmittelalterlichen Frauenkloster. Die sogennanten Söflinger Briefe', in *Meine in Gott geliebte Freundin*, ed. Gabriela Signori (Bielefeld: Verlag für Regionalgeschichte, 1995), pp. 107–16; and Schüppert, 'Söflinger Briefe und Lieder'.

21 Paravicini, 'Un amour malheureux au XVe siècle', pp. 140–56.

12

'And that was litel nede': Poetry's Need in Robert Henryson's *Fables* and *Testament of Cresseid*[1]

James Simpson

The last words of Cresseid in Robert Henryson's *Testament of Cresseid* (c. 1475) evoke the pained comment of Chaucer's narrator in *Troilus and Criseyde* (c. 1385). Cresseid dies thus:

> 'O Diomeid, thou hes baith broche and belt
> Quhilk Troylus gaue me in takning [tokening]
> Of his trew lufe', and with that word scho swelt.[2] [died]

Attentive readers of *Troilus and Criseyde* will remember the precise moment in Chaucer's narrative that Cresseid evokes, when she gives the brooch, which had belonged to Troilus, to Diomede:

> And eek a broche (and that was litel nede)
> That Troilus was, she yaf this Diomede.
> And eek, the bet from sorwe him to releve,
> She made him were a pencel of hir sleve.[3]

If we do recall the Chaucerian passage, we also are alerted to the issue of ethical need. Criseyde's donation of Troilus's gift to Diomede is simultaneously gratuitous and brutal, especially brutal because gratuitous. The gratuitousness underlines Criseyde's icy callousness toward Troilus even as she

1 I dedicate this essay with admiration and affection to Jill Mann, brilliant gem among scholars, colleagues and friends.

2 Robert Henryson, *The Testament of Cresseid*, in *The Poems of Robert Henryson*, ed. Denton Fox (Oxford: Clarendon Press, 1981), lines 589–91. All further references to this edition will be made by line number in the body of the text.

3 *Troilus and Criseyde*, in Geoffrey Chaucer, *The Riverside Chaucer*, 3rd ed., general ed. Larry D. Benson (Boston: Houghton Mifflin, 1987), 5.1040–43.

expresses apparent sympathy for Diomede ('the bet from sorwe him to releve').

Whether or not Henryson intended to evoke the striking, pained comment of Chaucer's narrator is impossible to say. That Henryson is intensely conscious of gratuitousness and its related category of need is, however, certain. For Henryson represents worlds of intense need, whether those worlds are inhabited by hungry animals or relentless astrological gods.[4] On the eve of a sixteenth-century Europe about to be hit by a predestinarian religion, the narratives of Henryson's worlds themselves follow fixed, predestined lines. They follow the law of Nature, where the word 'law' designates unbending regularity and predictability. Such worlds, the worlds of both animals and astrological gods, render human 'law', as the expression of justice, gratuitous. For, if the world is as it absolutely needs must be, then what's the point of trying to change it? One law (that of necessity) trumps another (that of justice). There is, in short, 'litel nede', which is to say no need at all, to change the world through moral exhortation. Ethical analysis slides off need, as water off a duck's back. Necessity, in the medieval formulation, has no law.[5]

At the same time, Henryson chooses literary genres whose explicit, stated aim is to elucidate and promote ethical justice. Out of the subtle ground of poetry springs, we read in the Prologue to the *Fables*, 'ane morall sweit sentence'.[6] The *Testament* is written to 'monische and exhort' (*Testament*, line 612). This is poetry's central function. If that is so, however, Henryson sets the bar of his poetic project especially high: he adopts moralizing genres for matter that most resists moralization. The narratives represent the iron 'law' of Nature observed by animals and astrological gods; the moralizations apply the pattern of those narratives to human practice, as if humans were somehow free from the unmoralizable necessity that rules both the natural and (therefore) the human worlds. That patent, disquieting lack of fit highlights the gratuitousness of most moralization, which is either a waste of time, or designed to occlude baser interests, or both.

4 For the nature and function of the planetary gods in Henryson, see Jill Mann, 'The Planetary Gods in Chaucer and Henryson', in *Chaucer Traditions: Studies in Honour of Derek Brewer*, ed. Ruth Morse and Barry Windeatt (Cambridge: Cambridge University Press, 1990), pp. 91–106: 'Their very role as planets instructs us in this: their motions – and thus their effects – are involuntary, determined by the physical laws of the universe' (p. 94).

5 For the maxim and its background, see Richard Firth Green, ' "Need ne hath no lawe": The Plea of Necessity in Medieval Literature and Law', in *Living Dangerously: On the Margins in Medieval and Early Modern Europe*, ed. Barbara Hanawalt and Anna Grotans (Notre Dame, IN: University of Notre Dame Press, 2007), pp. 9–30; see also Jill Mann, 'The Nature of Need Revisited', *Yearbook of Langland Studies* 18 (2004), 3–29.

6 Robert Henryson, *The Fables*, in *The Poems of Robert Henryson*, ed. Fox, line 12. All further references to this edition will be made by line number in the body of the text. For the defence of poetic fiction in the Prologue, see Douglas Gray, *Robert Henryson* (Leiden: Brill, 1979), p. 70. Gray's book offers the richest discussion of Henryson's *oeuvre* as a whole. For Henryson's defence of vernacular poetic authority, see also Tim William Machan, 'Robert Henryson and Father Aesop: Authority in the *Moral Fables*', *Studies in the Age of Chaucer* 12 (1990), 193–214.

Between the narratives of the fables and the 'morall sweit sentence' there is a radical lack of fit. The significant 'sentence' of Henryson's poetry is more often than not, as I will demonstrate, the dead end of the patently corrupt, unsweet legal judgment, or the dead end of natural law's 'decision'. Those sentences beggar, and render gratuitous, any moral, poetic sentence. Henryson's poetry consistently reveals, in short, that there is but 'litel nede' (i.e. no need) for poetry's sentence. Moral sentence is itself sentenced by the corrupt and/or ineluctable law perceptible in the narrative.

Nonetheless, under the great pressure of exposing its own potential uselessness, Henryson's poetry becomes a very refined instrument to isolate the precise need for poetry against the terrible pressures of the world's relentless need.

In this essay, then, I delineate the ways in which Henryson isolates the real need for poetry up against the need of the world. I do so with regard to both the *Fables* and to the *Testament of Cresseid*. I devote the first two sections of the essay to, respectively, the gratuitousness of ethics in Henryson's fictional worlds; and the consequent uselessness of poetic moralization in both the *Fables* and the *Testament*. In the final section I look to the ways in which Henryson reinstates the poetic voice in exceptionally unpropitious circumstances.[7]

I

I begin with a sequence from the *Fables* that would appear to undo the poetic project altogether, as it exposes the gratuitousness of all moralizing talk about a dog-eat-dog world driven by hunger.

Uniquely among fabulists, Henryson mixes the two great traditions of animal narrative, the Aesopian, beast fable tradition, and the Reynardian, beast-epic tradition.[8] These two traditions structure and interpret narrative

[7] Although I read it after the composition of this essay, I am working within the terms of the final sentence of Jill Mann's chapter on Henryson in her *From Aesop to Reynard: Beast Literature in Medieval Britain* (Oxford: Oxford University Press, 2009). She is discussing Henryson's rhetorical practice: '… through a rhetoric inflated to the point where, however serious its intent and however passionate its emotional charge, it carries with it a consciousness of its own potential redundancy' (p. 305).

[8] For the history and characteristics of both genres (animal fable and beast epic) see the magisterial account of Mann, *From Aesop to Reynard*, pp. 1–52. For a survey of European medieval beast literature, with bibliographical guide, see Jill Mann, 'Beast Epic and Fable', in *Medieval Latin: An Introduction and Bibliographical Guide*, ed. F. A. C. Mantello and A. G. Rigg (Washington: Catholic University of America Press, 1996), pp. 556–61. For a complete list of the branches of the *Roman de Renart*, see J. R. Simpson, *Animal Body, Literary Corpus: The Old French "Roman de Renart"* (Amsterdam: Rodopi, 1996), Appendix One. For the British material generally, see Mann, *From Aesop to Reynard*; see also the briefer surveys: N. F. Blake, 'Reynard the Fox in England', in *Aspects of the Medieval Animal Epic. Proceedings of the International Conference, Louvain, May 15–17, 1972*, ed. E. Rombauts and A. Welkenhuysen (Louvain: Nijhoff, 1975), pp. 53–65; and James Simpson, 'Beast

very differently: beast-fable offers short narratives followed by moralization. Its binary structure of fable and *moralitas* exemplifies a simplistic ethics that abstracts narrative in order to moralize and discard it.[9] Beast-epic, by contrast, offers continuous, unmoralized narrative, in which the fox constantly evokes the ethical only to exploit, neutralize and escape it through his narrative power.[10] The fox calls repeatedly upon ethical feelings, and shapes narrative rhetorically in order to provoke the sympathetic imagination. He does so, however, only to gain an advantage over his enemies. The ethical in his hands is only ever a weapon. Ethics turns out here, that is, to be simply one more consumable in a world driven only by desire to consume.

The fox in beast-epic is not simply amoral, as is his rival the wolf, for example; much more interestingly, he puts ethics into precise reverse. Instead, that is, of simply exercising brute force, as the unfunny wolf does, the fox activates the ethical in very precise ways. The only difference between his and properly ethical action is that he runs ethics backwards, as it were. He provokes ethical sentiments (especially pity), but exploits them to wholly unethical (pitiless) ends. This backwardness may explain the real mystery of why beast-epic is so funny; it allows us to laugh at the pretensions of the ethical, by observing the operations of ethical sympathy so closely. We do not laugh at the brute, voracious power of the wolf.

Henryson chose to import this Reynardian material into his collection of moral fables; he set it symmetrically and deeply into the chiastic structure of his collection, three narratives drawn from Reynard materials on either side of the central, Aesopian narrative of the Lion and the Mouse.[11] Such a choice underlines the high challenge that Henryson sets himself as a moralizing poet, for the Reynardian material threatens to eviscerate any attempt to make ethical, just sense of the world.

Epic and Fable', in *Medieval England: An Encyclopaedia*, ed. Paul E. Szarmach, M. Teresa Tavormina and Joel T. Rosenthal (New York: Garland, 1998), pp. 111–12.

9 See, for example, William Caxton, *Caxton's Aesop*, ed. R. T. Lenaghan (Harvard: Harvard University Press, 1967). For discussion of this brilliant text, see James Simpson, 'Consuming Ethics: Caxton's *History of Reynard the Fox*', in *Studies in Late Medieval and Early Renaissance Texts in Honour of John Scattergood*, ed. Alan Fletcher and Anne-Marie D'Arcy (Dublin: Four Courts Press, 2005), pp. 321–36.

10 For a survey of the entire medieval Reynard tradition, see John Flinn, *Le Roman de Reynart dans la littérature française et dans les littératures étrangères au moyen âge* (Toronto: University of Toronto Press, 1963). See also *Ysengrimus*, ed. and trans. Jill Mann (Leiden: Brill, 1987), 1–9.

11 For a precise account of the sources for individual animal narratives by Henryson, and the way he mixes both main traditions, see Mann, *From Aesop to Reynard*, pp. 264–7. The structure is very nearly chiastic: items 1–2 and 12–13 are Aesopian; 3–5 and 9–10 from beast epic (while 11 has debts to the Reynardian tradition); 6 and 8 Aesopian. In the middle stands the central tale, 'The Lion and the Mouse' (number 7), in which Aesop himself appears. For a defence of this order (derived from the Bassandyne print) as the authorial order, see Machan, 'Robert Henryson and Father Aesop', note 17 and further references. For a discussion based on this structure, see Edward Wheatley, *Mastering Aesop: Medieval Education, Chaucer, and His Followers* (Gainesville, FL: University of Florida Press, 2000), chapter 6.

In beast epic the relentless, comic self-interest of the fox finally consumes everything in its way, including the ethical and political orders. This humor is deeply subversive, since the fox escapes not only his enemies, but also the sacramental, political and legal systems in which we tend to put our trust. Furthermore, he escapes the power of writing itself to condemn him morally, partly because he is a better rhetorician than any learned writer. The fox of beast epic exposes and capitalizes on the potential violence of writing, and the self-delusions of reading.[12] Narratives about him are, in short, unmoralized because they are, effectively, unmoralizable.

Three narratives early in Henryson's collection highlight the subversive, barely containable power of animal narratives. Two related beast epic narratives, 'The Fox and the Wolf' and 'The Trial of the Fox' (the fourth and fifth narratives of the collection respectively), successively undermine the realms of sacramental practice, royal justice, and learned clerical expertise. They are followed by an especially grim Aesopian tale, 'The Sheep and the Dog', that exposes the sham of civil legal practice. In the space of three short narratives these not insignificant realms of discourse are comically exposed as hollow and gratuitous in a world whose real driver is hunger.

'The Fox and the Wolf' undoes sacramental practice. It begins with the fox's apparent moral doubt. He seems to experience remorse, and seeks absolution in Lent from his confessor the wolf, who enjoins forbearance of flesh until Easter. I say the fox 'seems' to experience remorse, since everything in this narrative, except hunger and power relations, is only apparent, and comically apparent at that. For the premise of any Reynardian story is that, however much the fox understands every nuance of the psyche, he is himself entirely invulnerable to any psychic promptings except those of self-interest. We can therefore be certain that his moral doubt is gameful. The wolf also plays his part:

> Freir Volff Waitskith, in science wonder sle, [cunning]
> To preiche and pray was new cum fra the closter,
> With beidis in hand, sayand his Pater Noster.
> (lines 667–69)

Reading animal narrative is governed by a tripartite, sequential logic of likeness/difference/likeness.[13] One begins by allowing a *likeness* (Stage 1): animals are like humans; this is clearly the enabling premise of the genre. Faced with the relentless brutality of the animal world, however, the reader insists on Stage 2: *difference.* 'They're animals, after all', we want to say. The capacity to hold the animal world at bay progressively diminishes, however, as the powerful animals exploit fundamentally human practices. Finally, the text

12 For these qualities in the Reynardian material, see Simpson, 'Consuming Ethics', pp. 326–27.
13 See Simpson, 'Consuming Ethics', p. 333.

insists (Stage 3), we're back in the land of *likeness*, though this time the likeness is the other way around: humans, that is, are revealed to be like animals.[14] This tripartite sequence of responses accounts for both the comedy (animals are like humans) and the shocking violence (humans are like animals) of animal narrative. It accounts for the fact that fables sometimes evoke Beatrix Potter (cute), and sometimes Swift (horrifying). Cute anthropomorphism is under siege in these narratives; it finally cedes to fierce zoomorphism. Human rulers are like lions.

In 'The Fox and the Wolf', for example, we begin with likeness: we stand amusedly detached from the fox as he pretends to be penitent to the 'doctor of divinity', a lean and pious-looking wolf who plays the part of spiritual advisor. That comedy then shifts to Stage 2 (unlikeness), since there's no penitence here at all. As they move through the stages of penitence, the fox reveals, as he must, that he is incapable of penitence: he is not contrite (hens are, after all, 'sa honie sweit'), nor will he promise not to repeat his sin ('how sall I leif, allace?'). Penitential satisfaction, however, he promises to make by not eating flesh until Easter, as long as his confessor permits him to lap a little blood, or to eat a head, some feet or a stomach in case he should lack flesh (lines 712–29). By the time the wolf agrees, we are in Stage 3 (humans are like animals).

The comedy shifts, that is, through the three stages isolated above; from the initial recognition of likeness, we realize that there are differences here: animals just cannot give up flesh, because they need it. Both fox and wolf underline the ineluctable force of need: the fox says that 'Neid causis me to steill quhair euer I wend' (line 709), while the wolf permits a little blood lapping to the penitent, since, after all, 'neid may haif na law' (line 731). Animals need to eat.

At this point, however, we move to the third, much more subversive stage of Reynardian perception, after moving through the stages of cute likeness and comforting dissimilitude: we now perceive that there is a profound likeness between animals and humans, but that it is we who are like them, not they who are like us.

After all, we also need to eat. The fox finds a young goat, and without hesitation preserves the game by simultaneously drowning and baptizing the kid as a Lenten salmon, before eating him. At this point we realize that we are the animals, and that the performance of penance is precisely that – a performance designed to provide the right appearances, but a performance also designed to mask and permit our animal natures to consume in the standard ways. The 'law' of penitence is subsumed by the 'law' of Nature. Penitence is gratuitous; there is 'litel nede' of it; it is a game that could easily have been dispensed with.

[14] For the flickering of difference and similarity in Reynard narratives, see J. R. Simpson, *Animal Body, Literary Corpus*, pp. 10–14.

In this particular narrative the third stage of fake penitence may not be shocking. Henryson is merely distracting us with gratuitous amusement, however, before he strikes us with a sudden, breakneck change of tone: the well-filled fox is struck dead by the goat-keeper's arrow, who then proceeds to flay the dead fox 'and made ane recompence' (line 774) for his lost kid. However much this might look like justice, it rather reinforces the likeness of humans to animals. The goat keeper has no interest in the recompense of penitential satisfaction: he wants payback for the loss of his goat. The goatherd, not unreasonably, enacts the law of nature rather than any law of justice. The brief *moralitas* (the shortest in the collection, at 21 lines) might enjoin repentance, but it gains its effect through the shock of death's brutal suddenness, rather than through any reflective, meditated understanding of the justice of the fox's end. The entire system of penitential law, then, seen from the perspective of humans being like animals, is exposed as wholly gratuitous, a dispensable game designed to provide some amusement, perhaps. Meanwhile, the routine, unstoppable patterns of consumption and recompense carry on undisturbed.

The next story, 'The Trial of the Fox', extends this gratuitousness to the political realm. It begins with a rhetorically playful lack of necessity. The dead fox had, we are unnecessarily told, no legitimate children. His one, illegitimate, son 'lufit weill', we are unnecessarily told, 'with pultrie to tig and tar' (line 802). These otiose details constitute rhetorically playful gratuitousness, talking about animals as if they were like humans, while we know all the while that we are safely in the realm of unlikeness (these are animals).

Henryson exaggerates the uselessness of vacuous criticism of animals from a human perspective. From within the narrative his narrator fulminates, for example, against the son's ill-treatment of the dead father fox: 'Fy, couetise, vnkynd and venomous!' (line 817). This hollow, playful criticism of the fox (how is a fox supposed to feel about his father's death?), takes us into what I earlier described as Stage 2 of animal fable, the stage of unlikeness (animals are not like us, since they're beasts). Stage 2, however, lulls a readership into a false sense of security. For it depends on us believing that animals are really not like us – of course, we think, the fox loves to attack poultry, and how amusing that a poet should take time out to say so, as if the fox were really like a human, who might, or probably might not, like to attack poultry. This sense of security is false, however, because the reach of the tale suddenly extends well beyond light comedy to the subversive, third stage of Reynardian perception, that dark stage in which we realize that it's we who are like the animals. For, on reflection, we do ourselves like to attack poultry, even if we get others to do it for us. But the fable exposes more than our taste for poultry: it exposes the entire political order as a gratuitous cover for the real business of needy consumption. It also exposes, as we shall see, the learned expertise of readers as no guarantee against the same, regular, base needs.

The narrative proper of 'The Trial of the Fox' begins with a general summons to the parliament of the Lion. This assembly displays the plenitude of nature, with each beast appearing. At its head sits the lion, the peak of the political order, whose wildness, however, underlines the bestial nature of that order:

> And in that throne thair sat ane wild lyoun,
> In rob royall, with sceptour, swerd, and crown. [robe]
> (lines 878–79)

As the lion declares the full force of his power, we perceive not only his error, but also the purely ideological status of his declaration, designed as it is to establish the rule of law as 'natural', when in fact that rule of law serves most to disguise the lion's own rapacity:

> Se neir be twentie mylis quhair I am [where]
> The kid ga saiflie be the gaittis side,
> The tod Lowrie luke not to the lam, [fox]
> Na reuand beistis nouther ryn nor ryde. [predatory]
> (lines 943–46)

This speech recalls the fox's eating of the kid in the previous narrative. It thereby exposes the consumption that is simultaneously the source and shame of the entire political order. The need to consume activates the political order and its apparently repressive justice, which seeks to disguise the fundamentally brutal character of the entire system. A narrative of this kind gives a very different meaning to Aristotle's claim that man is a political animal.

The fox not only exposes the gratuitousness of the political order, but also of learned expertise. For the lion sends the wolf and fox to summon the mare to parliament. The mare tells them that her written privilege is under her hoof. Come and read it, she invites the fox:

> 'I can not spell,' quod he, 'sa God me speid. [read]
> Heir is the volff, ane nobill clerk at all,
> And of this message is maid principall.
>
> He is autentik, and an man of age,
> And hes grit practik of the chanceliary.
> Let him ga luke, and reid your priuilage.'
> (lines 1010–1015)

The learned wolf succumbs to the fox's flattery of his clerical expertise as a legal reader, after which follows the mare's kick at the wolf's head as he reads. Together the mare and the fox prove that ' "The gretteste clerkes been noght wisest men,"/ As whilom to the wolf thus spake the mare'.[15] The learned and

15 The citation is from Chaucer, the Reeve's Tale, in Geoffrey Chaucer, *The Canterbury Tales*, ed. Jill Mann (London: Penguin, 2005), I. 4054–55. Henryson's Lion cites this very line (at line 1064).

the literate stand no better chance against the fox than the ignorant. They are both subject to exactly the same greed that drives the fox, and so are easily overturned by the fox's mastery of relentlessly self-interested rhetoric. This conclusion rings potentially true, of course, for ourselves as readers, inevitably subject as we are to imaginative desire, even the desire of reading this very text. From the impenitent, insouciant, gratuitous play of the fox in 'The Fox and the Wolf', then, unfolds an ever extending perspective capable of describing the entire world of sacramental and political law as gratuitous play designed to cover rapacity.

The next story in the collection, 'The Sheep and the Dog', completes this sombre understanding of the civilized order of law. For in this narrative we move to the process of civil law (in the modern sense of that term), only to find that care for due legal process is itself a form of savage rapacity. The moment the rapacious dog, illicitly claiming a loaf of bread, summons the defenceless sheep to court, the poor sheep's fate is sealed. From the beginning of this narrative we are in Stage 3, the subversive, shocking world of humans being like animals. Populated by officers such as raven, wolf, and fox, the court deploys the full panoply of literate legal procedure ('letteris', 'bill', 'indorsat has the write' [lines 1160–69]). As it does so, we observe the relentless process not of any law of justice, but only of nature's grim law working its way into, and overtaking, a system of justice. The sheep's careful set of legal objections to the nature of the judge (the wolf) and the court officers is met and easily absorbed by due legal process, 'as in the law is vsit' (line 1094). The bear and badger are appointed as arbiters to judge the force of the sheep's objections. They spend a good while working through decretals, glosses, and 'Of ciuile mony a volum they reuolue/ The codies and digestis new and ald' (lines 1216–17). Needless to say, they judge that the sheep should pass again before judge wolf, who judges him to be in default. The sheep must sell his fleece to pay the dog, and the story ends with the defenceless sheep 'naikit and bare' (line 1257).

Never for a moment in reading this grim tale do we think either that animals are cutely like humans, imitating our civilized ways, or that animals are, after all, different because so bestial; from beginning to end we are instead conscious of Henryson's deadly account of the way in which humans, like animals, are driven by necessity as they conduct the processes of justice's law. This process is very easily manipulated by the relentless needs of nature's 'law'. The fable evokes Henryson's Prologue, where he merges two kinds of properly distinct similitude between animals and humans. The fact that animals can argue suggests that they are like us, not that we are like them. Henryson, however, puts the matter thus:

> My author in his fabillis tellis how
> That brutal bestis spak and vnderstude,
> And to gude purpois dispute and argow,

> Ane sillogisme propone, and eik conclude;
> Putting exempil and similitude
> How mony men in operatioun
> Ar like to beistis in conditioun.
>
> (lines 43–49)

By this account, we are explicitly in Stage 3, that dark realm of likeness where humans are like animals.

II

Socially attuned medieval poetry finds its voice precisely as other discourses fail. As priests, counsellors, lawyers and the learned fail to speak up, so too does poetry derive its own authority to voice complaint. Always a marginal discourse, poetry nonetheless fills the discursive vacuum left by the discourses that are centrally responsible for the voicing of social critique. In the Prologue to the *Fables*, Henryson categorizes poetry as relaxation: it is necessary to mix serious matters with light, 'amangis ernist to ming ane merie sport' (line 20), just as he describes the reading of Chaucer's poetry as 'sport' in the *Testament* (line 40). From the tone of the fables discussed above, it will, however, be clear that Henryson's ambition for poetry extends well beyond light entertainment.

What, though, could Henryson as a moralist say in the face of the world he represents?

Henryson puts extraordinary pressure on many of his his *moralitates* partly by pitching them up against the rapacious world on which they are expected to comment. Also, more explicitly, the voice and function of the poet are subsumed from within those worlds of animal need. Take, for example, the judgment of the bear and badger as they deliver the fateful sentence on the sheep:

> Schortlie to make ane end off this debait,
> The arbiteris than summar and plane
> The sentence gaue, and process fulminait:
> The sheip suld pas befoir the vollf agane
> And end his pley. Than was he nothing fane, [plea]
> For fra thair sentence couth he not appeill. [could]
> On clerkis I do it, gif this sentence wes leill. [to scholars I appeal] [lawful]
>
> (lines 1223–29)

Henryson takes care to underline the striking similarities between legal and literary sentence in this passage. Like these legal figures, or like the legally learned wolf in the 'Trial of the Fox', Aesop, when he appears, is revealed to be both poet and lawyer; so too Henryson, like legal figures who deliver a sentence, offers a 'sad sentence' (line 1100), and often 'schortlie' (line 2970), to his fables.[16] These similarities suggest that recourse to poetry to right the ways of a crooked world may not be so straightforward: the rapacious themselves rely on the resources of poetry. And, what's more, they deliver their sentence from within the narrative, thereby subsuming the function of the poetic sentence outside the narrative. This phenomenon is made manifest by the court officials in 'The Sheep and the Dog'. It also appears in 'The Wolf and the Lamb', where the lamb's impeccable legal reasoning is met with the 'sentence' of brute force from within the tale. The hungry wolf simply beheads the learned lamb, drinks his blood and eats as much of his flesh as fills him; 'syne went his way on pace' (line 2703).

We also see brutal legal sentence delivered from within the narrative in the *Testament of Cresseid*, where Mercury, god of eloquence, is chosen as speaker of the parliament, since he can 'In breif sermone ane pregnant sentence wryte' (*Testament*, line 270). The actual 'legal' sentence on Cresseid is delivered by both Saturn ('a wraikfull sentence') and Cynthia the moon, whose even more vengeful sentence is described as a 'sentence diffinityue' (lines 329–34). Neither sentence has any grounding in justice.[17]

In the *Fables*, faced with the sheer brutality of 'legal' sentence, a sentence that enforces the cruel laws of nature that have nothing to do with justice, what discursive room is left for poetic sentence? Faced with the sheer, unstoppable processes of rapacious legal sentence, poetic sentence looks merely gratuitous. There is 'litel nede' of it. The legally learned lamb has said all that can be said about justice from within the tale, and he has had his head bitten off. What space does that leave for moralization? Henryson himself insists on the force of the question: 'Off his murther quhat sall we say, allace?' (line 2704).

What, indeed? What is left to say? Henryson sometimes conceives of interpretative comment as a measurable quantity: at the end of the entire collection, after the especially pessimistic 'Paddock and the Mouse' (sudden death for villain and victim), he says that he'll 'schortlie ... conclude' this story, and leave 'the laif vnto the freiris,/ To mak a sample or similitude' (lines 2971–72). After the measurable good of interpretation has been so efficiently swallowed and consumed by the all-powerful and pre-emptive law of nature, what is the scrap, the 'laif', that could be left to the friars? Or what the scrap that could be left the reader of Henryson's own collection?

16 For a profound meditation in rhetorical abbreviation in Henryson's *Testament of Cresseid*, see A. C. Spearing, 'Conciseness and the *Testament of Cresseid*', in his *Criticism and Medieval Poetry*, 2nd ed. (London: Edward Arnold, 1972), pp. 157–92. For Henryson's own activity as notary public, see Jana Mathews, 'Land, Lepers, and the Law in *The Testament of Cresseid*', in *The Letter of the Law: Legal Practice and Literary Production in Medieval England*, ed. Emily Steiner and Candace Barrington (Ithaca: Cornell University Press, 2002), pp. 40–66 (at pp. 43–44).

17 For the legal procedures of the planetary court and their severity, see Mathews, 'Land, Lepers, and the Law in *The Testament of Cresseid*', pp. 56–7.

Given the exiguous space left for moralizing, it is therefore unsurprising that Henryson should so often represent the dismissal of gratuitous moralization. From within the tale of the 'Cock and the Fox', Chantecleir's apparent capture by the fox is, for example, over-hastily moralized by his wives. Coppock in particular, who 'lyke ane curate spak full crous' (line 530), delivers a moralization that is as absurd as it is rhetorically competent. She describes Chantecleir's fall as 'ane verray vengeance from the heuin':

> Thairfoir it is the uerray hand off God
> That causit him be werryit with the tod.[18] [seized] [fox]
> (lines 542–43)

Coppock's fulmination is merely ridiculous. Henryson shapes poetic structures that work as a kind of winnowing machine for gratuitous talk. In the *Testament* the case is similar, though by no means ridiculous. There Cresseid delivers a rhetorically beautiful, expert, moving Complaint (lines 407–69) about the instability of fortune. Henryson takes care to set it off with full poetic honours: alliteration, apostrophe, tripartite syntactic sequences, and balanced clauses, along with the nine-line stanzas in which it is set, all mark out this passage as high style:

> O ladyis fair of Troy and Grece, attend
> My miserie, quhilk nane may comprehend, [which]
> My friuoll fortune, my infelicitie,
> My greit mischief, quhilk na man may amend.
> Be war in tyme, approchis neir the end,
> And in your mynd ane mirrour mak of me.
> (*Testament*, lines 452–57)

If any moralizing speech from within a narrative were to survive, it would be this rhetorically glorious, exhortative set piece. This complaint is a perfect example of the operations of morally persuasive fiction as defined by the prologue to the *Fables*: 'polite termes of sweit rhetore/ Richt plesand ... unto the eir of man' designed to 'repreif the of thi misleuing,/ O man' (lines 3–7). Henryson's winnowing machine is not, however, prepared to let the true moral sentiment, beautifully and persuasively expressed as it is, sit. Henryson's is an intensely situational ethics: if the moral sentiment ill fits its circumstance, it's dismissed as gratuitous. Beautiful expression is insufficient. And so Cresseid's fellow leper, an old lady, dismisses poet Cresseid's Complaint as wasted words that just make things worse:

> ... 'Quhy spurnis thow aganis the wall
> To sla thy self and mend nothing at all?

[18] See Mann, *From Aesop to Reynard*, pp. 291–92.

'Sen thy weiping dowbillis bot thy wo,
I counsall the mak vertew of ane neid;
Go leir to clap thy clapper to and fro, [learn]
And leif efter the law of lipper leid.' [live according] [leprous folk]
(lines 475–80)

Here only one law counts, that of the lepers. That is the one, ineluctable need, before which all other kinds of talk are so much 'wind inflate in vther mennis eris' (*Testament*, line 463). The articulate, rhetorically proficient voice of moral exhortation counts for nothing beside the one communicative sound demanded by the 'law of lipper leid', that of the clapping of the leper's clapper as it solicits alms. Of every other articulate, expressive sound (and especially of moral exhortation), there is but 'litel need'.

Given the acute scrutiny to which Henryson subjects poetry's moral discourse in the face of the world's need, it is also unsurprising that the great moralists at the centre of his text should either refuse to speak at all, or else be represented as speaking in vain to an insouciant audience. I think of 'The Lion and the Mouse' and 'The Preaching of the Swallow', centrally placed in the structure of the collection. When Henryson's narrator meets his auctor Aesop himself in a dream, as narrated in the prologue to 'The Lion and the Mouse', Aesop is equipped with the tools of writing. He bears a roll of paper in his hand, an inkhorn at his belt, and a swan's pen tucked elegantly behind his ear (lines 1356–58). All this writing gear, however, now lies idle, however much Aesop might confess to having written fables that 'ar full of prudence and moralite' (line 1381). Circumstance being essential to rhetorical value, Aesop denies that he could compose a 'prettie fabill/ Concludand with ane gude moralitie' (lines 1386–87) in the current circumstances:

... My sone, lat be,
For quhat is it worth to tell ane fenyeit taill, [what]
Quhen haly preaching may na thing auail?
(lines 1388–90)

The next tale in the collection, the beautiful 'Preaching of the Swallow', plays out, across the rhythm of an entire seasonal cycle, the painful point that Aesop makes.[19] For just as Aesop sees no point in speaking when the 'eir is deif, the hart is hard as stane' (line 1393), so too is the preaching swallow repeatedly ignored by the insouciant larks as they recklessly and determinedly head to perdition. Henryson says that Aesop wrote this tale as a marginal recreation, 'quhen that he waikit from mair autentik werk' (line 1890). But if the swallow is a proxy for the poet, as he is, then the 'autentik' author is represented as

[19] See the subtle essay by John Burrow, 'Henryson: *The Preaching of the Swallow*', *Essays in Criticism* 25 (1975), 25–37.

wasting his time. Once more, the law of nature, the need of the world, trumps any ethical choice. Poetry is a waste of time; there is of it but 'litel nede'.

III

Both Henryson's brilliant and bleak *Fables* and *Testament*, then, pitch one kind of sentence against another: the traditional moral sentence of poetry is set into fierce competition with the sentence of a law that has no interest whatsoever in justice. Henryson repeatedly stages encounters wherein the reliable, ethical outcome of an animal fable or of classical exemplum is demolished by the severities and relentlessness of the law of nature's sentence. Given the ineluctable severity of nature's brutal law, a 'law' that is simultaneously irresistible and wholly innocent of ethical concern whatsoever, ethical sentence is made to look gratuitous: what is the point of ethics when the law of need is so ferocious and all powerful in any case?

Does Henryson reconstruct ethical sentence from its apparent demolition? Does Henryson discover places for poetry in the space invaded by natural need? Animal fable may derive as a pedagogic exercise for children, but it attracts great writers. It offers the pleasure-giving possibilities of mimesis, as we see likeness where we expected none. It also offers a fundamental literary challenge of representing and constraining the body, and not just any body, but the hungry animal body. Fable must do that through a rhetorical practice that can persuasively represent the animal body, and yet constrain that body by appeal to the human-animal reader's rational soul. In the hands of great writers, sudden switches of rhetorical level will therefore be characteristic of the genre. Those sudden switches of style, in the service of interpretation and exhortation, produce pyrotechnic rhetorical and hermeneutic displays. In fact the pyrotechnics can easily become the subject of the work itself, as we observe the sometimes pleasurable, sometimes shocking impossibility of the rhetorical and hermeneutic task.

Thus Chaucer's brilliant Nun's Priest's Tale is the most skeptical and post-modern of the Canterbury tales. Chaucer urges the application of high philosophy to the trivia of the barn yard with such rhetorical insistence that skepticism invades the entire project of applied literature. Trying to make the application from animal to human might be fun, but there will, finally, be nothing but the fun of trying, since the application will collapse at every turn. We are left instead with competing discourses, very conscious of, and celebrating, their lack of '*hors-texte*'.

Or in Lydgate's brilliant early fifteenth-century *The Churl and the Bird*, the bird undoes the very premises of the fable tradition.[20] Embedded within the

[20] For which see James Simpson, ' "For al my body . . . weieth nat an unce": Empty Poets and Rhetorical Weight in Lydgate's *Churl and the Bird*', in *John Lydgate: Poetry, Culture, and Lancastrian England*,

fable tradition is the idea of embedding itself. The weighty, precious truth is *within*, despite an unpropitious surface; as Lydgate puts it in his own *Isopes Fabules*:

> And, who that myneth downe lowe in the grounde,
> Of golde and syluer groweth the mynerall;
> Perlys whyte, clere and orientall
> Ben ofte founde in muscle shellys blake,
> And out of fables gret wysdom men may take.[21]

In contrast, the startling, candid message of *The Churl and the Bird* is that there is *nothing* inside. Against the grain of the whole fable tradition, *The Churl and the Bird* strips the surface down to reveal nothing within. The point of this demolition is to strip any but a rhetorical content from the poet's advice. There is nothing here but advice about listening carefully. To identify the 'message' of the poem with its stated morality is to fall victim to the bird's own warning against giving credence to 'every tale brouht to the of newe' (line 303). This is a text about the importance of rhetorical process above sentential meanings.

Or again, in Caxton's very great *History of Reynard the Fox* (1481), we see the possibility of a relentlessly subversive, wholly anti-ethical text. The only minimalist way the text might salvage the ethical is by setting it within a complex psychological and discursive field. We can only take ethics seriously, that is, by seeing it as *threatened. Reynard* puts pressure on ethics by rendering it potentially gratuitous because severely threatened in a world populated only by animals. Ethics is most interestingly threatened in this text not through aggressive dismissal by the likes of the wolf Ysengrymus. Instead, *Reynard* threatens ethics through the fox, the figure who understands ethical discourse very precisely, so precisely that he can reverse it. This moment is the only point at which ethical discourse might find its true voice. At all other moments it is potentially complacent, idle, or, at worst, a cover for the immoral exercise of power. Or it is itself an immoral exercise of power. Ethics only becomes demanding when maximal pressure is put on it, and Caxton's *Reynard* does precisely that by setting all the powers of the ethical, already under pressure from relentless animal hunger, into reverse.

Henryson, as we have seen, admits exceptionally subversive Reynardian material into his collection. We have also seen how intensely sensitive he is to the gratuitousness of ethical discourse both across the animal narratives and in

ed. Larry Scanlon and James Simpson (Notre Dame, IN: University of Notre Dame Press, 2006), pp. 129–46.

[21] John Lydgate, *Isopes Fabules*, in John Lydgate, *The Minor Poems*, 2 parts, ed. Henry Noble MacCracken, EETS, e.s. 107, 192 (Oxford: Oxford University Press, 1911, 1934; repr. 1961), no. 21, 2:566–99, lines 24–28. Any further citation of this edition will be made by line number in the body of the text.

the *Testament.* Despite the pressures he puts on the ethical, he is, in my view, uninterested in pursuing what we now call postmodern insights into the nature of discourse. On the contrary, he wishes to maintain the ideal of an applied poetry, a poetry that evokes and addresses the world outside the realm of discourse. He wishes, within the unpropitious circumstances of nature's need, to redefine the need for poetry. I end this essay with two examples, one from the *Fables* and one from the *Testament*, to substantiate this claim.

As mentioned above, Henryson ends the narrative of 'The Wolf and the Lamb' by asking what he might possibly say about the lamb's murder: 'Off his murther quhat sall we say, allace?' (line 2704). 'The Sheep and the Dog' also ends with a beggared voice: what, asks Henryson, could he possibly say about the wholly unjust fleecing of the sheep? – 'Off this sentence, allace, quhat sall I say?' (line 1248). In fact he makes no ethical judgment in his own voice at all. Instead, he begins his *moralitas* simply by elucidating what was in any case obvious: the sheep represents the 'pure commounis, that daily ar opprest/ By tirrane men' (lines 1259–60). The morality continues in barely allegorical form: the wolf represents the sheriff, the raven the coroner and so on. It is less allegory and more description of what we have already seen. If the tale offered us 'game' of a kind, in the fiction of the legal animals, the *moralitas* denies us even that, with its assertion of the unfictional reality that the tale signifies. Henryson refuses to say anything beyond what is worth saying, which is, effectively, to repeat what we already know.

Powerfully, however, Henryson does not leave the matter there. If in some tales the morality enters the tale, here we have the reverse: the tale re-enters the morality, since it is in the *moralitas* that Henryson reports that he heard the sheep's lamentation. So the suffering sheep, not Henryson, has the last word; and the speech act of that word is not one of exhortation, but rather prayer.[22] Just as the sheep has been exposed, so too, powerfully, is the tale itself deprived of the protective covering of its *moralitas.* That stripping reveals, implicitly, that *moralitates* offer protective comfort, leading us as they do to believe that the brutalities of the needy world can be covered and changed. The supervention of the poet's voice in the standard morality also implicitly suggests that the word of wisdom lies outside the experience of the world. This tale refuses both those comforts: it strips the fable of any moral whatsoever, and has the only possible wisdom expressed by the only one who has understood the real structure of discourse, here the sheep:

> Seis thow not, lord, this warld ouerturnit is, [Do you not see]
> As quha wald change gude gold in leid or tyn? [who] [lead]

22 For recourse to prayer in the context of the failure of other discourses, see R. James Goldstein, 'Discipline and Relaxation in the Poetry of Robert Henryson', in *A Companion to Medieval English Literature and Culture c. 1350–c. 1500*, ed. Peter Brown (Oxford: Blackwell, 2007), pp. 604–18.

> The pure is peillit, the lord may do na mis, [poor] [stripped]
> And simonie is haldin for na syn.
> Now is he blyith with okker maist may wyn; [usury]
> Gentrice is slane, and pietie is ago.
> Allace, gude lord, quhy tholis thow it so? [why do you suffer]
> (lines 1307–13)

All other forms of discourse except description and prayer are now bankrupt. The fact that the prayer is made to an entirely unrepresented, silent God who never intervenes only heightens the voice's power and isolation.

The Testament of Cresseid also ends with minimal moralizing. Yes, Henryson does declare that he composed the poem for the purpose of exhortation (line 612), and yes, he does actually offer a single line of moral advice: 'Ming not your lufe with fals deceptioun' (line 613). This bit of *moralitas* is not, however, the poem's significant conclusion; that is rather Cresseid's ghastly death as a leper, struck down by the pitiless operations of the gods, who have punished her in a manner wholly excessive to any fault she may have committed. In the *Testament*'s conclusion, we are not confronted by a comforting, concluding moralization that wraps the poem within the fleece of warm wisdom; on the contrary, we are left exposed to the brutalities of nature's standard operations, before which we fall silent:

> Beir in your mynd this sore conclusioun
> Of fair Cresseid, as I haue said befoir.
> Sen scho is deid I speik of hir no moir.
> (lines 614–16)

As in 'The Sheep and the Dog', however, the narrator's own silence does not necessarily beggar all speakers and all forms of discourse. For Cresseid has spoken, and spoken as a poet. After her glorious but irrelevant speech about Fortune's fickleness (lines 407–69), Cresseid says nothing further until prompted by the gift of an initially unrecognized Troylus. Once she understands that it was Troylus who gave the alms, she makes a less rhetorical, but much more striking speech of self accusation. Now she blames not Fortune but herself as she addresses Troylus:

> Thy lufe, thy lawtie, and thy gentilnes [fidelity]
> I countit small in my prosperitie,
> Sa efflated I was in wantones,
> And clam vpon the fickill quheill sa hie. [wheel] [high]
> All faith and lufe I promissit to the
> Was in the self fickill and friuollous:
> O fals Cresseid and trew knight Troilus!
> (lines 547–53)

Whether or not we judge Henryson's Cresseid, in the light of what we know about Chaucer's Criseyde, as harshly as Cresseid judges herself, is not my concern here. It may not be Henryson's concern, either, since Cresseid does not convict herself. Her speech act is rather an accusation: 'Nane but my self as now I will accuse' (line 574). In the light of the argument of this essay, the key thing is that Cresseid does the talking and the writing (after her final complaint we read a record of her testament).[23] No one else, Henryson recognizes, is capable of reactivating a moral voice after its demolition by the gods and the leper lady. Cynthia might deliver a 'sentence diffinityue' in the legal judgment, but Henryson offers none as poet. As with 'The Sheep and the Dog', the only ethical voice that counts is from within the narrative, a voice of the victim, and a voice whose ethical purchase is under maximal pressure.[24] Everyone else should fall silent: the gods, the leper lady, Troylus, Henryson as narrator, and we as readers. It is true that Cresseid dies in the need of debt: she cannot return Troylus's broach, which she gratuitously gave to Diomede, which 'was litel nede'. Cresseid's recognition of debt and need serves, however, to reactivate non-gratuitous ethical possibility. However much the law might exclude a leper from having a will, or testament, in this final document Cresseid resuscitates the ethical will, or *voluntas* from the crushing forces that would repress it.[25] Poetry's function has been subjected to fierce pressure; the sentence of the gods would silence poetry's sentence. Out of that bleak silencing, however, we hear Cresseid's clear, needful voice of self-recognition.

23 For an account of the way Henryson takes us into Cresseid's meditations once she has abandoned Troy, see David Benson, 'Critic and Poet: What Lydgate and Henryson did to Chaucer's *Troilus and Criseyde*', *MLQ* 53 (1992), 23–40 (at pp. 39–40). Reprinted in *Writing after Chaucer: Essential Readings in Chaucer and the Fifteenth Century*, ed. Daniel J. Pinti (New York: Garland, 1998), pp. 227–42. Cresseid's testament conforms to legal testamentary form, for which see Julia Boffey, 'Lydgate, Henryson, and the Literary Testament', *MLQ* 53 (1992), 41–56.

24 See Mann, 'The Planetary Gods in Chaucer and Henryson': 'Henryson's Cresseid … allows the past to reconstitute itself with the force of a terrible destructive challenge to the present …. It is Henryson's generosity to Cresseid that he allows her this passionate re-integration with her former self, an identification so intense that her present life is consumed by her dead past' (p. 100).

25 For which see the excellent point by Mathews, 'Land, Lepers, and the Law in *The Testament of Cresseid*': 'By documenting her *voluntas* – and having it carried out after her death – Cresseid turns the law of personhood inside out. She manipulates established law in order to create a new law that in turn enables her to inscribe on herself an identity that no one can repress or eradicate' (p. 65).

13

The Art of Swooning in Middle English[1]

Barry Windeatt

> Plurent des oilz si baron chevaler;
> Encuntre tere se pasment .XX. millers ...
> [His brave knights' eyes are brimming with tears;
> Twenty thousand fall to the ground in a swoon ...][2]

Swooning occurs so frequently in many medieval narratives, and so extravagantly in some, as to pass for almost commonplace behaviour that prompts puzzlingly little comment or explanation by medieval authors, or reaction from bystanding characters within the texts. Such swooning belongs to a convention-governed lexicon of medieval body language, with its own rules, patterns and expectations, and swooning often characterizes the accretions to medieval narratives typically added by the embellishing imaginations of subsequent translators and adaptors of earlier texts. It is this ubiquity and clustering of swoons in medieval literature that is the focus of this essay, together with the pointers emerging from such swooning for continuity and change in reception and interpretation of body language and behaviour.

One modern response to such ubiquitous medieval swooning might be to caution that 'a swoon is not a swoon', warning against taking these swoons literally, rather than as rhetorical flourishes and generalized tokens of responsiveness. Yet the many references in medieval texts to swooning characters lying long on the ground, or as if dead, tend to indicate that their swoon is indeed a swoon, unlikely to be intrinsically different from modern understanding of a swoon as an abrupt loss of consciousness (and with that, usually, a physical collapse) brought on by psychological and physiological factors. A

[1] It is a great pleasure to offer this essay in grateful recognition of Jill Mann, who was initially my teacher, later the best of colleagues for many happy years, and always the most loyal and generous of friends. In what follows I am indebted to the inspiring example of her pioneering essay on 'Troilus' Swoon' (see n. 72).

[2] *The Song of Roland*, ed. Gerard J. Brault, 2 vols. (University Park: Pennsylvania State Press, 1978), lines 2415–16.

swoon distinguishes itself from other reactions to feelings or events by being such an absolute response that further ability to think and feel is temporarily overpowered. According to medieval physiology, swoons occur through movement to the body's interior of the three vital spirits located in the heart, liver and brain, so that 'the heart suffers through contraction of the spirit, and the body is weakened in sensation and movement'.[3] Swoons register an excess of distress, including shame and embarrassment, but also may reflect overwhelming excitement and joy, not least from love. Almost by definition, swoons are seen to be spontaneous, although the pretended swoon also has a literary role. Lying outside the suffering individual's control or discretion, swoons are often viewed as revelatory outward signals of hidden states of mind. Although, naturally, small children will also become unconscious through illness or injury, swoons tend to be seen as belonging to adult experience, with implications for the thoughts and feelings that swoons are held to register. At least on the evidence of the numerous swoons by men recorded in medieval literature, swooning was not necessarily regarded as the gendered behaviour that we now understand it to be (not unexpected in women, but unconventional and even effeminate in men). To a degree, swoons are defined and socialized by observation and reception, for while it is entirely possible in reality to swoon and revive in solitude, swoons in literature tend to be witnessed events, implicitly dramatic and performative occasions.

As a loss of consciousness, swoons imply cessation of utterance, although in literature swoons occur in close interchanges between speech and silence. As a cessation of conscious thought, swoons may represent a rehearsal and reminder of a sudden death, and are sometimes mistaken for death: medieval medical writers emphasize the short step that may separate swooning from death.[4] As a cessation and a special form of absence, swoons can mirror and parallel those absences through separations, partings and bereavements to which the swooners respond; as absences, swoons mime the losses and disjunctions that they register. The self-absenting that occurs during swooning – the self-vacating of the character from its bodily presence and awareness – can be read as a self-distancing, at whatever level of consciousness, from some abhorrent situation or predicament. Swoons of shame and embarrassment may reflect a temporary inability to bear being with oneself. Swooning is also a suspension of normal time, although it differs from extended trances or enchanted sleeps in being more temporary. In some narratives the interval of unconsciousness is followed by an adopted resolve in response to the shock that precipitated the swoon, so that swoons highlight not simply emotional response but also the inward realization of characters in moments of pathos

3 *Compendium medicine Gilberti anglici*, 1510, Book IV, fol. cci.

4 This proximity is implicit in the verb 'swelten', which can mean both to die and to swoon; it often occurs ambiguously in doublets with 'swounen'. See *Middle English Dictionary*, ed. Hans Kurath et al. (Ann Arbor: University of Michigan, 1954–), s.v. 'swelten v.'

and predicament. Strangest of all is how misery is measured by multiplication of swoons. Repeated swoonings by the same individual, whether in rapid or protracted succession, indicate that to medieval perceptions such serial swooning – however comically improbable in 'real' life – betokens and accords value to an estimable intensity of feeling, whether in suffering or joy, love or loss.

For medieval audiences, the most familiar and affecting exemplar of swooning would be the swoon (or indeed, swoons) of the Virgin Mary during the Passion, even though there was no biblical authority for such swooning.[5] Among the gospels, John 19.25 records only that Jesus's mother stood by the cross with her sister and Mary Magdalene. However, at Mary's purification Simeon had foretold to her 'Yea, a sword shall pierce through thy own soul also' [et tuam ipsius animam pertransiet gladius] (Luke 2.35), which licensed representations of Mary's piercing grief at the Passion and, by elaboration, her loss of consciousness.[6] By extension, the reference in Revelation 12.1–2 to 'a woman clothed with the sun' [mulier amicta sole] who 'being with child cried, travailing in birth, and pained to be delivered' [et in utero habens et clamat parturiens et cruciatur ut pariat] might be adduced in support of the tradition that those labour pangs that Mary was spared at the miraculous birth of Christ were experienced instead in labour-like agonies of empathetic *compassio* for her son's Passion, which came to include swooning.[7] The pervasive popularity of Mary's swoon in text and image did not develop without theological reservations, yet these were evidently ineffectual in curbing the enthusiasm of writers and artists for depicting the swooning Mary.[8] As early an authority as St Ambrose (339–97) writes as if resisting a tendency to invest Mary's manner with emotion ('I read that she stood, but I do not read that she wept' [Stantem illam lego, flentem non lego]), and Jacobus de Voragine's *Legenda Aurea* (c. 1260) is still propounding this orthodox view ('Mary stood at the cross because her faith held her erect, because no sin bowed her to the earth, and because her will corresponded to God's will' [stabat enim fide elevata, stabat peccato non inclinata, stabat Dei voluntate conformata]).[9] For the obvious

5 Gertrud Schiller, *Iconography of Christian Art*, 2 vols. (Greenwich, NY: Lund Humphries, 1972–), 2.152–3.

6 Here and throughout quotations from the the Bible will be from *Biblia sacra iuxta vulgatam versionem*, ed. R. Weber et al., 2nd rev. ed. (Württembergische Bibelanstalt: Stuttgart, 1975). Translations will be taken from the King James version (for a convenient edition see *The Holy Bible*, rev. ed. [Oxford; London: University Press, 1934]).

7 Amy Neff, 'The Pain of *Compassio*: Mary's Labor at the Foot of the Cross', *The Art Bulletin* 80 (1998), 254–73. Cf. Mosche Barasch, *Gestures of Despair in Medieval and Early Renaissance Art* (New York: New York University Press, 1976), chs. 6–7.

8 Harvey E. Hamburgh, 'The Problem of *Lo Spasimo* of the Virgin in *Cinquecento* Paintings of the *Descent from the Cross*', *The Sixteenth Century Journal* 12 (1981), 45–75.

9 J.-P. Migne, *Patrologiae cursus completus, series latina*, 221 vols. (Paris, 1844–64), 16, col. 1431; *Legenda aurea vulgo historia lombardica dicta*, ed. Th. Graesse, 2nd ed. (Leipzig: Impensis Librariae Arnoldianae, 1850), p. 937.

implication of Mary's swooning was a lack of faith in God's ordinance, and much ingenuity was expended in explaining that Mary's *compassio* was on a spiritual plane where her unshakeable faith was not belied by outward sorrow and swoon. Petitioned to authorize a new feast, *De Spasimo Beatae Virgine Mariae*, and to associate indulgences with it, Pope Julius II commissioned an investigation of its canonical nature from Cardinal Cajetan, who in 1506 concluded not only that the swoon is unmentioned by the gospels but also that, since physicians judged swooning to be a morbid state resulting from contraction of the sinews, 'it is not proper to attribute this to the Blessed Virgin'.[10] Moreover, since it was more pleasing to God that Mary shared her son's Passion both in her feelings and in her mind, it was necessary that her lower sensitivities be governed by an exercise of reason by her fully conscious mind, which was impossible if her sorrows made her 'beside herself'.

This sixteenth-century dismissal reflects the popularity of the Virgin's swoon as part of the iconography of the Passion and as a focus of devotion. One widely disseminated twelfth-century instance occurs in the Pseudo-Bernard's *Lamentation on the Passion*, which tells how Mary's 'living soul grew pale as she lay prostrate' [immo ista strata iacens pallebat anima viuens] after Christ dies on the cross.[11] There are fine mid-thirteenth-century English illuminations of the Crucifixion showing a swooning Mary,[12] although these depict Mary swooning not to the ground but into the arms of supporting women, and this motif of the 'slumping Mary', her fall broken by half-collapsing into the arms of others, becomes a persistent feature of how Mary's swoon is represented through both texts and images.[13] Highly influential for the popularity of Mary's swoon, both in itself and through its translated redactions, was the pseudo-Bonaventuran *Meditationes vitae Christi*. At her son's dying Mary is here described as 'so absorbed by the multitude of her sorrows as to be insensible or half-dead' [propter angustiarum multitudinem absorpta erat. et quasi insensibilis facta, vel semimortua facta est],[14] as she is to

10 *De spasmo gloriossime virginis maria matris dei*, in Tommaso de Vio, Cardinal Cajetan, *Opuscula & quolibeta* (Venice: G. Arrivabenum, 1514), p. 52.

11 Thomas H. Bestul, *Texts of the Passion: Latin Devotional Literature and Medieval Society* (Philadelphia, PA: University of Pennsylvania Press, 1996), pp. 176–77.

12 As in the Missal of Henry of Chichester and the Bible of William of Devon: see N. J. Morgan, *Early Gothic Manuscripts 1250–1285*, 2 vols. (London: Oxford University Press, 1988), catalogue nos. 100 and 159.

13 As in the Despencer Retable (c. 1370–1406) in Norwich Cathedral, see Jonathan Alexander and Paul Binski, eds., *Age of Chivalry: Art in Plantagenet England 1200–1400* (London: Royal Academy of Arts in association with Weidenfeld & Nicolson, 1987), cat. no. 711; or in alabaster panels of the Crucifixion, see Francis Cheetham, *English Medieval Alabasters* (Oxford: Phaidon-Christies, 1984), cat. nos. 172–6, 179.

14 *Meditations on the Life of Christ: An Illustrated Manuscript of the Fourteenth Century*, ed. Isa Ragusa and Rosalie B. Green (Princeton, NJ: Princeton University Press, 1961), p. 337. *S. Bonaventurae Opera Omnia*, ed. A. C. Peltier, vol. 12 (Paris: L. Vivès, 1868), p. 607. Hereafter translations and the Latin of the *Meditations* will be taken from these volumes and cited by page number in the text. Mary's swoon during Christ's carrying of his cross is found as early as *The Gospel of Nicodemus*: see

see her son carrying his cross. When Longinus's lance wounds Christ's side 'the mother, half-dead, fell into the arms of the Magdalen' [Tunc mater semimortua cecidit inter brachia Magdalenae] (339 [608]) who also 'seemed to faint with sorrow' [videbatur deficere prae dolore] (343 [609–10]) as she helps prepare Christ's body for burial. Fifteenth-century English readers could find versions of these swoons in Nicholas Love's translation,[15] and might also know the *Speculum humanae salvationis*, where Mary 'swoons as if dead' at the Passion.[16] In his version of the *Meditationes*, Robert Mannyng had already presented a more emotively demonstrative account of Mary's swoon at her son's death,

> For whan she say hym drawe to ende
> Y leue she wax out of here mynde;
> She swouned, she pyned, she wax half dede,
> She fell to the ground and bette here hede[17] –

just as Richard Rolle's *Meditations on the Passion* draw a more emotive picture than the *Meditationes* of Mary's meeting with her son on his *via dolorosa*: 'now she cast hir armes abrode; þe watyr of hir eyghne dropped at hir fete; she fel in dede swoune oft tymes for peynes and sorowe'.[18]

Another account that influenced widely the iconography of the Crucifixion and of Mary's swoons was the revelation received by St Bridget of Sweden in the Mount Calvary chapel inside the Church of the Holy Sepulchre. In this account, Bridget notices that the Virgin is 'lying on the earth, as if trembling and half-dead' [vidi tunc matrem eius mestissimam in terra iacentem et quasi trementem et semimortuam].[19] Mary rises to her feet and then 'supported by her sisters, she stood there all dazed and in suspense, as though dead yet living, transfixed by the sword of sorrow' [et sic sustentata stabat a sororibus, tota stupore suspensa et velut mortua viuens, gladio doloris transfixa] (7.15.16). Later in the same vision, when Christ dies, Mary 'would have fallen on to the

The Apocryphal New Testament, ed. and trans. Montague Rhodes James (Oxford: Clarendon Press, 1924), p. 116.

15 *The Mirror of the Blessed Life of Jesus Christ*, ed. Michael J. Sargent (Exeter: University of Exeter Press, 2005), 171/36, 178/34–5, 180/36.

16 *Speculum humanae salvationis*, ed. J. Lutz and P. Perrizet, 2 vols. (Leipzig: K. W. Kiersemann, 1907), I, 144; *The Mirour of Mans Saluacioun: A Middle English Translation of Speculum humanae salvationis*, ed. Avril Henry (Aldershot: Scolar Press, 1986), 'she was so feynt and ouercomen', 147/2913.

17 *Meditations on the Supper of Our Lord, and the Hours of the Passion*, ed. J. Meadows Cowper, Early English Text Society o.s. 60 (London, 1875), 783–6.

18 *Richard Rolle: Prose and Verse*, ed. S. J. Ogilvie-Thomson, Early English Text Society o.s. 293 (Oxford, 1988), 77/333–5.

19 *Birgitta of Sweden: Selected Revelations*, ed. M. T. Harris (Mahwah, NJ, 1990), 7.15; *Den Heliga Birgittas Revelaciones Bok VII*, ed. Birger Bergh (Uppsala: Almqvist & Wiksells Boktryckeri Ab, 1967), 7.15.13. Hereafter translations and quotations from the *Revelations* will be taken from these volumes and cited in the text. See also *The Liber Celestis of St Bridget of Sweden*, I, ed. Roger Ellis, Early English Text Society o.s. 291 (Oxford, 1987), 480–81.

earth if she had not been supported by the other women' [volens cadere in terram, nisi quod sustinebatur ab aliis mulieribus] (7.15.25). By 1594 the Counter-Reformation scholar John Molanus is disapproving of some medieval iconography. Reiterating that Mary's swoon is unmentioned by the Gospel and that her upright posture reveals that she stood firm in her heart through an unwavering faith, Molanus squarely blames St Bridget: 'Some represent her in a swoon beneath the cross or collapsing to the ground according to the passage in the Revelations of St Bridget', and his distinction between 'in a swoon' and in process of collapsing apparently registers the varying representations of the swooning and slumping Mary.[20] Such widely read texts as the *Meditationes* and St Bridget's revelations lent support to a noticeable trend in which Mary's swoon was multiplied into a serial swooning: 'þou fel swonynde doun ofte, als I wene'.[21] Stage directions for the N-Town Play of the Crucifixion specify that Mary swoons twice, before and after an eight-line lamentation, while later, as she leaves her dead son on the cross, Mary swoons for a third time.[22] The Digby Play of Christ's Burial also features Mary's repeated swoonings: Mary Magdalene reports 'Ryght many tymes emanges vs here/ Sche swounyd'; and at the deposition of her son's body from the cross, the stage direction stipulates 'Mary Virgyn sais, falles in swown'.[23] In fifteenth-century painting and later, Mary's swoon at the Deposition allows for a mirroring – which the meditative Digby Play also promotes in the mind's eye – between the posture of Christ's body, crumpling as it is unfastened from the cross into the arms of Joseph and his helpers, and the swooning mother's body crumpling into the arms of the other Marys.[24] After Mary's lamentation recalling Simeon's prophecy, the Digby stage-direction stipulates 'et cadit in extasia' and Mary Magdalene exclaims 'Ye swown stille on pase [frequently] with dedly suspiration [sighing]' (509). Such frequent swooning recurs in lyrics,[25] and in the late fifteenth-century *De arte lacrimandi*, subtitled 'Prosopopaeia B. Virginie', where Mary herself recollects swooning some six

20 'Eam quidam sub cruce pingunt deliquium patientem, aut in terram corruentem, iuxta illud Revelationum Sanctae Birgittae: Tunc ego exinanita corrui in terram. Sed plerique alii improbant hanc picturam', *De historia sacrarum imaginum et picturarum* (Louvain, 1570; rev. ed., 1594), iv.8.176.

21 *A Talking of Þe Love of God*, ed. M. Salvina Westra (The Hague: Martinus Nijhoff, 1950), p. 54.

22 *The N-Town Play*, ed. Stephen Spector, 2 vols., Early English Text Society s.s. 11–12 (Oxford, 1991), 328, 335.

23 *The Late Medieval Religious Plays of Bodleian MSS Digby 133 and E Museo 160*, ed. Donald C. Baker, John L. Murphy and Louis B. Hall Jr., Early English Text Society o.s. 283 (Oxford, 1982), 154–5, 455, 459.

24 Mary's slumping body thus mirrors that of Christ in *The Descent from the Cross* altarpiece painted c. 1435 for a Louvain church by Rogier van der Weyden and now in the Prado.

25 Mary recalls herself twice swooning on Calvary in one lyric: see *Religious Lyrics of the XVth Century*, ed. Carleton Brown (Oxford: Clarendon Press, 1939), 6.41, 50; see also 9.30. In a narrative of the Hours of Compassion 'At prime scho followit him to Pilotis place/ With sobing, siching, lik to fall in swone', *Devotional Pieces in Verse and Prose*, ed. J. A. W. Bennett, Scottish Text Society, 3rd series 23 (Edinburgh, 1949), 234–6.

times: she felt she would swoon at her baby's circumcision; she swoons when Christ coolly transfers her to John's keeping on Calvary; at the moment of Christ's death and again at the foot of the cross; when she sees all creation mourn his death; and at the deposition.[26]

In her own visions of the Passion, Margery Kempe records seeing Mary fall in a dead faint on six occasions. First, Kempe witnesses Mary falling down swooning at the sight of Christ coming on his way to Calvary and at the conclusion of their exchanges, a passage in which Kempe is probably recollecting some version of the *Meditationes*.[27] When Kempe sees Mary swoon during the pathetic scene where the mother tries to help her son carry his cross but cannot and 'fel down and swownyd and lay stille as it had ben a ded woman' (80.346), she is remembering how in Jerusalem her guides had shown her the very site of this swoon of Mary's (29.169). In Kempe's account, Mary experiences two swoons during the crucifixion, the first occurring when – as in the Gospel – Christ laconically transfers to John the responsibility for his mother (80.349), and then again at the point when Christ dies (80.349–50). Christ's's death is traditionally the most common moment for Mary's swoon – as in Lydgate's poem on *The Fifteen Joys and Sorrows of Mary*[28] – when the mother's overpowering grief makes her swoon into a quasi-death in parallel with her son's: ' "*Consummatum est*," quod Crist, and comsede for to swoune',[29] as Langland represents Christ's passing. Finally, Kempe sees a slumping Mary leave the scene of Christ's entombment (81.351), held up by St John and Mary Magdalene on either side. Mary's swoons in the face of anguished bereavement provided the most potent model for conveying intense emotion and complaint gesturally. On Calvary Kempe falls to the ground roaring and so apparently does not faint herself, but she does record what is evidently her own swoon at the site of Christ's sepulchre ('sche fel down wyth hir candel in hir hand, as sche schuld a deyd for sorwe' [29.168]). Such a Marian link resonates in the stricken mother's swoon over her son, dead yet undead, in the Prioress's Tale –

> His moder swowning by his beere lay;
> Unnethe mighte the peple that was there
> This newe Rachel bringen fro his beere[30] –

26 R. M. Garrett, 'De arte lacrimandi', *Anglia* 32 (1909), 269–94 at 273, 282, 284–6.

27 *The Book of Margery Kempe*, ed. Barry Windeatt (Harlow: Longman, 2000), ch. 79, pp. 340, 342. Hereafter citations from the *Book* will be by chapter and page number in the text.

28 *The Fifteen Joys and Sorrows of Mary*, pp. 268–79 in *Minor Poems of John Lydgate*, ed. H. N. MacCracken, Early English Text Society e.s. 107 (London, 1911), line 264 (p. 278).

29 *The Vision of Piers Plowman: A Complete Edition of the B-text*, ed. A. V. C Schmidt, 2nd ed. (London: J. M. Dent, 1995), 18.57. Hereafter citations from *Piers Plowman* will be from this edition of the B-text and cited by passus and line number in the text.

30 Geoffrey Chaucer, *The Canterbury Tales*, ed. Jill Mann (London: Penguin Books, 2005), VII.625–7. Hereafter quotations from the *Canterbury Tales* will be taken from this edition and cited by fragment and line number in the text.

for Rachel's sorrow over her child was a prefiguration of Mary's grief on Calvary, and represented as such in the *Speculum humanae salvationis*.[31]

The grief and shock of confronting another's death and of mourning over a body is conveyed so frequently through swooning that such body language becomes a stock response. In the story of Pyramus and Thisbe, when Ovid's Thisbe finds Pyramus dead she displays various gestures of shock and grief,[32] but Gower's Thisbe in *Confessio Amantis*[33] and Chaucer's Thisbe in the *Legend of Good Women*[34] both fall down in a faint. Of Emily's swoons in the Knight's Tale at Arcite's death and at his funeral (I.2819, 2943), only the second derives from the *Teseida*.[35] In the Prioress's Tale the abbot swoons to the ground upon witnessing the child's death (VII.675–6), and in Marie's *Les Deuz Amanz* the father falls in a swoon over the two youngsters' bodies on the mountaintop.[36] In Robert Henryson's *Testament of Cresseid*, on hearing the news of Cresseid's death, Troilus 'swelt for wo and fell doun in ane swoun'.[37] The same pattern unfolds in Malory's *Morte Darthur*, where Lancelot swoons at the moment of Guinevere's interment, and Ector swoons when he chances upon Lancelot's funeral and so discovers that he is dead[38] – neither of these swoons occurs in the French *Mort Artu*.[39] Viewed in this context, Chaucer's *Complaint unto Pity* follows convention when the speaker discovers the figure of Pity dead upon her bier and 'Adoun I fell when that I saugh the herse,/ Ded as a ston while that the swogh me laste' (15–16). Similarly, there are many climaxes to medieval narratives where characters swoon over tombs, in discovery, recognition and grief. At her lover's tomb at the end of *Yonec* the lady reveals his parentage to her son before fainting over the tomb, never to revive and hence absenting herself from her son's instant beheading of his father's killer (537–40).

31 *A Medieval Mirror: Speculum humanae salvationis 1324–1500*, ed. Adrian Wilson and Joyce Lancaster Wilson (Berkeley: University of California Press, 1984), p. 190.

32 Ovid, *Metamorphoses*, 2 vols., ed. and trans. F. J. Miller (London: Heinemann, 1966–68), 4.137–41. Hereafter this poem will be quoted from this edition and cited by book and line number in the text.

33 *The English Works of John Gower*, ed. G. C. Macaulay, Early English Text Society e.s. 81–2 (London, 1900–01), 3.1455.

34 *The Riverside Chaucer*, ed. Larry D. Benson, 3rd ed. (Boston: Houghton Mifflin, 1987), line 872. All subsequent references to Chaucer's works other than the *Canterbury Tales* and *Troilus and Criseyde* will be to this edition and cited by line number in the text.

35 See *Teseida delle Nozze d'Emilia*, ed. Alberto Limentani, in *Tutte le Opere di Giovanni Boccaccio*, 2, ed. Vittore Branca (Milan: Mondadori, 1964), 11.44.

36 *Marie de France: Lais*, ed. Alfred Ewert (Oxford: Basil Blackwell, 1944), line 232. Hereafter Marie's *lais* will be cited from this edition by line number in the text.

37 *Testament of Cresseid*, pp. 187–214, in *The Makars: The Poems of Henryson, Dunbar and Douglas*, ed. J. A. Tasioulas (Edinburgh: Canongate Books, 1999), line 599. Hereafter the works of these poets will be cited from this edition by line number in the text.

38 *The Works of Sir Thomas Malory*, ed. Eugene Vinaver, 3rd ed. rev. P. J. C. Field, 3 vols. (Oxford: Clarendon Press, 1990), 1256/21; 21.11 and 1259/6–7; 21.13. References to Malory hereafter will be to this edition, cited by page number and line number in the text, followed by Caxton's book and chapter number.

39 *La Mort le roi Artu*, ed. Jean Frappier, Textes littéraires français, 3rd ed. (Geneva: Droz, 1964), pp. 254, 262. Hereafter this work will be quoted from this edition and cited by page number in the text.

Swoons are the body language that bespeaks the shock in such moments of recognition: the lady in *Yonec* swoons over her fatally wounded lover when she rediscovers him (399); the guilty mother in *Lai le Fresne* swoons at rediscovering her abandoned daughter (452–3), a swoon that in the Middle English version becomes near-fatal;[40] the lady swoons at the joyful rediscovery of identities at the close of *Sir Degare*.[41] Swooning also accompanies and betokens moments of realization and remorse. Dorigen, informed by Aurelius that the rocks are away, goes home and 'wepeth, waileth, al a day or two,/ And swowneth that it routhe was to se' (V.1348–9). When Henryson's Cresseid realizes that it is Troilus who has given her the generous alms, she swoons (539), and Rigmel nearly swoons at the reproach in the disguised Horn's words.[42] Such swoons of remorse and self-reproach are related to those swoons brought on by an overwhelming sense of shame: Langland's Haukyn swoons for shame at his sinfulness (14.326), and Sloth swoons away when challenged to repent (5.443). When, in Malory's Tale of the Sankgreal, Perceval realizes how narrowly he has escaped losing his virginity to a devilish seductress, 'thys noble knyght was sore ashamed of hymselff, and therewith he fylle in a sowne' (919/26–7; 14.10) – a token of acute feeling that is absent from Malory's source.[43]

Some such swoons of recognition register shock at separation and loss, at partings and abandonment. When Guinevere 'sways in swooning' at Arthur's departure for his continental campaigns,[44] or Gower's Medea swoons at parting with Jason (*Confessio Amantis*, 5.3647), such swoonings – as self-absentings – mime the greater partings they dread. When Ywain is reminded of his folly at losing his wife he falls into a swoon,[45] as do Marie's Lanval (342) and the English Launfal[46] when realizing their folly in losing their fairy mistress. The Ariadnes of both Gower (*Confessio Amantis*, 5.5466–7) and Chaucer fall down in a swoon on the seashore in the shock and fear of their realization that they have been abandoned. Chaucer's Ariadne 'fyl aswoune upon a ston' (*Legend of Good Women*, 2207), just as Sir Orfeo, after his wife has been spirited away 'into his chaumber is go,/ & oft swoned opon þe ston'[47] – their fainted bodies insensible on the hard ground. In Henryson's *Orpheus and*

40 *Lai le Fresne*, pp. 81–94 in *The Breton Lays in Middle English*, ed. Thomas C. Rumble (Detroit: Wayne State University Press, 1965), line 387. Hereafter this poem will be quoted from this edition and cited by line number in the text.

41 *Sir Degare*, pp. 45–78 in *Breton Lays in Middle English*, ed. Rumble, line 982.

42 *The Romance of Horn*, ed. Mildred K. Pope, vol. 1 (Oxford: Blackwell, 1955), lines 4213–15.

43 *La Queste del Saint Graal*, ed. Albert Pauphilet, Classiques français du Moyen Age 33 (Paris: E. Champion, 1972), pp. 110–12. Hereafter this work will be quoted from this edition and cited by page number in the text.

44 *Alliterative Morte Darthur*, pp. 115–238 in *King Arthur's Death*, ed. Larry D. Benson (Exeter: University of Exeter Press, 1986), lines 715–16. Hereafter this poem will be quoted from this edition and cited by line number in the text.

45 *Ywain and Gawain*, ed. A. B. Friedman and N. T. Harrington, Early English Text Society o.s. 254 (Oxford, 1964), line 2064.

46 *Sir Launfal*, ed. A. J. Bliss (London: T. Nelson, 1960), line 755.

47 *Sir Orfeo*, ed. A. J. Bliss (Oxford: Clarendon Press, 1966), lines 196–7.

Eurydice the hero collapses 'And lay a quhyle in swoun and extasy' (399) when he loses Eurydice, where classical accounts represent him as stunned.

As with the lamentations of Mary, swooning becomes identified with situations in which pleas and petitions for pity are voiced, or complaints and lamentations uttered. Gower's Canace 'fell doun swounende' at her father's feet (as she does not do in the *Heroides*)[48] at the end of her speech, pleading for his mercy regarding her incest with her brother (*Confessio Amantis*, 3.232–4). As a silence and absence of the speaker, swooning is often juxtaposed with beginnings and endings of utterance. In the *Book of the Duchess*, Alcyone 'Ful ofte she swouned and sayed "Alas" ' (103) before her prayer to Juno, and once she has finished 'And with that word she heng doun the hed/ And fel aswowne as cold as ston' (122–3). Comparably, the Theban widow who petitions Theseus near the start of the Knight's Tale only begins her entreaty 'Whan she hadde swowned with a deedly cheere' (I.913), and Chaucer's Dido swoons as she frantically petitions Aeneas to let her go with him (*Legend of Good Women*, 1314). Here swoon acts as an embodied gestural rubric, marking prologue and epilogue to petition and prayer, but the boundaries between swooning and speech can also seem blurred: Kempe sees Mary falling swooning, yet addressing Christ (79.340), and Cresseid's swooning punctuates rather than precludes lamentation: 'And ever in hir swouning cryit scho thus:/ "O fals Cresseid and trew knicht Troylus!" ' (545–6). Like pleas, prayers and petitions, complaints and lamentations tend to be sites of swooning. Chaucer's Anelida swoons once she has finished penning her complaint (*Anelida and Arcite*, 353–4), and the complaint of Chaucer's Dido to her sister is concluded by her swooning (*Legend of Good Women*, 1342–4). Nor is such swooning before or after complaint confined to women: in the Knight's Tale, after Arcite utters his soliloquy in the grove, overheard by Palamoun, he swoons, as he does not do in *Teseida* (I.1572–3). Similarly, in the Franklin's Tale, after Aurelius concludes a lengthy plea for Apollo's compassion 'And with that word in swowne he fil adoun/ And longe time he lay forth in a traunce' (V.1080–1), while in a different key the fatally wounded Arthur in the *Alliterative Morte* falls down in a swoon before rising to his knees to utter a final lament (4273–90). At the end of his complaint in the *Book of the Duchess*, overheard by the dreamer, the Man in Black's 'sorwful hert gan faste faynte' (488), and the dreamer forestalls a post-complaint swoon here by introducing himself. In John Lydgate's *Complaynt of a Loveres Lyfe* the poet transcribes the overheard lament of the knight once he revives 'out of his swogh'.[49]

In the body language of swooning, as in other respects, the Squire's Tale interrogates courtly conventions, and this recognizable pattern of swoons as

48 Ovid, *Heroides and Amores*, ed. and trans. Grant Showerman (London: Heinemann, 1963), epistle 11.

49 *Complaynt of a Loveres Lyfe*, pp. 47–66 in *John Lydgate: Poems*, ed. John Norton-Smith (Oxford: Clarendon Press, 1966), line 154.

preface and epilogue to complaint is followed by the lamenting falcon that Canacee overhears. First, the falcon falls from her perch 'And lith aswowne, deed and lyk a stoon' (V.474), only beginning her complaint on her life as a lover after gradually reviving from her swoon (V.475–8), while much later, at the conclusion of her long lament she 'swowned eft in Canacees barm' (V.631). Indeed, this is only the latest of her multiple swoons, since when Canacee first notices the falcon in the tree 'everemoore as she stood/ She swowneth now and now for lak of blood' (V.429–30). As such, the fainting falcon exemplifies the widespread convention in medieval texts of multiple and serial swooning: Gower's Ariadne swoons 'fulofte' (*Confessio Amantis*, 5.5467); Alcyone in the *Book of the Duchess* 'Ful ofte she swouned', and when Henryson's Cresseid realizes that her benefactor has been none other than Troilus 'Than swounit scho oft or scho culd refrane' (*Testament*, 544). In the *Stanzaic Morte* Guinevere swoons thrice at banishing Lancelot for his supposed disloyalty to her, Arthur swoons thrice at Mordred's fatal blow, and Guinevere swoons thrice upon seeing Lancelot in her nunnery.[50] The lady in *Yonec* swoons four times at hearing bells announcing her lover's death (448), and Chaucer's Dido 'Twenty tyme yswouned hath she …' while lamenting to her sister (*Legend of Good Women*, 1342). Nor is such serial swooning confined to women: when Arcite is banished from Athens and unable to glimpse Emily anymore 'Ful ofte a day he swelte and seide alas' (I.1356); and, in retelling the story of Apollonius of Tyre, Gower has the young husband swoon first when his wife dies in childbirth and then, after his speech of lamentation, he falls swooning repeatedly over her body (*Confessio Amantis*, 8.1060, 1077), although these swoons do not occur in the *Historia Apollonii Regis Tyri*.[51]

For the heroines of his Clerk's, Man of Law's and Physician's Tales, Chaucer rewrites his sources so as to include a double faint near the climax of their tales. Chaucer's Griselda swoons upon hearing that her children are alive (IV.1079) and again on embracing them (IV.1099). Chaucer's Custance 'Twies she swowneth in his owene sighte' (II.1058) when she is brought face to face with her husband again in Rome, which represents a marked intensification of Trivet's original, in which she faints once on realizing that he has arrived there.[52] Whereas Gower has the Constance of his version swoon with fear at finding Hermengyld's murdered body beside her in bed and when she is to be set adrift from the Northumberland coast (*Confessio Amantis*, 2.846, 1063), Chaucer opts to concentrate a double swooning at the emotional climax of his own account. As for Virginia: in Livy she is abruptly stabbed by her desperate

50 *Stanzaic Morte Darthur*, pp. 3–111 in *King Arthur's Death*, ed. Benson, lines 774, 3399, 3626. Hereafter this poem will be quoted from this edition and cited by line number in the text.

51 Elizabeth Archibald, *Apollonius of Tyre: Medieval and Renaissance Themes and Variations* (Cambridge: D. S. Brewer, 1991), pp. 112, 138.

52 *Sources and Analogues of the Canterbury Tales*, II, ed. Robert M. Correale with Mary Hamel (Cambridge: D. S. Brewer, 2005), p. 325.

father and in the *Roman de la Rose* she is summarily beheaded.[53] It is in the Physician's Tale that Virginia experiences a double swoon, during the much fuller interview with her father that Chaucer develops. Her first swoon occurs when her father pronounces her doom and after she pleads for an interval to complain upon her death, such as Jeptha granted his daughter (VI.245). Rising up from this first swoon, Virginia urges her father to 'smite softe', before falling down in a second swoon and being beheaded while unconscious (VI.253–7).

Virginia's resolve when reviving after her initial swoon belongs with other instances where a swoon registers not only a self-absenting from something abhorrent but also precedes a resolution. In Gower's tale of Apollonius the king's daughter swoons repeatedly when confessing to her father's incestuous raping of her (*Confessio Amantis*, 8.332). In their accounts of Lucretia, both Gower (*Confessio Amantis*, 7.4986) and Chaucer have their heroine swoon at the crucial point, so that she is raped while unconscious ('... and wex so ded/ Men myghte smyten of hire arm or hed;/ She feleth no thyng, neyther foul ne fayr' [*Legend of Good Women*, 1814–16]). At other junctures, swoons induced by shock and fury lead on to resolution, whether just or unjust. Layamon – who has an eye for body language but little interest otherwise in swooning – rewrites Wace's account of Lear's umbrage at Cordelia's low-key expression of love, so that Lear grows so enraged he falls down in a swoon, before slowly rising up to deliver his speech disinheriting her.[54] Once Gower's Procne sees Philomela's tapistery and understands that her sister has been raped and mutilated by Procne's husband 'In swoune tho sche gan doun falle' (*Confessio Amantis*, 5.5788), as she does not do in *Metamorphoses* (6.583–6). Yet the self-absenting of this swoon signals not only shock and abhorrence but also a shift in self-possession, so that she revives as if newly resolved and now implacable for revenge (' "Of suche oultrages",/ Sche seith, "wepinge is noght the bote" ' [*Confessio Amantis*, 5.5792–3]). If weeping is implicitly identified here with female behaviour, there are few indications that swooning is more associated with women than men. It is true, for example, that in the *Stanzaic Morte* the brother of the knight poisoned by an apple at Guinevere's dinner party follows convention by falling in a swoon over his brother's tomb when he discovers that he is dead (903). It is also true that in *Morte Darthur*, Malory transfers this swoon from a male to a female character, removing it from the grieving brother and turning it instead into Guinevere's swoon when accused of the murder ('And the quene was so abaysshed that she cowde none otherwayes do but wepte so hartely that she felle on a swowghe' [1049/32–4; 18.3]). Yet Malory's concern is less with the gender of the swooning character

53 For these passages in Livy and the *Roman de la Rose* see *Sources and Analogues*, vol 2. ed. Correale and Hamel, pp. 546–7 and 550–1.

54 *Laȝamon's Brut*, ed. W. R. J. Barron and S. C. Weinberg (Harlow: Longman, 1995), lines 1535–7.

than with deploying a swoon to highlight the moral predicament of a key player: Guinevere's overpowering shame at being wrongfully accused in public.

To read Malory's last two tales in comparison with his sources is to observe many of these patterns and conventions of swooning coming together in the practice of one later medieval English author. *Mort Artu* already records a significant amount of swooning in recounting the last days of the Arthurian world, but Malory reorganizes and much extends this swooning for his own effects. Although he revises the contexts of some swoons, and paces differently the occurrence of others, Malory overall shows himself concerned to emphasize and intensify the instances of swooning in his *Morte*. These include: swooning over bodies and tombs, swooning in conjunction with lamentation, and some serial and simultaneous swooning, in a world where knights swoon freely and often. In rewriting his Tale of the Fair Maid of Astolat, it is Malory who adds to his source a number of swoons which intensify the Maid's reactions towards Lancelot. When the French Maid discovers that Lancelot is seriously wounded she is very sad (*Mort*, 40), whereas when Malory's Maid beholds him lying sick and pale in his bed she experiences a protracted double faint ('suddeynly she felle downe to the erthe in a sowghe. And there she lay a grete whyle. And when she was releved she shryked … And than she sowned agayne …' [1082/4–9; 18.15]). Later, when Lancelot cannot reciprocate her proffered love, the French Maid simply takes to her bed, never to rise again (68), whereas Malory envisages how the Maid reacts to her rejection by swooning ('Than she shryked shirly and felle downe in a sowghe; and than women bare hir into her chambir' [1090/8–9; 18.19]).

In the closing stages of the *Morte* Malory paces events so as to produce a veritable climax of swooning. In *Mort Artu* Arthur swoons successively over the bodies of Agravain and Gaheriet when he discovers them on the battlefield and Gawain swoons twice over Gaheriet (128, 129, 131). Since in Malory's *Morte* both Arthur and Gawain hear tell of these deaths instead of finding the bodies, the effect is somewhat different. Malory's Arthur faints for sorrow when he hears of the deaths of Gareth and Gaherys, and he continually weeps and faints (in an instance of intermingled speaking and swooning) as he complains upon the malice of Agravain and Mordred (1183/5, 1184/12–13; 20.9). Malory's Gawain falls in a lengthy dead faint upon hearing the news of Gareth's death (1185/9–10; 20.10). Gawain and Arthur then meet and fall into a simultaneous swoon (1185/18–19; 20.10), an occurrence that Malory has already encountered and retained in translating his sources, as in the wondrous simultaneous swoon that intervenes to prevent Bors from slaying his brother Lionel in the Quest (974/6; 16.17; see also *Queste del Saint Graal*, 193). When the French Arthur encounters the dying Gawain, he weeps bitterly yet does not swoon before Gawain dies (*Mort Artu*, 220–1), but Malory could hardly forget the equivalent scene in the *Alliterative Morte* where Arthur swoons in terrible grief after lamenting over Gawain's body (3969). Here

Malory seems intent on out-swooning his sources, for his Arthur swoons three times (1230/9; 21.2), and Arthur and the dying Gawain weep and swoon (1232/11; 21.2). In a cumulative pattern Malory paces the incidence of swooning so that the most climactic events prompt the most public swooning and he outdoes his sources in swooning. From the *Stanzaic Morte*, Malory retains Guinevere's triple swoon upon seeing Lancelot again in her nunnery, yet he embellishes it in order to present Guinevere as a slumping Mary ('And anone as she saw hym there, she sowned thryse, that all ladyes and jantyllwomen had worke inowghe to hold the quene frome the erthe' [1251/31–1252/1; 21.9]). But whereas in the *Stanzaic Morte* Lancelot and Guinevere simply swoon at parting, Malory has them fall into a serial and simultaneous swooning ('for there was lamentacyon as they had be stungyn wyth sperys, and many tymes they swouned' [1253/31–2; 21.10]). On several occasions Malory's narrative is exceptional in including questions within its narrative as to the value of some swoons. Lancelot asks the Maid of Astolat 'Why fare ye thus?' (1082/13; 18.15) when she swoons on seeing his wounds, and when Lancelot 'swouned and laye longe stylle' at Guinevere's burial the hermit who revives him declares 'Ye be to blame, for ye dysplese God with suche maner of sorow-makyng' (1256/24–5; 21.11). Lancelot's counter-argument, excusing his swoon to the hermit, rather unusually makes a swoon's larger implications a focus for contention.

Does the cumulative incidence of swooning across medieval literature suggest that, for this bodily practice at least, cultural attitudes to human behaviour have shifted perceptibly? It is not hard to find cases where instances of swooning were added to medieval versions of stories from earlier times and different cultures, and these cases might be presented as evidence that a demonstrative sensibility is more pleasing to medieval taste than to taste before or since. In addition to the swooning and slumping Virgin herself, other biblical examples arise. In an episode after the Fall in the apocryphal medieval lives of Adam and Eve, when Eve realizes that she has let herself be deceived yet again by the devil 'Sche swoned and fel to grounde' in a protracted swoon (which in one version lasts most of a day),[55] while the Northampton *Play of Abraham* features an Isaac who in his fear talks of swooning: '… I falle in swowne,/ Deþe haþe enbrasid myn hert'.[56] Ovid's tale of Iphis and Anaxarete from book 14 of *Metamorphoses* (14.698–761) – in which a humbly born youth hangs himself when his love is rebuffed by a stony-hearted young lady – undergoes a plot-reversal in Gower's *Confessio*, so that a now humbly born girl swoons frequently before and after her remorseful complaint at having caused her princely admirer to die for love (*Confessio Amantis*, 4.3619, 3631–2).

55 *The Apocryphal Lives of Adam and Eve*, ed. Brian Murdoch and J. A.Tasioulas (Exeter: University of Exeter Press, 2002), A.279–80, B.203–6.

56 *Non-Cycle Plays and Fragments*, ed. Norman Davis, Early English Text Society s.s. 1 (Oxford, 1970), lines 202–3.

Swoons become inseparable from the medieval stereotype of a lover's conduct, as in such sophisticated romances as *Partonope of Blois* or *Ipomadon*, and a potent prototype for swooning lovers is the figure of Amant in the *Roman de la Rose*, who falls in a swoon when struck by Love's arrow and subsequently.[57] Writing in this tradition, Charles d'Orléans describes his lover's heart variously as 'swelty' and 'faynty' in English, where his equivalent French poems do not.[58] The speaker of Chaucer's *Complaint of Mars* is only voicing the mentality that Troilus leaves unspoken when he declares that he positively ought to swoon by way of a suitable response his lady's distress, even though, as the god Mars, he experiences no other harm nor fear (215–17). Yet who could have predicted that by the fifteenth century, in Bokenham's version of her legend, St Margaret's unwanted lover and oppressor, the vicious tyrant Olybrius, would be described as reviving from a swoon after she rejects his advances?[59]

Some of the different associations with medieval swooning arise because in Middle English a swoon describes a range of outwardly unconscious states, from concussion as the result of blows or falls to dream vision and mystical experience. In *The Kingis Quair* the poet's vision begins as he rests 'Half sleping and half swoun';[60] at the close of Gavin Douglas's *Palis of Honour* the dreamer 'Out of my swoun I wallkynnyt quhare I lay', but 'langyt sare for till have swounyt agane' (2090, 2097); and when Venus intimates that he is too old for love, John Gower's Amans falls in a swoon (*Confessio Amantis*, 8.2449), during which he sees Cupid's parliament of lovers until he revives, restored to reason. At the mere mention of Piers Plowman the dreamer swoons for pure joy and 'lay longe in a love-dreem', his inner dream-within-a-dream of the Tree of Charity (16.18–20). 'As long as I lai in þat swownyng', the dreamer of Clanvowe's *The Cuckoo and the Nightingale* can comprehend the language of the birds,[61] while a spiritual director, advising on how to avoid deception and differentiate spiritual visions remarks: 'whiche rauyshyng, aftir Seint Austyn, mai properli be clepid a swounyng, as whanne þe inward wille is fulli turned

57 Guillaume de Lorris and Jean de Meun, *Le Roman de la Rose*, ed. Félix Lecoy, 3 vols., Les classiques français du moyen âge 92, 93, 98 (Paris: Honoré Champion, 1965–70), lines 1699–1700, 1767, and 1828. Partonope swoons at emotional crises: see *The Middle English Versions of Partonope of Blois*, ed. A. T. Bödtker, Early English Text Society e.s. 109 (London, 1912), 6735–9, 7389–90. However, when Ipomadon swoons his attendant comments: 'I wold not se the sowune soo/ Fore good men gyff me myghte': see *Ipomadon*, ed. Rhiannon Purdie, Early English Text Society o.s. 316 (Oxford, 2001), 1635–6.

58 *Fortunes Stabilnes: Charles of Orleans's English Book of Love*, ed. Mary-Jo Arn (Binghamton, NY: Medieval & Renaissance Texts & Studies, 1994), 768, 1136.

59 *Osborn Bokenham: Legendys of Hooly Wummen*, ed. M. S. Serjeantson, Early English Text Society o.s. 206 (London, 1938), lines 460–1.

60 *James I of Scotland: The Kingis Quair*, ed. John Norton-Smith (Oxford: Clarendon Press, 1971), line 510.

61 *The Cuckoo and Nightingale*, pp. 249–65 in *Middle English Debate Poetry*, ed. John W. Conlee (East Lansing, MI: Colleagues Press, 1991), 256/107.

awei fro þe bodili wittis'.[62] Moral instruction and divine admonition may also come during swoons: a young wife and an amorous squire are on the verge of an affair and flirting together in church when 'it happed by open myracle that soo grete a maladye tooke the said lady that sodenly she swouned', and during this swoon her long-dead parents appear to her and warn that she risks damnation.[63]

Yet the foil to such solemn swoons are those instances in which medieval conventions of swooning are evidently viewed with wry detachment or at least ambivalence. Insofar as swooning bespeaks a larger refinement of sensibility in many medieval contexts, once romance becomes popular entertainment a brisker treatment of its characteristic subjects and behaviours may include such conventions as swooning. When, at the end of *Octovian* the emperor's wicked mother learns that she is to be burnt 'Swownyng yn hur chaumbur she felle' and cuts her throat with a dagger, but 'Therat all the kyngys loghe .../ What wondur was þowe þer were no swoghe?',[64] for here a villain's swoon meets only with laughter, as if in defiance of the convention of simultaneous swooning. The tradition of the swooning lover is spoofed by Chaucer in the Miller's Tale through Absolom's wooing speech ('No wonder is thogh that I swelte and swete;/ I moorne as dooth a lamb after the tete' [I.3703–4]), and Henryson wryly alludes to the swoons of shock and loss in more pompous narratives when, in his *Moral Fables*, the poor widow sees the fox running off with her cock in its mouth, tears her hair, beats her breast and 'Syne paill of hew, half in ane extasy/ Fell doun for cair in swoning and in sweit' (490–1). In what happens next, Henryson burlesques the overlooked aftermath of so many literary swoons, when the widow's period of absence through unconsciousness creates an interval of which the hens may calmly and coolly take advantage in order to hold a debate ('With that the selie hennis left thair meit,/ And quhill this wyfe wes lyand thus in swoun,/ Fell of that cace in disputatioun' [492–4]). The sheer absoluteness of such a swoon, usually understood as irresistible, may be questioned by the near-swoons occurring in some narratives, even if many such almost-faintings seem genuine tokens of responsiveness. Margery Kempe nearly faints and falls from her horse at her first sight of Jerusalem (28.161), just as Criseyde nearly sinks down from her horse upon arriving at the Greek camp (5.182), while the guilty mother in the Middle English *Lai le Fresne* nearly swoons (as she does not in the French original) when she recognizes the brocade in which her abandoned daughter was wrapped (372). Some almost-swoons, however, may imply manipulation of effect and appearances: such is the Merchant's Tale's perspective on romance that Damyan in his pangs of love 'Almoost he swelte and swowned ther he stood' (IV.1776). Just

62 *The Chastising of God's Children*, ed. J. Bazire and E. Colledge (Oxford: Blackwell, 1957), p. 170.

63 *The Knight of the Tower*, ed. M. Y. Offord, Early English Text Society s.s. 2 (Oxford, 1971), 55.

64 *Octovian*, ed. Frances McSparran, Early English Text Society o.s. 289 (Oxford, 1986), lines 1715, 1720–1.

occasionally, there is even a faked swoon: in Dunbar's *Tretis of the Twa Mariit Wemen and the Wedo* one speaker – who reports with disgust that her impotent husband's penis is in a permanent fainting fit of its own – confesses how she got rid of her husband's unwanted fumblings by pretending to swoon (175, 225). Yet that such avowedly pretended swoons occur so exceptionally is itself evidence for the status of swooning in medieval tradition. The Wife of Bath's 'swogh' – knocked out cold on the bedroom floor by her toyboy – is no pretended swoon, but she well knows how to stage-manage its aftermath as some near-death revival from swooning ('Er I be deed, yet wol I kisse thee ...' [III.802]).

Revisiting the swoons of *Troilus and Criseyde* in the context provided by a survey of swooning in medieval English literature is to recognize the distinctiveness of Chaucer's account. Criseyde's swoon in her room at the prospect of separation[65] is modelled on the equivalent scene in *Filostrato* (4.114–24), itself probably inspired by Briseida's serial swoonings in Guido's *Historia*, XIX.[66] Troiolo's public swoon (which Chaucer omits) at the Trojan assembly where Criseida's exchange is agreed (4.18–21) prompts Chaucer's invention of his hero's different and earlier swoon in Criseyde's bedroom (3.1086ff.). Both Boccaccio's lovers and Chaucer's Criseyde swoon out of distress, but Troilus's swoon becomes an especially revealing crisis, brought on by acute embarrassment and shame when reproached by his upset lady with charges against which he cannot defend himself without admitting Pandarus's trickery. The scientific precision of Chaucer's physiological explanation of the process that Trevisa terms 'swowenynges for defaute of spiritis'[67] is strikingly unusual in literary narratives ('Therwith the sorwe so his herte shette .../ And every spirit his vigour in knette,/ So they astoned or oppressed were' [3.1086–9]). This description goes beyond Chaucer's account of Criseyde's swoon, where allusion to the spirits leaving and re-entering their allotted places is unusually scientifically aware, possibly implying both lovers swoon simultaneously before Criseyde's swoon (4.1142–3, 1152, 1221–2). Even more exceptional is the attention paid to how the swoon is received, for perhaps the strangest aspect now of medieval literary accounts of swooning is the relative indifference to what happened next, to how bystanders responded or cared for the fainted person. It was not that medieval medical authorities did not provide

65 *Troilus and Criseyde: A New Edition of 'The Book of Troilus'*, ed. B. A. Windeatt, 2nd ed. (London: Longman, 1990), 4.1149ff. Hereafter both this poem and Boccaccio's *Il Filostrato* will be quoted from this edition and cited by book and line number in the text.

66 'Que dum queratur de sua separaccione a dilecto suo Troilo, sepius intermoritur inter brachia eam uoluencium sustinere ... Briseida inter brachia Troili labitur sepius semiuiua ...' [while she was bemoaning the separation from her beloved Troilus she often swooned in the arms of those wishing to sustain her ... Briseida often fainted in the arms of Troilus]. *Guido de Columnis: Historia Destructionis Troiae*, ed. Nathaniel Edward Griffin (Cambridge, Mass., 1931), Book XIX, p. 163.

67 *On the Properties of Things: John Trevisa's translation of Bartholomaeus Anglicus, De Proprietatibus Rerum*, 3 vols. ed. M. C. Seymour (Oxford: Clarendon Press, 1975), 1.348/19.

advice on first aid – including rubbing the extremities and dashing water on the face[68] – and when Pandarus and Criseyde apply these remedies (3.1114–15), Chaucer is borrowing from the techniques used by Troiolo's family to revive him (*Filostrato*, 4.19). Equally unusual is the realistic sense that Chaucer's narrative gives of the physical awkwardness of Troilus's crumpled unconscious body, which Pandarus must somehow manhandle into bed (3.1097). Few authors demonstrate the alertness to the clumsy ungainliness of swooning that Chaucer shows when noticing how the fainted Anelida falls awkwardly, painfully cramping her limbs ('She wepith, waileth, swowneth pitously;/ To grounde ded she falleth as a ston;/ Craumpyssheth her lymes crokedly' [*Anelida and Arcite*, 169–71]). It is also Chaucer who sets both swoons in *Troilus* in tension with time by underlining how alarmingly protracted and silent the unconscious interval seems to its witnesses. Exceptional too is Troilus's extreme embarrassment at having swooned (3.1122). Chaucer's Griselda is 'abaised' on awakening from her second swoon (IV.1108), perhaps because of its unwonted display of inward feeling in public, but Troilus's swoon occurs in private, albeit in his lady's presence. Both Pandarus and Criseyde reproach Troilus for swooning as if they regard it as effeminate behaviour (' "Is this a mannes herte?" … "Is this a mannes game?" ' [3.1098, 3.1126]), despite abundant male swooning in medieval literature. Finally – in that Troilus is 'sodeynly avysed' (3.1186), and Criseyde proceeds to her misguided determination to comply with the exchange (4.1254–1414) – both swoons are followed by that new resolve occurring after swoons in other narratives.

As late as c. 1535, in its witty *hommage* to Chaucer, *The Court of Love* makes the lover's swoon the turning-point that signals change in both lover and lady,[69] as it had in the lover's swoon in his lady's bedroom in the fifteenth-century romance of *Generydes*.[70] To set the swoons in *Troilus and Criseyde* in the context of the patterns deriving from a wider survey of medieval swooning is to be reminded of how Chaucer's poem both draws upon and works changes on traditions. Indeed, if the swoons implied by reported fallings down are included, fainting and incipient fainting become an even more pervasive feature of the representation of feeling. Like the dreamer of *The Book of the Duchess*, who reports himself as 'Alway in poynt to falle a-doun' (13), both Troilus and Criseyde are described as nearly falling down with emotion (2.770, 5.532), or falling as if dead (4.733), just as Cecilia's husband 'as deed fil doun for drede' in the Second Nun's Tale (VIII.204), and Hypermnestra is so

68 John of Gaddesdon, *Rosa anglica practica medicinae* (Venice: B. Locatellus, 1502), ch. 13, fol. 69.

69 *The Court of Love*, pp. 409–47 in *Chaucerian and Other Pieces*, ed. W. W. Skeat (Oxford: Clarendon Press, 1897), l. 995.

70 *Generydes: A Romance*, ed. W. A. Wright, Early English Text Society o.s. 55 and 70 (London, 1878), lines 4700–34 ('Whanne she hadde sayde that pleasid hir to say,/ Thanne was Generides a wofull man:/ Anone he felle in swouneng and ther he laye …/ And furthwith remembre she beganne/ What man he was …').

frightened that 'thryes doun she fyl' in distress (*Legend of Good Women*, 2686), rather than raising her sword three times as in *Heroides* (14.45–6). In different contexts, Chaucer's Pandarus variously identifies with the convention that swooning betrays powerful emotions, yet also distances himself: he begs Criseyde not to make him rehearse Troilus's suffering for love of her unless she wants to see him swoon (2.574), yet when he drily advises Troilus not to endanger further progress by any serial swooning ('Swouneth nought now ... !' [3.1190]), Pandarus characteristically challenges convention by implying that swoons might not actually be beyond human control. Something similar is implied when Langland's Wrath reports that his aunt, an abbess, would rather swoon than suffer any pain (B.5.151–2), or when the *Ancrene Wisse* warns how the heart, reconciled to its lusts, gives in to the devil 'as softe swohninde'.[71] Pandarus's aside also implies that some swooning might be taken less than wholly at face value and that a swoon out of place may burlesque convention, as when the old carpenter in the Miller's Tale almost collapses with sorrow to hear from Nicholas that his young wife may drown in a second Noah's Flood (I.3524).

Writing of Troilus's swoon, Jill Mann eloquently recommended:

> If this discussion, then, has any implications for new directions in Chaucer studies, they are that we should, in a sense, go back to the old directions and abandon some of our self-conscious historicism in order to examine Chaucer's representations of human relationships with no other preconceptions than our belief that a poet of profound humanity will have something complex and enriching to show us in them.[72]

This is wise advice that can still guide us in the challenge of reading any medieval literature through an accommodation between historicist and critical interpretation. The powerful continuities that emerge from an overview of medieval swooning suggest that such swooning does have a distinct and particular cultural and historical value, and needs to be read in relation to that value in order to be properly comprehended. The evidence from medieval literary texts of this special, performative and definingly overwhelming bodily practice does have the potential to enforce a realization of the past's difference, even if this realization is qualified by the sense that literary texts provide no monolithic interpretation of swooning. A modern reader notices the rarity of any interrogations of swooning (such as the hermit's rebuke to Lancelot), the paucity of defences or regrets (as in *Ipomadon*), and the lack of reported reactions to swoons: whatever happened next, after Charlemagne's whole army tumbled over in a swoon? All such features point to a marked difference

71 *Ancrene Wisse: A Corrected Edition of the Text in Cambridge, Corpus Christi College, MS 402, with Variants from Other Manuscripts*, ed. Bella Millett, Early English Text Society o.s. 325 (Oxford, 2005), 4.1590–1; 'as if in a pleasurable swoon' is the translation in *Ancrene Wisse: Guide for Anchoresses*, trans. Bella Millett (Exeter: University of Exeter Press, 2009), p. 110.

72 'Troilus' Swoon', *Chaucer Review* 14 (1980), 319–35 (p. 332).

between modern assumptions that swooning is something extreme and exceptional and an apparent predisposition, found in so many medieval texts, to take swooning as nothing more remarkable than one among prevalent conventions for representing powerful feeling. The longest of Malory's rare additions to his source in his Book of Sir Tristram de Lyones climaxes with the moment when La Beall Isode 'felle downe in a sowne and so lay a grete whyle', upon recognizing a Tristram much altered by madness and exile (502/5–6; 9.21; c.f. 1473–4). Yet when the Roman Emperor falls into a near-fatal swoon upon hearing that William of Palerne is unwell, there is no implication in context that this is anything but an emotionally appropriate response, further dignified by the rank of the swooner, and creditable to both the emperor and William.[73] Does both the prevalence and the seeming unremarkableness of swooning – at least as a convention of literary texts – provide specific evidence for a real shift in sensibility between a more emotionally demonstrative medieval culture and succeeding times? How to interpret the cultural difference that is swooning goes to the heart of the perennial question of how to evaluate texts now far removed in time, as also in terms of representing and stylizing behaviour. The modern student of medieval literature necessarily strives for an accommodation negotiated between how much scholarship can inform us about the instructive differences between past and present, and how much criticism may discover in such literature that both respects yet transcends the distance and distinctiveness of the past – of which the art of swooning in Middle English is so striking an illustration.

[73] *William of Palerne: An Alliterative Romance*, ed. G. H. V. Bunt (Groningen: Bouma's Boekhuis bv, 1985), lines 1493–5; the swoon does not figure in *Guillaume de Palerne*, ed. H. Montherlant, Société des anciens textes français (Paris: Librairie Firmin-Didot, 1876), 2755–7. For other swoons in *William*, see lines 1516, 1755, 2098 (six times), 3882, 4268.

14

The Theory of Passionate Song

Nicolette Zeeman

At various points in the narratives of Chaucer's *Book of the Duchess*, *Troilus and Criseyde*, *Canterbury Tales*, Lydgate's *Fall of Princes*, and Henryson's *Testament of Cresseid*, protagonists or narrators express passionate feeling in the form of song, that is, in verse imagined to be musically performed, or at least marked by one or more formal features associated with song.[1] And of course much medieval song – although by no means all of it – purports to express erotic and religious desire, joy, regret or complaint. But these later English poets seem to go further, implying that for them song is *generically* associated not only with the expression but also with the excitation of various kinds of feeling.[2] By inserting emotionally expressive songs into their ethical, philosophical – and in varying degrees religious – tales, they use song to experiment with the possibility, and the problematics, of the passionate response.[3]

This insertion inevitably encourages a theoretical reflection on the formal properties of song, including those that might make it a particularly effective means of expressing, exciting, and in some way containing, passion. These inserted songs are always, after all, marked or formally differentiated from the rest of the narrative; this is effected by means of narrative information (we may be told it is 'sung'), by formal or metrical shape (often the text has a distinct song form), or by rubrication (in the English writers mentioned above

1 For their help and advice, special thanks to the editors of this volume, and to Elizabeth Leach and Christopher Page, who also kindly showed me in advance a section from his *The Christian West and its Singers. The First Thousand Years* (New Haven: Yale University Press, 2010).

2 Medieval rhetoric tends to assume that the verbal expression of feeling, or at least the appearance of it, has the potential to excite a felt response (see below, note 24); in this essay on songs with words I shall assume that, for the words at least, these two effects are often related.

3 On the terminology of the 'passions' and their devotional and ethical use, see Simo Knuuttila, *Emotions in Ancient and Medieval Philosophy* (Oxford: Clarendon Press, 2004); more briefly, Nicolette Zeeman, *Piers Plowman and the Medieval Discourse of Desire* (Cambridge: Cambridge University Press, 2006), pp. 84–9; and below, note 76.

inserted songs are variously described as *song*, *lai*, *envoie*, *canticus*, *compleynt*, or *exclamatioun*). A number of recent studies have in fact laid out the various critical grounds for identifying lyric insertion in later medieval French and English narrative.[4] If some inserted songs are complete, others are brief citations or allusions, what Michel Zink has called the 'evocation' of an idea of song.[5] Whole or fragmentary, however, such insertions inevitably draw attention to any one of a number of distinctive features of song: its grounding in musical pattern, recursion and contrast; its association with performance, social or liturgical ritual; its exploitation of verbal obliquity and ambiguity; its expression of the forms of inwardness, psychological vulnerability, solipsism – or passion.

Chaucer inserts a number of emotionally expressive songs into his narrative works: the love songs and laments of the Black Knight, Troilus, Absolon, January, and Mars in 'The Complaint of Mars', as well as the Marian prologue of the Prioress's Tale with its song-like use of the *ballade* rhyme royal stanza, and the Marian votive antiphon, *Alma redemptoris mater*, that is referred to, though not actually inserted, in that tale. The texts of all of these songs express some intense form of feeling, and also, surely, demand a felt response from the hearer. Several of them contain substantial philosophical or devotional materials (Troilus's philosophical songs or the Prioress's song-prologue); they are all part of a complex negotiation between desire (secular love, worship of the Virgin) and other discourses present in the narrative, whose concerns with conduct, life and loss are ethical, philosophical and political: Chaucer repeatedly asks about the place of sexual or religious desire in the social and metaphysical order.[6] But in each case these song insertions also draw attention to the formal qualities of song itself – not least the qualities that make it a possible means of passionate self-expression.

Maura Nolan has recently claimed, in a study of what she calls the 'aesthetic' of *chantepleure* in Lydgate's *Fall of Princes*, that Lydgate acquires from Chaucer a concern with multiple affective response to the complexities of history,

4 For French narrative, see Maureen Barry McCann Boulton, *The Song in the Story. Lyric Insertion in French Narrative Fiction, 1200–1400* (Philadelphia: University of Pennsylvania Press, 1993); on the insertion of both affective and non-affective forms of song, see p. 78; also Ardis Butterfield, *Poetry and Music in Medieval France from Jean Renart to Guillaume de Machaut* (Cambridge: Cambridge University Press, 2002); for Chaucer, see Ardis Butterfield, 'Interpolated Lyric in Medieval Narrative Poetry' (unpublished Ph.D. dissertation, University of Cambridge, 1987), chapter 6; Barry Windeatt, *Oxford Guides to Chaucer. Troilus and Criseyde* (Oxford: Clarendon Press, 1992), pp. 163–9; on Lydgate see Nolan, below, note 7.

5 Michel Zink, '*Suspension and Fall*: The Fragmentation and Linkage of Lyric Insertions in *Le roman de la rose (Guillaume de Dole)* and *Le roman de la violette*', in *Jean Renart and the Art of Romance. Essays on* Guillaume de Dole, ed. Nancy Vine Durling (Gainesville: University Press of Florida, 1997), chapter 4 (p. 108).

6 For Chaucerian critiques of the language of affect see Anne Middleton, 'The Physician's Tale and Love's Martyrs: "Ensamples mo than ten" as a Method in the *Canterbury Tales*', *Chaucer Review* 8 (1973), 9–32; David Aers, *Chaucer* (Brighton: Harvester, 1986), pp. 51–7.

whether happy or sad.[7] The 'tragedies' of the *Fall of Princes* are punctuated with highly charged lyric *compleynts* or *exclamacions* and conclude with tragic *envoyes*. In the *Fall* song functions as the expression and sign of a moral and affective response to the poem's complex amalgam of biblical and antique, Christian and classical ethics and philosophy.

Henryson's *Testament of Cresseid* also negotiates an engagement between classical narrative and an ethical and Christian penitential ethos. Spliced into this poem are a series of metrically distinct song-like inserts, amongst which Cresseid's four emotional *complaints*, which Douglas Gray, in his 'tragic' reading of the poem, describes as *planctus*.[8] The poem also contains other formally distinct and emotionally charged inserts, whose exploitation of the poem's stanza form (or part of it) gives them the quality of interpolated song: the narrator's own laments and exclamations, Cupid's complaint against Cresseid, possibly the gods' formal curses, and certainly the *envoie*-like last stanza and Troylus's refrain-like epitaph.[9] These emotive 'songs' also solicit from the reader an engagement with feeling as part of a moral response to the poem's complex events. But their various formal properties (whether exclamatory, dirge-like, penitential or tersely factual) also draw attention to the peculiar properties of the song, or the song-stanza, which enable it to signal and intensify the expression of different kinds of passionate feeling.

The existence of many medieval songs articulating various forms of emotion need not presuppose a parallel body of self-theorisation. Nevertheless, these English narrative poets' use of song certainly suggests that they were alert to, and reflected on, song as a means of both articulating and exciting feeling. Given that the Middle Ages furnishes nothing comparable to a Romantic or New Critical association of the 'lyrical' poem with the expression of emotion, in this essay I am asking what models or theories lie behind these passionate songs.

The grammatical, rhetorical and speculative-musicological picture is surprisingly inchoate. Neither the Latin grammarians' *accessus ad auctores* ('introductions to the authors') nor the Latin and vernacular poetical rhetorics or 'arts of composition' offer any comprehensive theory of affect in song. They recognise several affective genres that overlap with categories of song (Latin *planctus* and *elegia*), but these remain subcategories of song, and do not seem to imply any more comprehensive theory of song. The Occitan and French arts of composition focus on song and prescribe at length for various types of song associated with love; and yet they do so, not in terms of rhetorical expressivity, but exclusively in terms of form and technique. This is also true of the

7 See Maura Nolan, ' "Now wo, now gladnesse": Ovidianism in the *Fall of Princes*', *ELH* 71 (2004), 531–58; 'Lydgate's Literary History', *Studies in the Age of Chaucer* 27 (2005), 59–92.

8 Robert Henryson, *The Testament of Cresseid*, in *The Poems*, ed. Denton Fox (Oxford: Clarendon Press, 1981), pp. 111–31 (lines 126–40, 351–7, 407–69, 545–74); Douglas Gray, *Robert Henryson* (Leiden: Brill, 1979), pp. 166, 178–9, 197–9, 202.

9 Lines 78–84, 323–9 (see Gray, *Henryson*, p. 192), 274–94, 313–22, 334–43, 607–16.

dominant, Boethian and Neoplatonising medieval tradition of speculative music theory. In the first pages of this essay, I document this contrast between the great number of medieval songs that claim to express feeling and the lack of any synthesised view of affective expressivity in song to be found in the main theoretical traditions that comment on them.

It may be, however, that the most relevant claims about song's capacity to express a range of feeling occur in religious contexts: in the later part of this essay, therefore, I document, first, some rhetorico-expressive theories of music and its modes developed in monastic and ecclesiastical milieux; and, second, the theories about affectivity in biblical song to be found in scriptural exegesis. I believe that the impact of these musicological and exegetical theories of song can be seen in later medieval secular literature.

As a preamble, we should note the ambiguity of the medieval terminology of song: often it is simply unclear whether what we might describe as song was actually musically performed. At one level this may not matter, given that the 'songs' of Chaucer, Lydgate and Henryson were probably not sung anyway, and that what we are interested in is really an 'idea' of song. Nevertheless this exacerbates the problem of what it means to invoke the idea of song and how one might do it.

The Latin terminology is very various. Although some terms, especially liturgical ones, clearly describe forms of musical composition (*sequentia*, *conductus*, *hymnus*, and the contested term *tropus*), many others can be used both for sung and non-sung poetry: *cantilena*, *cantio*, *cantus*, *canticum*, *versus*, *cantus versualis* ('mixed forms') and *planctus* ('lament', 'complaint').[10] From the classical period onwards *carmen* ('song', 'poem') can refer to musical song, but more often it describes poetry;[11] *canere* can mean 'to sing', but also 'to recite' and 'to compose poetry'.[12] Such terminological overlap is compounded by the fact that a substantial amount of sung liturgical verse was in classical, quantative poetic metres.[13] Many aspects of our knowledge about the performance of medieval song remain unsure, moreover: songs may appear without

10 John Stevens, *Words and Music in the Middle Ages. Song, Narrative, Dance and Drama, 1050–1350* (Cambridge: Cambridge University Press, 1986), pp. 3, 49–50; Richard Crocker, 'Medieval Chant' and John Stevens, 'Medieval Song', in *The New Oxford History of Music 2. The Early Middle Ages to 1300*, ed. Richard Crocker and David Hiley (Oxford: Oxford University Press, 1990), chapters 7 and 9; on *planctus*, see also below, p. 237.

11 Used for non-sung poetry, see Ovid, *Heroides and Amores*, trans. Grant Showerman, rev. G. P. Goold, Loeb Classical Library (Cambridge, MA: Harvard University Press, 1986), *Amores*, 1.1.5; on the limited use of this term for musical song, see Stevens, *Words and Music*, pp. 49–50. In the *Consolation of Philosophy* Boethius refers to the *metra* both as *carmina* and *cantus*: see *The Theological Tractates. The Consolation of Philosophy*, trans. H. F. Stewart, E. K. Rand and S. J. Tester, Loeb Classical Library (Cambridge, MA: Harvard University Press, 1918), 1.m.1.1; 3.pr.1.1–2; 3.m.2.6.

12 Used for non-sung poetry, see Virgil, *Eclogues; Georgics; Aeneid I–VI*, trans. H. Rushton Fairclough, rev. G. P. Goold, Loeb Classical Library (Cambridge, MA: Harvard University Press, 1999), *Aeneid*, 1.1; Ovid, *Amores*, 1.1.24.

13 See Crocker, 'Medieval Chant', pp. 235, 250–51, 268, 285.

melodies in manuscripts, but this does not mean that melodies did not exist; in the Middle Ages the practice of *contrafactum* (setting new words to known melodies), for example, was widespread. Stevens' claim that the famous *Cambridge Songs* 'were perhaps all intended to be sung', despite the fact that 'only two of them have musical notation', is not unusual.[14] At the other end of the spectrum, there is evidence for the neuming of classical Latin poetry in the tenth to the twelfth centuries, opening up the possibility that even classical and medieval Latin poetry may have been performed in varying rhythms and pitches:[15] although we might reasonably assume that, when Boethius's Lady Philosophy 'sings' (*Consolation*, 4.pr.1.2, for example), this is metaphorical, poetic 'singing', in fact we have evidence for the neuming of Boethian *metra*;[16] and yet neuming may denote not singing but rhythmical and rhetorical pointing.[17] It remains hard to know which of these 'songs' were actually sung and what this might mean.

The thirteenth-century *chansonniers* containing the main collections of twelfth- to thirteenth-century Occitan and Old French troubadour and trouvère songs certainly suggest that many of these songs were musically performed: the manuscripts provide melodies for about a tenth of the troubadour corpus and almost two thirds of the trouvère corpus (in this case a total of some 2,000 melodies).[18] However, things seem to change over the thirteenth and fourteenth centuries, and manuscripts give evidence of a complex dialogue between musical and written 'performance'.[19] Deschamps' *Art de dictier* (1392) distinguishes 'musique artificiele', the musical setting and performance of song, from 'musique naturele', the verbal art of composing the song text;[20] Deschamps was a prolific poet, but, unlike his earlier predecessor Guillaume de Machaut, he did not also compose music. And yet many of the songs found without melodies in later manuscripts may well still have been

14 Stevens, *Words and Music*, p. 114.

15 Sam Barrett, review of *Melodien aus mittelalterlichen Horaz-Handschriften. Edition und Interpretation der Quellen*, ed. S. Wälli (Kassel: Bärenreiter, 2002), in *Early Music History* 23 (2004), 285–305; Jan M. Ziolkowski, *Nota bene. Reading Classics and Writing Melodies in the Early Middle Ages* (Turnhout: Brepols, 2007).

16 See Christopher Page, 'The Boethian Metrum "Bella bis quinis": A New Song from Saxon Canterbury', in *Boethius. His Life, Thought and Influence*, ed. Margaret Gibson (Oxford: Blackwell, 1981), chapter 12; on later French and English writers' interest in Boethius's *metra* as 'lyric', see Butterfield, 'Interpolated Lyric', pp. 195–203, 221–7.

17 Barrett, review cited in note 15 (p. 287); Ziolkowski, *Nota bene*, pp. 88, 109.

18 Samuel N. Rosenberg, Introduction, in *Songs of the Troubadours and Trouvères. An Anthology of Poems and Melodies*, ed. Samuel N. Rosenberg, Margaret Switten and Gérard le Vot (New York: Garland, 1998), p. 4, and passim; Margaret Switten, 'Music and Versification: "Fetz Marcabrus los motz e.l so" ', in *The Troubadours. An Introduction*, ed. Simon Gaunt and Sarah Kay (Cambridge: Cambridge University Press, 1999), chapter 9.

19 See Sylvia Huot, *From Song to Book. The Poetics of Writing in Old French Lyric and Lyrical Narrative Poetry* (Ithaca: Cornell University Press, 1987); Butterfield, *Poetry and Music*, pp. 25–35 and chapter 10.

20 Eustache Deschamps, *L'Art de dictier*, ed. Deborah M. Sinnreich-Levi (East Lansing: Colleagues Press, 1994), p. 60.

sung. This uncertainty is even greater in English, where there is a notable lack of music for the great majority of thirteenth- to fifteenth-century short poems and songs; many of these texts signal their song-like qualities in a variety of ways, but without offering firm musical evidence as to performance.[21] It is with these terminological provisos that I turn to the question of expressing affect in song – and the surprising lack of any systematic theorisation of this phenomenon in the Latin and vernacular introductions to the authors and arts of composition.

Matthew of Vendôme recognises various poetic genres and their characteristic subject matters, but neither he nor Geoffrey of Vinsauf identifies a genre clearly recognisable as song. John of Garland certainly invokes the idea of music, but it is the formalist, Neoplatonic view of music as the pleasurable mathematical harmony that structures the cosmos, of which instrumental music is an altogether lesser manifestation; this is the view that was influentially disseminated by Boethius and that dominated medieval speculative music theory.[22] John of Garland uses this view of music to reinforce a highly formalist view of poetic versification as another, lesser manifestation of this cosmic 'music':

> Rithmica est species artis musice. Musica enim dividitur in mundanam, que constat in proporcione qualitatum elementorum, et in humanam, que constat in proportione et concordia humorum, et in instrumentalem, que constat in concordia instrumentali. Hec dividitur in mellicam, metricam, et rithmicam.
>
> [Rhymed poetry is a branch of the art of music. For music is divided into the cosmic, which corresponds to the harmony of the properties of the elements, the human, which corresponds to the harmony and concord of the humours, and the instrumental, which corresponds to the concord of instruments. This is divided into song, quantative verse, and rhymed verse.][23]

There is nothing rhetorical or expressive about this 'musical' description of poetry, which, if anything, stresses the generally pleasurable effects of music over and above any more specific feelings it might articulate or encourage.

Rhetoricians from Aristotle onwards, of course, recognised that the expression and the manipulation of emotional states is a central function of rhetoric;[24] and yet medieval grammarians and rhetoricians have rather sporadic

21 See Stevens, *Words and Music*, p. 1.

22 See Elizabeth Eva Leach, *Sung Birds. Music, Nature and Poetry in the Later Middle Ages* (Ithaca: Cornell University Press, 2007), chapter 1.

23 John of Garland, *The Parisiana poetria*, ed. and trans. Traugott Lawler (New Haven: Yale University Press, 1974), pp. 158–61 (translation altered); on this formalist view of poetry, see Stevens, *Words and Music*, pp. 19–25, 413–34.

24 Aristotle, *Rhetoric*, 1.1 (1354a16–19); 1.2 (1356a14–18); Latin text in *Rhetorica: Translatio anonyma sive vetus et translatio Guillelmi de Moerbeka*, Aristoteles latinus XXXI, 1–2, ed. Bernhardus Schneider (Leiden: Brill, 1978), pp. 5 and 159; pp. 10 and 164. Cicero is clear that the orator should be moved by the same passions that he hopes to arouse in his hearers: see *De oratore: Books I–II*,

things to say about songs in this respect. They identify at least three genres of verse that express emotion, some of them spanning the secular/religious divide,[25] but all three are problematic in different ways, and, even when linked, do not add up to a comprehensive view of affect in song.

The first of these is Latin *planctus* ('lament'), Occitan *planh*, French or English *(com)plaint*, which is certainly associated with the expression of grief.[26] Some *planctus*, including the Occitan *planh* (which is a form of song), are versified laments for the dead, but the subject matter can also be more varied – and both religious and secular: there are laments of Rachel, Mary, and Abelard's biblical *planctus*; there are also *planctus* by 'captives', figures from antiquity, and 'Nature'; and there are many secular and Ovidian amorous complaints.[27] *Planctus/(com)plaint* can certainly refer to a through-composed musical song that, similar to the sequence and the lyric *lai*, develops by 'progressive repetition' (usually non-repeated couplets); it can also be 'grand chant';[28] and in vernacular contexts there is substantial overlap between the *planctus/(com)plaint*, the lyric *lai* and the love song.[29] And yet, as illustrated by the poetic *planctus* of Abelard and the verse and prose *planctus* of Alain of Lille's *Complaint of Nature*, *planctus/(com)plaint* is not always sung, nor even necessarily poetic. It is, I suggest, an affective genre that includes song, but cannot be used to generalise about song.

The second genre to be mentioned here is primarily poetic. According to Ovid and Boethius, *elegia* is a lesser form of poetry – neither heroic nor philosophical, but associated with the expression of feeling;[30] it is, often, though not always, devoted to the matters of love and complaint. Matthew of Vendôme personifies 'Elegia' with 'a most pleasing brow, eyes almost provocative, and a pert expression. Her lips, full of sweetness, seem to sigh for kisses' ('favorali

trans. E. W. Sutton and H. Rackham, Loeb Classical Library (Cambridge, MA: Harvard University Press, 1948), 2.43.182–46.194.

25 Stevens speaks of the tendency of medieval Latin song 'to run in and out of the liturgy' (*Words and Music*, p. 50); medieval *contrafacta* and motets (often vernacular, but containing Latin, liturgical tenors) also testify to the close interplay between sacred and secular song throughout the Middle Ages.

26 John of Garland, *Parisiana poetria*, pp. 180–81 (here called *querela*); *The* Razos de trobar *of Raimon Vidal and Associated Texts*, ed. J. H. Marshall (London: Oxford University Press, 1972), pp. 39, 96, 98.

27 See *Songs of the Troubadours*, ed. Rosenberg, pp. 39, 106–7, 225–6, 320–21, 355; Stevens, *Words and Music*, pp. 110–55, 353–61; 'Medieval Song', pp. 394, 428–33; Nancy Dean, 'Chaucer's *Complaint*, A Genre descended from the *Heroides*', *Comparative Literature* 19 (1967), 1–27; Nolan, 'Lydgate's Literary History'.

28 Stevens, *Words and Music*, pp. 113–14; Daniel Poirion, *Le poète et le prince. L'évolution du lyricism courtois de Guillaume de Machaut à Charles d'Orléans* (Paris: Presses universitaires de France, 1965), pp. 399–426.

29 See Dean, 'Chaucer's *Complaint*'; James Simpson, *The Oxford English Literary History 2, 1350–1547. Reform and Cultural Revolution* (Oxford: Oxford University Press, 2002), pp. 128–48.

30 For Ovid, see *Amores*, 1.1.1–30; for Boethius, see Anna Crabbe, 'Literary Design in the *De Consolatione Philosophiae*', in *Boethius*, ed. Gibson, pp. 237–74 (pp. 244–9); Simpson, *Reform and Cultural Revolution*, chapter 4; Nolan, ' "Now wo" '.

supercilio, oculo quasi vocativo, fronte expositiva petulante, cuius labellula prodiga saporis ad oscula videntur suspirare'), while, according to the twelfth-century *accessus ad auctores*, the matter of *elegia* is love, and in particular 'miseries and adversities in love' ('in amore miseriae et adversitates').[31] But although classical and medieval elegiac poetry certainly feeds into the later medieval literature – and song – of love and amorous *complaint*, *elegia* itself is not regarded as song, but as a form of *poetria* that influences song; Ovid and Boethius use the ambiguous Latin terminology of poetic 'singing' (*carmen*, *canere*) for their elegiac verses and *metra*; the medieval grammatical *accessus* and arts of composition link *elegia* with other genres of poetry, not with musical song.

The third genre of verse associated with the expression of feeling is the first-person love song, which often takes the form of the high-style, strophic Occitan *canso*, French *grand chant* (*chanson d'amour*), or Latin *cantio* or *cantus coronatus*. By the later Middle Ages, however, the love song is not limited to this form, and includes other song forms such as the *ballade*, the *rondeau*, the *lai* and so on; it can also express both secular and religious love (as in the French *chanson pieuse*).[32] A crucial feature of the love song, however, is that it comes with its own internal expressive 'theory' of affectivity in song – the reiterated claim that 'love makes me sing': 'Singing can hardly have any value/ if the song does not come from the heart,/ and the song cannot come from the heart/ if there is no heartfelt love there'.[33] In later French secular poetry, this claim is so pervasive that some poets say they cannot compose/sing because they do not love, as in the opening lines of Machaut's lyric-interpolated *Voir Dit*.[34] A version of this is the claim that joy makes the love poet sing, which in due course leads to the complaint that the poet cannot sing because he is unhappy in love: 'Every happy mood of mine is gone,/ and since I have no joy,

31 Mathei Vindocinensis, *Ars versificatoria*, in *Opera* 3, ed. Franco Munari (Rome: Edizioni di storia e letteratura, 1988), 2. 8 (p. 136); translated in *The Art of Versification*, trans. Aubrey E. Galyon (Ames: Iowa State University Press, 1980), pp. 64–5 (altered); *Accessus ad auctores, Bernard d'Utrecht, Conrad d'Hirsau: Dialogus super auctores*, ed. R. B. C. Huygens (Leiden: Brill, 1970), pp. 36–7; also pp. 62–3; John of Garland, *Parisiana poetria*, pp. 24–5, 102–3; Vincent of Beauvais, *Speculum doctrinale* (Venice, 1494), 2.112 (fol. 48r).

32 Stevens, *Words and Music*, chapter 1 and pp. 63–73; 'Medieval Song', pp. 363–95, 412, 433–51; Roger Dragonetti, *La téchnique poétique des trouvères dans la chanson courtoise: contribution à l'étude de la rhétorique médiévale* (Bruges: De Tempel, 1960); many Occitan and French examples in *Songs of the Troubadours*, ed. Rosenberg.

33 Bernart de Ventadorn, 'Chantars no pot gaire valer', in *The Songs*, ed. Stephen G. Nichols and John A. Galm (Chapel Hill: University of North Carolina Press, 1962), pp. 80–82; also 'Non es meravelha s'eu chan' (pp. 132–4); and Adam de la Halle, 'Puis ke je sui de l'amourouse loi', in *The Chansons*, ed. J. H. Marshall (Manchester: Manchester University Press, 1971), pp. 69–72; Dragonetti, *La téchnique poétique*, pp. 21–30, 139, 143–4; Poirion, *Le poète et le prince*, pp. 148–51, 175–7; Nicolette Zeeman, 'The Lover-poet and Love as the Most Pleasing "Matere" in Medieval French Love Poetry', *Modern Language Review* 83 (1988), 820–42.

34 Guillaume de Machaut, *Le livre dou voir dit (The Book of the True Poem)*, ed. Daniel Leech-Wilkinson, trans. R. Barton Palmer (New York: Garland, 1998), lines 54–70; Zeeman, 'The Lover-poet', pp. 832–7.

it is right/ that with my joy my song should cease'.[35] Variants of these forms of affective inspiration also appear in religious love songs.[36]

However, when we look at the Occitan arts of composition and Deschamps' French *Art de dictier*, which describe songs on a variety of topics, by no means all of them affective, we find no equivalent to this theory of love and song. Perhaps it is just assumed. Nevertheless, at an overt level, these theoretical texts are instead dominated by the formalist, Boethian view of poetic composition, with its stress on pleasurable effect over expressivity; it is manifest in their exclusive attention to metrical and versificatory technique, perhaps especially dramatically articulated in Deschamps' separate description of poetic composition as 'musique naturele'.[37] Nor is this preoccupation with form only manifest in the arts of composition, moreover, for, as many readers have observed, it is reflected in the elaborate construction of many of the songs themselves, especially in Occitan and French. It is possible that this is less true of English song.[38] Nevertheless, the great mass of Occitan and French song, even when it claims to express intense affect, and insists that song cannot be composed without it, tends in fact to foreground its dazzling technical virtuosity.[39]

What we have here, then, is a divided picture. On the one hand, emotional expressivity is acknowledged to be an important feature of several local genres of song and poem – *planctus*/(*com*)*plaint*, the *lai*, poetic *elegia* and the love song in its many forms; but, on the other hand, the theorisation of these songs, especially in the vernacular arts of composition, is dominated by Boethian theories of music, which stress the pleasures that derive from formal patterning over rhetorical expressivity, both in music and in verse. This contrast is reflected in what Switten describes as the modern tension between 'structural and rhetorical' readings of medieval song: 'the former emphasises parallel patterns or shapes (metrical rather than semantic); the latter emphasises the production and communication of meaning'.[40] What we do not find in songs, poems or this body of theory, however, is any claim that song *as a general category* involves or is especially apt for the expression of a range of

35 Le Châtelain de Couci (d. 1203), 'Merci clamans de mon fol errement', in *Lyrics of the Troubadours and Trouvères*, ed. Frederick Goldin (Garden City, NY: Anchor Books, 1973), pp. 358–63, lines 6–8; a claim predicated on the view that poetry is a form of pleasurable 'music'.

36 Stevens, *Words and Music*, pp. 394–6.

37 See Roger Dragonetti, ' "La Poesie … ceste musique naturele": Essai d'exégèse d'un passage de l'*Art de dictier* d'Eustache Deschamps', in *Fin du moyen âge et renaissance: Mélanges … Robert Guiette* (Anvers: Nederlandsche Boekhandel, 1961), pp. 49–64; Margaret Switten, 'Music and Words: Methodologies and Sample Analyses', in *Songs of the Troubadours*, ed. Rosenberg, pp. 14–28 (pp. 15–16).

38 Many of the texts in *English Lyrics of the XIIIth Century*, ed. Carlton Brown (Oxford: Clarendon Press, 1932), for instance, have a distinctly affective orientation; there are, unfortunately, no arts of composition directly addressing English song at this period.

39 Switten, 'Music and Versification', pp. 143–7; a feature influentially identified by Robert Guiette, *D'une poésie formelle en France au moyen âge*, 2nd ed., *Romanica gandensia* 8 (1960), 9–23.

40 Switten, 'Music and Versification', pp. 147–9; also 'Music and Words', pp. 15–16; Stevens is less at ease with this tension (*Words and Music*, pp. 386–409).

passions; and even when we do find songs claiming to express emotion, it is often compromised by the songs' (and manuals') emphasis on the songs' technical brilliance.

If we turn to notions of song developed in monastic and ecclesiastical music theory, things look very different; these texts may be for the large part highly technical, but, as Page and Holsinger have in rather different ways suggested, some of them also allow for the possibility of affective impact, and even expressivity, in song.[41]

In the Introduction to the widely read Book I of his *De institutione musica*, Boethius himself notes that it is proper to human nature 'to be soothed by pleasant modes' ('remitti dulcibus modis') and 'disturbed by their opposites' ('adstringi contrariis'). Music calms rage and 'sweetens' sorrow (though does this lessen or intensify it?): 'Why is it that mourners, even though in tears, turn their very lamentations into music? This is most characteristic of women, as though the cause for weeping might be made sweeter through song' ('Quid enim fit, cum in fletibus luctus ipsos modulantur dolentes? Quod maxime muliebre est, ut cum cantico quodam dulcior fiat causa deflendi'). Because like draws to like, moreover, 'a lascivious disposition itself takes pleasure in more lascivious modes ... a rougher spirit either finds pleasure in more exciting modes or becomes aroused by them' ('lascivus quippe animus ... ipse lascivioribus delectatur modis ... asperior mens vel incitatioribus gaudet vel incitatioribus asperatur').[42] Augustine too knows that 'because of their diversity, all the feelings of our spirit have their proper modes in song and voice, according to which they are stimulated, due to some mysterious relationship' ('omnes affectus spiritus nostri pro sui diversitate habere proprios modos in voce atque cantu, quorum nescio qua occulta familiaritate excitentur').[43] Although such statements, like Isidore's much cited 'Music sways the emotions, leading and changing the disposition of feelings' ('Musica movet affectus, provocat in diversum habitum sensus'),[44] are primarily focused on

41 Christopher Page, *Discarding Images. Reflections on Music and Culture in Medieval France* (Oxford: Clarendon Press, 1993), chapter 1, and pp. 198–200; see also below, note 52; Bruce W. Holsinger, *Music, Body, and Desire in Medieval Culture* (Stanford: Stanford University Press, 2001), Introduction and passim.

42 *Anicii Manlii Torquati Severini Boetii De institutione arithmetica. De institutione musica*, ed. Godofriedus Friedlein (Leipzig: Teubner, 1867), 1.1 (pp. 179–80, 184–7); *Fundamentals of Music*, ed. Claude V. Palisca, trans. Calvin M. Bower (New Haven: Yale University Press, 1989), pp. 2, 5–8 (altered).

43 *Confessionum libri XIII*, ed. Martin Skutella, rev. Lucas Verheijen, Corpus Christianorum, Series Latina 27 (Turnhout: Brepols, 1981), 10.33.49 (p. 181).

44 *Isidori Hispalensis Episcopi Etymologiarum sive originum libri XX*, ed. W. M. Lindsay, 2 vols. (Oxford: Clarendon Press, 1911), 3.17 (see also 3.16); a search under the term *affectus* in the *Thesaurus musicarum latinarum* (http://www.chmtl.indiana.edu/tml/start.html) reveals many medieval citations of this line in medieval music theory.

musical effect, it seems possible that they implicitly also attribute some kind of expressivity to it.

This certainly seems to be the case for a statement attributed to the late tenth-century Winchester cantor Wulfstan (known from citations in a fifteenth-century Oxford commentary on Boethius's *De institutione musica*):

> Musica est ... virtus modorum vel troporum musice artis, ut gaudentes plus gaudere faciant et plus dolere dolentes; unde Job 30° capitulo: *versa est in luctum cithara mea et organum meum in vocem flentem.*
>
> [Music ... is the power of modes or tropes of musical art, so that they may make those rejoicing to rejoice more and those grieving to grieve more: as in Job 30: 'My harp is turned to mourning and my organ into the voice of those that weep'.][45]

In what seems to be a simultaneous description of musical impact and expressivity, Wulfstan offers a different kind of claim, one that, instead of associating certain forms with certain emotions, suggests that music and its modes have the power to intensify whatever the hearer – or composer/performer? – is feeling. In Wulfstan's use of the term *tropus*, Rankin has seen evidence of the rhetorically expressive ethos of the liturgical culture of Winchester, the cathedral that was to produce within a generation the polyphonic Winchester Troper, with its 'remarkable' rhetoricising rubrics, which, although they do not attribute to music the power to express different emotions, emphatically affirm liturgical music's power to please: 'here begin the honey-flowing measures (melodies) of organa upon the sweetest heavenly proclamations' ('incipiunt melliflua organorum modulamina super dulcissima celestia preconia').[46] But the 'intensificatory' theory of music attributed to Wulfstan was widely available in the later Middle Ages: in the fifteenth-century Boethius commentary, it appears alongside a version of the same view from the twelfth-century Peter Comestor: 'as the natural philosophers tell us, this is the nature of music: if it finds a happy person, it makes them happier, and if it finds a sad person, it makes them sadder' ('ut tradunt physici – hanc esse musice naturam: si letum invenerit, leciorem facit, si tristem tristiorem reddit');[47] we will come across this intensificatory theory again.

[45] *Commentum Oxoniense in musicam Boethii. Eine Quelle zur Musiktheorie an der spätmittelalterlichen Universität*, ed. Matthias Hochadel (Munich: Verlag der Bayerischen Akademie der Wissenschaften, 2002), p. 60; trans. Susan Rankin in *The Winchester Troper. Facsimile Edition and Introduction*, Early English Church Music 50 (London: British Academy, 2007), pp. 73–4. I thank Susan Rankin for this reference.

[46] Rankin, *Winchester Troper*, pp. 63, 73–4; compare Crocker: 'the Franks started from the problems of singing and teaching chant; they were aware of, and admired, the model of rational theory in Boethius, but ... found little use for it' ('Medieval Chant', p. 279).

[47] *Commentum Oxoniense*, p. 60, citing Peter Comestor, *Historia* 1.16 for which see J.-P. Migne, *Patrologiae cursus completus, series latina*, 221 vols. (Paris, 1844–64), 198, col. 1310; see also *Commentum Oxoniense*, p. 104.

The *Musica enchiriadis*, an early theorisation of liturgical polyphony (850–900) articulates a fully affectively expressive theory of music:

> Nam affectus rerum, quae canuntur, oportet ut imitetur cantionis effectus: ut in tranquillis rebus tranquillae sunt neumae, laetisonae in iocundis, merentes in tristibus, quae dura sunt dicta vel facta, duris neumis exprimi[,] subitis, clamosis, incitatis et ad ceteras qualitates affectuum et eventuum deformatis; item ut in unum terminentur particulae neumarum atque verborum.
>
> [For it is necessary that the performance of the song should imitate the emotional characteristics of the things which are being sung about: thus in peaceful matters the neumes are peaceful; in pleasant matters, they are glad-sounding; in sad, they are mournful; those things which have been harshly spoken or done [should be] expressed with harsh notes, or with ones that are sudden, clamorous, excited, according to the other aspects of the ugliness of desires and events; and likewise, so that the details of the neumes and words should tend to one end.][48]

This type of theory, which prescribes using musical form to imitate affective 'content', has been seen to echo classical rhetorical teaching, such as that of Quintilian, for whom form, including that of music, should both please and elicit the relevant emotional response: 'with voice and modulation [music] sings sublime thoughts loftily, pleasing thoughts with sweetness, and ordinary thoughts with easy grace; and with all its art, it matches itself to the emotions required by the things that are spoken of' ('et voce et modulatione grandia elate, iucunda dulciter, moderata leniter canit; tota arte consentit cum eorum quae dicuntur adfectibus').[49] The *Musica enchiriadis* passage is similarly notable for the emotional range it attributes to song regarded as an affective genre (this is rather different from identifying one or two subcategories of song with their affective 'content'). In the *Micrologus* (c. 1026–8), Guido d'Arezzo influentially articulates a similar view of the imitative, expressive powers of song:

> ut rerum eventus sic cantionis imitetur effectus, ut in tristibus rebus graves sint neumae, in tranquillis iocundae, in prosperis exultantes et reliqua.
>
> [just as the effect of the song should imitate events in the matter [of the song], so in sad affairs the neumes should be low, in peaceful affairs pleasant, in prosperous affairs exulting, and so on.][50]

48 *Musica et scolica enchiriadis una cum aliquibus tractatulis adjunctis*, ed. Hans Schmid (Munich: Verlag der Bayerischen Akademie der Wissenschaften, 1981), chapter 19 (p. 58); on this and the treatises cited below, see Sarah Fuller, 'Early Polyphony', in *The Early Middle Ages*, ed. Crocker and Hiley, chapter 11.

49 Quintilian, *The Orator's Education*, ed. and trans. Donald A. Russell, Loeb Classical Texts, 5 vols. (Cambridge, MA: Harvard University Press, 2001), 1.10.24 (1:225); Stevens, *Music and Words*, pp. 403–4.

50 Guido d'Arezzo, *Micrologus*, in *Le Opere*, ed. Angelo Rusconi (Florence: Galluzzo, 2005), pp. 4–65 (chapter 15, p. 38); see Stevens, in *Words and Music*, pp. 406; later texts citing Guido include Guido Pannain, 'Liber musicae. Un teorico anonimo del XIV secolo', *Rivista musicale italiana* 27 (1920),

In the *De musica* (c. 1100), Johannes Affligemensis alludes explicitly both to rhetoric (theories of stylistic aptness and ornament) and also to the liturgical music which exemplifies his theories of the musical 'modes':

> Secundum sensum verborum cantus varietur ... quosdam [modos] enim curialitati, quosdam lasciviae, quosdam etiam tristitiae aptos monstravimus. Sicut autem laudem desideranti poetae studendum est ut facta dictis exaequet ... sic laudis avido modulatori annitendum est ut ita proprie cantum componat, ut quod verba sonant cantus exprimere videatur.
>
> [The music shall be varied according to the sense of the words ... we have shown that some modes were appropriate to courtliness, some to jollity, and some to sadness. Just as a poet who is desirous of praise must study aptly to relate deeds to words ... so the praise-loving composer must take pains to construct a melody with decorum so that the melody is seen to express what the words declare ...]

Continuing, he refers to Horace by name and cites specific antiphons to illustrate his theories:

> ita reprehendi potest modulator, si in tristi materia salientem modum adduxerit, vel in laeta lacrimabilem. Providendum igitur est musico, ut ita cantum moderetur, ut in adversis deprimatur et in prosperis exaltetur. Hoc autem non adeo praecipimus ut semper necesse sit fieri, sed quando fit, ornatui esse dicimus.
>
> [in the same way a composer can be criticised if he introduces a sprightly mode when the subject is sad, or a tearful mode when it is happy. So the musician has to take care to manage his melody, so that in dealing with adversity it has a low pitch and in dealing with happy events it is elevated. We do not, however, insist that this must always be done, but when it is done ... it is an added beauty.][51]

All these statements of course offer notoriously few clues as to how such effects might technically be achieved, and, from a musicological point of view, they pose more problems than they solve. Nevertheless, they do still suggest that there was an alternative, but widespread,[52] strand of liturgical theory, according to which music and song were thought to be capable of, and even

407–40 (pp. 431–2); 'Cuiusdam carthusiensis monachi Tractatus de musica plana' in *Scriptorum de musica medii aevi nova series a Gerbertina altera*, ed. E. de Coussemaker, 4 vols. (Paris: A. Durand, 1864–76), 2:434–83 (I.8 [2:448–9]).

51 Johannes Affligemensis, *De musica cum tonario*, ed. J. Smits van Waesberghe, Corpus scriptorum de musica 1 (Rome: American Academy of Musicology, 1950), pp. 117–18; see also Stevens, *Words and Music*, pp. 404–9.

52 Texts influenced by Johannes Affligemensis and combining an emphasis on effect and expressivity include *The* Summa musice*: A Thirteenth-century Manual for Singers*, ed. and trans. Christopher Page (Cambridge: Cambridge University Press, 1991), lines 2097–2223 (pp. 118–21, 195–8; also 24–30) (arguing for a later date for the *Summa*, see Michael Bernhard, 'La *summa musice* du Ps.-Jean de Murs: son auteur et sa datation', *Revue de musicologie* 84 [1998], 19–25); and 'Ein unbekannter Musiktraktat des 12. Jahrhunderts', in Marius Schneider, *Geschichte der Mehrstimmigkeit*, 2 parts (Berlin: Gebrüder Borntraeger, 1934, 1935), 2: 106–20 (2: 109).

characterised by, a whole range of passionate expressivity – an expressivity that might impact on both singer and audience.

Are such views of liturgical song paralleled in medieval scriptural commentary? Augustine's training in late-classical rhetoric and poetry may have contributed to his sense of the Psalms' emotional appeal: 'How I cried out to you, my God, when I read the Psalms of David, those hymns of faith, those songs of a pious heart ... how [Psalm 4] worked on me ... I quivered with fear, yet at the same time I was boiling up with hope and rejoicing in your mercy, my Father. All these things were revealed in my eyes and my voice ...' ('Quas tibi, deus meus, voces dedi, cum legerem psalmos David, cantica fidelia, sonos pietatis ... quid de me fecerit ille psalmus ... Inhorrui timendo ibidemque inferui sperando et exultando in tua misericordia, pater. Et haec omnia exibant per oculos et vocem meam'). Augustine 'boils' and 'burns' ('inferui', 'ardebam') as he reads the Psalms.[53] In Book 10 of the *Confessions* Augustine stresses the verbal meaning of the Psalms, expressing ambivalence about the risky sensory pleasures of performed church music, though he retains a sense of its devotional value: 'I am inclined to approve of the custom of singing in church, in order that through the pleasure of the ears the weaker spirit may ascend to devotional feeling' ('adducor ... cantandi consuetudinem approbare in ecclesia, ut per oblectamenta aurium infirmior animus in affectum pietatis adsurgat').[54] Nevertheless, in the *Enarrationes in Psalmos*, he rarely focuses on musical performance.[55]

One result of the later medieval interest in matters of authorship, textual form and often emotive effect that have been so extensively documented by Minnis was that commentators focused on the song form of the Psalms in newly analytical and theorised ways.[56] The *Glossa ordinaria* (early twelfth century) describes the Psalms as 'hymns', because 'a hymn is where there are words and praise with song' ('quia hymnus est ubi habentur verba et laus cum cantico').[57] About the same time, Gilbert of Poitiers says that the psalmist intended to teach about Christ but also 'in teaching to draw the affections of

53 *Confessionum libri*, 9.4.8–9, 11 (pp. 137–40); see also 9.6.14–7.16 (pp. 141–2); see Holsinger, *Music, Body*, chapter 2.

54 *Confessionum libri*, 10.33.49–50 (pp. 181–2); for other 'moderate' views of musical affectivity, see Bernard of Clairvaux, *Sermones super canticum canticorum* in *Opera*, ed. J. Leclercq, C. H. Talbot and H. M. Rochais, 8 vols. (Rome: Editiones Cistercienses, 1957–77), Epistola 398, 2 (8:378); also, citing Augustine, Aelred of Rievaulx, *Speculum caritatis*, 2.23.69 (Corpus Christianorum, Continuatio Medievalis 1: 98); Aelred is cited in the 'Commendacio artis musice secundum quendam Gregorium', edited by Hochadel in *Commentum Oxoniense*, pp. 413–33 (p. 430).

55 See, for instance, the lack of musical reference in the highly affective commentary on Psalm 41 in *Enarrationes in Psalmos*, 3 vols., Corpus Christianorum, Series Latina 38–40 (Turnhout: Brepols, 1956), pp. 459–74; for a slightly different emphasis, see Holsinger, *Music, Body*, pp. 73–8.

56 See A. J. Minnis, *Medieval Theory of Authorship. Scholastic Literary Attitudes in the Later Middle Ages* (London: Scolar Press, 1984), whose influence will be manifest here.

57 *Patrologia Latina* 113, col. 841.

carnal men to the same end of praise' ('in docendo affectum carnalium hominum ad eandem laudem trahere'):

> Unde et metrice scripsit et diversis loquendi generibus opus ornavit et ante archam voce et instrumentis et maxime cum psalterio ipse cum multis et coram multis cantavit.
>
> [For this reason he wrote in metre and ornamented his work with various kinds of speaking, himself singing along with many others before the ark with voice, instruments and especially the Psalter, in the presence of many more.][58]

According to a commentary that later circulated with the works of Bonaventure, the psalms express several types of feeling, both penitence and rejoicing: David is like a trumpet (*tuba*), used 'for war, banquets and festivities' ('in bello, in conviviis, in festis'); his laments express sorrow and his singing mental joy (*hilaritas*). In the early fourteenth century Peter Aureol says that some psalm songs (*cantica*) are 'called "alleluia", from a richer inner cry' ('dicuntur Alleluia a iubilo uberiori interiori'), and with such psalms, 'David expressed the great cry of his heart, which burst out in praise of God' ('exprimebat David maximum iubilum cordis sui, erumpentis in laudem Dei').[59] Indeed, as Gillespie says, commentators treat 'the individual psalms as lyric or elegiac verse'.[60]

However, later medieval notions of biblical song include not only the Psalms, but also the Old and New Testament canticles, the Song of Songs, and (perhaps more surprisingly) Lamentations; the possibility of an interface here with liturgical musicology remains strong, for these scriptural texts also provide many passages used in the liturgy. However, the main theoretical result of bringing together these other scriptural texts seems to be a newly comprehensive category of song, one characterised in terms of its expression and encouragement of multiple forms of feeling. Within this large category, the Song of Songs and Lamentations are defined in terms of the affective genres we have already looked at, love song and *planctus*. Of course, once again generic questions remain about the sense in which the (albeit highly poetic) Song of Songs and Lamentations are 'song', but it will be clear that both their titles and their subject matters connect them with the forms and materials of song. The underlying assumption seems to be that all these texts are types of passionately expressive song.

58 Gilbert of Poitiers, Oxford, Balliol College, MS 36, fol. 2r (before 1117), cited in Minnis, *Theory of Authorship*, pp. 50, 239, notes 59 and 60.

59 *Summa expositio in Psalterium* in *Sancti Bonaventurae Opera*, 6 vols. (Cologne, 1609), 1, 73–293 (praef. and on Psalm 7; pp. 84, 87); on this, see *Repertorium biblicum medii aevi*, ed. Fridericus Stegmüller, 11 vols. (Madrid: Matriti, 1940), no. 5638; *Petri Aureoli Compendiosa in universam sacram scripturam commentaria* (Paris, 1585), fol. 23r.

60 Vincent Gillespie, 'The Study of the Classical Authors: From the Twelfth Century to c.1450', in *The Cambridge History of Criticism 2, The Middle Ages*, ed. Alastair Minnis and Ian Johnson (Cambridge: Cambridge University Press, 2005), pp. 145–235 (p. 152).

Some examples. The *Glossa ordinaria* states that the purpose of the Song of Songs is the love of God; it excels all other songs (*cantica*) and, under the appearance of the love discourse of the bride and bridegroom, teaches about the love of God; it works affectively, 'exciting the soul to love of celestial things and inviting it to the fellowship with God that is to follow' ('animam ad amorem celestium excitans perveniendum ad Dei consortium provocat', prothemata vi–vii [Corpus Christianorum, Continuatio Mediaevalis 170, 76–9]). For Bernard of Clairvaux, in his highly affective twelfth-century reading of the Song of Songs, the biblical canticles are all *cantica* of thanks; but Solomon, who needed nothing, 'divinely inspired, sang the praises of Christ and the church, the gift of holy love, and the sacrament of eternal union; simultaneously, he expressed the desire of the spiritual soul, and, exulting in spirit, joyfully composed a wedding song' ('divinitus inspiratus, Christi et ecclesiae laudes, et sacri amoris gratiam, et aeterni connubii cecinit sacramenta; simulque expressit sanctae desiderium animae, et epithalamii carmen, exsultans in spiritu, iucundo composuit').[61] Introducing his commentary on the Song, Giles of Rome (d. 1316) cites Boethius and Augustine on the concord between musical number and the motions of the soul, but he goes on to stress the Song's affective expressivity:

> Modus autem in isto libro specialiter videtur esse affectivus, desiderativus, & contemplativus … Unde modus agendi huius libri convenienter notatur per huiusmodi dulcedinem, cum dicit (Vox tua dulcis), quia complacentia, affectio, & desiderium quandam dulcedinem amoris important.
>
> [The mode in this book seems to be especially affective, desirous and contemplative … Hence the mode of proceeding of this book is fittingly described in this manner as *sweetness*, when it says 'your voice is sweet', because pleasure, love and desire bring a certain sweetness of love.]

If the purpose of this book is love of God, how does it differ from the other books of the Bible, whose purpose is the same?

> In hoc autem libro specialiter manuducimur ad divinam dilectionem, considerando divinam benignitate[m], & meditando quanta affectione Christus sponsam suam diligat, & quanto desiderio moveri debet anima sancta ad gustandum dulcedinem divinam.
>
> [In this book in particular we are guided to divine love, by considering divine benevolence, and by meditating with how much love Christ loves his bride, and with how much desire the pure soul ought to be moved to taste the divine sweetness.][62]

Such comments on the Song of Songs take on a much sharper significance in relation to the affective genre of *planctus* or *threnos* ('mourning song') of

61 Bernard of Clairvaux, *Sermones super Canticum canticorum* in *Opera*, vols. 1–2 (1.4.8 [1:6]).

62 *In librum Solomonis qui cantica canticorum inscribitur commentaria D. Aegidii Romani* in his *Opera exegetica: Opuscula I* (Rome: Antonio Blado, 1554–5; repr. Frankfurt: Minerva, 1968), fol. 2v.

Lamentations.[63] The *Glossa ordinaria* directly pairs and contrasts the genre of *lamentatio* with other *cantica*, along with their respective emotions, such as sorrow and joy; each, however, also expresses intense desire:

> Sicut in divinis Litteris diversa leguntur cantica, ita et spiritu sancto reserante lamentationes diversae: et sicut proprie appellatur liber Salomonis Cantica Canticorum, ita et appellari queunt Threni Jeremiae Lamentationes lamentationum: quia sicut omnino praecellunt illa, in quibus sponsus ac sponsa dulcibus fruuntur amplexibus, ita et lamentationes istae vincunt omnia Scripturarum lamenta, in quibus abscessus sponsi ab sponsa magnis cum fletibus vehementius deploratur.
>
> [Just as in the Holy Scripture various songs are read, so there are diverse lamentations revealed by the Holy spirit; and just as the Book of Solomon is properly called The Song of Songs, so the mourning songs of Jeremiah can be called The Lamentations of Lamentations: because, just as those in which the bridegroom and the bride enjoy sweet embraces excel in every respect, so these lamentations supersede all the laments of the scriptures, in which the absence of the bridegroom from the bride is bemoaned more intensely and with great weeping.]

Although the commentary describes Lamentations as unhappy *lamentationes* or *threni*, the implied parallel between these and the joyous *canticum* of the Song of Songs is clear:

> In illis quippe canticis, diversae introducuntur ad gaudia nuptiarum personae, in istis vero diversae planguntur. Illa siquidem decent in patria: ista vero in hac nostra peregrinatione.
>
> [In those songs, different people are brought together for the joys of nuptials, in these different people are lamented. Those songs are fitting in heaven; but these are fitting in this our exile.][64]

Various citations from the Psalms reveal 'that the saints are moved by many feelings' ('quod multis sancti moventur affectibus'). Although on earth *planctus* is the 'natural' song, it too has a wide emotional range – it is 'an infusion of the heart either with grief or with desire for eternal life' ('aut moerore, aut ex desiderio aeternae vitae cordis infusio').[65]

The thirteenth-century Franciscan John Pecham actually describes Lamentations as a 'carmen maestitiae' ('a song/poem of sorrow'), which he contrasts with biblical 'cantica laetitiae' ('songs of joy'), such as the Song of Songs:

> Deus igitur in scriptura sacra utrumque istorum affectum, planctum scilicet et saltum in nobis volens alternari, condidit cantica laetitiae ad fovendam devotionem, et carmina moestitiae, ad exitandum in nobis salutiferum dolorem.
>
> [In holy scripture, therefore, God, desiring that each of these feelings, that is

63 See also Vincent of Beauvais, *Speculum doctrinale*, 2.112 (fol. 48r).

64 *Patrologia Latina* 120, col. 1061.

65 *Patrologia Latina* 120, cols. 1061–2.

lament and the leap [of joy], should alternate in us, created songs of joy to encourage devotion, and songs of sorrow, to excite salutary grief in us.][66]

'All singers, and also women singers,' he says, 'repeat [these] lamentations right up to the present day …' ('omnes cantatores, atque cantatrices, usque in presentem diem lamentationes replicant'). Although John reiterates the formalist, Boethian and pleasure-oriented view of song (it is 'triply adorned with music and rhetorical ornament. First of all … it is written metrically'; 'triplici adornatur musica, & rhetorica venustate. Primo, in eloquentia, quia scribitur metrice'[67]), this is also a profoundly affective rhetorical reading. He discusses the different feelings expressed by *planctus* – detestation of sin – and by *ululatio* (howling, wailing) – particular vehemence in detestation – and explores the rhetoric of the text's attempts to solicit the hearer's pity, compassion and sense of offence.[68] John also reiterates the now-familiar view that 'it is the nature of music that whom it finds sad it may make sadder, and whom it finds happy it may make happier', adding, 'hence the musical or metrical mode suits lamentation' ('natura musicae est, ut quem invenit tristem reddat tristiorem, & quem laetum reddat laetiorem, unde modus musicus, vel metricus, congruit lamentationi', p. 409).

In the thirteenth century Hugh of St Cher also repeatedly describes Lamentations as a *planctus*, which he too glosses as a sad song:

> Carmen fecit lamentabile, quod antonomasice Lamentationes lamentationum vocavit, sicut Cantica Canticorum Salomonis, metrice illud describens, versusque lamentationum incipiens per litteras alphabeti …
>
> ([Jeremiah] made a song of lament, which, using the figure of antonomasia [epithet/phrase substituted for a proper noun], he called the Lamentations of Lamentations, just like the Song of Songs, arranging it metrically and beginning the lines of the lamentations with letters of the alphabet …)[69]

Lamentations is the prototype of the sad song of lament, in which 'the heart's sorrow and distress' ('dolor et angustia cordis') are sung with 'a bitter spirit' ('amaro animo'); it is emotively enhanced with a variety of rhetorical colours, on which Hugh also elaborates at length.[70] In commentaries such as these, with their comparisons between the various forms of affective song, we see what looks remarkably like a comprehensive theory of song and feeling, in which the books of the bible offer a compendium of spiritual songs, along with their characteristic emotions.

66 *In Lamentationes Hieremiae prophetae*, in *Sancti Bonaventurae Opera*, 1, 408–45 (p. 409); on this attribution, *Repertorium*, ed. Stegmüller, no. 4847; Minnis, *Theory of Authorship*, p. 130.

67 *Lamentationes Hieremiae prophetae*, p. 409; also cited in Stevens, *Words and Music*, p. 409.

68 *Lamentationes Hieremiae prophetae*, pp. 408–9.

69 *Hugonis de S. Charo Opera omnia in universum vetus et novum testamentum*, 8 vols. (1621), 5, fol. 282v.

70 *Hugonis de S. Charo Opera omnia*, 5, fol. 283r.

Finally, there is Peter Aureol's *Compendiosa commentaria*, which introduces the term *elegia* to the mix. For Peter, the 'third part' of the Bible (the Psalms, Song of Songs and Lamentations) is 'hymnidica, et quasi poetica et decantativa' ('hymn-like, and as if poetical and sung'); once more, although I shall emphasise musical song, we recognise the simultaneous reference to poetry and its sub-categories:

> Cantus poeticus dividitur in tria genera. In carmina quae sunt cantus laetitiae: unde Boetius primo *de consolatione*: *carmina qui quondam studio florente peregi.* In elegias quae sunt cantus moestitiae, sicut ibidem sequitur: *et veris elegi fletibus ora rigant.* Et in dramatica, quae sunt cantus amicitiae. Et secundum hoc pars decantativa scripturae divinae ad modum sacrae poetriae dividitur in librum psalmorum, qui continet carmina laetitiae et dulcoris, & librum Threnorum, qui continet elegias miseriae et doloris, & canticum canticorum, qui continet dramata gratiae & amoris.
>
> [Poetic song is divided into three types. Into *carmina*, which are songs of joy, to which Boethius refers in the first book of the *Consolation of Philosophy*: *Verses I once made glowing with content.* Into elegies, which are songs of sorrow, as the same passage continues: *And with unfeigned tears let these elegies drench my face.* And into dramatic ones, which are songs of friendship. And according to this [system], the sung part of scripture is divided in the manner of sacred poetry into the book of Psalms, which contains *carmina* of joy and sweetness, and the book of Lamentations, which contains elegies of misery and sorrow, and the Song of Songs, which contains dramas of grace and love.][71]

Here, then, Peter even recuperates the poetic genre of *elegia* in his description of Lamentations;[72] the startling degree of this recuperation is made very clear by his citation of the initial elegiac lament of the *Consolation*, Boethius's example of dangerously 'unphilosophical' affective song.[73] Peter goes on to speak movingly about the affective variety of the psalms, and the multiple rhetorical techniques of Lamentations, which, as he says, use all the rhetorical techniques identified by Cicero, the supposed author of the *Rhetorica ad Herennium*, for soliciting both indignation and pity. He illustrates how the scriptural commentators recognise the variety of affect to be expressed in song – and comment on it in psychologically and textually inventive ways.

Hugh of St Cher provides one last example of this lively scholastic thinking; just as Peter's use of the term *elegia* brought him into dialogue with secular poetics, so here Hugh is in dialogue not only with Boethian, formalist music

[71] *Compendiosa*, fol. 22v, citing Boethius, *Consolation of Philosophy*, 1.m.1.1 and 4.

[72] Lamentations contains, he says, 'elegias, cantus scilicet tristitiae et moeroris', or four *planctus* (fol. 26r).

[73] Boethius nevertheless also attributes a consolatory role to poetry (*Consolation*, 4.pr.1.1–2): see Crabbe, 'Literary Design', pp. 249–52, 258–61; Butterfield, 'Interpolated Lyric', pp. 203–8; Sarah Kay, 'Touching Singularity: Consolation, Philosophy, and Poetry in the French *Dit*', in *The Erotics of Consolation. Desire and Distance in the Late Middle Ages*, ed. Catherine E. Leglu and Stephen J. Milner (New York: Palgrave MacMillan, 2008), chapter 1.

theory, but even, perhaps, with secular and vernacular song: 'But it is asked, if these lamentations are written metrically, in what way do they express grief, when in metre there is usually pleasure?' ('Sed hic quaeritur, si metrice scriptae sunt hae lamentationes, quo modo lamentabiles, cum in metro soleat esse delectatio?'). Here Hugh points to the tension between the formalist Boethian view, that song causes pleasure through its musical/metrical form, and the rhetorical view, that song expresses various emotions, including sorrow. His formulation of this tension could indicate that he is thinking of it in the contradictory form articulated by secular love poets, who both subscribe to the idea that song should express and give joy, and yet often sing about sorrow. The Chatelain de Couci, cited above, articulated this, like many of his peers, as a 'courtly contradiction',[74] beyond which he was unwilling to move. However, Hugh solves his problem with the alternative expressive theory of affectivity in music: 'It is the nature of music that when it finds anyone sad, it renders them sadder, and when it finds anyone happy, it renders them happier' ('natura musice est, quod quem invenit tristem reddit tristiorem, si letum laetiorem').[75] Unlike the Latin and vernacular arts of composition, with their limited acknowledgement of the expression of affect in song, Hugh associates song with affect and suggests that the range of feeling it can express is completely open. His is the intensificatory – and essentially rhetorical – view, which attributes to song the power to give expression to, but also to enhance, whatever passions the hearer, or singer, is experiencing.

In the work of Chaucer, Lydgate and Henryson, we see these rhetorico-affective views of liturgical and scriptural song, originally formulated in religious and Latin-speaking contexts, reformulated in secular and philosophical terms. No doubt such theories have very different implications when extracted from the milieux within which they were first developed. However, this transfer of theoretical assumptions from a devotional to a secular context may not be quite so surprising as might first appear: there is, as Jill Mann has movingly shown, a renewed interest in the language of sentiment and affect among these later English poets and their contemporaries. If this includes their interest in amorous sentiment, Ovidianism, suffering and the modes of tragedy and elegy,[76] it also includes Chaucer's very experimental interest in the language of religious pathos and devotion,[77] Lydgate's religious verse, and

74 See Sarah Kay, *Courtly Contradictions. The Emergence of the Literary Object in the Twelfth Century* (Stanford: Stanford University Press, 2001).

75 *Opera omnia*, 5, fol. 282v.

76 Jill Mann, *Geoffrey Chaucer*, Feminist Readings (New York: Harvester Wheatsheaf, 1991), chapters 3 and 4. On the late-medieval poetics of affect, see Simpson, *Reform and Cultural Revolution*, pp. 127–90; Sarah McNamer, 'Feeling', in *Oxford Twenty-first Century Approaches to Literature. Middle English*, ed. Paul Strohm (Oxford: Oxford University Press, 2007), chapter 16.

77 Robert Worth Frank, 'The *Canterbury Tales* III: Pathos', in *The Cambridge Companion to Chaucer*, ed. Piero Boitani and Jill Mann, 2nd ed. (Cambridge: Cambridge University Press, 2003), chapter

Henryson's often trenchantly painful moral tales, in the *Fables* as in the *Testament*. These poets' engagement with the language of religious affect is both overt and complex, for they are critically concerned with the ethical and political issues raised by the language of passion.

In conclusion, I can only gesture once more at Henryson's *Testament of Cresseid*. Perhaps the poem is his 'Laments of Laments', written in response to Chaucer's 'Song of Songs'. In this 'cairfull dyte', Cresseid utters her one formally rubricated 'complaint' 'In ane dark corner of the hous allone', a bit like the lamenting *civitas* who 'sits alone' in Lamentations, bewailing her exile and loss of goods, friends and life, and, finally, lamenting her sins. The *Testament* undoubtedly exemplifies the use of inserted song to express various extremes of passion and feeling:

> *The Complaint of Cresseid*
> O sop of sorrow, sonkin into cair,
> O cative Cresseid, now and ever mair
> Gane is thy joy and all thy mirth in eird;
> Of all blyithnes now art thou blaiknit bair ...[78]

Although Cresseid's four 'songs' are all *planctus*, their orientation is subtly varied: the first represents a pathetic and entirely comprehensible response to what she first sees, like the 'unconsoled' Boethius, as her misfortune; the second and third represent differently grounded reactions to hardship and divine judgementalism, as do the narrator's own surprised and passionate interjections. Although her last complaint (lines 407–69) may represent the most orthodox Christian-penitential response, all of these complaints excite through their very situation a complex and conflicted set of ethical and philosophical responses. I am not the first to claim that this poem's morality is full of doubt about what it means to make judgements and inflict punishments. Nevertheless, these complex reader responses are surely focused by the passion expressed in the song-like outbursts and the spare, concentrated stanzas of feeling that punctuate the poem. It may be that Troylus's terse, mordant and not especially Christian 'epitaph' is in fact the poem's most telling, funereal *planctus*.[79] Like Chaucer and Lydgate, Henryson harnesses what may ultimately be devotional resources to some rather moving but also philosophical ends.

11; *Chaucer's Religious Tales*, ed. C. David Benson and Elizabeth Robertson (Cambridge: D. S. Brewer, 1990).

[78] *Testament of Cresseid*, lines 1, 405–10.

[79] On *epitaphium* as *carmen*, see Vincent of Beauvais, *Speculum doctrinale*, 2.112 (fol. 48r).

List of Contributors

Siobhain Bly Calkin, Associate Professor of English, Carleton University, Ottawa

Christopher Cannon, Professor of English, New York University

Rebecca Davis, Assistant Professor of English, University of California, Irvine

Peter Dronke, Emeritus Professor of Medieval Latin and Fellow of Clare Hall, Cambridge

A. S. G. Edwards, Professor of Textual Studies, De Montfort University

Elizabeth B. Edwards, Professor of Humanities, University of King's College, Halifax

Maura Nolan, Associate Professor of English, University of California, Berkeley

Paul J. Patterson, Assistant Professor of English, St. Joseph's College of New York

Derek Pearsall, Gurney Professor Emeritus of English, Harvard University and Honorary Member, Centre for Medieval Studies, University of York

Ad Putter, Professor of Medieval English Literature, Bristol University

Paul Gerhard Schmidt, Emeritus Professor Ordinarius für Lateinische Philologie des Mittelalters und der Neuzeit, Albert-Ludwigs-Universität Freiburg im Breisgau

James Simpson, Donald P. and Katherine B. Loker Professor of English, Harvard University

Barry Windeatt, Professor of English and Fellow of Emmanuel College, Cambridge

Nicolette Zeeman, Fellow of King's College, Cambridge

Index

Tabula Gratulatoria

Elizabeth Archibald
Laura Ashe
Arthur W. Bahr
Gillian Beer
Fred Biggs
Siobhain Bly Calkin
Julia Boffey
Piero Boitani
Charlotte Brewer
John Burrow
Ardis Butterfield
Christopher Cannon
Neil Cartlidge
Cristina Maria Cervone
Howell Chickering
Andrew Cole
Helen Cooper
Edwin D. Craun
Richard Dance
Rebecca Davis
Carolyn Dinshaw
Ivana Djordjevic
Peter Dronke
A. S. G. Edwards
Elizabeth B. Edwards
Richard Firth Green
John Ganim
Shannon Gayk
Alan T. Gaylord
Antony Hasler
John C. Hirsh
Anne Hudson
Christa Jansohn
Terry Jones
Sarah Kay
John Kelly
Laura Kendrick
Pamela King
Ebbe Klitgård
V. A. Kolve
Lisa Lampert-Weissig
David Matthews
Dieter Mehl
Ludo and Greta Milis
Bella Millett
Maura Nolan
Katherine O'Brien O'Keeffe
Christopher Page
Paul J. Patterson
Derek Pearsall
Nicholas Perkins
Ad Putter
Mark Rasmussen
Stephen R. Reimer
Elizabeth Robertson
Miri Rubin
Martha Dana Rust
Wendy Scase
Misty Y. Schieberle
Paul Gerhard Schmidt
James Simpson
A. C. Spearing
David Staines
Paul E. Szarmach
Toshiyuki Takamiya
Andrew Taylor
Kathleen A. Tonry
Anna Torti
Lawrence Warner
Barry Windeatt
R. F. Yeager
Nicolette Zeeman
Jan M. Ziolkowski